PUBLIC DISTRIBUTION SYSTEM IN INDIA

Editors

ANIL KUMAR THAKUR
KALPANA PAL

REGAL PUBLICATIONS
New Delhi - 110 027

PUBLIC DISTRIBUTION SYSTEM IN INDIA

ISBN 978-81-8484-107-7

Typeset by
RAHUL COMPOSERS
358, Pocket-B, Phase-2, Sector-16 B, Dwarka, New Delhi - 110 075

Printed in India at
MAYUR ENTERPRISES
WZ Plot No. 3, Gujjar Market, Tihar Village, New Delhi - 110 018

Published by
REGAL PUBLICATIONS
F-159, Rajouri Garden, New Delhi - 110 027 • Phone : 45546396
E-mail : regalbookspub@yahoo.com

Contents

Section II
FUNCTIONING OF PDS IN BIHAR

Section III
VARIOUS ASPECTS OF PDS

Preface

Public Distribution System in India was started in 1960 with the aims of protecting the general public against the price rise of essential commodities such as, foodgrain, sugar, Kerosene oil and edible oils; rectifying the existing imbalances between supply and demand for goods of mass consumption and ensuring food security to the people. The PDS in its original form was severely criticised for its failure to serve the BPL population, its urban bias, negligible coverage in the states with the highest concentration of the rural poor and lack of transparent and accountable arrangements for delivery. The programme was revamped as Targeted Public Distribution System (TPDs) in June 1997 to protect the interest of poor in the country with the provision of 10 kg/20 kg/25 kg of food grains per month as specially subsidised prices. Currently the PDS operates through a large distribution network of around 4.89 lakh fair price shops. The PDS suffers from high exclusion and inclusion errors, non-viability of FPSs, failure in fulfilling the price stabilisation objective, and widespread leakages.

In the backdrop of these observations the present book reviews various dimensions of Public Distribution System in India in general and the state of Bihar in particular. The book examines the main features of PDS in the state of Bihar and elsewhere, its impact on the level of food security, price stabilisation and distributional aspects of essential commodities.

The book includes 41 selected research papers presented at the 12th Annual Conference of Economic Association of Bihar held at the TM Bhagalpur University, Bhagalpur (Bihar). The papers are a part of presentation and discussion on the theme—"Public Distribution System in India". We extend our sincere thanks to all those who took active participation in the deliberations of the session on the above theme of the conference.

We express our sincere gratitude and thanks to the Economic Association Bihar in general, and Prof. Bikrama Singh, the Executive President in particular for giving us this excellent opportunity to bring this book. All the contributors of this book deserve our sincere thanks for their efforts. We are also thankful to Shri R.D.S. Bhatia of M/s Regal Publications, New Delhi for bringing this book in an excellent manner.

ANIL KUMAR THAKUR
KALPANA PAL

List of Contributors

Abhay K. Pandey, Department of History, Mahadev Singh College, Bhagalpur (Bihar).

Abhishek Kumar, Manager, TATA AIG, Kalyani, Muzaffarpur (Bihar).

Amita Sinha, Research Scholar, University Department of Commerce and Business Administration, TM Bhagalpur University, Bhagalpur (Bihar).

Anjana Kumari, Faculty of Social Sciences, B.R.A. Bihar University, Muzaffarpur (Bihar).

Anju Jain, Lecturer of Economics, R.P.M. College, Patna City, Patna (Bihar).

Anju Singh, Department of Home Science, MAM College, Naugachia.

Anju Sinha, Department of Economics, J.D. Womens College, Patna (Bihar).

Aprana Bhardwaj, Final Year, M.A. in Economics, A.N. College, Patna (Bihar).

Arun Kumar Thakur, Head, Department of Economics, R.D.S. College, Muzaffarpur (Bihar).

Arun Kumar, C/o Dhaneshwar Yadav, Krishnapuri, Alalpatti, Darbhanga (Bihar).

Arun Kumar, H.S. Makhdumpur (Jehanabad).

Arvind Kumar Singh, Lecturer, Department of History, Mahadeo Singh College, T.M. Bhagalpur University (Bihar).

As Mahammad, Research Scholar, P.G. Department of L.S.W., M.U. Bodh-Gaya (Bihar).

Asha Dubey, Department of Home Science, Mahadeo Singh College, Bhagalpur (Bihar).

Ashok Kumar Jha, Lecturer, Department of Economics, B.N. College, Bhagalpur (Bihar).

Asim K. Karmakar, Lecturer, Department of Economics, Jadavpur University, Kolkata (W.B.).

B.K. Pandey, Department of Economics, SKM College, Nawada (Bihar).

Bindeshwar Kumar, Nawadih, Bazura, Gaya (Bihar).

Binod Prasad, Department of Commerce, Gaya College, Gaya, M.U. (Bihar).

Bipin Pd. Singh, Department of Education, A.S. College, Deoghar.

Bishwanath Gupta, Lecturer in Commerce, Gaya College, Gaya (Bihar).

Chandra Bhushan Kumar, Research Scholar, P.G. Department of L.S.W., M.U. Bodh-Gaya (Bihar).

Chandra Kant Singh, Lecturer, Department of Economics, Nitishwar Singh College, Sarmastpur, Muzaffarpur (Bihar).

Chandrika Prasad, Department of Economics, Balanda College, Biharsharif, Nalanda (Bihar).

D.K. Bhattacharya, Senior Lecturer, Department of Economics, H.D. Jain College, Ara.

Debes Mukhopadhayay, Guest Faculty, Presidency College, Kolkata and Former Teacher-in-charge, St. Paul's CM College, Kolkata (W.B.).

Dhananjay Kumar, Department of Geography, S.G.G.S. College, Patna City, Patna (Bihar).

G.S. Dokania, Research Scholar, University Department of Rural Economics and Cooperation, TM Bhagalpur University, Bhagalpur (Bihar).

Gori Shankar, Research Scholar, PG Department of Economics, TM Bhagalpur University, Bhagalpur (Bihar).

H.C.L. Das, M.S. College, Motihari (Bihar).

Iswari Prasad, Habu Nagar, Aliganj, Jammu.

Jagdish Prasad, Department of Commerce, College of Commerce, Patna (Bihar).

Kalanand Singh, Department of Political Science, Mahadeo Singh College.

Kalpana Pal, Department of Applied Economics and Commerce, Magadh University, Bodh Gaya (Bihar).

Kamini Jha, Lecturer, Department of Economics, Patna Women's College, Patna (Bihar).

Kamlesh Kumar, Lecturer, Department of Commerce, Dr. J.M. College, B.R.A. Bihar University, Muzaffarpur (Bihar).

Kumari Sudama Yadav, Lecturer, Department of R. Economics, MAM College, Naugachia.

Laxmi Kumar, Research Scholar, B.R.A. Bihar University, Muzaffarpur (Bihar).

Md. Aiyub Rayeen, At-Bherlyahi, P.O. Koelasthan, Darbhanga (Bihar).

Mirza Ehshan Haidar "Sham", Lecturer, Department of Rural Economics of Cooperation, SNSRKS College, Saharsa (Bihar).

Mritunjay Prasad Singh, Research Scholar, University Department of Rural Economics and Cooperation, TM Bhagalpur University, Bhagalpur (Bihar).

Mukul Kumar Singh, M.A. (Economics), Shastri Nagar, Jail Press, Gaya (Bihar).

N.C. Jha, Reader and Head, Department of Economics, Madhupur College, Madhupur, S.K.M. University, Dumka.

Navendu Shekhar, Department of Economics, A.N.S. College, Barh.

Niranjay Kumar, Research Scholar, Department of Economics, M.U., Bodh-Gaya (Bihar).

Nisha Kumari, (P.G. Department of Economics), T.M. Bhagalpur University, Bhagalpur (Bihar).

Niyati Chakraborty, Lecturer in Economics, Barahea Degree College, Munger.

Pankaj Kumar, Research Scholar, Department of Commerce, V.K.S.U., Ara (Bihar).

Pankaj Purushotam, B.B.A., M.D.D.M. College, B.R.A. Bihar University, Muzaffarpur (Bihar).

Prita Yadav, Research Scholar, Department of Economics, M.U. Bodh-Gaya (Bihar).

R. Rahman, Department of Commerce, College of Commerce, Patna (Bihar).

Rajesh Kumar, Research Scholar, P.G. Department of Geography, M.U. Bodh-Gaya (Bihar).

Rakesh Kumar Singh, Department of Economics, R.D.S. College, Muzaffarpur (Bihar).

Ram Dular Singh, Singh Pokhar, Dobhi, Gaya (Bihar).

Ram Kumar Prasad, H.O.D. of Economics, S.S.J.S. Namdhari College, Garhwa (Jharkhand).

Ramanuj Sharma, Department of Economics, T.S. College, Hisua, Nawada (Bihar).

Ranjana Singh, Department of Economics, R.D. and D.J. College, Munger, T.M.B.U. Bhagalpur, (Bihar).

Ratan Lal Basu, Former Teacher-in-Charge, Bhairab Ganguly College, Kolkata.

Sandhya Rani, Lecturer in Economics, Maharaja College, Arrah (Bihar).

Sangeeta Kundu, Research Scholar, Planning and Development Unit, Department of Economics, Jadavpur University (Bihar).

Sanjay Kumar, Faculty Member, Department of Commerce, S.K.M. University, Dumka, Jharkhand.

Sanjay Kumar, Vill-Makhadumpur, P.O.-Kerap, P.S. Rafiganj, Aurangabad (Bihar).

Saroj Kumar, Guest Faculty of BBA, G.B. College, Ramgarh, Kaimur (Bihar).

Satyendra Narayan Singh, Gandhi H/S Prabhat Nagar, Makhadumpur (Jehanabad).

Shabnam Parween, Department of Economics, H.D. Jain College, Arra, V.K. University (Bihar).

Shailesh Kumar, Department of Economics, H.N.B. Govt. P.G. College, Kumaun University, Nainital (U.P.).

Subodh Kumar Sinha, Lecturer, Department of Economics, S.N.S. College, Muzaffarpur (Bihar).

Sudama Singh, Retd. Prof. and Head, Department of Economics, M.U., Bodh Gaya (Bihar).

Suresh Kumar, T.D.B.V. H/S, Bichkorwa Jamui.

Swarnim Ghosh, (UGC-Net Qualified and Research Scholar), Guest Faculty of B.B.A.-S.M. College, Bhagalpur (Bihar).

Syed Alay Mujtaba, Lecturer, Department of Commerce, Rameshwar College, B.R.A. Bihar University, Muzaffarpur (Bihar).

Umesh Kumar Jha, Department of Home Science, M.L.S.M. College, L.N. Mithila University, Darbhanga (Bihar).

Vandana Kumari, A/101, Raj Kishori Complex, Kankarbagh, Patna (Bihar).

Vinod Kumar Sinha, Department of Philosophy, S.N.S. College, Muzaffarpur (Bihar).

Introduction

Public Distribution System in India is a major intervention aimed at ensuring food security to all the poor, especially the vulnerable sections of the society. It not only provides essential commodities, including foodgrains, to more than 6 million families on regular basis, but also ensures the price stability in the market. The PDS operates through a large distribution network of around 4.89 lakh fair price shops. Originally the PDS was started in 1960 and later on redesignated as Targeted Public Distribution System in June 1997. Functioning of the PDS is the joint responsibility of the Central Government and State Governments, while the Central Government is responsible for the procurement and transportation of wheat/rice, sugar, kerosene oil, edible oils, etc. up to the principle distribution centers, the state governments are responsible for the identification of families living below the poverty line, issue of ration cards, appointment of dealers for the distribution of essential commodities to the vulnerable sections of the society through FPSs.

Various studies, undertaken by especially appointed enquiry committees/commissions and independent researcher come to conclusion that PDS or TPDS have failed in serving the objective of making foodgrains available to the poor. If it had, the consumption levels of cereals should not have fallen on average—as it has consistently over the last two decades

(GoI, 2007, Vol. III, pp. 134-35). The programme evaluation organisation establishes in one of its studies (2005) that TPDS has large scale exclusion and inclusion errors with a large number of ghost cards. The share of leakages in off-take from the Central Pool is abnormally high. PDS has also failed in its objective of price stabilisation, observes the study, because of faulty allocation system, which often ignores demand-supply constraints. Central Vigilance Committee in PDS, under the chairmanship of Justice D.P. Wadhwa (2009) observes that there is lot of pilferage at every level in PDS along with multiple ration cards under a single name. Planning Commission has no hesitation to accept that 'for every Rs. 4 spent on PDS, only Re 1 reaches the poor and 57% of PDS foodgrains does not reach the intended people'. Several studies confirm that a thriving nexus is in operation between transporters, fair price shops and officials of the department including anti-hoarding cell and the entire network of civil supplies.

In the light of above general observations about the Public Distribution System, the present book contains 41 research papers in all presented at 12th Annual Conference of Economic Association of Bihar held at TM Bhagalpur University, Bhagalpur (Bihar) which are divided in three sections. The session on Public Distribution System in India, in which these research papers were presented and discussed.

I. PUBLIC DISTRIBUTION SYSTEM AND THE FOOD SECURITY

Research papers of Debes Mukhopadhayay, Ratan Lal Basu, H.C.L. Das, Anju Singh, Kalanand Singh and Asha Dubey, Subodh Kumar Sinha and Vinod Kumar Sinha, N.C. Jha and Navendu Shekhar, Ranjana Singh, Kumari Sudama Yadav and Shabnam Parween, Chandra Kant Singh and Rakesh Kumar Singh, Mritunjay Prasad Singh, Amita Sinha and G.S. Dokania, Niranjay Kumar, Arvind Kumar Singh, Sanjay Kumar and Abhay K. Pandey, Arun Kumar Thakur and Umesh Kumar Jha, Sandhya Rani and Chandra Bhushan

Kumar, Bishwanath Gupta, Bindeshwar Kumar and As Mahammad deal with the Public Distribution System in relation to food security.

Debes Mukhopadhayay suggested the variable to judge whether a country is food secure: (i) per capita availability of food, and (ii) distribution of food among the people particularly the vulnerable sections of the society. Ratan Lal Basu traces the (i) falling income and employment of the poor, and (ii) failure of PDS as the basic reasons for the recent increasing trend of food insecurity. H.C.L. Das very categorically emphasises that PDS is essential to ensure food security at household land. Anju Singh *et. al.* assess the food security through time series data on the availability of foodgrains in India for the period 1956-98. Subodh Kumar Sinha and Vinod Kumar Sinha examine the problem of food security through the base of PDS.

According to their views the present system of support price for the procurement and maintenance of buffer stocks of foodgrain did not help much to provide food security to the vulnerable sections of the society. N.C. Jha and Navendu Shekhar analysed the food security to the downtrodden people in the state of Jharkhand. They found that majority of the poor people in Jharkhand consumed only 6 kg. to 10 kg. foodgrains per month, which is insufficient even for their survival. The current system of PDS in Jharkhand is in shamble because of large scale pilferage of the foodgrains and other essential commodities distributed through PDS. Ranjana Singh is of the view that PDS can be helpful in mitigating the poverty and providing food security on mass scale. The Paper entitled—Management of PDS in Bihar: A Goal of Food Security by Kumari Sudama Yadav and Shabnam Parween provides a micro-view of food security through a well conceived study in the district of Bhagalpur. Chandra Kant Singh and Rakesh Kumar Singh's paper provides a grim view of PDS in Bihar where the food security is a distant dream unless the whole system of foodgrain distribution is not revamped. Paper by Mritunjay Prasad Singh *et. al.* emphatically makes it clear that faulty system of transportation, storage and distribution of foodgrains greatly hampered the efficacy of the PDS. Niranjay Kumar's paper reveals that income transfer through PDS is very low in the state of Bihar, Orissa, Rajasthan and U.P. Arvind Kumar Singh *et. al.* provide an historical view of PDS and its impact on food security. They conclude that the first phase of battle against raw hunger is more or less won. However, the battle ahead, in the form of food security, is still more difficult. Therefore, it must be waged with great resolve on the part of everybody concerned, including of course, the affected people themselves.

The paper—"Impact of Food Security on Nutritional Health of Rural Women" by Arun Kumar Thakur and Umesh Kumar Jha examines the level of nutrition among rural women. The authors suggest that nutritional deficiency among rural women can be mitigated by providing food security to them. Sandhya Rani and Chandra Bhushan Kumar discuss the issue of Food Security for poor people and problem of PDS in India. The authors are of the view that PDS, despite its certain weaknesses, has certainly helped millions of poor to overcome hunger and deprivation. Bishwanath Gupta *et. al.* paper provides a generalised view of PDS and its role in food security.

II. FUNCTIONING OF PDS IN BIHAR

The *Second Section* of the book presents the research paper on the functioning of PDS in the state of Bihar. Sudama Singh in his paper, 'A Reflection on PDS: Its Operation and Challenges', presents a detailed description of PDS in Bihar. According to Prof. Singh the whole system in Bihar suffers from allotment gap, weak delivery mechanism, poor off-take and widespread leakages. Anju Jain observes in her paper that effectiveness of the PDS in Bihar lies in the viability of FPSs, and control of black marketing, adulteration, under weighing, quality control of commodities supplied. Ramanuj Sharma's paper entitled—Significance of PDS in context of food in Bihar discusses various schemes that ensure food security in the state. A paper entitled "PDS and its Functioning in Bihar and

Jharkhand by Laxmi Kumar provide a generalised view of PDS in both the states. Anjana Kumari and Anju Sinha review the functioning of PDS in Bihar. Satyendra Narayan Singh *et. al.* examines PDS in present scenario.

III. VARIOUS ASPECTS OF PDS

In the *Third Section* the contributors presents the Public Distribution System in various aspects. Abhishek Kumar and Aprana Bhardwaj examine the existing regional imbalances in PDS. According to authors, regional imbalances in the productivity and production of foodgrains creates heavy burden on PDS. D.K. Bhattacharya and Niyati Chakraborty discuss the global food crisis and its impact on India. Kamini Jha's paper entitled, "Who does the Public Distribution System Target" examines the issue of targeting in relation to two points: (i) Persons needing food subsidy, and (ii) How to eliminate those who do not need food subsidy. She criticised the TPDs on account of faulty mechanism of identification of beneficiaries. Shailesh Kumar in his paper "Strengthening Public Distribution System" suggests some measures of far reaching consequences.

Saroj Kumar's paper—PDS and PRIs finds a ground for the active involvement of PRIs in the functioning of PDSs. Functionaries of PRIs can act watchdog under PDS. People's participation is vital for the effective functioning of PDS. PRIs are the best model of peoples' participation. That is what says the paper of Sanjay Kumar. Binod Prasad and Pankaj Kumar discuss the role of PRI in the implementation of PDS in Bihar and Jharkhand.

Research papers of Syed Alay Mujtaba *et. al.* Nisha Kumari and Swarnim Ghosh, Chandrika Prasad, Ashok Kumar Jha *et. al.,* Mukul Kumar Singh, Jagdish Prasad and Arun Kumar, R. Rahman and Md. Aiyub Rayeen, Vandana Kumari, Ram Kumar Prasad and B.K. Pandey, Asim K. Karmakar and Sangeeta Kundu, Dhananjay Kumar *et. al.* Prita Yadav and Ram Dular Singh, present different aspects of Public Distribution System in India ranging from the empowerment of women and gender justice, poverty eradication through PDS, social aspects and good governance, etc. Some of the contributors are of the view that problem of food and hunger has no place in a well conceived PDS. Bipin Pd. Singh and Md. Aiyub Rayee categorically emphasised that PRI's involvement in PDS would certainly improve the benefits of PDS.

United Progressive Alliance and its Government at the centre under the able leadership of world renowned economist Dr. Man Mohan Singh is committed to provide food security to all the citizens of the country by making "Right to Food" a legal right through a well designed central legislation. This right will be operationalize through Public Distribution System which has some in-built shortcomings, such as bogus ration cards, identification of genuine poor families, widespread leakages, and malfunctioning of Food Corporation of India. Unless these issues are dealt in an effective matter any move towards 'right to food' or the 'food for all' will be a distant dream.

The variety of research papers presented in this book make significant contribution to the understanding of food security, nutritional requirements and the entire working of the Public Distribution System. Some of the papers provide concrete suggestions of far reaching consequences for the smooth functioning of the PDS. The book will help the policy planners to find efficient and equitable ways to make the proposed right to food a great success. Ultimately this will ensure the growth with inclusiveness.

ANIL KUMAR THAKUR
KALPANA PAL

SECTION I

Public Distribution System and the Food Security

Public Distribution System
A Poor Delivery System

Debes Mukhopadhayay

As long as our food policy keeps shifting between tweedledum and tweedlede, and we have been doing precisely this year after year to this day, we shall not be able to procure adequate stocks of grain for the maintenance of a stable public-distribution system. It will fail, as has happened in the past, when it is most needed." —*B.S. Minhas*

". . . the PDS is a grossly inefficient instrument for reaching the poor."

—*Vijay Joshi and IMD Little*

INTRODUCTION

Being mostly agriculture-dominated economies, LDCs/ UDCs are inflation-sensitive countries. Thus, the goal of price stability remains elusive as agricultural output is subject to seasonal fluctuations. Anyway, failure in the price front means a rise in (both rural and urban) poverty level. One has to look into the public distribution system (henceforth PDS) against the backdrop of inflationary pressures so that a balance between supply of and demand for foodgrains is maintained. This demands the building up of adequate reserves of foodgrains (i.e., buffer food stock) round the year to meet the exigencies. Maintenance of foodgrains stock/reserve requires an increase in supplies through increased outputs and ultimately imports if shortages persist. Procurement and maintenance of sufficient buffer stock of foodgrains and distribution of the same to the vulnerable sections of the population is an important instrument of GOI's foodgrains policy.

Share of food in total consumer expenditure in rural areas has fallen from 73 p.c. to 55 p.c. and from 64 p.c. to 42 p.c. in urban areas. Share of cereals has fallen from 41 p.c. to 18 p.c. of total consumer expenditure in rural areas and the same declined from 23 p.c. to 10 p.c. in urban areas. There has been a change in the type of cereals consumed by the lowest income group. Data from the last three NSSO surveys (during the period 1993-94 to 2004-05) tell that there has been progressive increase in consumption of wheat and rice while consumption of coarse cereals like jowar, bajra, maize, etc., have fallen because of the availability of such cereals under PDS—a healthy change in the food consumption. One then sees changing fortunes of peasants. But ironies of food insecurity and starvation among these people persist and recur.

OBJECTIVES MANAGEMENT OF FOOD ECONOMY—DECLINING PER CAPITA AVAILABILITY OF CEREALS

The PDS took shape against the backdrop of the catastrophic Bengal famine of 1943. In the 1950s and 1960s it aimed at providing the benefit of support price that assures producers a certain minimum price on the one hand, and providing food subsidy to the consumers. The underlying philosophy of foodgrains policy of the GOI was to counter the scourge of terrific food crisis (a 'ship to mouth' condition) and the consequent high food prices. Raj Krishna (1967) has given a synthetic list of objectives : (i) steady growth of per capita supply of foodgrains, (ii) equitable distribution of foodgrains at a "fair" price, etc., and many others in the Government's operations in foodgrains. Echoing the same objective, Economic Survey, 2007-08 has articulated that the country's food management policy has three basic objectives: 'procurement of foodgrains from farmers at remunerative prices, distribution of foodgrains to the consumers particularly the vulnerable sections of the society at affordable prices, and maintenance of food buffers for food security and prices stability'. However, Raj Krishna's Comment on the government operations in foodgrains over the last 16 years since the planning era began Raj Krishna, "Thus", observed "a legal, rational, two-market two-price system would have existed instead of the illegal two-market, two-price regime, which overambitious rationing and price control have brought into being."

Food policy demands a balance between the supply of foodgrains and the demand for foodgrains. In the initial years of planning, foodgrains imports (e.g., under PL 480) was an important element of the food policy so as to maintain balance between demand and supply. This is evident in Table 1 where we find that the country had to import 10.3 million tonnes of foodgrains from abroad in 1966 because of three consecutive droughts years. For the obvious reasons, there had never been a steady growth of per capita availability of foodgrains (cereals and pulses only). This is also true of the green revolution years when the foodgrains production rose to a great height. As years rolled on, the number of population living below the poverty line also declined, of course, by mathematical jugglery. Anyway, the table reveals an interesting phenomenon: per capita availability of foodgrains for the first 30 years (1951-80) averaged at 426.02 gms. per day, but for the next 26 years (1981-2006), it marginally increased to 464.70 gms per day—a linear trend indeed. However, per capita mean availability (the difference between maximum and minimum availability) of foodgrains for the first 30 years was higher (523.3 gms per day) as compared to 466.3 gms per day for the next 26 years. Per capita availability tends to fluctuate around the mean value, if a year-to-year availability is studied. Thus, the

TABLE I

Net Availability of Cereals and Pulses

Year	Population (million)	Cereals			Pulses		Per day (grams)
		Net production (million tonnes)	Net imports (million tonnes)	Change in Govt. stocks (million tonnes)	Net availability (million tonnes)	Net availability (million tonnes)	Cereals + Pulses = Total
(1)	(2)	(3)	(4)	(5)	(6)	(7)	(8)
1951	363.2	40.1	4.1	+0.6	44.3	8.0	394.9
1952	369.2	40.7	3.9	+0.6	44.0	8.0	384.5
1953	375.6	45.5	2.0	-0.5	48.0	8.6	412.6
1954	382.4	53.6	0.8	+0.2	54.2	9.7	457.8
1955	389.7	51.7	0.6	-0.8	53.1	10.1	444.0
1956	397.3	50.4	1.4	-0.6	52.4	10.2	430.7
1957	405.5	52.8	3.6	+0.9	55.5	10.6	447.1
1958	414.0	49.5	3.2	-0.3	52.9	8.8	439.0
1959	423.1	57.4	3.9	+0.5	60.8	11.6	468.3
1960	432.5	57.1	5.1	+1.4	60.8	10.4	449.6

(*Contd.*)

TABLE I (*Contd.*)

(1)	(2)	(3)	(4)	(5)	(6)	(7)	(8)
1961	442.4	60.9	3.5	-0.2	64.6	11.1	468.7
1962	452.2	61.8	3.6	-0.4	65.8	10.2	460.9
1963	462.0	60.2	4.6	–	64.8	10.1	443.8
1964	472.1	61.8	6.3	-1.2	69.3	8.8	452.0
1965	482.5	67.3	7.4	+1.1	73.7	10.8	480.1
1966	493.2	54.6	10.3	+0.1	64.8	8.7	408.1
1967	504.2	57.6	8.7	-0.3	66.6	7.3	401.4
1968	515.4	72.6	5.7	+2.0	76.2	10.6	460.2
1969	527.0	73.1	3.8	+0.5	76.5	9.1	445.1
1970	538.9	76.8	3.6	+1.1	79.3	10.2	455.0
1971	551.3	84.5	2.0	+2.6	84.0	10.3	468.8
1972	563.9	82.3	-0.5	-4.7	86.5	9.7	466.1
1973	576.8	76.2	3.6	+1.1	79.3	10.2	455.0
1974	590.0	82.8	5.2	-0.4	88.4	8.8	451.2
1975	603.5	78.6	7.5	+ 5.6	80.6	8.8	405.5
1976	617.2	94.5	0.7	+10.7	84.4	11.4	424.3
1977	631.3	87.3	0.1	-1.6	89.0	10.0	429.6

1978	645.7	100.1	-0.8	-0.3	99.6	10.7	468.0
1979	660.3	104.8	-0.3	+0.4	104.1	10.8	476.5
1980	675.2	88.5	-0.5	-5.8	93.8	7.6	410.4
							Minimum 384.5
							Maximum 448.8
							Mean 523.3
1981	688.5	104.1	0.5	-0.2	104.8	9.4	454.8
1982	703.8	106.6	1.6	+1.3	106.8	10.1	454.8
1983	718.1	103.0	4.1	+2.7	104.4	10.4	437.3
1984	734.5	122.0	2.4	+7.1	117.4	11.3	479.7
1985	750.4	116.9	-0.3	+2.7	113.9	10.5	454.0
1986	766.5	119.9	-0.1	-1.6	121.5	12.3	478.1
1987	782.7	115.2	-0.4	-9.5	124.4	10.4	471.8
1988	799.2	113.2	2.3	-4.6	120.1	10.7	448.5
1989	815.8	136.6	0.8	+2.6	134.7	12.5	494.5
1990	832.6	138.4	–	+6.2	132.3	12.5	476.4
1991	851.7	141.9	-0.6	-4.4	145.7	12.9	510.1
1992	867.8	136.8	-0.7	-1.6	137.7	10.9	468.8

(*Contd.*)

TABLE I (*Contd.*)

(1)	(2)	(3)	(4)	(5)	(6)	(7)	(8)
1993	883.9	145.8	2.6	+10.3	138.1	11.7	464.1
1994	899.9	149.6	0.5	+7.5	142.6	12.2	471.2
1995	922.0	155.3	-3.0	-1.7	154.0	12.7	495.5
1996	941.6	147.1	-3.5	-8.5	152.1	11.3	475.2
1997	959.8	162.0	-0.6	-1.8	163.2	13.0	503.1
1998	978.1	156.9	-2.9	+6.1	147.9	11.7	447.1
1999	996.4	165.1	-1.5	+7.5	156.1	13.3	465.7
2000	1014.8	171.8	-1.4	+13.9	156.6	11.7	454.4
1901	1033.2	162.5	-4.5	+12.3	145.6	11.3	416.2
1902	1050.6	174.5	-8.5	-9.9	175.9	13.6	494.1
1903	1068.2	143.2	-7.1	-23.2	159.3	11.3	437.6
1904	1085.6	173.5	-7.7	-3.3	169.1	14.2	462.7
1905	1102.8	162.1	-7.2	-2.4	157.4	12.7	422.4
1906(P)	1119.8	170.8	-3.8	-1.5	168.5	13.3	444.5
							Minimum 422.4
							Maximum 510.1
							Mean 466.3

Source : Economic Survey, 2007-08.

objective of 'steady growth in consumption' has not been achieved even after 55 years of economic planning. Only population growth and price level have been showing steady growth!

FOOD MANAGEMENT—POORLY TARGETED ON POVERTY-STRICKEN PEOPLE

PDS is an important component of supply management of essential commodities. This is an essential element of government's safety net for the poor. Now we consider the distributive objective of PDS that aims at protecting the interests of the weaker sections of the community by providing minimum supply of foodgrains at reasonable prices. However, the PDS that we had before 1992 was the universal public distribution of foodgrains variety. Objective is indeed laudable, but difficult to attain because of many reasons like inefficiency, corruption, leakages, etc. 42nd Round NSS data of 1986-87 showed that hardly 16 p.c. the poor were dependent on the PDS. In other words, this amounts to saying that poor people were largely dependent on the market for their purchases of cereals. It has been reported that in 1999-2000, as many as 36 p.c. BPL families purchased rice or wheat from the PDS as contrasted to 31 p.c. non-poor households. If additional data are analyzed, one may reach the conclusion: 'that while the PDS includes significant members of the non-poor, it also excludes the bulk of the poor'. It has also been observed that more than 90 p.c. of rural population of the seven Northern states of the country bought nothing from the PDS. Taking only the poorest 20 p.c. of all rural and urban households, more than 85 p.c. made no purchases from the PDS in these seven states. The essence of these studies is that the bulk of the cereal subsidy had not been directed to the not-so-poor. Kirit Parikh observed: "For every rupee spent, less than 22 paise reach the poor in all states, excepting Goa, Daman and Diu where 28 paise reach the poor." Karnataka's figure is more pathetic: only 13 paise out of a rupee of the cereal subsidy on PDS reached the poor.

But why? Leakage of foodgrains is considered to be one of the major problems of PDS. Such leakage may be attributed to the losses in movement of cereals by transport and storage and diversion of foodgrains to the free market. Commenting on the inefficiency and corruption of the FCI and the Food Departments of different State Governments, Ashok V. Desai put the following eloquently: "At least 15 p.c. of the foodgrains procured by FCI disappears without trace . . . These losses are passed off as wastage, but are actually siphoned off by the staff and sold. The proportion is far higher in the State Food Departments." Often shop owners make fake entries in ration cards of poor illiterate people: "For example, in a village in Dahanu Taluka in Maharashtra, the tribals have not tasted sugar for over a year. But, one family's ration card tells a different story. According to an entry made for June 1995, this undernourished tribal bought 26 kgs. of sugar on a single day!" The delivery systems particularly in rural areas are very poor. Even if a fair price shop exists, foodgrains are not available in many places. It had been estimated by the 1999 Tata Economic Consultancy Services Report that 38 p.c. of wheat, 36 p.c. of rice, and 55 p.c. of edible oil did not reach the actual users due to diversion of foodgrains to the free market. The extent of such diversion, as per the said Report of the Tata Economic Consultancy Services has been shown in Table 2.

TABLE 2

Extent of Diversion of Rice, Wheat and Sugar

(*in %*)

	Rice	*Wheat*	*Sugar*
Bihar	44	64	47
West Bengal	40	34	24
Andhra Pradesh	15	19	16
All-India average	36	31	23

It is clear from the table diversion was the largest in Bihar, much above the national average. West Bengal's position is no less good than either the national average or Bihar. As far as diversion of foodgrains is concerned, Andhra Pradesh is in a better shape. It is indeed true that the dual pricing system—

APL and BPL prices—has made the process of diversion and leakage of foodgrains easier. Most importantly, the coverage of the PDS has become narrow because of targeting. Even a large chunk of BPL families have not been brought under the TPDS net.

An estimate based on a 2005 study by the Planning Commission revealed that during 2003-04, out of 14.07 million metric tonnes of rice and wheat released for distribution to the vulnerable sections of the population of 16 states, less than one-third of the allotted quota (exactly 5.93 million metric tonnes) actually reached the BPL ration card holders. Table 3 shows the nature of distribution of foodgrains among the target group to have inkling about the unholy and deep nexus between the FPS owners or ration dealers, black marketers and officials of the State Food Departments.

TABLE 3

Characteristic Feature of Distribution of Foodgrains among the Target Group

(in %)

	National average	*Bihar*	*West Bengal*
1. Legitimate FPSs within 1 km. of Residence	60	56	64
2. People getting rationed quota regularly	23	10	9
3. People getting the right quantity	8	6	2
4. People getting the right quality	9	14	1

Regarding the quality of foodgrains, less the said the better. Nutritional deprivation of poor hungry millions can be imagined from a Report of the World Bank. It said that in 2000 half of FCI's food stock is at least 2 years' old, 30 p.c. lying between 2-4 years' old and some grain was as old as 16 years.

Diversion is higher in Northern, Eastern and North-Eastern regions diversion (e.g., 64 p.c. of rice in Bihar and Assam, 100 p.c. of wheat in Nagaland) as contrasted to Southern and Western regions.

One also observes glaring regional disparities in the allocation of foodgrains under the PDS, circumventing the requirements of the poorer states. States having largest concentration of poverty-stricken population like Bihar, Rajasthan, Orissa, Madhya Pradesh, etc., got lower allocations of foodgrains. In other words, food subsidies are not intended to the poorest households of the poorest states. High-sounding words (that is, pro-poor slogans and statements) are enough to bamboozle the public. That is why drumbeating amidst failure in implementing policies is made repeatedly. Being an anti-poverty programme, Joshi and Little had to say that the PDS is 'extremely poor targeted on poverty, and is believed to be a hotbed of inefficiency and corruption'.

DUAL PRICE SYSTEM AND THE CONSEQUENT CROWDING OUT EFFECT

Anyway, the PDS is 'untargeted' and has an urban bias. In rural India, more than 17 p.c. households do not have ration cards and 18 p.c. BPL households do not own ration cards. Thus, the targeting of the poor gathered momentum in 1992 when the PDS was considerably extended in selective tribal-rural backward blocks (1775) under the Revamped PDS. Under this new scheme additional quantities of cereals were made available at prices lower than the issue price for universal PDS. A Targeted PDS—a two-tier subsidized pricing system, one each for Above the Poverty Line (APL) and another for Below the Poverty Line (BPL) families—was introduced in June 1997. Since its inception, both APL and BPL prices as well as allocation of cereals have been revised. Presently (since April 2002), the allocation of foodgrains to the BPL families is 35 kg per family per month. What is disturbing is that in most areas APL families withdrew large quantities of cereals from the FPSs since BPL families could not afford to purchase 35 kg of foodgrains per month at a time. This kind of leakage in the distributional channels bears testimony to the fact that even the TPDS has failed to reach the poor. What is disturbing is the crowding out effect—APL families, in the ultimate analysis, crowd out BPL families in the distributional channels.

One significant development of the newly introduced TPDS is the higher, if not more than double, allocation of foodgrains in UP, Bihar and Assam but the offtake by the States (e.g. 48 p.c. in Bihar, 38.26 p.c. in Madhya Pradesh and 50 p.c. in Pondicherry as per data available for the period 2008-09 up to September, 2008) is poor and by actual BPL beneficiaries even poorer.

Thus the TPDS fails in reaching the poor for whom it is intended. While dissecting the TPDS, the Planning Commission in its evaluation study in 2005 found: (i) errors in targeting the genuine poor people, (ii) ghost BPL cards, and (iii) diversion foodgrains away from the distributive channels.[9] Diversion of foodgrains could be attributed to the low rate of return from the capital invested in FPSs. It was observed that not more than 23 p.c. of FPSs did earn a rate of return of just 12 p.c. on capital. Possibly, this low rate of return is an inducement on the part of ration dealers to sell their products in private markets where high prices rule.

PARADOX OF PLENTY AND THE ISSUE OF FOOD SECURITY

Cut in food subsidy in the neo-liberal economic regime has brought into the issue of food security in sharp focus, although provisioning of food subsidy is an important element of the food security system in India. Since the beginning of the reform era, the Government has been serious in reducing its flab by targeting the subsidy to the household specific.

Food security necessitates building up of adequate food stocks to meet the exigencies. Food security is very much connected with the volume of output in the foodgrains sector, their prices (minimum support prices, prices in fair price shops, etc.) and the policies relating to distribution, holding of food stocks, etc. Two variables may be used to judge whether a country is food secure: (i) per capita availability of food, and (ii) distribution of food among the people particularly the vulnerable populations. It is indeed correct to assume that the spectre of food insecurity will come to the surface with an ugly head if sufficient food stocks as per the country's requirements are not built up. Consequent upon good agricultural production in the late 1990s and early 2000s, more than 50 million tonnes of foodgrain stocks had been accumulated by 2002. But the country experienced 'the scandalous phenomenon of mounting food stocks against the background of widespread hunger.' Authors, frustrated over such unprecedented accumulation of food stock at massive public expense amidst shortfall in the supply of foodgrains in FPSs, regretted: "To put these staggering numbers in perspective, it may help to think of the current stock as the equivalent of one tonne of food for each household below the poverty line. If all the sacks of grain in state warehouses were lined up in a row, the line would stretch for one million kilometers or so—more than twice the distance from the earth to the moon." Thus, the objective of attaining food security could not be achieved as the massive food stocks deprived a large number of people of food entitlements.

In this connection, the political economy of PDS may be reviewed. Over the years, food subsidy—both in the Central and State budgets—has gone up as such kind of subsidy is deployed as a political weapon. One of the contentious issues in the PDS operation has been how to contain the food subsidy within reasonable levels. The Government intends to appease rich privileged farmers through Minimum Support Prices (MSP) even against expert recommendations of the Commission for Agricultural Costs and Prices (CACP). Again, to win the hearts of rich farmers, Government also raises Procurement Prices (PP) to procure foodgrains, food subsidies to the consumer through the PDS. Subsidies to the Food Corporation of India to cover up all its costs are also given. 'By fulfilling the obligation towards distributive justice, the Government incurs food subsidies.' Food subsidy has been remaining stable around Rs. 25,000 crore since 2003-04. Only in 2007-08, such subsidy went up beyond Rs. 31,000 crore. May be in absolute terms, food subsidy constitutes less than 1 p.c. of GDP, and it comprises 3-4 p.c. of the total Government expenditure, it is expensive because of (illegal) diversion of foodgrains to the private market and excess distribution costs of the PDS. On the contrary, rich farmers are the only beneficiaries of rising MSP. Further, the bulk of the subsidy

Table 4
Allocation of Subsidies and Population below Poverty Line

State	*Food subsidy for TPDS*			*Per cent of total food subsidy*	*Percentage of people below poverty line (based on URP)*
	2005-06	*2006-07*	*Average*		
Bihar	975.1	625.1	800.1	3.5	41.4
Punjab	119.2	49.6	84.4	0.4	8.4
Jharkhand	678.1	429.4	553.7	2.4	40.3
Rajasthan	882.4	388.5	635.4	2.8	22.1
Madhya Pradesh	1571.4	949.0	1260.2	5.5	38.3
Uttar Pradesh	4024.3	2766.3	3395.3	14.8	32.8
Maharashtra	2183.5	1499.6	1841.6	8.0	30.7
Haryana	275.0	139.1	207.1	0.9	14.0
Orissa	1111.8	1130.9	1121.4	4.9	46.4
Gujarat	744.4	438.7	591.6	2.6	16.8
Goa	18.6	8.3	13.5	0.1	13.8
Chhattisgarh	787.9	663.4	725.7	3.2	40.9
West Bengal	1903.2	1593.4	1748.3	7.6	24.7
Karnataka	1611.9	1409.0	1510.5	6.6	25.0
Delhi	373.0	239.4	306.2	1.3	14.7
Kerala	821.6	674.7	748.1	3.3	15.0
Tamil Nadu	2636.1	2595.2	2615.7	11.4	22.5
Andhra Pradesh	2415.3	2243.0	2329.1	10.2	15.8
Total of all States	25813	19945.5	22879.3	100	27.5

Note : 1. Subsidies have been calculated on the basis of offtake and difference between economic cost and issue price.

2. Share of BPL population is as per Planning Commission, 2004-05, based on Uniform Recall Period.

3. Totals cover all States and UTs including the ones not specifically mentioned.

Source : Economic Survey, 2007-08 and Planning Commission.

(more than 85 p.c.) goes to the FCI for procurement and distribution.

Despite the annual rise in subsidy bill over the last 4-5 years, State-wise allocations of subsidy do not match with the incidence of poverty level of different States. Orissa, being the poorest State in India as per Planning Commission's latest estimate of 2004-05, total food subsidy it received was just 4.9 p.c., Bihar's food subsidy amounted to a meager of 3.5 p.c. *vis-à-vis* percentage of BPL population of 41.4 p.c. On the other hand, states like Andhra Pradesh having less population living below the poverty line received more than 10 p.c. of the total food subsidy (Table 4).

Consequent upon this kind of inefficiency and the rampant corruption in the delivery channels, West Bengal witnessed 'ration riots' in as many as six districts in late 2007 when people violently agitated against some unscrupulous ration dealers who afforded the risk of diverting cereals to the black market so as to reap the gain. Such immoral and illegal activities of these ration mafias denied the poor people of much-needed food.

CONCLUSION

Right to food is a human right and denial of such means unfreedom. So this human right needs to be protected at any cost. Unfortunately, PDS/TPDS in India has jeopardized the food security to the target group not only in recent years but also in the early years of 2000 when the country had piled up colossal food stocks. The level of hunger and starvation is linked to this slapdash attempt of maintaining food security. Had there been food security, some of the starvation deaths could have been avoided. We are afraid that the strategy that is being pursued is rather wrong-headed and hence food security seems to be a challenging proposition. Issues of politics, power and the nature of violence perpetrated by mobs in rural Bengal (where the majority of poor people live) recently in the State of West Bengal may be visible in a more vigorous form as today's food insecurity is too linked to the global food crisis and the global capitalist system. However, as a provider of food security of poor families, the PDS must not be made slimmer. The need of the hour is the universal PDS rather than TPDS. Livelihood security and right to food have to be the policy focus of any government (either left-wing or right-wing) in power.[12]

References

Alternative Survey Group, *Alternative Economic Survey, India, 2006-07, Pampering Corporates, Pauperizing Masses*, Daanish Books.

Alternative Survey Group, *Alternative Economic Survey, India, 2007-08, Decline of the Developmental State;* Daanish Books.

Bharat Ramswami's write up in Kaushik Basu (ed.), *The Oxford Companion to Economics in India* (2007), OUP.

Government of India, *Economic Survey, 2007-08.*

Government of India (2008), *Economic Survey, 2007-08.*

Ibid., 1.

Ibid., 5.

Ibid., 5.

J. Dreze and A. Sen, (2002) *India: Development and Participation*, OUP.

Kirit, S. Parikh (ed.) (1997), *India Development Report*, IGIDR, OUP.

Objectives of foodgrains operations policy of the Government of India are: (i) steady growth of per capita supply of foodgrains; (ii) equitable distribution of foodgrains at a "fair" price; (iii) purchase and sale of marketed surplus by the Government to realize the second objective; and (iv) self-sufficiency. Raj Krishna (1967) *Governments Operations in Foodgrains in Some Problems of India's Economic Policy (1973)*, Ed. Charan D. Wadhva, Tata McGraw Hill Publishing Company Ltd.

V. Joshi and IMD Little (1996), *India's Economic Reforms, 1991-2001;* Clarendon Press, Oxford.

Public Distribution System in India and Food Security

Ratan Lal Basu

INTRODUCTION

Food insecurity for the poor and vulnerable sections of both rural and urban areas of India, which had been a chronic problem since independence, aggravated alarmingly since the inception of the Economic Reforms in 1991. Slow growth of agriculture in the face of rapid growth of population has no doubt intensified the problem but deeper analysis would reveal that the main cause of food insecurity of the majority of the population in India lies not in supply failure but in increasing unemployment, rapid fall in income of the poor in the rural and urban areas and the miserable failure of the PDS in India.

Since 1951, food production increased almost steadily (except for a few bad years) and overstepped the growth rate of population and the Buffer Stock of the Food Corporation of

India (FCI) exceeded the required minimum except for the last few years. Still food insecurity increased during the 1990s although there had been a falling trend during the 1980s.

If we look at the buffer stock position of the FCI we come across a paradoxical situation. On the one hand buffer stock has been more than sufficient till 2006 to meet the requirements. For the last few years it has fallen marginally below the minimum required, which could be met by food imports. On the other hand, intensity of food insecurity of the vulnerable segments of rural and urban population has been continuously increasing ever since the 1990s. The percentage of hungry people fell marginally during the period but absolute number increased considerably.

So it becomes clear that supply deficiency is not the basic cause of hunger and food insecurity of the majority of the population. Historical evidence also shows that famines and food insecurity in India in the past arose not because of supply failure but because of wrong policy of the government. Amartya Sen has shown that during the Great Bengal Famine of 1943, there was no scarcity of foodgrains (Sen, 1999).

After independence India has not experienced any acute food crisis in the form of famine which had been a recurrent catastrophe during the British regime, but we have been inflicted with chronic hunger which has been intensified since the 1990s. Here also the basic cause does not lie in supply deficiency but in wrong policy of the government in two ways. First, the policy of liberalization has resulted in fall of income and employment of the vulnerable segments of population and second, the PDS and other safety measures for the poor have become less efficient. So in brief, the basic reason for the recent increasing trend of food insecurity are:

(i) Falling income and employment of the poor, and
(ii) Failure of the PDS.

FOOD INSECURITY IN INDIA

According to report of the Food and Agricultural Organization (FAO) of the United Nations, number of hungry people in India had been:

1979-81: 261.5 million (38%)
1990-92: 215.6 million (25%)
1998-2000: 233.3 million (24%) (FAO, 2002)

From the above data it is found that both percentage and number of hungry people declined in India between 1979-81 and 1990-92, but the absolute number increased between 1990-92 and 1998-2000 (although proportion declined marginally).

The Food Insecurity Atlas prepared by M.S. Swaminathan Research Foundation (MSSRF) used two composite Indices of Food Insecurity (one for rural area and the other for urban area) to show that both urban and rural poor in most of the States in India are afflicted with extreme food insecurity (MSSRF, 2003, 2004).

According to a United Nations report (Feb. 20, 2009) about 20 per cent of the world's 1 billion hungry poor live in India and the number of undernourished in India is increasing. India ranks 94th in the Global Hunger Index of 119 countries and about half of Indian children are underweight. [Website-1]

In a recent study Ranjan Ray has used household calorie

TABLE I
Bufer Stock with the FCI

Year (Jan.)	*Buffer Norms (Million Tonnes)*	*Actual Stock (Million Tonnes)*	*Year (Jan.)*	*Buffer Norms (Million Tonnes)*	*Actual Stock (Million Tonnes)*
1994	15.4	22.0	2002	16.8	58.0
1995	15.4	30.3	2003	16.8	48.2
1996	15.4	28.5	2004	16.8	24.4
1997	15.4	27.0	2005	16.8	21.7
1998	15.4	18.3	2006	20.0	18.8
1999	16.8	24.4	2007	20.0	17.4
2000	16.8	31.4	2008	20.0	19.2
2001	16.8	45.7			

Source : Economic Survey, 2000-01 (Table 5.8, p. 92); 2002-03, (Table 5.12, p. 92); 2007-08 (Table 7.25, p. 179).

intake data from recent National Sample Survey rounds to compose a Prevalence of Under-Nutrition Index. On the basis of this index percentage of undernourished rural household in India rose from 48 per cent at the time of NSS Round 43 (1987-8) to 67 per cent at NSS Round 57 (2001-2); undernourished urban households rose from 37 per cent during the same period (Ray, Ranjan, 2008).

Now it would appear a real paradox if we consider the buffer stock position of the FCIs in 1994. This is shown in the following Table.

The above table shows that actual stock of FCI exceeded the minimum requirement in all the years till 2005. Only for 2006-08 it has been marginally lower than the minimum. In fact the problem does not lie in deficiency in buffer stock but inefficient operation of the PDS, especially the targeted PDS introduced since 1997.

PDS IN INDIA AND ITS FAILURE

One of the major objectives of the Agricultural Price Policy in India, during the plan period, was to assure steady supply of essential foodgrains to the consumers, especially the poor, at affordable prices. The objective of the price policy of the government was stated as: "The objective of the Government's food security policy is to ensure availability of foodgrains to the public at an affordable price. The Public Distribution System, which has existed in the country since the Second World War, strives to meet these twin objectives." (Economic Survey, 1994-95, p. 80)

The so-called Green Revolution added additional importance to PDS. With the introduction of HIV technology the North Western States like Punjab, Haryana, Western U.P., etc. became the main producers of the major cereals and 4 Southern States, Assam, etc. concentrated more on cash crops. (Patnaik, 2001).

This regional specialization called for administered price and distribution policy by the central government to stabilize prices of foodgrains. Thus the existing PDS system assumed added importance. The Food Corporation of India (FCI) was established by the FCI Act, 1964 to facilitate procurement of foodgrains, maintenance of buffer stock and distribution of foodgrains through fair price shops.

Under the PDS, mainly wheat and rice, the two principal cereal food crops in India, are issued by the Central Government at uniform Central Issue Prices (CPIs) to the States and the Union Territories for distribution under PDS. The FCI procures and issues the crops to the States and the Union Territories. The economic cost of the FCI involves costs for procurement, storage, distribution and wastage of foodgrains. The gap, between economic cost of FCI and realization based on the CPIs, is filled by the Central Government through 'food subsidy'.

Till 1996 the PDS in India was universal, *i.e.* essential foodgrains were distributed to everyone irrespective of level of income. In spite of many flaws, the PDS in India till the 1990s played an important role in stabilization foodgrain prices over the country and averting food crisis. During the severe drought of 1987-88, the PDS played an important role in averting famine and death from hunger. (Chaturvedi, 1994).

During the early 1990s the PDS system was criticized on many grounds. One of the criticisms was its marginal impact (on food security) which was considered to be a function of its universality of coverage. (Nawani, 1994)

Moreover, universality of coverage was considered to be a cause of high food subsidy. Structural reform measures in India aimed at reducing revenue deficit and fiscal deficit and reduction of food subsidy was considered as a means to fulfil this objective. So from 1997 the universal PDS was replaced by a targeted PDS (TPDS). The new system attempted to divide the population into two categories: Above Poverty Line (APL) and Below Poverty Line (BPL), the latter entitled to receive foodgrains at lower prices through the fair price shops.

In fact introduction of TPDS created more problems than it solved and made the public distribution mechanism more inefficient. The most serious flaw lies with the definitions of the poverty line and selection of the BPL population who are entitled to food ration at lower prices (Swaminathan 2003).

The problem may be formalized in the following manner:

Let us define (simulating statistical definition) Two Types of Errors:

First Type of Error E-I: Wrong Exclusion: This error occurs if those who should have been included are excluded.

Second Type of Error E-II: Wrong Inclusion: This error occurs if those who should have been excluded are included.

Now under universal PDS, E-II error is likely to be high leading to unnecessary high subsidies. TPDS would exclude those who are included due to E-II. It has been shown by some studies that introduction of TPDS reduced E-II considerably (Dutta and Ramaswami 2001; Misra and Swaminathan 2001). Keeping aside the question of E-I error, reduction of E-II is likely to reduce food subsidies, but the available data gives the contrary indication as in the following table.

TABLE 2

Food Subsidy

Year	*Subsidy (Rs. Crore)*	*Year*	*Subsidy (Rs. Crore)*
1991-92	2850	2001-02	17494
1996-97	6066	2002-03	24176
1997-98	7500	2003-04	25160
1998-99	8700	2004-05	25746
1999-00	9200	2005-06	23071
2000-01	12010	2006-07	23828

Source : Economic Survey, 2000-01, p. 96; 2007-08, Table : 7.27, p. 180.

The above table shows that cost due to food subsidy has steadily increased even after introduction of TPDS.

Now coming to E-I error, it is found that the TPDS has resulted in alarming increase in this type of error leading to exclusion of a large proportion of the poor and the vulnerable sections because of wrong and erratic method of selection of the BPL category.

According to many studies, there is no scientific criteria for identify the BPL household, the criteria used is arbitrary and varies from State to State. (Patnaik, 2003). A study found that over half the proportion of households in the lowest 5 per cent of population did not get BPL cards (Kriesel and Zaidi, 1999).

Various studies have shown that the poverty line, which is the basis of dividing APL and BPL population, as defined by the Planning Commission, fails to give a true picture of poverty in India as it excludes many people who should be considered poor (Patnaik, 2004, Ray and Lancaster 2005).

According to a United Nations Report (*op. cit*) the TPDS failed miserably due to lack of adequate data and incorrect definition of hunger. In theory, essential foodgrains were to be sold only to those who really needed help, but in practice the TPDS excluded large number of the poor and reclassified them as better off than they actually were. Thus according to the report, the TPDS led to greater food insecurity for large sections of the poor and the near-poor [Website-2].

Some other strong opinions against the TPDS are noted below:

1. After 1991, intense pressure from the IMF and the World Bank to reduce the budget deficit brought first a sharp rise in the PDS price of foodgrains unmatched by higher prices for farmers, and then the introduction of "Targeted PDS" in 1997. Within ten years all that had been gained over a generation was lost. "Targeting" involved the near-criminal use of indefensible "Poverty Lines" to subject a vast impoverished population to paying prevailing market prices for essentials. Though accompanied by hypocritical expressions of concern for the poor from both World Bank and Indian neo-liberals, targeting was a deliberate and successful attack on the PDS system as a whole [Website-3].
2. According to NSS Report on Public Distribution

> System and Other Sources of Household Consumption, 2004-05, 58 per cent of subsidised foodgrains do not reach Below Poverty Line ("BPL") families, as 22 per cent reach Above Poverty Line ("APL") families, while 36 per cent are sold in the black market. Only 57 per cent of BPL households have ration cards, while the homeless often do not have any. Only 28 per cent of the rural poor have benefited from any type of government food assistance schemes, and for urban areas the figure is just 9.5 per cent. Over half (51%) of rural households with the smallest landholdings (less than 0.01 hectares) do not possess ration cards that entitle them to monthly rations of rice, wheat, sugar and kerosene under the PDS [Website-4].

Thus we see that introduction of the TPDS since 1997 has failed to reduce E-II error appreciably. On the other hand it has led to alarming increase in E-I error nullifying the basic objective of the PDS to ensure food security for the majority. Moreover, introduction of the TPDS has made the rationing system non-viable in many areas of the country. In the new system off-take by the APL population fell drastically. On the other hand, off-take by the BPL population also declined due to fall in income. These made the system inoperative in many areas (Chakravarty and Dand, 2005).

CONCLUSION

From the above analysis we find that the basic causes of food insecurity in India lie not in supply failure but in declining income and employment in the unorganised sector and failure of the TPDS that excludes a large segment of the poor because of definitions and methods of implementation. So far as policy of introducing the TPDS is concerned, it may be said that the policy as such is not unsound but the real problem lies in the way it is implemented. The following guidelines may improve the functioning of the TPDS:

1. Correct definition of the poverty line following international norms and updating definition regularly.
2. Measures for collecting adequate data on the basis of which people below poverty line are to be selected.
3. Measures to improve functioning of the fair price shops removing inefficiency and corruption.
4. Regular supply of essential articles to the fair price shops.
5. Reduction of wastage and other unnecessary costs of the FCI.
6. Bringing the tribal population residing in remote areas under the cover of rationing system.
7. Measures to raise income and employment of the extreme poor through direct poverty removal schemes.

References

Chakravarty, Sujay and Dand, Sejal, A. (2005), "Food Insecurity: Causes and Dimensions", p. 14, <http://ideas.repec.org/p/iim/iimawp/2005-04-01.html>

Chaturvedi, S. (1994), "India Tries for Drought Tolerance", *Biotechnology and Development Monitor*, No. 18, p. 8.

Dutta, B. and Ramaswami, B. (2001), "Targeting and Efficiency in the Public Distribution System, Case of Andhra Pradesh and Maharashtra", *EPW*, Vol. 36, No. 18, May 5, pp. 1524-32.

FAO (2002), "State of Food Security in the World", <http://www.fao.org/documents_cdr.asp?url_file=/docrep/005/v7352e/v7352e00.htm>

Govt. of India, *Economic Survey*, 2000-01, 2002-03, 2007-08.

Kriesel, S. and Zaidi, S. (1999), "The Targeted Public Distribution System in Uttar Pradesh, India—An Evaluation", *Working Paper*, World Bank, Washington DC, August.

Misra, N. and Swaminathan, M. (2001), "Errors of Targeting: A Case Study of Public Distribution System of Food in a Maharashtra Village, 1995-2000", *Ithaca*: Mario Einaudi Centre for International Studies, Cornell University

MSSRF (2003), "Food Insecurity Atlas of Rural India", *Report* of MSSRF and World Food Programme (WFP) of the Food Aid Organization of UNO.

MSSRF (2004), "Food Insecurity Atlas of Urban India", *Report* of MSSRF and World Food Programme (WFP) of the Food Aid Organization of UNO.

Nawani, N.P. (1994), "Indian Experience on Household Food and Nutrition Security", *FAO Report*, Regional Expert Consultation, FAO-UN, Bangkok.

Patnaik, U. (2001), "Concentration of Regional Food Output and the Public Distribution System", *People's Democracy*, XXV (23), June 2001.

Patnaik, U. (2003), "Food Stocks and Hunger: Causes of Agrarian Distress", *Social Scientist*, Vol. 32, Nos. 7-8, July-August.

Patnaik, U. (2004), "External Trade, Domestic Employment and Food Security: Recent Outcomes of Neo-Liberal Economic Reforms", Conference ('the Question of Asia in Global Order') Paper, Asia Pacific Institute, Duke University, Oct. 1-2.

Ray, Ranjan (2008), "Diversity in Calorie Sources and Undernourishment during Rapid Economic Growth," *EPW*, February 23.

Ray, R. and Lancaster, G. (2005), "On Setting the Poverty Line Based on Estimated Nutrient Prices: Condition of Socially Disadvantaged Groups during the Reform Period", *EPW*, Vol. 11, No. 1, January.

Sen, Amartya (1999), "Food, Economics and Entitlements" in Drèze, Jean, Sen, Amartya and Hussain, Arthar (eds.), *The Political Economy of Hunger*, Oxford University Press, New Delhi, pp. 50-68.

Swaminathan, M. (2003), "Strategies towards Food Security", *Social Scientist*, Vol. 31, No. 9-10, Sept.-Oct., p. 58.

Website-1: <http://tvnz.co.nz/world-news/indian-food-policy-failing-2497797>

Website-2: <http://tvnz.co.nz/world-news/indian-food-policy-failing-2497797>

Website-3: <http://www.monthlyreview.org/mrzine/amr160508.html>

Website-4: <http://www.cseindia.org/programme/nrml/infocus-august07.htm>

Inevitability of Public Distribution System for Food Security in Bihar vis-à-vis India

H.C.L. Das

In India the need for a Public Distribution System (PDS) as an effective instrument of price stabilisation in the national economy was felt for the first time during the Second World War. The Foodgrains Policy Committee in 1943 recommended setting up of a procurement and rationing machinery by the government to meet the war time situation, complicated by the Bengal Famine of 1943. The Ashok Mehta Foodgrains Enquiry Committee (1957) had argued for a measure of relief to consumers through assuring them the benefit of government procurement operation at reasonable prices by selling foodgrains through the institutions like co-operative societies, and/or employers' organizations.

India has lived with food shortage for a very long period. Famines, wars and droughts causing acute scarcity conditions forced the government to undertake 'firefighting' measures from time to time like suspending normal activities of markets and trade through wholesale trade, organization of food zones (for purpose of procuring foodgrains from surplus zones and distributing them to deficit zones), introduction of statutory rationing in selected urban areas, etc. However, a developing economy like India needs a food security system looking much beyond management of scarce supplies and critical situation (Rao, 1995) India took a quantum leap in 1965 when the Food Corporation of India (FCI) and the Agricultural Price Commission, renamed as Commission for Agricultural Costs and Prices (CACP) later, were set-up.

OBJECTIVES OF THE PUBLIC DISTRIBUTION SYSTEM

The broad objectives of the PDS are:

1. To make sure the availability of foodgrains at reasonable prices especially to the vulnerable sections of the society,
2. To rectify the existing imbalances between the supply of and demand for consumer goods,
3. To hold up the hoarding and black marketing in essential commodities,
4. To ensure social justice in the distribution of basic necessities of life,
5. To even out the fluctuations in the prices of mass consumption goods, and
6. To ensure food security to all its citizens and their families.

The purpose of this paper is to examine the working and performance of PDS in context of providing food security for the people in India and highlight the measures to make the system effective in achieving its objectives.

METHODOLOGY

The present paper is based purely on secondary data taken from the *Economic Survey (2007-08)*, Government of

India, New Delhi. The paper covers the period of 57 years from 1950-51 to 2006-07, divided into 5 periods—Period I (Pre-Green Revolution Period : 1950-51 to 1967-68), Period II (Green Revolution Period: 1968-69 to 1980-81), Period III (Wider Technology Dissemination Period: 1981-82 to 1990-91), Period IV (Early Reform Period: 1991-92 to 1996-97) and Period V (Ninth and Tenth Plan Period: 1997-98 to 2006-07).

The exponential trend equation of the type $y = ab^x$ has been fitted into the time series data on net production, net imports, net availability, distribution, and per capita net availability of foodgrains in India during the period from 1950-51 to 2006-07. This trend equation has also been fitted into the time series data on net import as per cent of net availability of foodgrains, procurement as per cent of net production of foodgrains, and the distribution as per cent of net availability of foodgrains. The Student's t-distribution has been applied to test the significance of the estimates (Croxton *et. al.*, 1973). The following formulae have been applied:

1. Exponential trend equation:
   $y = ab^x$
2. Logarithmic form of the equation:
   $\log y = \log a + x.\log b$
3. Corresponding normal equations :
   $\Sigma \log y = N.\log a + \log b.\Sigma x$
   $\Sigma X.\log y = \log a.\Sigma x + \log b.\Sigma x^2$
4. Compound Growth rate :
   $GR = 100(b-1)$
5. $$Syx = \sqrt{\frac{\sum \log y^t - \log a.\sum \log y - \log b.\sum x.\log}{N-K}}$$
6. $$Sb = \sqrt{\frac{Syx}{\sum (X-X)^2}}$$
7. $$t = \frac{\log b - 0}{Sb}$$

where

y	=	Net production of foodgrains/Net imports of foodgrains/Net availability of foodgrains/ Procurement of foodgrains/Distribution of foodgrains under PDS/Per capita availability of foodgrains/Net import as per cent of net availability of foodgrains/Procurement as per cent of production of foodgrains/Volume of distribution of foodgrains under PDS as per cent of net availability of foodgrains.
a	=	Intercept (parameter)
b	=	Trent value (parameter)
GR	=	Compound growth rate per cent per annum
Syx	=	Standard error of estimates
x	=	Number of years
N	=	Number of years
K	=	Number of constants in the equation = 2
Sb	=	Standard deviation of b
t	=	Student's t-statistics.

ANALYSIS

The trends in different variables of public distribution system have been presented in the Table 1. It is evident from the table that net production of foodgrains has shown an increasing trends, in all the five periods from 1950-51 to 2006-07. but it is important to note that during the periods IV and V the production has increased at the decreasing rate. While its growth rate declined from 2.99 per cent per annum in the period III (1981-82 to 1990-91) to 2.59 in the period IV (1991-92 to 1996-97) and further to 0.40 per cent in the period V (1997-98 to 2006-07).

The net import of foodgrains has shown an increasing trend during the period I (1950-51 to 1967-68). But its growth rates have been found negative during the periods II to V. The availability of foodgrains has shown positive trends in all the five periods from 1950-51 to 2006-07. Similartly, the procurement of foodgrains has shown increasing trends in all the five periods from 1950-51 to 2006-07.

TABLE I

Trends in Production, Imports, Procurement, Distribution and Availability of Foodgrains in India (1950-51 to 2006-07)

Item Parameter	*Period*				
	Period-I (1950-51 to 1967-68)	*Period-II (1968-69 to 1980-81)*	*Period-III (1981-82 to 1990-91)*	*Period-IV (1991-92 to 1996-97)*	*Period-V (1997-98 to 2006-07)*
(1)	*(2)*	*(3)*	*(4)*	*(5)*	*(6)*
1. Net Production of Foodgrains					
GM	64.34	96.19	131.14	160.77	176.35
GR	2.24	2.35	2.99	2.59	0.40
t	9.636	4.061	4.693	6.094	6.092
S	0.001	0.001	0.001	0.001	0.001
2. Net Imports of Foodgrains					
GM	3.50	2.13	0.91	1.01	-3.16
GR	9.07	-19.91	-9.51	-7.37	-7.43
t	3.996	5.021	5.105	5.904	6.037
S	0.001	0.001	0.001	0.001	0.001

3. Net Availability of Foodgrains					
GM	68.46	97.75	132.83	159.58	172.78
GR	2.60	2.09	3.21	3.45	11.26
t	8.76	5.005	6.016	6.738	6.355
S	0.001	0.001	0.001	0.001	0.001
4. Procurement of Foodgrains					
GM	1.56	9.32	17.96	25.74	37.38
GR	3.48	5.19	2.42	0.55	1.11
t	4.959	6.657	6.097	6.046	5.105
S	0.001	0.001	0.001	0.001	0.001
5. Per day Per capita availability of Foodgrains					
GM	433.53	443.75	470.05	470.58	448.37
GR	0.53	6.75	1.06	1.36	-1.25
t	6.246	5.489	5.392	6.009	6.266
S	0.001	0.001	0.001	0.001	0.001

Note : GM = Geometric mean in million tonnes for items from 1 to 4, and in grams per day per capita for item 5.
GR = Compound growth rate per cent per annum.
t = Student's t-statistics.
S = Level of significance.

TABLE 2

Trends in Per cent Changes in Imports, Procurements and Distribution of Foodgrains in India (1950-51 to 2006-07)

Item Parameter	*Period*				
	Period-I (1950-51 to 1967-68)	*Period-II (1968-69 to 1980-81)*	*Period-III (1981-82 to 1990-91)*	*Period-IV (1991-92 to 1996-97)*	*Period-V (1997-98 to 2006-07)*
(1)	(2)	(3)	(4)	(5)	(6)
1. Net Imports as Per cent Net Availability of Foodgrains					
GM	5.13	2.73	1.72	1.53	-2.02
GR	7.16	-9.88	-4.71	-4.07	-13.69
t	2.782	5.217	5.553	6.065	5.483
S	0.02	0.001	0.001	0.001	0.001
2. Procurement as Per cent of Net Production of Foodgrains					
GM	2.73	9.62	13.64	14.14	20.08
GR	-2.71	3.7	-0.53	-2.06	3.54
t	6.509	6.587	5.015	6.064	4.487
S	0.001	0.001	0.001	0.001	0.001

3. Distribution as per cent of Availability of Foodgrains					
GM	7.64	10.93	12.52	10.42	11.05
GR	4.63	1.27	-0.4	-3.02	4.93
t	2.132	5.221	5.002	4.365	4.386
S	0.05	0.001	0.001	0.005	0.005

Note : GM = Geometric mean in per cent.
GR = Compound growth rate per cent per annum.
t = Student's t-statistics.
S = Level of significance.

There has been observed an increasing trend in the per day per capita availability of foodgrains in the first four periods from 1950-51 to 1996-97, while during the fifth period (1997-98 to 2006-07), there has been observed decreasing trend.

The trends in percentage changes in imports, procurement and distribution of foodgrains have been shown in the Table 2. The per cent change in imports has shown positive trend during the first period (1950-51 to 1967-68), but negative trends in second to fifth periods (from 1968-69 to 2006-07).

In the case of procurement of foodgrains the per cent change has shown increasing trends during the second and fifth periods and decreasing trends in the first, third and fourth periods.

Finally, the per cent change in the distribution of available quantity of foodgrains has shown positive trends during the periods I, II and V, but negative trends during the periods III and IV.

GREEN REVOLUTION AND AVAILABILITY OF FOODGRAINS

The Government of India went for seed-water-fertilise policy popularly known as the 'Green Revolution'. This policy ushered in a revolution in production of foodgrains in India and dispensed with imports of foodgrains altogether. India achieved self-sufficiency in foodgrains by the year 1976 and since then the imports of foodgrains have remained negligible (even negative). In the words of Etienne, "Despite the gloomy and perfectly ill-founded forecasts or 'prophecies' about India's future distress which were fashionable in the 1960s, the country is no longer exposed to real famines". (Estienne, 1988, p. 196).

Progress on Foodgrains front Reveals the Following:

(a) Between 1950-51 and 2001-02, foodgrains production had increased from 51 million tonnes to 212 tonnes—more than four-fold increase; the production of foodgrains, however, declined to 174 million tonnes in 2002-03.

(b) The various components of cereals production indicate that whereas cereals accounted for 84 per cent in foodgrains in 1950-51, their share has increased to 91 per cent in 2001-02, but as against them, the share of pulses has declined from 16 per cent to just 4 per cent during the same period.

(c) Within cereals the share of the two superior cereals—rice and wheat—which was only 53 per cent in 1950-51, had improved to 78 per cent in 2001-02. During the same period, the share of coarse cereals had declined from 30 per cent to 18 per cent. This indicates a substitution by the weaker sections in favour of rice and wheat as against coarse cereals consumed earlier.

PUBLIC DISTRIBUTION SYSTEM AND FOOD SECURITY

One of the basic objectives of the PDS is to provide food security to people of the vulnerable section of the society. Broadly speaking, food security means ensuring that all people at all times have both physical and economic access to basic food they need. Food security involves physical availability of food to the entire population in a country. People have enough purchasing power so that they can acquire the food they need for healthy life, the food available should be adequate in quantity as well as quality to meet nutritional requirement. A nation may acquire self-sufficiency in food at a point of time, but the concept of food security necessitates that timely, reliable and nutritionally adequate supply of food should be available on long-term basis. This implies that a nation has to ensure the growth in food supply so that it takes care of the increase in population as also the increase in demand resulting from increase in the income of the people.

NINTH FIVE YEAR PLAN AND FOOD SECURITY

The Ninth Five Year Plan (1997-2002) discussed the problem of food security at the national level as well as household level. The Planning Commission states : "An approach to national food security which relies largely on domestic production of food needed for consumption as well as for building buffer stock, can be described as a strategy of self-sufficiency" (Planning Commission, 1999, p. 4).

There is no doubt that as the result of these efforts, India was able to avert famines and acute food scarcity, yet it has not been able to provide food needed for an active and healthy life to its population. In other words, the goal of a balanced diet is still a distant dream. Reviewing the 50 years effort in this direction the Ninth Five Year Plan stated: "Even though self-sufficiency of food production has been achieved, the population still lacks access to balanced food. It is a matter of concern that even though cereal production has kept pqr with the increasing requirements and average per capita intakes have remained satisfactory, there have been a fall in the per capita consumption of pulses. It is important not only to improve pulses production but also make them available at affordable cost. The production and consumption of vegetables continue to remain low. Special efforts have to be made to improve production and improved access to vegetables especially green leafy vegetables at affordable cost both in rural and urban areas" (Planning Commission, 1999, p. 54).

At the household level food security implies having a physical and economic access to food articles which are adequate in terms of quantity, quality and affordability. This raises the question of prices of food articles and the purchasing power in the hands of the population. To help the poor sections, the Government of India introduced the public distribution system (PDS) and adopted dual pricing mechanism. At the PDS outlets the issue price of food articles was kept lower than the market price to enable the poor to purchase subsidized food. But due to political pressure, the Government adopted a universal PDS and poor were not able to take full advantage of the PDS supplies. The PDS which was conceived as a key mechanism in the Government food security system, did not achieve the desired results. The Ninth Five Year Plan reviewing the situation underlined the stark reality : "In spite of mounting food subsidies, evaluation studies indicate that supply of subsidised foodgrains through PDS has not resulted in improvement in household level food security. Self-sufficiency of foodgrains at national level and availability of foodgrains at affordable cost at local level have not got translated into household level food security for the poor" (Planning Commission, 1999, p. 529).

To achieve household level food security efforts were made and directed on the following fronts:

(a) Accelerating growth in food and agricultural sectors which provides direct sources for food and income with which to buy food;
(b) Development strategies and macroeconomic policies which would create conditions for growth with equity;
(c) Promoting rural development which focuses on the poor;
(d) Improving access to land and other natural resources;
(e) Providing cheap credit for poor households;
(f) Increasing employment opportunities;
(g) Introducing income transfer scheme including provisions of public distribution system of subsidized cheap food;
(h) Stabilising food supplies and food prices; and
(i) Improving emergency preparedness planning for providing food aid during natural calamities and disasters like droughts, floods, earthquakes, etc.

TENTH FIVE YEAR PLAN AND FOOD SECURITY

The Tenth Five Year Plan (2002-07) has drawn the attention to the changes in consumption pattern which have taken place in the Post-Green-Revolution period. It stated : "Between 1972-73 and 1993-94 the food basket has become much more diversified, with the share of cereals seeing a dramatic decline of 10 per cent in most regions. At the all India level, cereals consumption in the rural areas declined from 15.3 kg per capita per month in 1972-73 to 13.4 kg per capita per month in 1993-94. The corresponding decline in the urban areas was more modest—from 11.3 kg to 10.6 kg over the same period. At the same time, consumption of milk and meat products as well as vegetables and fruits has increased. Such changes are a natural outcome of economic development" (Planning Commission, 2002, p. 365).

The Tenth Five Year Plan provided the following outline for restructuring of PDS :

(a) Since wheat and rice are the basic necessities of the poor, the items other than these two should be excluded from the scope of food subsidies.
(b) Sugar should be kept outside the purview of PDS.
(c) The subsidy on kerosene should be phased out by raising its supply price for PDS shops, since studies show that the subsidy on kerosene is cornered by the non-poor. Alternatively, if kerosene is to be retained under PDS, the extent of subsidy provided should be reduced so that there is less incentive for diversion.
(d) The coverage of Targeted Public Distribution System (TPDS) and food subsidy should be restricted to below poverty line (BPL) population. Any attempt to revert to the old concept (BPL as well as APL population) of a universal PDS would be a retrograde step and needs to be resisted.
(e) To reduce malpractices, food stamps should be issued to female members of the family who can be designated as heads of households for the purpose. Under the system of food stamps, the state governments should issue a subsidy entitlement cart (SEC) instead of ration card.
(f) A food card system could be a superior alternative to the prevalent Fair Price Shops (FPS) system and perhaps even a food stamp system. The customers could use food credit/debit cart to buy subsidized foodgrains from the market and the retailers can claim the subsidy from the government.
(g) A food coupon scheme was introduced in Andhra Pradesh in 1998-99 for distribution of rice and kerosene through PDS. This system resulted in saving about 20,000 tonnes of rice, 71 lakh liters of kerosene every month. The Andhra Pradesh

experiment may be replicated with suitable adoption in the other states.

Despite the huge stock of foodgrains available in FCI godowns, stray cases of hunger and death are still being reported. PDS should, therefore, be reformed and made more efficient. The present system can be replaced by a system of food stamps and eventually by a food credit card system. The excess stock of foodgrains which have accumulated with the Government, is partly the result of the high Minimum Support Price (MSP) which often exceeds the levels recommended by the Commission for Agricultural Costs and Prices (CACP), There is, therefore, a need to adhere to the recommendations of the CACP.

The scheme for decentralised procurement of foodgrains should be encouraged and more states could be brought under its fold. Similarly, the operation of PDS could be decentralised with the states taking their own decisions regarding issue prices and quantum of foodgrains to be supplied. The national level food subsidy could be distributed among the states according to a prescribed formula.

The Essential Commodities Act should be amended to make it an emergency provision that will have to be formally invoked by notification for a limited period for specific commodities.

All restrictions on inter-state movement of foodgrains should be removed. Octrio and all sorts of taxes/levies on food articles should be eliminated. The ban on future trading in all agricultural commodities should be lifted.

To help the private sector to play an enhanced role in the distribution system, 26 per cent foreign direct investment (FDI) should be in food retailing and 100 per cent FDI in insurance for agriculture and rural areas.

MISMANAGEMENT OF FOOD ECONOMY

In India the structural adjustment policies (SAP) implemented by the successive governments since the early 1990s have led to an increase in food prices, making foodgrains high priced for the majority of rural and urban population (Kak, 2008, p. 201). Nearly 836 million of India's 1.1 billion people live on less than Rs. 20 per day and 300 million on less than half of this amount (The Report of the National Commission for Enterprises in the Unorganised Sector). The National Family Health Survey Report (NFHS-III), The Global Hunger Index and the State of the World's Children Report, 2008 by UNICEF have pointed out the absymal levels of malnutrition prevalent amongst small women and poor adults in rural and urban areas.

The food economy of India has remained thoroughly mismanaged by various governments. Foodgrains were allowed to pile up in the downs in the previous decades to let them rot or were exported at low prices, in fact, at lower than the prices at which the poor people in India were supplied foodgrains under PDS. In 2006-07, the procurement target were kept low and procurement operations were undertaken in a manner where even these low targets were not achieved. Private grain traders and corporate business houses were allowed to purchase wheat from the farmers. Then to meet the shortfall in the PDS, imports of wheat were made at higher prices than what was paid to Indian farmers for purchasing their crop. These have had a disastrous impact on the farming community in the country. A large segment of people in India lives on agriculture directly or indirectly. With the preponderance of small and medium farmers in the country, the agricultural sector in India consists of predominantly subsistence farmers. It is only from states like Haryana, Punjab, parts of Uttar Pradesh and other regions with large production that surplus foodgrains come to the market. The majority of the rural population including small and medium farmers in India are net buyers of foodgrains. Therefore, policies regarding food production and prices and food distribution affect their food security. The raging agrarian crisis is the indicative of the failure of the government policies in all these areas. It is often repeated these days that small scale agriculture is not profitable or feasible and the solution to these crises is through diversifying the cropping pattern into high value crops ranging from floriculture to horticulture particularly in Punjab and Haryana. According to the *Economic Survey (2007-08)*, the area under foodgrains had average

TABLE 3

Offtake of Rice and Wheat (2003-04 to 2007-08)

(In million tonnes)

Year	*Targeted Public Distribution System*				*Welfare Schemes*	*Open Market Sales*	*Total (5+6+7)*
	BPL	*APL*	*AAY*	*Total (2+3+4)*			
(1)	*(2)*	*(3)*	*(4)*	*(5)*	*(6)*	*(7)*	*(8)*
2003-04	15.80	4.20	4.20	24.20	13.50	11.60	49.30
2004-05	17.50	6.70	5.50	29.70	10.60	1.20	41.50
2005-06	15.60	8.30	7.40	31.40	9.70	1.10	42.10
2006-07	14.20	8.70	8.70	31.60	5.10	0.00	36.70
2007-08*	11.20	7.00	6.50	24.70	2.60	0.00	27.30

Note : *April to December 2007.

Source : Government of India (2008), *Economic Survey (2007-08)*, Ministry of Finance, New Delhi, p. 175.

annual decline of 0.26 per cent during 1989-90 to 121.6 million hectares in 2005-06. This decline has been of the magnitude of 6.2 million hectares.

The target for procurement of cereals has not been fulfilled for several years now. The procurement targets remain unfulfilled. It makes the government bring down the allocation of foodgrains for the PDS. The government bring down the allocation of foodgrains for the PDS. The government seems to worry more about the private trade in grain, especially by the big corporate and multinational companies (to the detriment of the small and medium traders operating in more than seven lakh *mandies* all over the country) than fulfilling its duty to ensure that no Indian citizen goes to bed hunger. The procurement of wheat in 2007-08 was short by nearly 40 lakh tonnes (Table 3). The government covered up this shortfall by bringing down the allocation to various states. Table 4 shows the decline in the off-take of grains for various welfare schemes such as the mid-day meals for schools and the Integrated Child Development Schemes (ICDS) among others. The decline in the actual offtake of wheat and rice for TPDS has also taken place in these years from 42.1 million tonnes in 2005-06 to 36.7 million tonnes in 2006-07, like the mid-day meal and ICDS among others.

PUBLIC DISTRIBUTION AND FOOD SUBSIDY

The importance of universalizing the public distribution of foodgrains has been highlighted in a number of studies. Various public hearings conducted by social activists and the right to food campaign have brought out the prevalence of hunger in the country. A very significant measure of welfare in the country, the universal public distribution system of foodgrains, has been abandoned. As a result, the above poverty line (APL) people are supposed to depend totally on the private trade, while earlier a part of their needs was supplied by the PDS. This was a disciplining factor on the private trade, because whenever market processes and players forced the prices to unreasonable heights, even the well-to-do took recourse to the PDS, and thus reduced their dependence on the private trade and produced a sobering effect on the prices of foodgrains. The targeted PDS divides the vulnerable population into below the poverty line and above the poverty line categories as defined by the Planning Commission. A number of studies have questioned the official poverty line which translates into an expenditure level of less than Rs. 12 per day per person (Kaur, 2008, pp. 245-62). The market driven grain prices have made the access to foodgrains more difficult for the poor. The future trading in commodities have led to speculation by the corporate grain traders, thus leading to a rise in prices of these commodities. The withdrawal of the government from active intervention in terms of PDS of foodgrains has allowed the volatility in the grains prices to stay. The neglect of the farm sector in terms of investment allocation of public funds, distressed condition of the farmers, trade policy *vis-à-vis* foodgrains, mainly wheat, rice, pulses and edible oils all combined to work against food security at the household level and the rise in foodgrains prices had made the universal PDS a crucial lifeline for a large number of households.

In recent years the government has been talking about the rising food subsidy. Food subsidies comprise subsidies to farmers through minimum support prices (MSP) and purchase operations of the FCI, consumer subsidy through the PDS and subsidies to FCI to cover all its cost. The significance of retaining food subsidies to provide affordable foodgrains to vast section of the Indian population should not be underestimated. The need for such subsidies is a creation of the policies and plans which push social exclusion below subsistence level for most of the Indians and squanders public revenue on supplying the fancy mimetic whims of a tiny minority of the well-to-do and well connected, who are so ironically termed VIPs and VVIPs in a democracy for purposes of accessing publically provided scarce but high cost facilities. Ever since the dismantling of the universal PDS in the mid-1990s on the advice of the world Bank/IMF combine, attempts are being made to 'reform' the PDS and the institutions engaged in implementing the programme. The government argues that the PDS has to be reformed due to a tremendous hike in subsidy and leakages in the distribution system. Both these claims are totally misplaced as the misallocation and diversion are policy induced and reflect a faulty delivery mechanism, leaky and defective implementation. One cannot expect any thing different from an administration whose other name is corruption and corruption from top to bottom. In any case the subsidies given on food account are not necessarily the subsidies delivered to the buyers and consumers of publicly supplied food, as this subsidy bill includes the cost of buffer stock maintained for meeting the macro-economic needs of the economy as a whole for tiding over supply failures on the national scale or for large parts of the country and exclusively for helping the food deficient families as a supplement to what they are expected to buy from the private market, that is, if and when they are in a position to do so. In any case, the food subsidy bill has remained less than 1 per cent of the gross domestic product and forms a small part of the incentives and supports provided to the large corporates. According to the *Economic Survey (2006-07)*, the food subsidy bill as a per cent of gross domestic product declined from 0.91 per cent in 2003-04 to 0.83 per cent in 2004-05 and to 0.66 per cent in 2005-06 the food subsidy declined in money terms from Rs. 25,746 crore in 2004-05 to Rs. 23,071 crore in 2005-06 and Rs. 23,828 crore in 2006-07 in real terms this is a substantial decline over the past three years when inflation is taken into account (Government of India, 2008, p. 178).

The Government has been curtailing the foodgrains on the pretext of rationalizing the system on the basis of 'each state's' average offtake during the earlier three years or last year takeoff which ever was low (*Economy Survey*, 2007-08, p. 179). The Rice consuming states have got a cut of 25 per cent in the allocation. Further, allocation for the APL category is made depending upon the availability of strocks in the central pool. The allocation of Antyoday Anaaj Yojana (AAY) and BPL categories is made at 35 kgs per family per month. This is highly insufficient for the manual labour that these people are generally engaged. The multiple objectives achieved from subsidized operations are expected to lead minimum guaranteed prices to the farmers, maintenance of buffer stocks, supply of subsidised foodgrains which are used for different programmes carried out by the government, relief programmes, food for work programmes and other welfare

TABLE 4

Allocation of Subsidy and Population Below Poverty Line

State	*Food Subsidy for TPDS (Rs. Crore)*			*Per cent of total food subsidy*	*Population below poverty line*	*Ratio of % of subsidy & % population below poverty line*
	2005-06	*2006-07*	*Difference (2-3)*			
(1)	*(2)*	*(3)*	*(4)*	*(5)*	*(6)*	*(7)*
Bihar	975.1	625.1	350.0	3.5	12.2	0.3
Punjab	119.2	49.6	69.6	0.4	0.7	0.5
Jharkhand	678.1	429.4	248.7	2.4	3.9	0.6
Rajasthan	882.4	388.5	493.9	2.8	4.5	0.6
Madhya Pradesh	1571.4	949.0	622.4	5.5	8.3	0.7
Uttrar Pradesh	4024.3	2766.3	125.8	14.8	19.6	0.8
Haryana	275.0	139.1	135.9	0.9	1.1	0.9
Maharashtra	2183.5	1499.6	683.9	8.0	10.5	0.8
Orissa	1111.8	1130.9	-19.1	4.9	5.9	0.8
Gujarat	744.4	438.7	315.7	2.6	3.0	0.9
Goa	18.6	8.3	10.3	0.1	0.1	1.0

(Contd.)

TABLE 4 (*Contd.*)

(1)	(2)	(3)	(4)	(5)	(6)	(7)
Chhatishgarh	787.9	663.4	124.5	3.2	3.2	1.1
West Bengal	1903.2	1593.4	309.8	7.6	6.9	1.1
Karnataka	1611.9	1409.0	202.9	6.6	4.6	1.4
Delhi	373.0	239.4	133.6	1.3	0.8	1.9
Kerala	821.6	674.7	146.9	3.3	1.6	2.0
Tamil Nadu	2636.1	2595.2	40.9	11.4	4.8	2.4
Andhra Pradesh	2415.3	2243.0	172.3	10.2	4.2	2.4
Total of all states	25813.0	19945.5	5867.5	100.0	100.0	

Note : Subsidies have been calculated on the basis of offtake and difference between economic cost and issue price.
Share of BPL is as per Planning Commission, 2004-05.
Total covers all states and union territories including the ones not specifically mentioned.

Source : Government of India (2008), Economic Survey (2007-08), New Delhi, p. 180.

schemes. Based on the magnitude and coverage of these programmes and activities, the government needs to intervene either for price stabilization or for providing rations to the needy and starving. It is interesting to note that once the buffer component is separated, the subsidy as proportion of GDP remained more or less stable around 0.43 per cent during the period 1996-97 to 2000-01. However, it went up marginally to 0.49 per cent during 2001-02. This further supports the finding that fluctuation in food subsidy is more a function of the quantity procured and the stock of foodgrains maintained during a year. Food subsidy proper remained more or less stable as proportion of the GDP.

With the current situation of price rise in foodgrains and general inflation accompanied by limited and low wage jobs, the role of the government for providing affordable foodgrains is extremely crucial. To be able to do so, food subsidy needs to be maintained with efficient and universal public distribution of foodgrains. This requires adequate allocation of foodgrains for distribution under PDS economically and financially viable, programmes to augment the purchasing power of the people. Livelihood guarantee and right to food have to be the policy focus of whichever government is in power.

References

Croxton, Frederick E., Dudley, J. Cowden., and Sidney Klien (1973), *Applied General Statistics*, Prentice Hall of India, New Delhi.

Estienne, Gilbert (1988), *Food and Poverty*, Oxford University Press, London and New Delhi.

Government of India (2007), *Economic Survey (2006-07)*, Ministry of Finance, New Delhi.

Government of India (2008), *Economic Survey (2006-07)*, Ministry of Finance, New Delhi.

Kak, Shakti (2008), "Food Insecurity", *Alternative Survey (2007-08)*, Danish Books, New Delhi.

Kaur, Smriti (2008), "Poverty Measurement Blues: Some Reflections", *Alternative Economic Survey (2007-08)*, Danish Books, New Delhi.

Planning Commission (1999), *Ninth Five Year Plan*, (Vol. I & II), Government of India, New Delhi.

Planning Commission (2002), *Tenth Five Year Plan*, (Vol. I & II), Government of India, New Delhi.

Radhakrishna, R. (2008), *India Development Report (2008)*, Oxford University Press, New Delhi.

Rao, V.M. (1995), "Beyond 'Surplus': Food Security in Changing Context", *Economic and Political Weekly*, January 28, p. 216.

Reddy, D.N. and Surjit Mishra (2008), "Crisis in Agriculture" in R. Radhakrishna (ed.) *India Development Report (2008)*, Oxford University Press, New Delhi.

Management of Public Distribution System in India
An Arrangement for Food Security

ANJU SINGH, KALANAND SINGH
AND ASHA DUBEY

INTRODUCTION

The Public Distribution System initially visualized in term of checking inflation protecting vulnerable section from the vagaries of the market mechanism, is an organizational asset of considerable significance for achieving wider socio-economic objectives. In so far as improving the nutritional status of poorer groups touching the core of the anti-poverty programme, PDS has a direct bearing on their success. The concept of minimum need, coupled with enlarging scope of PDS, served to underline to its dynamic character. As we move from the rigorous of primary poverty to a happier position, the system can be used to concretize the quest for "Quality of

Life", as it may be defined from time to time in politico-administrative terms.

India has lived with food shortages for a very long period. Famines, wars and drought causing actual scarcity and they forced the government to undertake fire-fighting measures from time to time like, suspending normal activity of markets and trade through nationalization of wholesale trade, organization of food zones, introduction of statutory rationing in selected urban area. However, a developing economy like ours needs a good security system looking much beyond management of scarce supplies and critical situation. India took a quantum leap in this direction in the mid-sixties when the *Food Corporation of India* and *Agricultural Prices Commission* (Renamed Commission for Agricultural Cost and Price later) were set-up.

In an agricultural country like India the prices of agricultural commodities, especially of foodgrains hold a key position in the price structure of the country. The effectiveness of the government operation in foodgrain market in order to have smooth in public distribution system depends on the size of stocks foodgrain operation are primarily aimed at regulation the movement of grains prices by making purchases from the farmers and arranging the regular supply of foodgrains to the public distribution system to improve the food situation it become imperative for the government to create sufficient buffer stock in years of good monsoon and utilized them in periods of lean monsoon. Keeping in this view, the government step up the Food Corporation of India in 1965 as a monopoly institution to undertake purchase handling transport, storage and distribution of foodgrains and other food status on behalf of the government. Foodgrains procured by the government are sold throughout the public distribution system (PDS) which operates throughout the fair price shops or ration shops.

The basic aim of fair price shops is to provide essential commodities such as rice, wheat, sugar, edible oil, soft cake and kerosene at subsidized prices within the ration limit.

Since the mid-1980s, the coverage of the PDS was extended to rural areas in some states. Thus, it acquired the status of a welfare programme. An effort was made to extend subsidized foodgrain in 1985s in all tribal block covering about 57 million persons. The revamped PDS later expanded to cover 1752 blocks with high incidence of poverty covering 164 million persons. The numbers of fair price shops were increased in rural areas to provide agencies for distribution of subsidized foodgrain.

OBJECTIVES OF THE STUDY

The following objectives have been framed to assess the impact of economic reforms in public distribution system in India:

1. To study the organization structure of public distribution system.
2. To analyzed the historical development of PDS in India.
3. To study the problems of PDS.
4. To examine the impact of economic reform in PDS.

METHODOLOGY

This socially relevant study consists of both primary data secondary data. Primary Data have been collected from the department of Food and Civil Supplies, Government of India and also by interacting central officials attached to ministry of Food and Consumer Affairs for strengthening subject by way of asking pricing mechanism, subsidy, and method of procurement practice and the like. The secondary data were also collected from various research findings, periodic journals and newspapers related to PDS.

WORKING OF PDS

The department of Food and Civil Supplies in the ministry of food, has the primary responsibility for policies of food procurement and food distribution throughout PDS. The Food Corporation of India (FCI) set-up under the jurisdiction of this department, is the soul central agency in charge of procurement, storage, transportation and distribution of food commodities. The FCI is an implementing body and implement the government's policies on procurement, storage, transportation and distribution. Often, procurement is undertaken by state cooperative marketing federation's and supplied to the FCI. From the FCI, state government purchase the commodities required for distribution within their state, and the states are, then, responsible for supplying the commodities to Fair Price Shop. Thus, the responsibility for implementing, monitoring and enforcing legal provisions relating to public delivery rests with state government. The implementing agency at the state level is the state civil supplies department or corporation.

PDS is a rationing mechanism that entitles household to specified quantities of selected commodities at subsidies prices. In most parts of the country, PDS has been universal and all households, rural, urban, with a registered residential address are entitled to rations. Eligible households are given a ration (Varying with household size and age composition) of selected commodities. The exact entitlement (quantity, range of commodities and prices) varies across states.

The six essential commodities supplied through PDS nationally are rice, wheat, sugar, edible oil, kerosene and coal. Additional commodities like pulses, salt, tea are commodities that are made available through a network of Fair Price Shops. In 1998, there were a total of 4.5 lakhs Fair Price Shops in the country of which 3.6 lakhs were in rural areas, as of 1998 there were a total of 182.8 million families with ration cards in the country and an average, there were 406 ration cards assigned to each Fair Price Shop.

HISTORICAL DEVELOPMENT OF PUBLIC DISTRIBUTION SYSTEM IN INDIA

Public Distribution System was first started in 1939 as a war time rationing measure. The British Government introduced it in Bombay and later on extended it to six other cities and a few regions. The drought and food storage of the mid-sixties highlighted the need for strengthening and containing with a system of food distribution and Public Distribution System was made a universal scheme in the 1970s record of net production, import, net availability, procurement and Public Distribution of foodgrain from 1951 to 1998 is given at Table 1.

TABLE I
Availability, Procurement and Public Distribution of Foodgrain in India (1951-98)

Year	*Net Production*	*Net Imports*	*Net Availability (NA)*	*Procu-rement*	*Public Distribution (PD)*	*PDNA (%)*
(1)	*(2)*	*(3)*	*(4)*	*(5)*	*(6)*	*(7)*
1956	60.7	1.4	62.6	Neg.	2.1	3.4
1957	63.4	3.6	66.2	0.3	3.1	4.7
1958	58.3	3.2	61.8	0.5	4.0	6.5
1959	69.00	3.9	72.3	1.8	5.2	7.2
1960	67.5	5.1	71.2	1.3	4.9	6.9
1961	72.00	3.5	75.7	0.5	4.0	5.3
1962	72.1	3.6	76.1	0.5	4.4	5.7
1963	70.3	4.5	74.8	0.8	5.2	6.9
1964	70.6	6.2	78.1	1.4	8.7	11.1
1965	78.2	7.4	84.6	4.0	10.1	11.9
1966	63.6	10.3	73.5	4.0	14.1	1.1
1967	19.2	65.0	08.7	73.9	4.5	13.2
1968	83.2	5.7	86.8	6.8	10.2	11.8
1969	82.3	3.8	85.6	6.4	9.4	11.0
1970	87.1	3.6	89.5	6.7	8.8	9.9
1971	94.9	2.0	94.3	8.9	7.8	8.3
1972	92.00	0.5	96.2	7.7	10.5	10.9
1973	84.9	3.6	88.8	8.4	11.4	12.8
1974	91.6	5.2	97.1	5.6	10.8	11.1
1975	87.4	7.5	89.3	9.6	1.3	12.6
1976	105.9	0.7	95.8	12..8	9.2	9.6
1977	97.3	0.1	99.0	9.9	11.7	1.8
1978	110.6	0.6	110.2	11.1	10.2	9.2
1979	115.4	0.2	114.9	13.8	11.7	10.2

(1)	(2)	(3)	(4)	(5)	(6)	(7)
1980	96.00	0.3	101.4	11.2	15.0	14.8
1981	113.4	0.7	114.3	13.0	13.0	11.4
1982	116.6	1.6	116.9	15.4	14.8	12.6
1983	113.3	4.1	114.7	15.6	16.2	14.1
1984	133.3	2.4	128.6	18.7	13.3	10.4
1985	127.4	0.4	124.3	30.1	15.8	14.7
1986	131.6	0.5	133.8	19.7	17.3	12.9
1987	125.5	0.2	134.8	15.7	18.7	13.8
1988	122.8	3.8	130.8	14.8	18.6	14.2
1989	148.7	1.2	147.2	18.9	16.4	11.1
1990	149.7	1.3	144.8	24.0	16.0	11.0
1991	154.3	0.1	158.6	19.6	20.8	13.1
1992	147.3	0.4	148.4	17.9	18.8	12.7
1993	157.5	3.1	149.8	28.0	16.4	10.9
1994	161.2	1.1	154.8	26.0	14.0	9.1
1995	167.6	0.4	169.8	22.6	15.3	9.0
1996	157.9	1.2	168.2	19.8	18.3	11.0
1997	174.4	1.0	177.2	23.6	17.5	9.8
1998	169.00	2.0	170.4	25.5	18.4	

Source : Government of India, Economic Survey, 1998-99.

In the 1960s, there were major changes in the organization of food policy in India. In response to crop failures, food shortage and price fluctuation, it was decided to make PDS a permanent and universal programme two new organization the Agricultural Price Commissions (later renamed as the Commissions on Agricultural Costs and Prices CACP) and the Food Corporation of India were set-up in 1965. The drought of 1965-66 and 1966-67 provided a strong impetus for the expansion of PDS. Foodgrains distributed in PDS grew to more than 10 million tonnes in 1965. During the period 1965-68, PDS depended heavily on imports of food (imports peaked at 10 million tons in 1966). Gradually, as food production grew, imports fell and purchased from PDS also fell, but after the drought of 1972-73, the distribution of foodgrain in PDS peaked up again.

This phase is marked by the growth of comfortable buffer stock, and this provided the basis for the large scale expansion of PDS as well as food for work type employment programme. From 1978 onwards, there was a steady growth in the quantity of foodgrain distributed through PDS, with a peak provision of 20.8 million tons in 1991. During the late 1970 and 1980, PDS was viewed as a component of the strategy to alleviate property. The network of fair Price shop grew in the 1970, as did the number of commodities supplied in the shops. Special scheme were introduced in state such as Andhra Pradesh to expand the supply of cheap food to the poor.

After 1991, the start of the fourth phase, the amount of foodgrains distributed through PDS has fallen substantially, from 20.8 million tonnes in 1991 to 14 million tonnes in 1994. This fall in distribution has been accompanied by a rise of stock, and excessive holding of stocks. One of these reasons of this fall in purchase from PDS in the narrowing price differential between PDS and market prices. Although distribution of foodgrain through PDS has risen in the last few years, it remains below the peak of 1991. There have also been major changes in the structure of PDS in the 1990s, most importantly the introduction of targeting in 1997.

PROBLEMS OF PUBLIC DISTRIBUTION SYSTEM

Basic problems of the Public Distribution System which are identified in the course of investigation are as follows:

1. *High Transportation Charge*: As most of the villages were distant from the Public Distribution System shops, it resulted in higher transportation charges, which were as high as Rs. 20 to Rs. 40 per bag. But the rate allowed by the government is Rs. 8 for transportation of one bag from storage point to retail centre including the commission.
2. Quota fixed by the supply department for ration card holders are insufficient.

3. *Inaccessible Villages*: Most of the PDS points were in the remote area. So the consumers are facing problem to get the ration from the PDS.
4. *Black-marketing of PDS commodities*: According to Deepak Ahluwalia, a little more than a third of the foodgrains and sugar and over a half of kerosene oil do not reach the actual users of PDS, and goes to open market in the form of black-marketing.
5. *Lack of Supervision*: As the number of PDS centre is very high so the supervision is quite difficult for one marketing inspector in a block/division, it is difficult to keep track of all the dealers of PDS.

CONCLUSION

On the basis of the above analysis it may be conclude that 70 per cent of people living in villages and 40 per cent of landless labourers. Beside this 20 crores of the poor people are rural agricultural labourers. Food problems can be solved by the integration of the PDS with other anti-poverty programme like *Antyoday* and other programmes. The Public Distribution System is a vital programme to ensure *'distributive justice'* to the weaker sections of the community. Lastly, it may be quote the line of Mother Theresa, *"If we have no peace, it is because we have forgotten that we belong to each other"*.

References

Ahulwalia, D., Public Distribution of Food in India: Coverage, Targeting and Leakages, *Food Policy*. Vol. 1(18), Feb. 193.

Ahulwalia, Deepak, Public Distribution of Food in India Coverage. *Food Policy*, Vol. 18(1), 1993.

Chandrashekhar, C.P. and A. Sen, Foodgrain Stock: To Feed the Poor or Pay for Liberalized Imports? *Business Line*, 30 April, 1996.

Das, V. Tulasi and Rao, N. Sanjeeva, Second Generation Reform: Revamping Production and Distribution System to augment Food Security, *Third Concept*, May 2005, Vol. 19, No. 219.

Govt. of India, *Economic Survey*, Vol. 11, 1998-99.

Gupta, D.N., Public Distribution System—Involvement of Institutions, *Journal of Rural Development*, April-June, 1996, Vol. 15(2).

Indian Development Report, Oxford Press, 2002.

Markkendayan, N. and Ponniah, M., Economic Reform in PDS in India, *Third Concept*, April 2005, Vol. 19, No. 218.

Mohanty, P.C., Mounting Foodgrain Stocks in the Face of Vicious Circle of Hunger; *Third Concept*, Aug. 2004, Vol. 18, No. 210.

Rahim, C.A., Management of Public Distribution System in Andhra Pradesh: Administrative Arrangements in Delivery System, *Journal of Rural Development*, Jan.-March, 1997, Vol. 16(1).

Sen, A., Poverty and Famine: An Essay on Entitlement and Deprivation, Clarendon Press, Oxford, 1989.

Role of PDS and Food Security

Subodh Kumar Sinha and Vinod Kumar Sinha

The Public distribution is recognized as a permanent feature of the strategy to control prices, reduce fluctuations and achieve equitable distribution of essential goods. This PDS can be in the form of rationing or fair price shops or both. Under this system, a certain proportion of the output of commodities involved is procured by public agencies or agencies designated by the government at reasonable prices for distributing through approved channels, while remaining supplies may be disposed of by the produces at market prices. This would ensure availability of certain quantities of selected commodities to the consumers, particularly, the vulnerable sections, at reasonable prices and at the same time allow the producers to realize on the whole a fair price to their produce.

PRESENT STATUS OF PDS

The PDS is major State intervention in the country aimed at ensuring food security to all the people, especially the poor.

The PDS operates through a large distribution network of around 4.89 lakh fair price shops (FSS), and is supplemental in nature. Under the PDS, the Central Government is responsible for the procurement and transportation of foodgrains up to the principal distribution centres of the FCI while the State Governments are responsible for the identification of families living below the poverty line, the issue of ration cards, and the distribution of foodgrains to the vulnerable sections through EPSs. PDS seems to have failed in serving the second objective of making foodgrains available to the poor. If it had, the consumption levels of cereals should not have fallen on average—as it has consistently over the last two decades.

With a view to improving its efficiency, the PDS was redesigned as TDPS with effect from June 1997. The TDPS envisages identifying the poor households and giving them a fixed entitlement of good grains at subsidized prices. Under the TPDS, higher rates of subsidies are being given to the poor and the poorest among the poor. The APL families are also being given foodgrains under TPDS but with lower subsidy. The scale of issue under TDPS for Antyodaya cardholders began with 10 kg. per family per month, which has been progressively increased to 35 kg. per family per month with effect from April, 2002.

Under the TPDS, the identification of BPL families was to be carried out by the State Government based on criteria adopted by the Minister of Rural Development (MoRD). However, the total number of beneficiaries was to be limited to the State-wise poverty estimates (1993-94) of the Planning Commission projected to the population as on 01.03.2000. Against a total ceiling of 6.52 crore BPL households (as per the poverty estimates of the Planning Commission for 1993-94 and population projection of the Registrar General as on 01.03.2000), more than 8 crore BPL ration cards have been issued. Similarly, against the figure of 18.03 crore households in the country (as per the population projections as on 01.03.2000 of the Registrar General of India), the total number of ration cards issued is around 22.32 crore. This does raise problems at the field level.

MINIMUM SUPPORT PRICE AND PDS

Foodgrains are procured at the MSP fixed by the government mostly in a small number of grain-surplus states in the north of India, which are then transported across the country to deficit States (the latter mostly in the south and west of the country). MSPs are fixed on rate recommended by Commission of Agriculture Costs and Prices (CACP), which are set using mainly cost of cultivation. These grain stocks essentially supply the PDS of the country through the PDS, cereals are made available to BPL households, as well as to Above Poverty Line (APL) households- at differential prices. There is a third category of beneficiaries antyodaya card holders. Under the Antyodaya Anna Yojana (AAY), 35 kg of foodgrains are being provided to the poorest of the poor families at the highly subsidized rate of Rs. 2 per kg. for wheat and Rs. 3 per kg for rice.

During the years of accumulation of stocks in the Central Pool until 2001-02, it was believed that excess procurement was on account of the government's decision to fix the MSP for paddy and wheat in excess of the levels prescribed by the CACP. Grain stocks have declined since then.

Given the limited purchasing power of the poor, there is a need to contain cereal price rises. For this purpose government maintains foodgrains buffer stocks through the Food Corporation of India (FCI). Stocks had reached to 256.17 lakh tones (rice) and 324.15 lakh tonnes (wheat) for the year 20001-02. But in 2007, the stocks of these two foodgrains fell to 131.71 lakh tonnes (rice) and 45.63 lakh tonnes (wheat), respectively.

To achieve the cereal price stabilization objective of PDS, food stocks with FCI should be at a reasonable level. In recent years, both procurement and stocks with FCI have tended to fall. If the needs of procurement to maintain adequate stocks requires procurement prices to be higher than MSPO, a transparent mechanism is needed that enables government to undertake commercial purchases at prices comparable to those paid by private traders. This could be done if the procurement price (i.e. MSP plus bonus) was announced at the beginning of the purchase season, along with a procurement target in terms of quantity. After the procurement target was met, the bonus would be suspended. However, if procurement quantities, even with bonus are not met, FCI should be able to tender from both domestic as well as international markets, after standard procurement operations, to make up the deficit to maintain stocks with the FCI.

TABLE I

Food Subsidy

(Rs. in Crore)

Year	*Food subsidy*
1996-97	5166
1997-98	7500
1998-99	8700
1999-2000	9200
2000-01	12010
2001-02	17494
2002-03	24176
2003-04	25160
2004-05	25746
2005-06	23071
2006-07	23827

Source : N.S.S.

APPROACH TO FOOD SUBSIDY ON PDS

Food subsidy is provided in the Budget of the Department of Food and Public distribution to meet the difference between the economic cost of foodgrains procured by FCI and their sales realization at CIP for TPDS and other welfare schemes. In addition, the Central Government also procures foodgrains for meeting the requirements of buffer stock. Hence, part of the food subsidy also goes towards meeting the carrying cost of buffer stock.

The food subsidy bill of the GoI peaked in 2004-05 and declined as stocks declined. However, with higher MSPs declared more recently, there is a danger that the subsidy is likely to rise (See Table 1) due to increase in MSP, announcement of bonus, and carrying cost of FCI. The Table 1 gives the figures of food subsidy of the GoI.

DEFICIENCIES OF TPDS

As identified by various studies, the major deficiencies of the TPDS include : (i) high exclusion and inclusion errors, (ii) non-viability of FPSs. (iii) failure in fulfilling the price stabilization objective, and (iv) leakages.

The Programme Evaluation Organisation's (PEO's) Study (2005) establishes large-scale exclusion and inclusion errors in most Status (See Box Below).

BOX
Performance Evaluation of TPDS

- Only 22.7 per cent FPS are viable in terms of earning of return of 12 per cent on capital.
- The offtake by API cardholders was negligible except in Himachal Pradesh, Tamil Nadu and West Bengal.
- The offtake per BPL card was high in W.B., Kerala, Himachal Pradesh and Tamil Nadu.
- The offtake by the poor under TPDS was substantially higher than under universal PDS.
- There are large errors of exclusion and inclusion and ghost card are common.
- High exclusion errors mean a low coverage of BPL households. The survey estimated that TPDS covers only 57 per cent BPL families.
- Errors of inclusion are high in Andhra Pradesh, Karnataka and Tamilnadu. This implies that the APL households receive an unacceptable large proportion of subsidized grains.
- Leakages vary enormously between States. In Bihar and Punjab, the total leakage exceeds 75 per cent while in Haryana and U.P., it is between 50 and 75 per cent.
- Leakage and diversion imply a low share of the genuine BPL households of the distribution of the subsidized grains. During 2003-04, it is estimated that out of 14.1 million tones of BPL quota from the Central Pool, only 6.1 million tonnes reached the BPL families and 8 million tonnes did not reach the target families.

- Leakage and diversion raised the cost of delivery. For every 1 kg. that was delivered to the poor, GoI had to issue 2.32 kg. from the Central Pool.
- During 2003-04, out of an estimated subsidy of Rs. 7258 crore under TPDS, Rs. 4123 crore did not reach BPL families. Moreove, Rs. 2579 crore did not reach any consumer but was shared by agencies involved in the supply chain.

It also question the BPL methodology used for identification of households at State level. There are two problems here. One is the criterion used for allocation of foodgrains by the Central Government to States. The Central Government allocates foodgrains to State based on a narrow official poverty line. There is a need to look at this allocation criterion to States. If we go by the official poverty ration criterion, only 28 per cent of the population is eligible under PDS at all-India level in 2004-05. However, food-insecure households may be much higher than the official poverty rations. For example, under nutrition among children and households is much higher than this figure. The use of BPL estimates to determine Central allocations should be revisited because there is a significant mass of households just above the poverty line.

A second problem is the use of BPL method for identifying households by the States. This identification differs from State to State. For example, some of the south Indian States do not follow the official poverty ration for limiting the ration cards. In Andhra Pradesh, more than 70 per cent of the households have ration cards. This is one of the reasons for high inclusion errors in Andhra Pradesh.

NEED TO STRENGTHEN OF TPDS

One of long standing criticisms of the TPDS has been that offtake of PDS cereals (rice and wheat) by States from FCI does not match with NSS estimates of PDS consumption of those same grains. For instance, Table 2 shows that, according to NSS, over 1993-94, 1999-2000, and 2004-05, consumption of PDS grains rose. It also shows that offtake of PDS grain from FCI by States increased much more than consumption over the same decade. The difference between the two shows the extent of leakage of PDS wheat and rice. This leakage [defined as 1–{ration of (a) to (b)}] was 28 per cent for wheat and rice together in 1993-94, but it had risen to 54 per cent by 2004-05-a very significant increase in leakage. These facts clearly show that TPDS is in urgent need of reform.

TABLE 2

PDS Implied Leakage-Offtake *vs.* Consumption

	1993-94	*1999-2000*	*2004-05*
(a) NSS PDS Consumption (m. tonnes)			
Rice	7.20	9.30	9.98
Wheat	3.44	2.99	3.55
Total	10.64	12.29	13.53
(b) PDS offtake (m. tonnes)			
Rice	8.84	11.35	16.62
Wheat	5.86	5.76	13.02
Total	14.70	17.11	29.65
Ratio of (a) to (b)			
Rice	0.81	0.82	0.60
Wheat	0.59	0.52	0.27
Total	0.72	0.72	0.46

Source : N.S.S.

Drives home the point about the poor targeting by TPDS benefits. It estimates the benefits in rupees per household of PDS grin beneficiaries [calculated as PDS quantity consumed* (PDS Price-Average Market Price)]. It shows that the benefits to the household are dependent upon whether you have a card or not and which card you have—APL, BPL, or Antyodaya, and not on whether you are poor or non-poor. In fact, it demonstrates that there is very little difference between the benefits (in Rs./household) of poor and non-poor households when one compares poor BPL cardholders with non-poor BPL Cardholders, or when comparing poor AAY cardholders with non-poor AAY cardholders.

TABLE 3
PDS Benefits—Rice and Wheat

(Rs. Per Household)

State	Poor				Non-Poor			
	No. Card	APL Card	BPL Card	Antyodaya Card	No. Card	APL Card	BPL Card	Antyodaya Card
(1)	(2)	(3)	(4)	(5)	(6)	(7)	(8)	(9)
J & K	33.73	28.19	278.12	333.96	22.77	53.89	206.43	286.26
Himachal Pradesh	0.00	43.83	124.94	262.10	2.72	21.84	122.38	204.55
Punjab	0.00	0.00	1.96	111.54	0.58	0.07	1.38	0.00
Uttaranchal	0.00	8.32	88.22	202.61	0.06	10.52	54.73	115.10
Haryana	0.00	0.04	12.09	114.36	0.00	0.00	11.61	75.15
Rajasthan	6.23	6.42	70.93	169.27	6.18	3.77	54.35	93.80
Uttar Pradesh	2.48	0.92	39.96	132.88	0.17	0.68	23.79	107.40
Bihar	0.29	0.32	3.86	47.27	0.05	0.01	6.10	44.26
Assam	8.27	4.71	81.33	184.81	2.45	1.43	47.98	21.30
West Bengal	50.69	0.03	30.78	86.65	14.82	0.31	24.15	46.06

Jharkhand	0.00	0.48	30.43	112.80	0.15	0.94	10.84	65.06
Orissa	2.17	3.09	31.93	129.92	0.25	0.81	12.04	120.67
Chhattisgarh	5.72	13.69	70.05	213.53	2.97	6.36	43.01	104.49
Madhya Pradesh	4.27	8.02	60.37	146.03	0.80	1.42	40.20	100.32
Gujarat	4.38	1.99	86.17	182.58	0.57	1.86	79.17	29.02
Maharashtra	3.02	8.75	97.16	192.23	1.87	4.25	80.77	158.83
Andhra Pradesh	1.71	56.75	113.67	260.27	4.17	31.23	95.72	249.61
Karnataka	8.79	63.08	199.43	230.81	1.29	46.29	180.99	231.85
Kerala	22.04	68.16	166.06	242.23	4.82	18.33	94.03	209.85
Tamil Nadu	43.83	182.85	198.06	349.04	13.56	126.08	177.58	314.68
All India	6.69	15.64	81.45	176.18	2.28	12.56	74.59	146.92

Source : NSS 61st, 2004-05.

The TPDS in its current form as a anti-poverty programme clearly is not doing very well. Given these facts, a restructuring of the TPDS has been suggested are follows:

In this context, a recommendation of the HLC on Long Term Grain Policy (2000) was that instead of the current distinction between APL, BPL, and Antyodaya in terms of issue pricing for rice and wheat, there should be a single issue price for grain issued by the FCI from its warehouses. This recommendation, sometimes identified with the return to universal PDS from TPDS adopted in 1997, has been criticized on a number of grounds. First, that if the same price for BPL and APL households was charged, this would not be financially viable for the BPL. If existing AAY and BPL cardholders were charged a higher price, there would be a diversion of benefits from the relatively poor to the relatively rich. Second, there might be pressure to kept the uniform CIP low as high common price for BPL and APL would have adverse consequences for the poor. On the other hand, a low CIP would increase even further the fiscal subsidy. Third, any widening the effective reach of PDS due to its universalization would put unbearable pressures for the supply of grain into the PDS.

It needs, however, to be noted that the HLC had not altogether ruled out the continuation TPDS in States where this might be the best option. Its recommendation was that there should be a single CIP as far as FCI is concerned for each grain fixed at FCI's acquisition cost and that he existing subsidy beyond his should be passed on to the States on the condition that this be used for food-based schemes.

POLICY OF FOOD SECURITY AND FOOD MANAGEMENT

The concept of food security has been discussed mostly in making available minimum quantity of foodgrains to the entire population. India has set three pronged objectives for its food management initiatives viz., procurement of foodgrains from farmers at remunerative prices, distribution of foodgrains to the consumers particularly the vulnerable sections of the society and maintaining a buffer stock of foodgrains to ensure food security in the country. Through Minimum Support Prices (MSP), this initiative tries to ensure remunerative prices to the poor farmers by procuring foodgrains and through the Central Issue Price (CIP) mechanism, it distributes foodgrains with a view to ensuring stability in food prices. Being the nodal agency, FCI is responsible for procurement, distribution and. storage of foodgrains.

The years 2001-03 witnessed high levels of stock build up. The foodgrain stocks available with the FCI stood at an all time high of 64.7 million tonnes against an annual requirement of around 20 million tonnes for ensuring food security in June 2002. After the year 2002, there has been a steady decline in the food stocks because of relatively lower procurement of rice and wheat, reduction in the growth of agriculture sector, relatively high off-take of cereals. The stock position of foodgrains as on January 1, 2008 was 19.2 million tonnes against a buffer stock norm of 20 million tonnes comprising 11.5 tonnes of rice and 7.7 million tonnes of wheat. With reduced buffer stock of wheat has led to the government for resorting to import of wheat from abroad to meet the demand as committed towards targeted public distribution system and other welfare programmes for the poor. Since the world food price is at peak now, the domestic prices of wheat after the projected import is not expected to see a downward trend.

Further, the enhancement in MSP of foodgrains over the years has given rise to an increase in the economic cost and the distribution cost of the foodgrains. While the distribution cost of wheat and rice was Rs. 165.3 per quintal in 2003-04 the same rose to Rs. 286.7 in 2007-08. During the same period the economic cost of wheat and rice was Rs. 928.7 and 1371.3 per quintal. The Government's steps in price stability in food commodities for poor have not really benefited the poor farmers. Steps to insulate the poorer section of the society from price rise by distribution of essential food items through fair price shops, allocating foodgrains to Below Poverty Line (BPL) and Antyodaya Anna Yojana beneficiaries, and maintaining CIP a wheat and rice at July 2002 level could not ensure the availability of sufficient foodgrains to the poor due to inflationary situation and price rise in food articles. Further, there has been a huge gap between the MSP and CIP for BPL people under Targeted Public Distribution System (TPDS). This gap has encouraged the unscrupulous Fair Price Shop (FPS) owners to divert the foodgrains to open market. The policy on agricultural production after mid-60s focused on enhancement of agricultural production and reduction in the import demand. Researchers have documented that the mechanism of support price for procurement and maintenance of rice and wheat stocks for maintaining food security in the domestic economy has not really supported this drive of the government rather it has created price distortion in the food market, both in India and abroad.

CONCLUSION AND SUGGESTIONS

Despite the huge stock of foodgrains available in FCI godowns, stray cases of hunger and death are still being reported. PDS should, therefore, be reformed and made more efficient. The present system can be replaced by a system of food stamps and eventually by a food credit card system. The excess stock of foodgrains that have accumulated with the Government is party the result of the high Minimum Support Price (MSP) which often exceeded the levels recommend by CACP (commission for Agricultural Costs and Prices).

There is, therefore, a need to adhere to the recommendations of CACP.

The scheme for decentralized procurement of foodgrains should be encouraged and more states could be brought under its fold. Similarly, the operation PDS could be decentralized with the states taking their own decisions regarding issue prices, and quantum of foodgrains to be supplied. The national food subsidy could be distributed among the states according to a prescribed formula.

The Essential Commodities Act should be amended to make it an emergency provision that will have to be formally invoked by notification for a limited period fix specific commodities.

All restrictions on inter-state movement of foodgrains should be removed. Octroi and all sorts of taxes/levies on food articles should be eliminated. The ban on future trading in all agricultural commodities should be lifted.

To help the private sector to play an enhaned role in the distribution system, 26 per cent Foreign Direct Investment (FDI) should be allowed in food retailing and 100 per cent FDI in insurance for agriculture and rural areas.

The most important consideration affecting cropping pattern is the economic consideration. Even in a country like India which is dominated by farmer steeped in poverty and conservatisms and where farmers hold tiny bits of land cropping pattern can be changed through appropriate change in economic motive. Experience in recent years has been that the farmer does accept the logic for a change wherever he is shown a better cropping patter. The real difficulty in adopting a better cropping pattern is that the farmer may not have the requisite capital to invest now or possess the know-how that may be necessary for changing the crops, It is here that the Government may come to his help.

The recommendations listed in the Tenth Plan for PDS should result in making the system more vibrant and efficient and capable of meeting the requirements of a liberalised economy.

References

Bhatia, B.M. (1983), A Study India's Food Policy.

Radhakrishna, R., Subbarao, K., Indrakant, S. and Ravi, K. (1997), Public Distribution: A National and International Perspective, World Bank Discussion, Paper No. 380.

World Bank, World Development Report (1986).

Planning Commission, Ninth Five Year Plan (1997-2002), Vol. II.

Tenth Five Year Plan (2002-07), Vol. II.

Eleventh Five Year Plan (2007 to 2002), Vol. II.

Significance and Role of PDS in Food Security for Downtrodden in Jharkhand

N.C. Jha and Navendu Shekhar

Jharkhand which has multidimensional problems is characterised by widespread poverty, large scale unemployment and under employment massive illiteracy malnutrition, poor housing, ill-fractured infrastructure, very low level of living, low availability of cereals, very low-human development index, massive smoking and drinking habits especially among the Dalits, scheduled caste and scheduled tribes. The cultivable land area in Jharkhand is only 22.7 per cent, i.e. 18,09,50,780 hectares where cereals, pulse, oil seeds, vegetables are sown. The state is a deficient state so far as the food requirement is concerned because the required minimum needs of foodgrains for the state people should be 45 lakh metric tonnes but the total production remains equal to about 22 lakhs metric tonnes. This is due to the low yield rate of cereals, pulses and oilseeds in the state, although paddy is the prime crop sown throughout the state, the yield per hectare is only 1930 kg against the national average 3000 kg, for the maize and wheat, it is 1756 kg and 1811 kg respectively against the national average 4500 kg and 3000 kg.

In Jharkhand, agriculture is the central occupation for the people of the state because more than two third proportion of total population is directly or indirectly dependent for their fulfillment of minimum basic needs. The state's population growth rate is between 2.3 per cent to 2.5 per cent which has raised the demand for the foodgrains, which in turn reflects the higher income elasticity for food items—Agriculture in this state is not only an occupation but a significant means of subsistence or survival for total population, i.e. 2.69 crores of the state, in which 26.30 per cent is scheduled tribes, 11.84 per cent scheduled caste on the one land, on the other, 77.76 per cent population is the rural population. This sector is termed as totally undeveloped, backward or even hilly in nature. Out of S.T. and S.C. population, more than 80 per cent remains in rural area.

The rural population especially backward or dalits ST and ST is characterized with the highest illiteracy, poverty, crippled with the high dose of malnutrition. Out of the total household which is 74,99,081, according to 2001 census 37,36,524 households are rural which is 77.86 per cent, out of total rural households, 23,22,071, i.e. 61.57 per cent is under the poverty line between 1997-2000. During the 9th and 10th five year plans the total household living below the poverty line is 25,23,520 and 26,44,499 which shows that during these two plans, the incidence of poverty has increased we may explain the poverty level of the districts of the state with the help of Table 1.

From the Table 1 it is evident that between 9th plan (1997-2002) and 10th plan (2002-07), the families living below the poverty line show a rising trend in all districts except Latehar, Dumka, Bokaro, Ranchi and West-Singhbhum. According to the government estimate, 23.22 lakh families in the rural areas line below the poverty line. Out of which 3.91 lakh belong to scheduled tribes. These families fail to get minimum subsistence food even to survive in such a difficult time.

Various NGOs and other social organization had made a severe hue and cry regarding the scandalous situation of hunger deaths amidst plenty of foodgrains rotting in the godown of the food corporations of India.

TABLE I

District-wise Number of Poor Households in Jharkhand During 9th Plan (1997-2002 and 10th Plan 2002-07)

Name of the District	*9th Plan 1997-2002*	*10th Plan 2002-07*	*% Increase/ Decrease*
Garhwa	97508	017215	+9.96
Palmau	179529	190158	+5.92
Latehar	94281	53417	- 43.34
Chatra	10022	104880	+4.64
Hazaribag	197702	222810	+12.7
Koderma	46747	51077	+ 9.26
Giridih	176885	176885	+7.66
Deoghar	75536	81262	+7.58
Godda	98692	11719	+19.27
Sahibganj	115105	125342	+8.89
Pakur	73725	90007	+22.08
Dumka	132594	125701	-5.19
Jamatara	68040	82070	+20.60
Dhanbad	127078	135842	+6.89
Bokaro	110339	82665	- 25.08
Ranchi	230193	207187	-9.99
Lohardagga	23817	36355	+52.64
Gumla	163265	183470	+12.37
Simdega	65060	71635	+10.11
W. Singhbhum	158707	152560	-3.87
Saraikela Kharsawan	93094	128354	+36.69
E. Singhbhum	107196	117918	70.00
Jharkhand	2523520	2644499	

Source : Economic Study of Jharkhand—An Analysis By K Bahadur, p. 128.

Such is the condition where the role and importance of public distribution system is being realized where such poverty ridden families get the cereals either free or at a very subsidized rate, as prescribed by the government of India or the state. In India, during the mid sixties, for countering the problems of foodgrains shortage public distribution system was evolved so that the economy could overcome the problems of famine, hunger death and equitable distribution of food to the families living below the poverty line. Because of the increase recorded in foodgrains with the FCI, the food problems in the sense of inadequacy and shortage of foodgrains no longer exist. However food problems in the normative sense continues to exists as millions of poor suffer from persistent hunger and malnutrition and many others are at the risk of doing so in future. In 2003, FAO (Food and Agriculture organization) in its reports state of food Insecurity in the world, clearly expressed a great concern about the food insecurity for the families/persons living below the poverty line because 213.7 Millions, over a fifth of India's population still suffers from chronic hunger and almost one-fourth of the hungry people of the world are found in India alone. Thus the prime concern and the principal justification of the food security system or the public distribution system is to avoid or to nullify the persistence of hunger and malnutrition from the civil and developed human society.

The chief goal of the PDS in India as well as in Jharkhand is to provide essential consumer goods at cheap and subsidized prices to the consumers so as to insulate them from the impact of rising prices of these commodities and to maintain the minimum nutritional status of our population, especially for those who are spending a little on food material is the poorest of the poor. In the states or union territories of our country, the grain mainly wheat and rice, edible oils, sugar coal, kerosene and cloth have been distributed but later on only rice, wheat, sugar and kerosene are being distributed coarse grains do not figure in PDS or fair price shops. Recently only wheat and kerosene and being distributed in PDS or fair price shops in Jhrakhand PDS. The criterion is to issue ration cards to all those households that have proper registered residential addresses. The number of fair price shops has increased over the years from 0.47 lakhs at the end of 1960 to 3.12 lakhs in 1984 and 4.74 lakhs in 2003. PDS distributes commodities worth more than Rs. 30,000 core annually to about 160 million families and is perhaps the largest distribution network of its kind in the world. The PDS or the fair price shops are established especially in rural areas to protect the rural poor from the market price exploitation of the profiteers class.

Since in Jharkhand the general proportion of families living below the poverty line is 54 per cent, although the research fellows, social activists, NGO in Jharkhand do not agree with such percentage. In Jharkhand, government has divided the poor in three categories:

1. *Poorest of the poor:* Those families have been provided the food security under Annapurna Yojana so that there must not be any case of hunger death are termed as the poorest of the poor. In this programme approximately there are more than two lakhs families. Those families have been given 10 kg of cereals free of cost without taking a single paisa during a month.
2. *Poorer of the poor:* In this category in Jharkhand, there are about more than 7.26 lakh families who are attached with 'Antyodaya Anna Programme'. In this programme, the families are given wheat at rupees two (Rs. 2) and rice at rupees 3 and the quantity of the cereal is 35 kg per family.
3. *Family below poverty line or poor*: The third category is termed as the family living below poverty line or the poor. In this category there are 26.44 lakhs of families. Every family under the BPL scheme gets 35 kg of wheat and rice at Rs. 4.60 per kg and Rs. 6.61 per kg respectively. The central govt has increased the number of Antyodaya families in tribal dominated districts of Jharkhand in which Gumla, Palamu, Ranchi, Lohardaga, Chatra, Hazaribagh, Giridih, East-Singhbhum, West-Singhbhum, Dumka, Pakur and Sahibganj are the important districts because these districts are tribal dominated and the

poverty dominated families. In this scheme, additional 1,91,100 new Antyodaya families have been increased. According to the government estimates, there are 70 per cent families of SCs and STs or Dalits who live below the poverty line. In case of such STs and SCs poor families, *Economist, EPW de costa* has divided in three categories:

a. Severe destitutes.
b. Destitutes.
c. Poor.

According to him in three categories the percentage is 10.3 per cent, 14.4 per cent and 23.3 per cent of the total population of the poor families. In the first category Adam tribals community belongs but the other two categories has not even determined in the state too. Under this scheme 7.26 lakh families are being selected below poverty line. Every family under this scheme has been provided 21 kg of wheat at Rs. 2 per kg.

In Jhakhand, on the whole 41 per cent families at average have to face the Food insecurity, with the increasing rate of the incidence of poverty the fear of food insecurity is spreading fast especially among the BPL families or all the above three categories of the poor. It is estimated that about more than 3 per cent household is facing the severe food insecurity because they are seen to collect the cereals either fallen in the field or rotten cereals or forest food materials. According to the Institute of Human Development, in 2001, about 10.5 per cent household has to face the seasonal food insecurity and the 59 per cent household of agricultural labourers has the severe challenge of food insecurity. Here is the role of the public Distribution system or fair price shops which is an active protective agent of food insecurity for the BPL families. According to the all India report on food security Jharkhand is really far behind in providing the food security to the people of the state which is far below the national average 2.3 per cent. Thus the public distribution system is indeed an important organ of the present society, especially in the rural areas for providing the food security to the poorest of the poor in the society.

In this context it is essential to mention the basis of calorie norm and on an average cereals accounts for the poorer households, particularly in the rural sector. Hence cereal consumption is an important indicator of food security. In Jharkhand for the poorest of the poor, consumption of cereals is 6 kg to 10 kg, although, recently in rural areas improvement in cereal consumption indicates up to 10.95 kg where as in the urban area it is 10.03 kg. But it is a matter of great concern to the government of Jharkhand that the such level of cereal consumption is still below the subsistence level norm as determined by IMCR for the minimum cereal consumption is 11.58 per month. Thus from the point of view of food security, it is necessary to bring the cereal consumption to the especially to the weaker sections, Dalits, SCs, STs of the tribal dominated population of Jharkhand. Radha Krishna, R. in India's public distribution system—A National and International perspective, has remarked, 'The evidence shows that even now, efficacy of PDS in distribution food to the poor seems to be as bad as in 1986-87 and that some of the disquieting features persist-the virtual exclusion of backward state's such as Bihar and U.P. from the PDS network and the universal character of PDS in states in which PDS off-takes were significant. None of the four villages surveyed in Bihar received any PDS supplies, nor did three out of four villages surveyed in Uttar Pradesh."

One of the important goals of the beginning of PDS in India as well as in different states is "to transfer income to the poor via ration shops, fair price shops and control price shops by supplying essential commodities at subsidized prices. Income gain or transfer to a household from PDS is defined as the difference between the expenditure that the household would have incurred in the absence of PDS and the actual expenditure under PDS. It is measured by multiplying the quantity purchased from PDS with the difference between open market price and PDS price. R. Radha Krishna in its report remarks". The upshot is that the gains in terms income transfer from PDS were negligible to the poor for the country as a whole largely because of negligible impact in states with high incidence of poverty. The per Capita monthly income transfer was Rs. 1.84 to the very poor and Rs. 2.17 to the moderately poor in rural areas of India and Rs. 3.27 and Rs. 3.60 respectively in urban areas. In AP and Kerala, the poor did receive substantive income transfer but so did the non-poor and the impact, therefore is regressive. In case of Jharkhand the transfer of income to the poorest of the poor in the society as many social activists pointed out in its observations is very low or even a little marginal because due to illiteracy and lack of knowledge of the provisions of PDS with simple thinking, they are widely cheated and fooled by the food dealers or the owners of fair price shops. The ill-practice of the owner of PDS makes the food more available in the market. They generally used to sell the BPL foods to the shopkeepers of the open markets than to the real poorer of the society. It is also essential to make a comment on the dependency of the poorer or BPL families on the open market than the PDS or fair price shops for both rural and urban BPL families the dependency on open market is much higher than the expected one MH Surya Narayana in his PDS reform and scope for commodity based targeting at all India level compiled three dependency of rural and urban families commodity-wise data. The data is grouped under three heads and rural and urban basis and for all-India. Population dependents have been classified as :

(a) Wholly dependent on PDS,
(b) Partially dependent on PDS, and
(c) Not dependent on PDS.

The data reveals that in rural areas 44 per cent of the population is dependent on PDS for kerosene, 36 per cent for sugar, 26 per cent for wheat and 14 per cent for rice..... but if we take wholly and partially market dependents together, then PDS purchasers account for 68 per cent in case of sugar, 51 per cent for kerosene, 40 per cent for rice and 31 per cent for wheat in rural areas, This implies that the non-poor also take advantage of PDS purchase, more especially in sugar and kerosene. Nearly a similar situation prevails in urban areas where the share of wholly and partially dependents in PDS purchases was 76 per cent in case of kerosene, 39 per cent in rice and about 37 per cent in wheat. But now a day as we all know that in all sectors—Rural and Urban—all poor as well as non poor household are wholly dependent on PDS for kerosene oil since the free sale of kerosene is already banned. So far Sugar is concerned, there is no provision of sugar sale from fair price shops of Jharkhand. All are wholly dependent on the open market sale. The BPL families and APL families may get wheat from the PDS under fair price shops scheme. But the PDS system in Jharkhand fails totally on the expectation of the poorest of the poor both in rural and urban sectors. The PDS dealers openly do the practice of black marketing from their shops which are meant to provide kerosene, wheat at a subsidized rate under different programmes to the BPL families. Sometimes the real stocks are unknown to the households nor they try to get the real picture from the block officers/districts supply officers since they are simple; open heart and to believe on the statement or practice of the owner of the fair price shops.

More social activists researchers NGO make a severe allegations on the PDS as the regional based and the regional disparities is evident from the policy implementation. Among the states considerable regional disparities in the distribution of PDS benefits are evident because the four southern states AP, Karnataka, Kerala and Tamil Nadu accounted for almost one half (48.7 per cent) of total PDS off take of foodgrains in the country while their share in all India population below the poverty line in 1993-94 was just 18.4 per cent. As against this, the four northern states of Bihar, MP Rajasthan and UP or (BIMARU states) having as much as 47.6 per cent of all India population below the poverty line in 1993-94 accounted for just 10.4 per cent of all India off-take of foodgrains from PDS in 1995. The off-take of foodgrains for Jharkhand is not explicit in the official records. But the people belonging to BPL group suffer from the advantage what the government wants to provide.

In Jharkhand NGOs activists remind the government of Jharkhand times and number for safe guarding the common man's right to food. But it is felt that such warning has fallen on deaf ears of the government of Jharkhand. The organizations or activities who are working in the development fields, especially for the right to food believe that public problems and solution should be done on the basis of the public opinions as well as on the right thinking approach of the government policy PAI RAVI, a New Delhi-based organization and it is found that the participants had little faith in the state's Public distribution system that had become a hot bed of corruption and should be either abolished or made corruption free. According to a report of the controller and auditor general: A PDS dealer should make a profit of Rs. 358 in a month if he runs a PDS system without malpractice. Prof. Ramesh Saran an economist and teacher of Ranchi University in his findings of PDS system in Jharkhand remarks, "the low profit margin often tempted dealers to adopt unfair means to make a bigger profit'. To compensate him for his loss or minimal profit. The suggested the Government of Jharkhand that the state government should increase the profit margin of PDS to a respectable amount. He added that at present the Government distributes food and materials through PDS to 25 lakh families, though the actual number of the families living below the poverty line is 29 lakh in the state. Members expressed concern over the rising prices of essential commodities especially the foodgrains. But the government of the Jharkhand clarifies that the recent price rise of essential commodities is somehow related to global inflation. But the activists as well as NGOs have rightly said this price rise of essential commodities in Jharkhand is due to the mismanagement policy as well as inefficient, dishonest and irresponsible administrative set-up of the state Mr. A.K. Jha, Director of PAIRVI has remarked, "Since sixties the production of foodgrains in the country had tripled and the population doubled, thus the people should ideally have enough to eat". But day after day the situation of food security for the BPL families especially for Dalits, SCs and STs household is detoriating and there are same news regarding hunger death in such social poorest of the poor household in the state. But the reality of this situation does not exist because of the administrative set-up which denied flatly such a death.

In Jharkhand under central scheme, Mid-day Meal Programme is being started but it is also came under scanner. In part two session of Jharkhand vidhan sabha, not a single question was raised in the assembly on the right to food. This shows how far the government of Jharkhand is not only irresponsible but not even serious into such a serious problems. By getting so many irregularities and effective non-implementation of the principles of the PDS through fair price shop, the National Human right commission has decided to enquire the real facts about the right of food and has already asked it to the government of Jharkhand. For probing the PDS anomalies in Jharkhand and Bihar a central team under the spécial rapporteur, Snila Basant, a retired officer has come and focused on this issue and reported the weakness, anomalies as well as the drawbacks and anti-poor and anti-social activities of the dealers of fair price shops. It is remarked that it is indeed a herculiam task to cope with the corrupt states administrative set-up. The PDS members have urged the visiting central vigilance committee team to clean up the mess. The team finds that the system in the state has built on corruption at a large scale. The dealers appropriately remarked that they were not sure what to do to prevent themselves for presenting the demanded commission by the supply inspectors or District supply officer. Again they were in a dilemma about their steps by which they could prevent their losses. More over, they pinpointed that the FCI often failed to ensure distribution of quality of foodgrains as a result of which they had to face the ire of the people. The central team also stated the ill-maintained record as well as account of distributed foodgrains or kerosene. There is total lack of transparency in the present PDS working system in Jharkhand. At no point, there is any transparency and the people are the great suffer at the end.

In the state, the Government of Jharkhand under the leadership of Mr. Sibu Soren, six months ago, took an important decision under the chief minister Food Security Programme—"To provide wheat at Rs. 21 per kg for the families living below the poverty line. But it is still only a principle and in the core paper for the government The families living below the poverty line has hardly got any such package as revealed by the poor families during their talk at a meeting held by the NGOs of Madhupur sub-division. Recently a survey report of Jharkhand's tribal Institute published the number of tribal families of the state but it is found that such survey report is not complete because the paharia tribal of many sub-divisions such as the sub-division of Madhupur, Jamtara, etc. is not being included. This flaws in report makes such families debarred from the getting facilities of rice at Rs. 3 and wheat at Rs. 2 under Chief Minister food security programme. In Madhupur sub-division there is a great dissentment among these tribals because they are at a large number and it is reported on the 19th of Dainik Jagran daily. In Madhupur Municipal Area at ward no 22 there are 22 Paharia's house. Besides this, at Kolahatia Gram Panchyat there are about 300 Pujhar tribal, along with there are hundreds of households under Tanagori, Budai, Patwabad but their name's are not in the list published by Tribal Research Institute, Ranchi. Due to this these BPL families fail to get 25 kg rice and 10 kg wheat free of cost per family under Chief Minister's food security scheme. In Sarwan, Palojori, Sarath, Devipur, Deoghar, Mohanpur Karoawn blocks about 6415 Mal Pahavia's are registered in government record after the district survey. This also shows that the tribal Research Institute Ranchi fails to provide the correct household figures to the government and believed families are not getting the demarketed wheat and rice under the Chief Minister food security Scheme.

Having gone through the weakness of the PDS of Jharkhand, here we would try to suggest ways for the effective, efficient, equitable transparent public distribution system which could be a possibility in future. It is indeed the reality of PDS in Jharkhand that it is one of the most corrupts, inefficient, non-qualitative and in transparent system of the state. In this context the supreme court has constituted the team two years ago to study the loopholes in the functioning of the system which provided its report and made some specific suggestion to plug loopholes and strengthen the system.

"The centre allots around Rs. 52,000 crore per annum for foodgrains at a subsidized rate for the poor. Out of this Rs. 30,000 crore gets diverted which is a matter of concern and which the court wants to prevent . . . the allotted foodgrains worth Rs. 52,000 crore was for the poor and should gone to them", The vigilance team conducted an enquiry to listen to the probe of the people at a public hearing in Angara Block about 25 km away from capital of Jharkhand, Ranchi. The villagers charged that the dealers regularly took disproportionate price what is prescribed for the foodgrains. Due to the lack of co-ordination between the officials and civil supplies department and FCI, they fail to get allotment on time. At times delay is more than three months. The dealers association made a severe allegations against corrupt administrative set-up unless the urgent percentage has been paid or the size of allotment is delayed or cut-of which directly hampers the distribution of cereals among the public. More over it is indeed the reality that the commission of the dealers has not been revised for the last two decades. The present rate of the commission on one quintal rice and wheat is Rs. 11 and Rs. 7 respectively, thus total earning on commission is about Rs. 400 to 500 per month which prompts the dealers to practise corrupt means. These suggestions can be made for the efficient functioning of PDS in Jharkhand which are as follows:

1. Target the PDS only to the vulnerable and poor mass population.
2. Well-advanced demonstration of real stock of foodgrains by the dealers to the public.
3. Efficient and honest process of identification of BPL families.
4. Timely and regular supply of cereals in all the fair price shops under PDS.
5. Explicit Demarcation of the household under different schemes—Central and State sponsored.
6. Equal rate of cereals to all parts of state.
7. Enhance in the commission—of dealers so that they do not adopt corrupt practices.
8. Transfer of surplus cereals to the deficit regions in time with efficient management.
9. Burden of subsidy would only be borne of the BPL different categories families.
10. Family having no workforce be granted at subsistence level of cereals especially to the old aged persons at free of costs.

11. Decentralisation of PDS at a large scale.
12. To help the effective transfer of income to the poor at equitable level.
13. Implementation of PDS through different employment generation programmes.
14. Efficient co-ordination between centre and state government for the functioning of PDS.

Thus we may conclude that in Jharkhand the PDS should that in Jharkhand the PDS should have impressive coverage so that not a single poor If any category be left to get the proper benefit from different scheme which would be only possible if the PDS is efficient honest, upto-date, modernize; poor friendly and free from all loop holes and corruption. If it were the reality we are not only sure but also confident that it would provide full food security to the BPL families of the state.

References

Indian Economy, Ruddar Datt and KPM Sundharam.

Indian Economy, S.K. Mishra and V.K. Puri.

National Food Security, A Policy Perspective for India.

PDS Reform and Scope for Commodity-based Targeting.

Food Security in India—Ruddar Datt.

Public Distribution, A National and International Perspective—World Bank Discussion Paper No. 380, Radha Krishna R., Subbarao, K., Indrakants, Andravi, K.

Special Rapporteur of Rights Commission of Jharkhand and Bihar, S. Nila Basant, A Retired IAS Officer.

Report of NGO Pairvi, Director, A.K. Jha.

The Telegraph, Kolkata Jharkhand/Food/PDS, 14 Feb.

The Telegraph, Kolkata Central Team, 14 Feb.

Food and Power in Bihar and Jharkhand PDS and its Functioning, J. Mooij, *Economic and Political Weekly*, 2001.

Patterns in Social Expenditure Pre and Post-Reform Periods, M.S. Dev, J. Mooij, India Development Report, 2004.

Food Policy in India, The Importance of Electoral Politics in Policy Implementation, *Journal of International Development*, 1999.

Food Policy and *The Indian State J. Mooij*, 1999, Oxford University Press.

Impact of the Public Distribution System on Poverty and Food Security

RANJANA SINGH

INTRODUCTION

Indian economy emerged from the colonial rule as a food deficit economy. Notwithstanding the phenomenal progress made by the agricultural sector is the Post-Independence period, crop failures continue to occur at an interval of 3 to 5 years with the monotonic regularity. The consequent shortages of foodgrains lead to malnutrition, even starvation deaths, and massive migration of the rural poor to urban areas in search of food and work, on the one hand and highly marked rise in prices, on the other. Food security has, therefore, charged as a serious problem of public policy which has several facets in the Indian economy.

Over the past decade a series of events in India have brought the question of food security into sharp focus. According to the food and agricultural organisation, India alone accounts for over 400 millions poor and hungry people. Since reducing poverty is one of the major development challenges facing India, the country has introduce a wide range of economic reforms, including a direct anti-poverty programme the PDS. This quantity rationing food subsidy programme has contributed to the upward pressure on food prices and insured access of food to urban consumers.

PRODUCTION OF FOODGRAINS AND POVERTY

India is one of the largest producer of agricultural products. Rice and wheat are the two staple foodgrains of India and form major part of agricultural products. India with 15 per cent of world's rice and 21.12 per cent of world's wheat. Only in recent years India entered into the international trade in foodgrains.

India at present finds itself in the midst of a paradoxical situation, endemic mass hunger coexisting with the mountain foodgrains stocks. The foodgrains stocks available with the food corporation of India (FCI) stand at an all time high of 62 million tonnes against an annual requirement of around 20 million tonnes for ensuring food security. Still, an estimated 200 million people are underfed and 50 million on the brink of starvation, resulting in starvation deaths.

PUBLIC DISTRIBUTION SYSTEM

PDS provides rationed amounts of basic food item (rice, wheat, sugar, edible oils) and other non-food products (Kerosene, Coal, Standard Cloth) at below market prices to consumers through a network of fair price shops disseminated over the country. With a network of more than 400,000 fair price shops (FPS), the PDS in India is perhaps the largest distribution machinery of its type in the world. PDS is said to distribute each year commodities worth than Rs. 15,000 crore to about 16 crore families. A large subsidy each year keeps the system going. The level of food subsidies as a proportion of total government expenditure has gone up from about 2.5 per cent or below at the beginning at the 1990s to about 3 per cent towards the end of the decade. Since, June 1997 PDS turned into the Targeted public distribution system (TPDS). The aim is to target the poorest household by differentiating the access quantities and prices at which one is allow to buy. Those households below the poverty line (BPL households) are entitled with ration card that allows them to buy more quantity at a higher subsidized price. Under TPDS each poor family is entitled to 10 kg. of foodgrains per month, (20 kg. w.e.f) April 2000) at specially subsidised prices. This is likely to benefit about six crore poor families, to whom a quantity of about 72 lakh tones of foodgrains per year is earmarked. The identification of the beneficiaries is done by the states, based on state-wise poverty estimates of the Planning Commission. The thrust is to limit the benefit to the truly poor and vulnerable sections: Landless agricultural labourers, marginal farmers, rural artisans/craftsmen, potters, tappers, weavers, blacksmiths and carpenters in rural areas, similarly those covered by TPDS in urban areas are slum-dwellers and people earning livelihood on a daily wages in the informal sector like the porters and rickshaw pullers and handcart pullers, fruit and flowers sellers on the pavement, etc. The allocation of foodgrains to states is based on consumption in the past. In the terms of both coverage and public expenditure, the most important food safety net is the PDS.

Of the 200 million tonnes of foodgrains produced in 1999-2000, about 29 million where produced by the government under PDS, which now support the largest network of "Fair prices shops" in the world. 4,58,499 shops in 1999. The PDS is managed by state government. Location of the fair price shops are determined by the officials at the district level. In response to complaints, a study was conducted by the Tata economic consultancy services to know how much of PDS supplies were diverted from the system. At the national level it was found, there was a diversion of 36 per cent of wheat, supplies 31 per cent rice and 23 per cent sugar. It is significant to note that the diversion of rice, is estimated less in the case at sugar as compared to rice and wheat. The PDS is better organised in towns where sugar is consumed while its infra structure is weak in rural areas. Problem of lack of infra structure and shortage of funds with government agencies are not unique to Bihar, most states suffer such handicaps, except for a few in the West and South. The Public stocks are the only means of disaster management in a year of crop failures. Therefore, public stocks play not only a crucial role in the maintenance of price stability but they also constitute the main play of public policy for ensuring food security in the economy.

PROBLEM ASSOCIATED WITH THE PDS

- The low quality of PDS grains and the poor service at PDS shops forced many people to swithover to market, which offers better quality grains, allows purchase on credit and ensures flexibility to purchase in small quantities.
- The PDS entitlement meets only around 25 per cent of the total food-grains requirement of a BPL family and it has to depend more on the market for meeting its needs. Also with the APL families essentially opting for market purchases, the market demand has risen. Resulting in a relative rise a rates.
- Most storage godowns with FCI are small scale, low quality structures, sometimes grains are also stored in the open, leading to heavy losses.
- The poor do not have cash to buy 20 kg at a time, and often they are not permitted to buy in instalments.
- Low quality of food-grains—A world Bank report (June 2000) states that half of FCI's grain stocks is at least two year's old.
- Weak monitoring, lack of transparency and in adequate accountability of officials implementing the scheme.

SUGGESTED RECOMMENDATIONS

- There is a need to shift from the existing expensive inefficient and corruption ridden institutional arrangements to those that will ensure cheap delivery of requisite quality grains in a transparent manner and are self-targeting.

- There is need to amend law to ban controls and restrictions on trade between states. There should be free movement of all kinds of commodities including agricultural produce. Free trade will help make-up the difference between production and consumption needs, reduce supply variability, increase efficiency in resource use and permit production in regions more suited to it.
- To achieve cent per cent literacy, the food security need can be productivity linked to increased enrolment in schools. With the phasing out of PDS, food coupons may be issued to poor people depending on their entitlement.
- Items others than rice and wheat need to be excluded from the purview of TPDS.
- Subsidy on Kerosene should be gradually phased out and alternate avenues of marketing it needs to be explore. Because, subsidised Kerosene is used for adulteration with diesel.
- Remove licensing controls on Roller flour mills and other food processing industry.
- Scrap Essential Commodities Act.
- Completely decontrol sugar and take it out of PDS.
- Limiting Public Distribution of essential items to targeted groups.

We can conclude that, while it may me true that PDS has a poor records on reaching the poor, once they have access to PDS, the programme objective of increasing food security in India is effective.

References

R.K. Sen and R.L. Basu, Socio-economic Development in the 21st Century.

V.S. Mahajan, Studies in Indian Agriculture and Rural Development.

Sujoy Chakravarty, Food Insecurity in India.

B.M. Bhatia, India's Food Problems and Policy since Independence.

Rajeev, P.V., Planning for Social Reforms.

Management of Public Distribution System in Bihar : A Goal of Food Security

KUMARI SUDAMA YADAV AND SHABNAM PARWEEN

INTRODUCTION

The Public Distribution System (PDS) in India was set by the British after World War II to support the people hit by Bengal famine which had claimed more then three million lives. The inadequacy and ineffectiveness of the normal market channel were thoroughly exposed at that time, when, in spite of adequate stock, the same could not be made available in the affected area due to black marketing and hoarding by a section of unscrupulous traders. The failure of open market system to protect the interest of low income consumer and to maintain the overall stability of the general price level necessitated the central government to streamline the Public Distribution System. However, based on the warranted needs on the ground, the administrative mechanism adopted was to: (i) procure as much stock from as many sources by as many agencies at as low price as possible, (ii) arrange movement of procured stock to different areas, (iii) storage of stocks as dispersed as possible, and (iv) distribution to the consuming public at fixed scales and at regular interval. There had been, of course, the emphasis on holding the price line by curving the tendency of certain unscrupulous traders to indulge in profiteering during shortages.

The Public Distribution System initially visualized in terms of checking inflation protecting vulnerable section from the vagaries of the market mechanism, is an organizational asset of considerable significance for achieving wider socio-economic objectives. In so far as improving the nutritional status of poorer groups touching the core of the anti-poverty programme, PDS has a direct bearing on their success. The concept of minimum need, coupled with enlarging scope of PDS, served to underline to its dynamic character. As we move from the rigorous of primary poverty to a happier position, the system can be used to concretize the quest for *"Quality of Life"*, as it may be defined from time to time in politico-administrative terms.

Central Government, as a routine and regular process, has introduced various measures and even passed strict ordinances to be adhered to by the state government for achieving good result as the means to streamline and improve the system. There have been, however, the identically prevailing steps like revamping the PDS by which the means the supply of essential commodity would be affected to far-flung, remote, hilly and tribal areas; additional allocation of foodgrain and financial assistance to procured mobile vans for mobile fair price shops, etc. To add to this, the Prime Minister has been evincing keen interest in making the Public Distribution System really effective. On his suggestion, the Union Government determined to for revamp the system in identified areas viz., Integrated Tribal Development Programme (ITDP), Drought Prone Area Development Programme (DPAP), designated Hill Area (DHA) and Desert Development Programme (DDP) areas. The main thrust of this programme is that each and every family must be issued a supply card an adequate infrastructure like Fair Price Shops, Storage facility should be provided and the system of delivery of Essential Commodity at the door-step of Fair Price Shops should be introduced of course, system is in operation based on the line of these parameters. However, in so far expectation of yielding results are concerned, experience reveals that the degree of goals being achieved vary from state to state and place to place. It cannot be overruled that the administrative and executive arrangements framed and found in operation are partly responsible for partial successful results in different states and union territory.

Public Distribution System (PDS) is an important service mechanism in rural development. It ensures of availability of food material in the interior pocket. Public Distribution System is a subsidies scheme where the Govt of India is providing a subsidy of about Rs. 3000 crores in a year for procurement, storage and distribution of commodity. Public Distribution System involve procurement of foodstuff (like rice, wheat) by FCI (Food Corporation of India) and then State government purchase from FCI, as per the need and requirement of the state. Thereafter, it is transported to different storage point at the sub division and block-level through the storage agent under the State government's control. After this, the commodities are lifted by the retailer from the storage godowns in blocks to be sold in different villages. Ultimately, it is the retailer, who is responsible for selling of commodities to the people in different villages expending on the area of operation under the supervision of Civil Supplies Department and block staff.

OBJECTIVES

In the light of the perspective discuss in this paper, the specific objectives of the study are the following:

1. to examine the existing administrative arrangement for distributing of essential commodity,
2. to examine the working of distributive mechanism at the grass-root level focusing of the functioning of Fair Price Shop,

3. to analyze the perception of official and Fair Price Shop dealers working in the delivery system of essential commodity, and
4. to examine the issues delivery system of PDS with special reference to Bhagalpur district of Bihar.

METHODOLOGY

The study was conducted in Bhagalpur district of Bihar state. The district was on the basis of socio-economic indices. In this regard both official and non-officials concerned with development activities particularly associated with the implementation of the scheme of Public Distribution System at various level, and of different ranks were interviewed with a duly structure schedule and questionnaire. A lot of macro-level investigation gave insight to prove micro-level programmes prevailing in the delivery system. The survey covered 20 Fair Price Shops of PDS dealers, many relevant officials, leaders and others.

DISCUSSIONS

There is a network of about 4.61 lakhs PDS retail outlets in the country. PDS operates under the joint responsibility of the Central and the State governments. The Central government bears the responsibility of procurement storage, transportation and bulk allocation of foodgrain, rice and wheat at subsidized prices, while the responsibility of distribution to consumers through Fair Price Shops rest with the State governments.

The PDS as it operated earlier had been widely criticized for its failure to serve the population below the poverty line. Therefore based on the recommendations of the Chief Ministers' Conference held on July 1996, an effort was made to streamline the PDS through the introduction of the targeted Public Distribution System in July 1977. This system follows a two-tier subsidized pricing structure for families under BPL and those APL families. BPL populations receive rice and wheat at a much lower price (hence highly subsidized), where APL populations are supplied at a price, which is much higher and close to the economic costs. The identification of poor under the scheme is done by states as per the state-wise poverty estimates of Planning Commission based on the method of the Lakdawala Expert Group.

Policies of structural adjustment and liberalization in the 1990s have had a critical impact on the policies of the public provisioning food, namely the PDS. Driven by the goal of cutting food of subsidized, there have been major changes in policies with respect the PDS, most importantly, the shift from the principal of universal coverage to a principle of targeting, accompanied by changes in entitlement and policies. So the proposition that targeting of PDS on the basis of a narrow definition of absolute income poverty has failed, and is likely to continuously fail in providing even minimal food security to the food insecure and nationally deprived population of our country. According to the expert group 1993-94, 37 per cent of our rural population and 32 per cent of our urban population were qualified to be in the target group. For this type of policy the majority of the actual poor have been denied BPL ration card because they have been denied BPL ration card because they have identified as being poor. Off-take from the PDS have been drastically fallen as a result. This criterion includes weather the family has a *pucca* road of its house, whether any member is in service and whether owns a television set. If the household satisfies any of this condition, it is denied as BPL status: the absurdity of these criteria is obvious.

The reason is started peaking up after 19991, and has reached a crisis point today, is because purchasing power especially in villages had collapsed under a combination of governments concretionary fiscal policies after the effect of globally falling farm prices. This happen as a protection removed and the poor have been excluded from the PDS by the misconceived targeting of the food subsidy. This situation was aggravated in 1996-97 by their introduction of the targeted PDS, which image PDS less attractive to those APL and increased unit subsidy for those below poverty line, but on a reduced initial quota of only 10 kg per household per month. This immediately resulted in reduced off-take from 19.7 million tonnes for the next three years. The excess holding of stock is a very recent phenomenon and should not be viewed as a consequences of certain long-run tendencies in the food economy. The very price system of administered procurement that generates a massive supply keeps the hand so and the month of the poorer consumers away from food. The problem here is that the government has expanded neither the distribution system nor the purchasing power to ensure that the need actually receive the food that it has procured.

AVAILABILITY OF FOODGRAINS

The net per capita availability of foodgrain in term of gram per day is showing the failure of food strategy in Bihar. The data shows that the 1990s have witnessed no trend increases in per capita availability of foodgrain, and in recent years the situation has deteriorated even relative to the levels achieved thirty years earlier. The last four years in particular, exhibit decline per capita availability of both cereals and pulses.

The Table 1 represent the longer term trends in aggregate net production and availability of foodgrains. The difference between the two would give the extent of net import/export from the data it is quite certain that one important characteristic of 1990s has been the shift from the net import to net export.

Outflows through the Public Distribution System however varying from year to year have trended to decline in 1990s in two distinct phases. The decline of purchase from the Public Distribution System was in two stages, first in 1993-1995 and then after a recovery more precipitously in the last two year. In 2001 only 8.7 million tons were distributed in the first nine months of the year and the total for is unlikely to exceed 10 million tonnes. The huge build up of stock has taken place only in the last three years particularly 2004-05.

PUBLIC DISTRIBUTION SYSTEM IN BHAGALPUR DISTRICT

Bhagalpur, the silk city, is one of the 14th populous districts of Bihar. It is situated on 24°30′ to 25°30′ North latitudes and 86°30′ to 87°30′ East latitudes in the eastern parts

TABLE I
Average Net Production, Net Export, Net Availability, Procurement and Public Distribution

Period	*Average net period of foodgrain*	*Average net export of foodgrain*	*Average Net availability of foodgrain*	*Average procurement*	*Average public distribution*
1951-55	55.2	-2.4	58	2.42	4.64
1956-60	63.8	-3.44	67	0.78	3.86
1961-65	72.6	-5.04	78	1.44	6.48
1966-70	72.2	-6.42	82	5.68	11.14
1971-75	90.3	-3.56	93	8.44	10.36
1976-80	104.0	0.06	104	11.76	11.56
1981-85	120.8	-1.4	120	16.56	14.62
1986-90	135.7	-1.32	138	18.48	17.4
1991-95	157.6	-0.22	156	22.84	17.06
1996-2000	172.3	1.68	167	27.20	17.04
2001-04	171.6	2.7	156	42.20	11.3

of the state. The district has 16 CD Blocks and 2 Sub-divisions. It is situated over in 5,589 sq. km. The population of the district as per Census 2001 is 24,30,331 persons constituting 12,94,192 Male and 11,36,139 Females The overall literacy rate is 50.03 per cent.

In this case study problems have been analysed with regards to implementation of PDS and an attempt was made to streamline the PDS by involvement of institutions (Gram Panchayat and urban bodies) in order to make the commodities available to people timely and adequately.

PROBLEMS OF PUBLIC DISTRIBUTION SYSTEM

Basic problems of the Public Distribution System which are identified in the course of investigation are as follows:

1. *High Transportation Charge*: As most of the villages

TABLE 2

Poverty Status of the Households—Bhagalpur District

Sl. No.	*Block*	*Total HHs*	*Poorest of the poor (Yellow card-holders HHs)*	*BPL (Red card-holders HHs)*	*APL (Green card-holders HHs)*	*Total Ration cards issued*
	(1)	(2)	(3)	(4)	(5)	(6)
1.	Narayanpur	13237	1846	7031	13339	22216
2.	Bihpur	16543	2184	12680	12065	26929
3.	Kharik	17469	2317	13389	11715	27421
4.	Naugachia	20744	1902	9245	8446	19593
5.	Rangrachowk	12892	1635	9570	5541	16746
6.	Gopalpur	12974	1722	7144	8438	17304
7.	Pirpainti	36568	4939	28632	24502	58073
8.	Colgong	51327	6275	26994	30658	63927
9.	Ismailpur	6277	848	3172	4591	8611
10.	Sabour	18835	2467	11120	17450	31037
11.	Nathnagar	21875	2746	12043	13486	28275
12.	Sultanganj	33301	3560	22532	18155	44247
13.	Shahkund	26878	3449	17887	16093	37429
14.	Goradih	19289	2537	15870	8378	26785
15.	Jagdishpur	74281	2742	16107	17394	36243
16.	Sonhaula	29590	3919	21194	12470	37583
	Total	412080	45088	234610	222721	502419

Source : Compiled on the basis of census data-2001 and primary data collected at village/Panchayat-level.

were distant from the Public Distribution System shops, it resulted in higher transportation charges, which were as high as Rs. 20 to Rs. 40 per bag. But the rate allowed by the government is Rs. 8 for transportation of one bag from storage point to retail centre including the commission.

2. Quota fixed by the supply department for ration card holders are insufficient.
3. *Inaccessible Villages*: Most of the PDS points were in the remote area. So the consumers are facing problem to get the ration from the PDS.
4. *Black-marketing of PDS commodities*: According to Deepak Ahulwalia, a little more than a third of the foodgrains and sugar and over a half of kerosene oil do not reach the actual users of PDS, and goes to open market in the form of black-marketing.
5. *Lack of Supervision*: As the number of PDS centre is very high so the supervision is quite difficult for one marketing inspector in a block/division, it is difficult to keep track of all the dealers of PDS.

MEASURES TO STRENGTHEN THE PUBLIC DISTRIBUTION SYSTEM

1. Streamlining the Public Distribution System

One of the important recommendations made by the high level *Abhijit Sen Committee* in the context of huge stocks rotting in government godowns is that an expansion of the existing Antyodaya Scheme of food support to become a food security for the entire destitute population, in particular old people, the disabled widows and other single women without regular support. The committee also calls for the reservation to the universal Public Distribution System and the provision of foodgrains at half the present BPL prices, analyzing in details the gross failure of the PDS. Food for work programme also needs to be effectively implemented, especially in all the drought stricken regions of the country.

2. Streamlining Food Corporation of India (FCI)

FCI's role can be limited to price stabilization and

maintenance of buffer stocks. The central government's food subsidy to the state in form of grant, so that the agencies, private or public, can find the best way to procure the grains to serve their PDS. This would also lead to decentralization of storage activities.

3. Streamlining Prices

As has been stressed, better targeting of consumption subsidies and appropriate pricing is needed. The High level committee on Long-term Grain Policy recommended in its final report that the BPL price be reduced to 50 per cent and APL price to 80 per cent of the economic costs, excluding statutory levis. This would help improve the Fair Price Shops in the distribution network.

4. Avoid Dumping

In the face of rising subsidies and increasing dumping, import restriction and countervailing duties become a right and a necessity. The WTO has robbed countries of this right through article 5. The developing countries should focus on stopping dumping by eliminating article 4 of the AOA, the basis of the destruction of 'food security' and rural livelihood in the third world though dumping. Once this crippling clause is removed, countries can start building a global system on citizen initiatives and national priority that ensures sustainability, support small farmers, ensures just prices, prevents dumping, protects the country side and the environment and ensures good, safe, adequate food for all.

CONCLUSION

The Public Distribution System is a vital programme to ensure *'distributive justice'* to the weaker sections of the community. In actual practice through the micro analysis it is found to be less satisfactory. The defective procurement, unscientific management, consumers dissatisfaction, vested interest and many other issues like wrong classification of cards, and malpractice has rendered the programme less effective which is causing widening gap between promise and performance of a crucial public policy.

As democracy strikes deeper in the psyche of people, their satisfaction have a crucial bearing on the evaluatory framework for judging the performance of administrative structure like Public Distribution System including those with a political interface or public policy.

The present level of huge food stocks and annual export of the three million tons represent not only a surplus, but also a huge reduction from the necessary consumption of the people. The immediate and urgent measure is to be going back to the earlier universal system, issue ration card to all who want it, and make foodgrain available at the present BPL rates to all.

A temporary glut can be dealt with through unorthodox measure such as rising BPL quota and attempting to export if possible. However, if the surplus situation persist because of high Minimum Support Price (MSP) and inability of the domestic to adjust each year changes in MSP, there may be a need to reformulate the policy framework to make it more relevant in terms of the present domestic and global market realities. Longer term policies of restoring purchasing power needed to be started on an urgent basis and the stepping up of *'Food for Work'* programme to cover every state, whether drought effected or not, is the obvious answer. To keep abreast of the persisting regional imbalance in foodgrain production and surplus, the need for a national policy and national agency to maintain food security is required. The current food crisis of plenty-amidst-want reflect very basic economic mismanagement by the government.

References

Ahulwalia, D., Public Distribution of Food in India: Coverage, Targeting and Leakages, *Food Policy*, Vol. 1(18), Feb. 1993.

Chandrashekhar, C.P. and A. Sen, Foodgrain Stock: To Feed the Poor or Pay for Liberalized Imports? *Business Line*, 30 April, 1996.

Das, V. Tulasi and Rao, N. Sanjeeva, Second Generation Reforms: Revamping Production and Distribution System to Augment Food Security, *Third Concept*, May, 2005, Vol. 19, No. 219.

Gupta, D.N., Public Distribution System—Involvement of Institutions, *Journal of Rural Development*, April-June, 1996, Vol. 15(2).

Mohanty, P.C., Mounting Foodgrain Stocks in the Face of Vicious Circle of Hunger; *Third Concept*, Aug. 2004, Vol. 18, No. 210.

Rahim, C.A., Management of Public Distribution System in Andhra Pradesh: Administrative Arrangements in Delivery System, *Journal of Rural Development*, Jan.-March, 1997, Vol. 16(1).

Sen, A., Poverty and Famine: An Essay on Entitlement and Deprivation, Clarendon Press, Oxford, 1989.

Role of Public Distribution System in Food Security

CHANDRA KANT SINGH AND RAKESH KUMAR SINGH

"Public Distribution System has been launched in India as a panacea to safeguard the interest of poor by eliminating middlemen barriers and also to protect the consumers from malpractices of adulteration, overpricing, profiteering, under-weight, black marketing, etc. The present study in a lucid manner seeks to examine the network, status and role of PDS in the country as well as in Bihar. In order to contain the level of food subsidy within manageable limits, major reforms are require in the pattern of marketing of foodgrains in the country. The concept of having fair price shops over the length and breadth of the country should be looked into afresh. It may be more efficient to move towards a new system of providing food subsidy through the normal food supply shops that exist throughout the length and breadth of the country, supplemented by Fair Price Shops in remote and inaccessible regions where such shops may be absent. This could be achieved through the introduction of food stamps or the food credit card system as recommended by the Tenth Five Year Plan Working Group Report on Public Distribution System and Food Security".

The concept of Public Distribution System in India has some specific connotations. It is not a system of distribution under Public ownership as in the case of many socialist countries, nor is it an independent system of consumer cooperation of the type found in Scandinavian Countries. The Public Distribution System in India is a retailing system supervised and guided by the state.

The basic objective of the Public Distribution System in India is to ensure the distribution of essential commodities to the common man at reasonable prices. After examination of a number of alternatives as regards the Distribution System, the "Dharia Committee on Essential Commodities and Articles of mass consumption" came to the conclusion that long-term strategy for supply of essential commodities and articles to the common man at reasonable prices has to be centered on the creation of an adequate public procurement and distribution system. The efficiency and efficacy of the Public Distribution System should, therefore, gear itself towards the fulfilment of the basic objective of ensuring satisfactory, adequate and continuing arrangements for the distribution of essential mass consumption goods at reasonable and fair price to the vulnerable and weaker sections of the society in urban and rural areas.

It must be appreciated that the system is not merely a 'regulatory measure'. It is an extension of the philosophy of participation of public authorities and organization in matters of broader public interest in response to the changing requirements of the society globally. The organizational involvement in the Public Distribution System present an ideal instance of management of inter-linkage amongst a number of organizations in the private, public and cooperative sectors, under the overall direction and control of the Ministry of Civil Supplies at the Central and State levels. The coordination between the centre and the states is an added feature of this mechanism.

PDS AND DISTRIBUTION OF FOODGRAINS

Under the new Targeted Public Distribution System (TPDS) each poor family is entitled to 10 kilograms of foodgrains per month (20 kg w.e.f. April 2000, 25 kg w.e.f. July 2001, 35 kg w.e.f. April 2002) at specially subsidized prices. The thrust is to limit the benefit to the truly poor and vulnerable sections: landless agricultural labourers, marginal farmers, rural artisans/craftsmen, potters, tapers, weavers, blacksmiths, and carpenters in the rural areas; similarly those covered by TPDS in urban areas are slum-dwellers and people earning livelihood on a daily basis in the informal sector like the porters and rickshaw pullers and hand cart pullers, fruit and flower sellers on the pavements, etc.

At a Conference in September 1997, Chief Ministers reviewed the TPDS implementation and the states demanded that the additional allocations be made at APL rates. Accordingly, the additional quantities are being allocated at APL rates from December 1997 subject to availability of foodgrains in the Central pool and constraints of food subsidy. The BPL/APL rates (Rs./kg) have been as follows during the Ninth Plan:

Issue Price of Foodgrains (Rs.)

Category	*Date*	*Wheat*	*Rice (common)*
BPL	1.6.1997	2.5	3.5
-do-	1.4.2000	4.5	5.9
APL	1.6.1997	4.5	5.5
-do-	1.4.2000	9.0	11.35
BPL	1.4.2002	4.15	5.65
Antyodaya	1.4.2002	2	3

Source : Bharat, 2008.

PDS AND SOCIAL EXCLUSION

In striving for "efficiency" by means of narrow targeting, households that should be entitled to basic food security through the PDS have been left out. The data from the 61st round of the NSS make it quite clear that a high proportion of agricultural labour and other labour households, households belonging to the Scheduled Castes and the Scheduled Tribes, households with little or no land and households in the lowest expenditure classes, are effectively excluded from the PDS today.

In Bihar, the Targeted PDS was begun in 1996. In March 2000, the prices of grain for above-poverty-line (APL) cardholders where hiked and the gap between prices for below-poverty-line (BPL) and APL households widened. APL prices of grain were close to market prices and, as a result, households with APL cards stopped buying grain from the PDS. The Antyodaya programme introduced a new category, the "poorest of the poor", for whom rice and wheat are available at even lower prices than for BPL households. In the present situation, a person who belongs to a household that has neither a BPL nor an Antyodaya card is effectively excluded from the PDS.

The recent report of the National Sample Survey gives us an insight into the magnitude and nature of this exclusion from the PDS. At the all-India level, 70.5 per cent of rural households either possessed no card or held an APL card. In Bihar, 82 per cent of households held an APL card or no card.

DIVERSION OF PDS GOODS

In response to complaints, a study was conducted by the Tata Economic Consultancy Services to know how much of PDS supplies were diverted from the system. At the national level, it was found, there was a diversion of 36 per cent of wheat supplies, 31 per cent of rice and 23 per cent of sugar. Statistically at 90 per cent confidence level, the actual diversion of wheat would fall in the range of 32-40 per cent, rice in 27-35 per cent and sugar in 20-26 per cent. In Bihar, it was found, there was a diversion of 44 per cent of wheat supplies, 64 per cent of rice and 47 per cent sugar.

DELIVERY SYSTEM FOR PDS IN BIHAR

Problem of lack of infrastructure and shortage of funds with Government agencies are unique to Bihar. A study in Bihar has reported the following box.

Delivery System for PDS in Bihar

- Dealership and even membership of vigilance committees are seen as positions where money can be made.
- The procedure to appoint them is highly politicized, and mostly clients of MLAs are appointed.
- Sub-district infrastructure to handle foodgrains is poor.
- The Bihar state Food and Civil Supplies Corporation has no working capital to buy from Food Corporation of India; vans are in poor condition or have no money for petrol, staff does not receive salaries for months.
- On the whole, only Government staff, agents and retailers benefit from the scheme.

Source : T.E.C.S. Report.

Other problems associated with the scheme are:

- The poor do not have cash to buy 20 kg at a time, and often they are not permitted to buy in instalments.
- Low quality of foodgrains—A World Bank report (June 2000) states that half of Bihar State Food and Civil Supplies Corporation's grain stocks is at least two years' old, 30 per cent between 2 to 4 years old, and some grain as old as 16 years.
- Weak monitoring, lack of transparency and inadequate accountability of officials implementing the scheme.

- Price charged exceeds the official price by 10 per cent to 14 per cent.

FOOD SECURITY AND FOOD STAMPS

A food credit card system could be a superior alternative to the prevalent system of specialized Fair Price Shops and perhaps even to a food stamp system. Food credit/debit cards could be used by the customers to buy subsidized foodgrains from the market and the retailers can claim the subsidy from the government. Though the issue costs of a food credit card are likely to be higher than for existing ration card, the running costs may be lower than for specialized Fair Price Shops as the credit card can be used in any existing retail shops that accepts such cards. This will eliminate the need for an exclusive FPS system and consequently its entire overhead cost. This will partly compensate for the initial costs of setting up a leakage proof credit card system using smart card technology. The rest would be compensated for by the elimination of leakage at all stages of the current food procurement, storage and distribution system. To minimize the cost, existing credit card companies could be induced to set-up and run the food credit card system at cost in return for advertisement rights to this social service.

There is a fear among some academics committed to the current system that food stamps may be traded on the informal market and thus be effectively converted from a food subsidy to an income subsidy. The food credit card can obviate this problem as it is much more difficult to trade. Additional safety feature such as identifying characteristics of the card holder and periodic validation (and re-charging) can be built into the system, which will make it virtually non-tradable. The food credit can also have the inbuilt flexibility of changing over from a food subsidy to an income transfer system if there is a subsequent change in the policy. The food credit card can be made applicable to all cereals including coarse grains. If desired, a different subsidy rate can be specified for different cereals. As coarse cereals are consumed primarily by the poor, the smart card will allow some self-selecting/self-targeting features to be built into the system.

A ROLE OF PDS IN FOOD SECURITY

The level of grain stocks with Bihar State Food and Civil Supplies Corporation's has shot up. The problem is not one of scarcity but it has to do with how to manage surplus so that farmers are not adversely affected by decline in prices. In this connection, the Committee of Secretaries has directed the Department of Food and Civil Supplies to set-up a panel of eminent experts to make a study on foodgrain management in Bihar and related issues; the study is to include the role of Bihar State Food and Civil Supplies Corporation.

Provision of food subsidy is an important element of the food security system; an equally important role is played by food procurement and buffer stock operations. The agricultural production is subject to climatic swings and market forces and there is likely to be wide fluctuations in foodgrain prices. To bring about price stability, it is necessary to build and maintain an adequate level of buffer stock. For now, the challenge however is to reduce the present stock level to roughly half without detriment to farmers. This would need several legal and policy changes, which could enhance the role of private sector and make markets less distorted.

A key legislation, Essential Commodities Act was enacted during a time when state was faced with severe food shortage and scarcity. Restrictions under the Act, which were relevant 30 years back could hamper productive/commercial activity in the market in an era of self-sufficiency/surplus in foodgrain output and in other primary commodities. There are several licences and permits to be obtained from the authorities under the EC Act. Apart from this a large number of registers are to be maintained and returns filed periodically. Inspections are carried out to ensure compliance. All these have pushed operational costs to traders.

Control under EC Act are seen as a disincentive to production and distribution of essential commodities. Traders reportedly operate at high margins and share a part of these with inspectors. With the increased production in essential commodities, it is recommended that all agricultural produce and its products be deleted from the definition of "essential commodities" under Section 2(a) of EC Act and all Control

Orders relating to or affecting agricultural products be rescinded. Action in this direction may be initiated for wheat and sugar to begin with, it is suggested. Also, state intervention may now be directed to make the markets friendly to the poor.

In new initiatives, Bihar Government has initiated his own food procurement operations. More such initiatives are likely in the future. It is conceivable that some of Central agency FCI's godowns are transferred to the Bihar Government. In this context the task of maintaining buffer stocks will become a responsibility of State Government. There is also a possibility that Bihar State Food and Civil Supplies Corporation play a more active role in undertaking open market operations within a prescribed price band. It can release stocks in the open market when shortages are prevalent and prices are high. The Bihar State Food and Civil Supplies Corporation could also become an active player in the national foodgrains market.

Most storage godowns with Bihar State Food and Civil Supplies Corporation are small-scale, low quality structures; sometimes, grains are also stored in the open leading to heavy storage losses. On other issues, the present extraction for wheat and rice are about 10 per cent to 30 per cent below the national standards.

CONCLUSION AND RECOMMENDATIONS

- There is need to amend law to ban controls and restrictions on trade between States. There should be free movement of all kinds of commodities including agricultural produce.
- While it would be expedient to continue with support price for agricultural produce like wheat and paddy the need to abolish or monopoly purchase should be considered. Levy acts as a tax on the processors which is then passed on to the producers. Government should buy rice for its public distribution system through an open tender system.
- Remove licensing controls on Roller Flour Mills and encourage roller flour mills to buy from the farmers.

- Bihar State Food and Civil Supplies Corporation should be allowed to intervene in the foodgrains market within a predetermined price band to moderate prices and facilitate management of surplus food stocks.
- Scrap Essential Commodities Act, or at least take wheat, rice and sugar out of its purview.
- Limiting public distribution of essential items to targeted groups, abolishing PDS for APL while retaining TPDS.
- Completely decontrol sugar and take it out of PDS.

References

Atmanand, Public Distribution System: Role of Food and Civil Supplies Corporation, *Yojana*, New Delhi, 16-31 March 1990, p. 6.

Pathania, Kulwant Singh, Public Distribution System: Status, Challenges and Remedial Strategies, *Kanishka*, New Delhi, 2005, XI, p. 220.

Rudra Dutt and Sundaram, Indian Economy, S. Chand & Co. Ltd., New Delhi 2004, p. 266.

Rajeev, P.V., Public Distribution System and Food Stamps, Third Concept, New Delhi, June 2003, p. 42.

Sinha, Subodh Kumar, Wage Goods Model for Economic Development, 72nd Annual Conference Volume of IEA, Trivendrum, 1998, p. 141.

Sharma, O.P., Vishwabyapi Khadyan Sankat, *Kurukshetra*, New Delhi, July 2008, p. 22.

Tripathi, K.K., Food Securities and Food Management in India: A Review, *Kurukshetra*, June 2008, p. 23.

10

Public Distribution System (PDS), Food Security and Poverty Alleviation Programmes

A Case of Bihar

MRITUNJAY PRASAD SINGH, AMITA SINHA AND G.S. DOKANIA

Poverty-alleviation and eradication of hunger are two vital objectives of rural development programmes in India. Among various programmes of poverty alleviation and hunger mitigation, the Public Distribution System (PDS) is a conspicuous programme. PDS aims at eradication of rural poverty and inequality by providing justice to the poor (Pattanaik, 1997). It was clubbed with the Minimum Needs Programme (MNP) in the Seventh Five Year Plan.

With a network of about 4,51,000 Fair Price Shops (FPS) for the distribution of commodities worth over Rs. 150 billion to about 180 million households throughout the country, the

PDS in India is perhaps the largest distribution network of its type in the world (Meenakshisundaram, 2001). PDS, over the years, has become an important instrument of the governments' policy of ensuring availability of foodgrains to the public and providing food security to the poor.

PDS is a rationing mechanism that entitles households to essential commodities such as rice, wheat, sugar, kerosene, edible oils, clothes, etc. at subsidized rates through a network of ration and fair price shops. The responsibility of operating the system is shared by the central and state governments. The central government procures stocks and supplies the grains and absorbs the cost of these operations, while the state governments 'lift' the grains and distribute these to retail PDS outlets across the state. Therefore, the performance of the PDS depends upon foodgrain operations of the central government as well as its distribution at subsidized rates by the state governments. Largely, for this dual responsibility mechanism, regional as well as state diversity is noticed in PDS performance. The programme is working fairly efficiently in the four southern states, two western states and Himachal Pradesh and a medium pace in Madhya Pradesh. A comparative analysis of the working of PDS in Andhra Pradesh and Maharashtra shows that the programme has universal coverage in Andhra Pradesh, while nearly 30 per cent of the poor are excluded in Maharashtra for want of coverage (Dutta and Ramaswami, 2001). Moreover, high administrative costs also raise the question of cost-effectiveness of the system. In general, it is calculated that it costs the government Rs. 2 to Rs. 7 (with the highest value reported for PDS) to provide one rupee to the poor. (World Bank, 1993) feels that "a subsidized PDS for well-targeted groups is the best form of food security that we have been able to find out". The success of PDS depends on several aspects such as coverage, accuracy of targeting and efficiency and cost effectiveness of the schemes (Coondoo and others, 2000). Taking into consideration all these aspects, the Tenth Five Year Plan urged that "the PDS needs to be restructured and there is need to explore the possibility of introducing and there is need to explore the possibility of introducing innovative ideas such as smart cards, food credit/debit cards, food stamps and decentralised procurement, to eliminate hunger and make food available to the poor wherever they may be, in a cost-effective manner".

The predecessor of PDS is rationing system which has been introduced during 2nd World War to meet the contingency of scarcity or non-availability of foodgrains for the general people of the country. The rationing system limited the supplies of foodgrains to the people and guaranteed the price of the commodities. It was a temporary measure and an emergency measure to meet a particular situation. When India became independent it had inherited the legacy of Bengal Famine in 1943 when food was lying in the godowns but it could not reach the starving people on account of various factors such as, no money to purchase foodgrains and no transport of foodgrain to the places afflicted with scarcity and non-availability. There was danger that the miseries and calamities of 1943 Bengal might be repeated. Hence a kind of Public Distribution System was felt to be the need of the hour.

The PDS vitally and fundamentally differs from the previous rationing system. The former is elevated to a social policy instrument. It is a deliberate, purposive and planned policy measure to be followed on a permanent basis. The food has to be made available to persons who have no capacity to purchase. This necessitates the reduction of the price of foodgrains to suit the pockets of the poor. Technically the term poor has been defined to be below poverty line which has been fixed by the economists and policy-makers. It is true that PDS is a desirable and necessary measure but it raises another pertinent question—the question of its effectiveness. One of the instruments of PDS is the subsidized prices.

It guarantees adequate availability of foodgrains for the poor households. The word 'Public' is a misnomer. It connote public ownership. But the PDS is devoid of public ownership. It is not an independent system of consumer cooperation. It is not a private enterprise. In fact, it is a retailing system which is supervised and guided by the state. It has become an integral part of the National Food Policy. It aims at consumer protection. But when new agricultural strategy was formulated and implemented after 1957 it developed a powerful instrument to alleviate and eradicate poverty.

OPERATION OF PDS IN BIHAR

Under PDS four commodities are distributed among the people who are ration card holders. The commodities are wheat, rice, sugar and kerosene oil. In June 1997, the State Government implemented a new Targeted PDS which had been sponsored by the Central Government. The consumers were divided into two categories. The first category was known as APL (Above Poverty Line) which contains persons who have been identified as living above poverty line. Another category is BPL (Below Poverty Line) which covers persons living below poverty line. Those living below poverty line have been made beneficiaries of Antodaya Food Programme. At present there are 39,93,972 BPL families in the state of Bihar. Each family gets a total quantity of 35 kg. foodgrains—25 kg. rice and 10 kg. wheat. The beneficiaries get wheat @ Rs. 4.96 per kg. and rice @ Rs. 6.51 per kg.

The main question of PDS is the identification of the persons who are to be the beneficiaries. In 2006, the Department of Rural Development made a survey and found out the actual persons who should be beneficiaries. A list was published containing the identified BPL persons. This list is used by the Department of Food and Consumer Protection. It came to light that certain errors in identification process had crept and they needed to be corrected. A transparent list of BPL persons shorn of any mistake was made. After this it was reported that in rural area there were 1,13,40,990 BPL families in the state. In urban areas also the Department of Urban Development is carrying on survey work to identify BPL persons. It is estimated that there are 8 lakh BPL families in urban areas. Hence the total BPL families in Bihar come to 1,21,40,990. Out of these families only 65.23 lakh families receive foodgrains from the Govt. of India and hence the PDS does not cover all the deserving families. 56,17,990 families are left behind. This means that food security under PDS in Bihar is not available to all the needy persons.

When we came to the lifting of wheat by BPL persons, we find that it presents a sorry spectacle in 2006-07. The allocation of wheat was 6,22,982.61 mts. but the whole amount could not be lifted by the beneficiaries. The lifting was only to the tune of 2,27,441.91 mts. Thus there is a shortfall in lifting to the amount of 3,95,540.70 mts. The situation is worse when we come to rice. The allotment of rice is 13,13,288.4 mts. and the lifting is only 1,84,417.4 mts. This shows that 11,28,871 mts. could not be lifted.

During the year 2006-07 the allocation and lifting of wheat and rice under Antodaya Food Programme and Annapurna Programme present a different picture. The allocation of wheat under Antodaya Ann Programme was 2,75,333.658 mts. and the lifting was only 2,38,269.20 mts. Hence 3,70,644.52 mts. remained unlifted. The allocation of Rice during the year was only 3,86,745.506 mts. out of which only 86,329 mts. could be lifted. When we come to Annapurna Programme, the allocation of wheat was 11,995.20 mts. and that of Rice 7,996.80 mts. But the lifting of wheat was 9,622.19 mts. and that of rice was 6,384.89 mts. Hence the lifting of both wheat and rice during the year was quite lower.

In the year 2007-08 the allocation and lifting of wheat and rice under all the schemes indicate a decreasing trend. The allocation of wheat was 3,59,457.48 mts. under BPL schemes, 3,05,993.88 mts. under Antodaya Ann Programme and 8996.40 mts. under Annpurna Scheme whereas the lifting was 2,19,356.95 mts. in case of wheat, 23,279.64 mts. for rice and in case of Annapurna Scheme it was 6,367.23 mts. So far the allocation of Rice is concerned, it was 8,98,643.7 mts. for BPL scheme, 4,58,990 mts. for Antodaya Ann Scheme and 5,997.60 mts. for Annapurna Programme. The lifting of rice for BPL was 3,44,431.14 mts., 3,69,837.14 mts. for Antodaya. Ann Programme and 4,200.61 mts. for Annpurna scheme.

From these figures we find that the allocation of foodgrains is less than what is required to cover all deserving beneficiaries and whatever allocation is made, does not reach the beneficiaries who are not able to lift their alloted quotas.

In addition to these two factors there is a third factor which operates and tells upon the efficacy of the system. The question is about storage. A large quantity of allotted foodgrains is destroyed or damaged or becomes unfit for human consumption on account of several facts. If wheat or rice is kept in godown for two or three years the cereals naturally deteriorate. Again when there is no supervision and observation and inspection at needed intervals it becomes well-nigh impossible to detect the decaying condition of foodgrains. In most cases the building in which the foodgrains are stored is not properly and efficiently maintained, then the result is that deterioration takes place because of the unhygienic condition of godowns. When the foodgrains are managed by insects and pests they become unfit for human consumption. Their value tumbles down considerably and they have to be disposed of at less than the cost price. This causes tremendous loss and the goal of attaining food security becomes a distant dream.

Further there is the transport problem also. The foodgrains have to be transported to the godown for storage and from the godowns they have to be taken to the fair price shops. A very meagre amount is paid to the fair price owner and they make up their loss by adopting corrupt measures. Hence, the Government should undertake to transport the foodgrains or the transporter should be paid a sum adequate to defray the actual expenses of the transport.

References

FAO, FAO Production Yearbook.

FAO, The State of Food and Agriculture, 1992.

FAO, Agriculture Towards, 2010.

FAO, The State of Food and Agriculture, 1994.

FAO, Food Outlook (December 1994).

World Bank, World Development Report, 1995.

World Bank, Global Economic Prospects and the Developing Countries.

World Food Programme, Food Aid in Review (Rome, WFP, 1992).

World Bank, Global Economic Prospects and the Developing Countries, 1992 (Washington, D.C.: World Bank).

Possibility of Food Security in Bihar Through the Mechanism of Public Distribution System

Some Constraints

NIRANJAY KUMAR

Millennium global monitoring goal, targets, at rapid economic growth along with eradication of poverty and sustainability besides woman empowerment quality improvement in the field of education, health and governance. It also aims at monitoring the right flow of funds to the right place of the international monetary institutions. In aggregate term and inclusive prospects it can be learnt from past that economic development in the democratic system has inherent weaknesses on two fronts. First, distributional inequality and instability in the market mechanism on the normative count it is necessary all should have opportunity to leave with optimum potential of productivity nature provided to them.

Since, economic activities do not in corporate all with consideration of skill and opportunity, it is necessary that separate measures are require to be taken for the survival of the economically deprived section by the Government of the concerned countries. One of the grievous problems is to provide food security to all in this situation. Policy-makers are to pounder over the method and techniques both in short and long-term prospective to provide food security of its population. This can be done through increased production which a long-run planning requirement and availability of food steps to all through administered techniques of bridging the cap of supply demand deficit. Public distribution system is universally accepted method. Through public distribution system, problem of food security can be fought and income generation capacity can also be saved of the suffering sections which can be utilized for the diversified economic development. Thereby it is possible to minimize the incidents and extent of poverty. The present paper aims at finding the academic solution of the eradication of poverty through public distribution system. It also raises some question and suggests measures for the efficient working of the public distribution system.

The overall record of China on food security appears to be much better than that of India. If we compare with developed countries of the world, India has miles to go. There is a tremendous hidden potential which India needs to exploit. It appears that the green revolution has pattered out. A big push is needed to revive green revolution in the laggard states of India as well as in the so-called green revolution States like Punjab, Haryana, Western Uttar Pradesh and Tamilnadu.

The main purpose of the Public Distribution System (PDS) was to act as a price support programme for the consumer during the periods of food shortage of the 1960s. Thus, it acted as an instrument of price of price stabilization and became a countervailing force against private traders who were interested to exploit the situation of scarcity to acquire more and more profits. The basic aim was to provide essential commodities such as rice, wheat, sugar, edible oil, soft coke and kerosene at subsidized prices.

The trends in expenditure on food security shows that there has been a continuous increase in PDS expenditure, which rose from Rs. 650 crores in 1980-81 (at current prices) to Rs. 2,800 crores in 1992-93. But there was big jump in expenditure during 1993-94 to Rs. 5,537 crores. Thereafter in 1994-95, the expenditure registered a small decline to Rs. 5,100 crores. As a proportion of Central Government expenditure, it was in the range of 2.9 to 3.1 per cent during 1974-75 to 1985-86. Thereafter, it declined to a low level of 2.22 per cent during the first phase of economic reforms, but responding to popular pressure to continue the scheme as a welfare measure along with a price stabilization instrument, it went up sharply to 3.8 per cent in 1993-94 but was reduced to a level of 3.0 per cent in 1994-95. Even during 1995-96 and 1996-97, it remained between 2.8 to 2.9 per cent. In 1997-98 and 1998-99, it is expected to be 3.2 per cent of total Central Government expenditure.

As a proportion of GNP, PDS expenditure was 0.53 per cent in 1980-81 (at current prices) and reached a level of 0.71 per cent in 1985-86, but gradually declined to 0.45 per cent in 1992-93. It went up sharply to 0.75 per cent in 1993-94, but was reduced to 0.55 per cent in 1994-95 and it further declined to 0.48 per cent in 1996-97 and thereafter rising again and was 0.60 per cent in 1998-99.

Although rice, wheat, sugar, edible oil, soft coke and kerosene are sold through PDS outlets, but of these 4 items, viz., rice, wheat, sugar and kerosene account for 86 per cent of total PDS sales. Sugar alone accounts for 35 per cent, followed by rice (27 per cent), wheat (10 per cent) and kerosene (15 per cent). Coarse cereals (bajra, jawar and other coarse grains), which are largely, consumed by the poor account for less than one per cent of total PDS sale. The share of pulses, the main source of protein for the poor, is less than 0.2 per cent.

Dr. M.H. Suryanarayana is, therefore, right is drawing the conclusion : "A break-up for rural and urban sector separately shows that sugar, rice and kerosene are relatively more important items sold through the PDS in the rural sector, while rice, sugar, kerosene, wheat and edible oils in the urban. Thus, there is some basis for the general impression that the PDS commodity composition is weighted in favour of them supposed to be consumed largely by the relatively richer sections of the society."

A detailed analysis reveals that in rural areas 44 per cent of the population is dependent on PDS for kerosene, 63 per cent for sugar, 26 per cent for wheat and 14 per cent for rice. Obviously, it implies that this relates to poor who would like to purchase subsidized sugar and kerosene. Since the poor are themselves producers of rice and wheat and get part of their wages in kind (landless labourers), their dependence on wheat and rice is relatively less. But if we take wholly and partially market dependents together, then PDS purchasers account for 68 per cent in the case of sugar, 51 per cent for kerosene, 40 per cent for rice and 31 per cent for wheat in rural areas. This implies that the non-poor also take advantage of PDS purchases, more especially in sugar and kerosene.

Nearly a similar situation prevails in urban areas where the share of wholly and partially depending in PDS purchases was 76 per cent in the case of sugar, 64 per cent in the case of kerosene, 39 per cent in rice and about 37 per cent in wheat. It may be noted that about 27 per cent of market dependents were either wholly or partially dependent on PDS purchases for edible oils and for pulses, this percentage was 23 per cent. It is conceded that sugar and edible oils are not consumed by the poor, then it becomes obvious that bulk of the PDS purchases of these commodities go to benefit the non-poor.

To reduce malnutrition among the poor, it is imperative that consumption pattern of the poor which has remained stagnant in cereal consumption, be altered in favour of nutritious non-cereal items. But this should be resorted to only when the minimum subsistence level of cereal consumption is reached as prescribed by ICMR. Food security is intended in the first stage to achieve the minimum level of 11.8 kgs per month. It may be noted that the lowest decide has not been able to achieve even this minimum in the rural areas and in urban areas, even the lowest 30 per cent are not able to reach the minimum level of cereal consumption prescribed by ICMR by the year 1990. This is a sad commentary on our achievement towards food security.

It may be observed that monthly purchase from PDS was lowest for the very poor uniformly across all the states, both in rural and urban areas. Radhakrishan *et. al.*, therefore conclude "Impressive coverage and/or additional state-level spending on subsidy is no guarantee that the very poor are better served." They further state : "The conclusion is inescapable. PDS has remained an expensive and largely targeted programme. The central issue, therefore, is : how to improve the efficacy of PDS in transferring food to the poor cost-effectively. The policy initiatives should distinguish between the very poor and moderately poor, and attempt at improving the efficiency of PDS in transferring food to the former since the ultra poor suffer not only from chronic food insecurity but also severely exposed to the risk of uncertainly both in the food and labour markets."

A recent trend is the decline in off-take of cereals from PDS. Between 1991-92 and 1994-95, wheat off-take for PDS fell from 8.87 to 4.83 million tones and rice off-take fell from 9.94 to 8.0 million tones. The major factor responsible for decline in off-take was the abnormal increase in the issue price of wheat in recent years. The upward revision of issue prices has reduced the difference between issue price has reduced the difference between issue price and open market price. Moreover, the consumer has to accept whatever be the quality of wheat and rice sold at fair price shops, but he has the option to make a choice about the quality of rice and wheat in the open market sales. Both these factors have contribution to the shift of consuments from PDS to the open market, though the reduction of price differential between issue price and open market price has been a dominant factor.

"The per capita off-take was low in food surplus states with low incidence of poverty such as Punjab, Haryana, as well as in poorer states (with low fiscal capacity) such as Bihar, Orissa, Madhya Pradesh and Uttar Pradesh. The off-take was high in food-deficit, but relatively (fiscally) richer states such as Gujarat and Maharashtra."

To verify the relationship between off-take of rice and wheat from FCI and its correlates: (i) percentage of population below the poverty line, (ii) per capita State Domestic Product and (iii) State Government's per capita expenditure, regression analysis reveals that none of the correlates is significantly related to off-take. Obviously, it indicates virtual absence of an all-India pattern in off-take from FCI for PDS. This is rather disappointing. In fact, from the point of view of food security, States with higher poverty ration should have higher per capita off-take of PDS foodgrains. But his hypothesis is not confirmed by statistical analysis.

It is only social commitment of the state that is responsible for higher per capita off-take of foodgrains. This is true in case of Kerala and Andhra Pradesh. Besides, Jammu & Kashmir and Assam are two other states with higher off-take. Weak commitment to the programme is observed in Orissa, Bihar, Uttar Pradesh and Madhya Pradesh—the very poor states of India. Economically better-off states such as Punjab and Haryana have also a very low commitment to PDS.

The basic purpose of the PDS is to transfer income to the poor via ration shops, fair price shops and control price shops by supplying essential commodities at subsidized prices.

Income gain or transfer to a household from PDS is defined as the difference between the expenditure that the household would have incurred in the absence of PDS and the actual expenditure under PDS. It is measured by multiplying the quantity purchased from PDS with the difference between open market and PDS price.

Income gain to the household is expressed by the equation:

$$Y = Q\ (P_M - P_R)$$

where P_M is the open market price
P_R is the PDS price
Q is the quantity purchased
Y is the income gain or income transfer.

Income transfer in poor states such as Bihar, Orissa, Rajasthan and Uttar Pradesh was very small ranging from

Rs. 0.7 to Rs. per month, but as against them, income gain to the poor in Kerala and Andhra Pradesh was Rs. 9.4 and Rs. 7.8 per month respectively. Similarly, in Karnataka and Jammu and Kashmir, income transfer to the poor was Rs. 5.1 and Rs. 7.2 per month. Obviously, income transfer were biased against the poor states. Income gains to the non-poor were higher than those to the poor in the case of Jammu and Kashmir, Karnataka, Maharashtra, Orissa, Tamil Nadu and Uttar Pradesh. At the all-India level, income gain to the non-poor was Rs. 3.8 as against that to the poor of Rs. 3.4 per month. This is indicative of the regressive nature of PDS subsidies. R. Radhakrishna *et. al.*, therefore conclude: "The upshot is that the gains in terms of income transfer from PDS were negligible to the poor for the country as a whole largely because of negligible impact in states with high incidence of poverty. The per capita monthly income transfer was Rs. 1.84 to the very poor and Rs. 2.17 to the moderately poor in rural areas of India Rs. 3.27, Rs. 3.27 and Rs. 3.60 respectively in urban areas. In Andhra Pradesh and Kerala, the poor did receive substantive income transfer, but so did the non-poor; and the impact, therefore, is regressive."

Radhakrishna Report has also studied the decline in poverty as a result of PDS subsidies. The report comments "considering India as a whole, the impact of all consumer subsidies of poverty was moderate; subsidies reduced poverty (as measured by Head Count Ratio) by 1.66 percentage points in rural areas and 1.71 percentage points in urban areas. About 12.1 million persons (9.4 million in rural and 2.7 million in urban areas) may have moved out of poverty in 1986-87 due to income transfer from PDS. ... Given the large size of absolute number of poor (274 million in 1986-87), these numbers are small."

A close look however, impels us to differ from the conclusion drawn by Radhakrishna Report. To bring about 5.49 per cent decline in poverty in Kerala, 4.69 per cent in Andhra Pradesh, 4.33 per cent in Karnataka and 3.85 per cent in Gujarat indicates a significant contribution by these states in poverty reduction in 1986-87. Had the scheme been not universal, but properly targeted, this impact would have been much greater. Moreover, the poor impact of the scheme in poor states also underlines the need for strengthening PDS in these states. To underestimate the overall impact of the scheme in reducing poverty by 1.66 per cent in rural and 1.71 per cent in urban areas is to do injustice to the impact of the scheme.

However, it needs to be understood that the impact is transient and is not of an enduring nature. But so long as the development process is not able to reduce poverty effectively in Bihar, Uttar Pradesh, Madhya Pradesh, Orissa and Rajasthan, the continuance of the PDS in poor states stands justified. Rather the need of the hour is to encourage proper targeting to achieve better results and to build commitment on the part of the poorer states to pursue PDS.

The study by Radhakrishna *et. al*, shows cost in terms of direct transfers to the beneficiaries. This may be true in the case of PDS, but in the case of wage employment programmes like JRY and Maharashtra EGS, there are substantial indirect benefits like improvement in agricultural labourers wages, creation of assets, insurance and stabilization function, etc. Another benefit of employment generation schemes is that inclusion errors (covering the non-poor) will be much lower on account of the self-targeting nature of the scheme, but exclusion errors (covering all the poor) will be much lower on account of the self-targeting nature of the scheme, but exclusion errors (covering all the poor) will be much higher because of limited coverage of these programmes. As against it, in the untargeted PDS, which has been in operation in India, the 'inclusion errors' are much higher due to the universal nature of the scheme and 'exclusion errors' are expected to be relatively small. Radhakrishna *et. al.*, therefore, conclude : "The potential benefits from PDS to the poor could not be realized cost-effectively due to week targeting and leakages. The cost of income transfer was high mainly because the programme was open-ended and never targeted."

Radhakrishna *et. al.* Draw Four Conclusions on the Basis of International Experience.

Practically every country that adopted open-ended generalized price subsidy as a way to protect the poor found the policy not only fiscally unsustainable, but also significantly discretionary in its effect on the agricultural sector.

No particular method adopted in any country was found to be perfect; yet programs, which are imperfectly targeted, have proven to be better in reaching the poor and keeping costs down than no targeting at all. Moreover, leakages appear to be lowest in programs that selected beneficiaries base on beneficiary (or their children's) participation at primary schools or clinics and not on income-based means lest.

While the cost of transferring income to the poor is lower for food stamps and targeted food and nutrition programme, than for quantity rations or general subsidies, it is difficult to rank the targeted programmes in terms of their cost-effectiveness and incentive costs because of the significant variations in the design of programs. The cost effectiveness of a program depends very much on the choice of a particular targeting method and the design and delivery of the program, which, in turn, depend on the needs of beneficiaries and on country specific constraints.

Political economy considerations are a major constraint that need to be considered in designing Programs. No Government would like erosion of its support-base by subjecting the program to certain rigid tests. However, an imperfectly, yet politically acceptable program, may be preferred to a strictly targeted program.

References

Etienne, G. (1988), Food and Poverty: India's Half Won Battle.

Hanumantha Rao, C.H. and Radhakrishna, R., National Food Security: A Policy Perspective for India (Mimeo).

Suryanarayana M.H., P.D.S., Reform and Scope for Commodity-based Targeting (Mimeo).

World Bank, World Development Report (1986).

Role of Public Distribution System in Food Security

A Study in Historical Perspective

ARVIND KUMAR SINGH, SANJAY KUMAR
AND ABHAY K. PANDEY

BACKGROUND

Over the past decade a series of events in India have brought the question of food security into sharp focus (UNDP, 1999). According to the Food and Agricultural Organization, India alone accounts for over 400 million poor and hungry people. For a nation long inured to scarcity and starvation the problem is ironic: it is the one of plenty. Why in a food surplus nation where buffer stocks are three time what is required for food security, thousands still die of malnutrition and hunger? While the objective of food security has been reached, the fundamental individual right for food has not. The purpose of the present research is to evaluate the impact of the Indian

Public Distribution System (PDS) on poverty and food security. The results are of immediate policy interest with respect to the current debate and re-shaping of the Indian Public Distribution System.

Of all the safety net operations that exist in India, the most fare reaching in terms of coverage as well as public expenditure on subsidy is the PDS. PDS provides rationed amounts of basic food items (rice, wheat, sugar, edible oils) and other non-food products (kerosene, coal, standard cloth) at below market prices to consumers through a network of fair price shops disseminated over the country. While measurement of poverty is a heated issue in India (Deaton, 1999, Deaton *et. al.* 2000) to the best of my knowledge only one study has quantitatively evaluated the extend to which PDS alleviate poverty (Radhakrishna *et. al.*, 1997). The PDS had been criticized for its urban bias and its failure to serve effectively the poorer sections of the population. As main of studies on benefit incidence of fiscal transfer, this evaluation of PDS failed to consider the counterfactual and take the fiscal transfer as the net gain accruing to the poor using PDS. My claim here is that recent advances in program impact literature provide powerful tools to evaluate the benefit incidence of fiscal transfer through food subsidy on food security and poverty. The power of these methods is that by controlling for selection into the program the implicitly take into account behavioral heterogeneity and estimate the impact net of this heterogeneity. Since June 1997 PDS turned into the Targeted Public Distribution System, the aim is to target the poorest household by differentiating the access quantities and prices at which one is allow to buy. The differentiation is made with respect to the state official poverty lines. Those households below the poverty line (BPL households) are entitled with ration card that allows them to buy more quantity at a higher subsidized price. In the light of the above background the paper deals the role of PDS in the historical perspective.

HISTORICAL DEVELOPMENT OF PUBLIC DISTRIBUTION SYSTEM IN INDIA

Public Distribution System was first started in 1939 as a

war time rationing measure. The British Government introduced it in Bombay and later on extended it to six other cities and a few regions. The drought and food storage of the mid-sixties highlighted the need for strengthening and containing with a system of food distribution and Public Distribution System was made a universal scheme in the 1970s. In the 1960s, there were major changes in the organization of food policy in India. In response to crop failures, food shortage and price fluctuation, it was decided to make PDS a permanent and universal programme, two new organizations the Agricultural Price Commissions (later renamed as the Commissions on Agricultural Costs and Prices, CACP) and the Food Corporation of India were set-up in 1965. The drought of 1965-66 and 1966-67 provided a strong impetus for the expansion of PDS. Foodgrains distributed in PDS grew to more than 10 million tonnes in 1965. During the period 1965-68, PDS depended heavily on imports of food (imports peaked at 10 million tonnes in 1966). Gradually, as food production grew, imports fell and purchased from PDS also fell, but after the drought of 1972-73, the distribution of foodgrain in PDS peaked up again.

This phase is marked by the growth of comfortable buffer stock, and this provided the basis for the large scale expansion of PDS as well as food for work type employment programme. From 1978 onwards, there was a steady growth in the quantity of foodgrain distributed through PDS, with a peak provision of 20.8 million tonnes in 1991. During the late 1970 and 1980, PDS was viewed as a component of the strategy to alleviate property. The network of fair price shop grew in the 1970, as did the number of commodities supplied in the shops. Special schemes were introduced in state such as Andhra Pradesh to expand the supply of cheap food to the poor. After 1991, the start of the fourth phase, the amount of foodgrains distributed through PDS has fallen substantially from 20.8 million tonnes in 1991 to 14 million tonnes in 1994. This fall in distribution has been accompanied by a rise of stock, and excessive holding of stocks. One of these reasons of this fall in purchase from PDS in the narrowing price differential between PDS and market prices. Although distribution of foodgrain through PDS has risen in the last few years, it remains below the peak of

1991. There have also been major changes in the structure of PDS in the 1990s, most importantly the introduction of targeting in 1999.

Historical perspective of food management in India: Shortage of food has not been unknown to the societies world over throughout the ages. The most extreme form of such shortage, the famines, have also been experienced by societies in varying degrees. Some of the notable instances "beginning with 436 B.C. when thousands of starving Romans threw themselves in the Tibet; or in Kashmir in AD 918 when one could scarcely see the water of Vitasta (Jhelum) entirely covered as the river was with corpses; or in 1933-37 in China, when, four million people died in one region only; or in 1770 in India when the best estimates point to ten millions deaths; or in 1945-51 in Ireland when the potato famine killed about one-fifth of the total Irish population and led to emigration of a comparable number" (Amartya Sen, 1981).

India, with a vast population and uncertain harvest due to dependence on monsoon rains, has always been vulnerable to famines. The countries in the North also face year to year variation in precipitation and resultant fluctuations in harvests. Their buffer stocks and their ability to purchase, allows them to sail through such fluctuations with no adverse impact on food security. However, in countries like India, dependent as they are on vagaries of the monsoon, even one year of drought can, depress the production very substantially and also dry up the reserves and pipelines stocks. A second successive year of drought not only further depresses the production, but there is hardly anything left in the private or community stocks and the pipelines also get completely dried up. The situation then becomes ripe for a famine. The problem was further compounded earlier due to lack of transportation facilities and even if there were surplus foodgrains stocks in one part of the country, it would not be possible to transfer huge stocks from such parts to distressed areas. So, famines remained a part of India's history. Kautilya, the great statesman of ancient India, in his exhaustive chronicle on statecraft "Arthashastra" (321-301 BC), has advised the kings that during famine, the king should show favour to his people providing them with seeds and provisions. He may either do such works as are usually resorted to in calamities; he may show favour by distributing either his own collection of provisions or the hoarded income of the rich among the people. (Bhatia, 1970). In Vedic era, the parting direction of Guru to his disciples, was to go and grow foodgrains. The saying "Annam Brahmam" (grain is God) also illustrate the importance that was given to foodgrains. There was "a gradual evolution of an elaborate system of precautions against famines and for grappling with food problems. The Mauryas under whom India received her first unity—both cultural and political—laid down elaborate instructions to the higher officers with respect to the measures for dealing with famine and other natural calamities" (Acharya, 1983). Villages were encouraged to have their own "grain reserves" and kings used to maintain their own emergency stocks. "The Sohgaure Plate—another early Mauryas document discovered in Gorakhpur district, records an order to Mahamatya (Chief Minister) of Sravasti to the effect that certain store houses (Katha galani) at Triveni, Mathura, Cancu, Modena and Bhadra are to be opened to cultivators in season of distress" (Acharya, 1983). Occasional famines appear to have occurred in India in some sort of regularity all through—it is said that India faces a major drought once in fifty years. There were 14 famines between 11th and 17th century (Bhatia, 1985). It, however, appears that earlier these famines were localised and it was only after 1860 that famines come to signify general shortage of foodgrains in the country: Frequency of famines also seems to have increased, there being 20 between 1860 and 1909. However, the Governments remained unaffected by these famines and perhaps felt that, at worst, the prices of foodgrains in affected areas will go up but foodgrains will also reach those areas through the marketing channels in view of the attraction of high prices. In fact, "the Famine Commission (1880) had observed that each province in British India was surplus in foodgrains and annual surplus, including of Burma (then part of British India, later an independent country Burma and now Myanmar) was 5.16 million tonnes" (Bhatia, 1970). At that time, annual export of rice and other grains from India was to the tune of one million tonnes. Situation seems to have changed drastically on the eve of the Second World War and the Bengal Famine of 1943 is known to have claimed around

3.5 million lives though the official Famine Inquiry Commission had pegged the figure at 1.4 million. However, the Commission did make a general observation that "as many as 30 per cent of the people remained hungry." In any case, this famine jolted the Government out of its slumber and gave birth to a new era of food management in the country, resulting in introduction of policies of control on price and regulation of the distribution of foodgrains by the State.

FOOD SITUATION AT THE TIME OF PARTITION OF THE COUNTRY

Partition of the country in 1947 left India with 82 per cent of the total population of undivided India but only 75 per cent of the cereal production. The surplus province of Punjab was partitioned and West Punjab, which had a well-established network of irrigation canals, went to Pakistan, Sind province, which too was a surplus province also went to Pakistan. These two provinces together used to supply about one million tonnes of foodgrains to other provinces in undivided India. At the time of independence, thus, the new nation India started its tryst with destiny with lots of handicaps as far as food security was concerned.

Soon after becoming an Independent nation on 15 August 1947, India opted for planned economic development. Rapid economic growth to improve the standards of living of all, through appropriate distributive mechanisms was an important principle of Indian Planning. Gandhi's philosophy of aiming for contentment and happiness with wants being kept at a low level, and each village becoming more or less a self-reliant entity, was quickly given a go by. This was an universal phenomenon during that period, the days of psychological and spiritual happiness and contentment were getting replaced by materialistic well-being. Modernity was the concept in vogue. In fact, the idea of what constituted good life seemed to be not significantly different between the socialist and the capitalist modernisers. While "the Gandhian approach has always talked about the voluntary limitation of wants, the need for having self-reproducing village communities and about issues bearing a better balance between man and nature, Gandhi and his disciples looked more like moralizing old men than people who could be expected to change the direction of the society. Thus, the modernising school under Nehru won the day" (Sukhamoy Chakraborty, 1988). Since then, Indian planning has consciously and consistently accepted "growth with equality" as the cornerstone of its strategy. The equality concept requires, among other things that market forces would not be allowed to have unrestrained free play and will be controlled to an extent that will help superimpose social policy over the economic policies. Striving for equality, in practical terms at least the minimum level of standard of living, including of the household food security, was an important practical manifestation of such equality. The concept of attainment of a minimum standard for all the people becomes all the more relevant in case of commodities like foodgrains which are required by all to satisfy one of their most basic human needs and critical lack of which had resulted in loss of millions of lives in the pre-Independence history of this country. The equity concept in respect of food becomes absolutely compelling in a country like India, where around 300 million people were still living below the poverty line; their physical and mental growth being stunted on account of poverty-led malnutrition. India's food policy seeks to achieve the social justice through its price, foodgrain production and distribution policies; through the mechanism of world's biggest public distribution system; through various poverty alleviation programmes, in some of which foodgrains is distributed as part of the wages and through programmes launching a direct attack on malnutrition. This superimposition of social policy over the food policy to control, albeit as minimal as possible, the freeplay of open market forces is nothing peculiar in India; most of the countries do it. "The necessity for food stamps programme in the U.S., however, suggests that market-oriented economies may never become rich enough for all consumers to be able to afford adequate diets from their own earned incomes. Even rich countries will have hungry people if there are not food interventions" (Timmer, 1986). We will have, later on, an occasion to refer to these programmes and policies as these have a strong bearing on the status of the food and nutrition security scenario.

EMERGENCE OF A COMPREHENSIVE FOOD POLICY IN INDEPENDENT INDIA

The food policy of independent India was examined by a Foodgrains Policy Commission under the chairmanship of Sir Purshottam Das Thakur Das in 1947 which submitted its report in April 1948. It came to the conclusion that imports were necessary to enable maintenance of central reserves to guard against crop failures and such reserve could be of the tune of two million tonnes. It simultaneously recommended that the commitment to maintain the rationing system, introduced during the World War II, as also the need to import foodgrains, should be liquidated in phases. The Commission also recommended that the indigenous foodgrains production should be increased by 10 million tonnes per annum till self-sufficiency is achieved. Without saying so in as many words, this Commission did ask the country to move towards the first stage of national food security by attaining self-sufficiency and can be justifiably termed as the first major policy initiative towards the achievement of food security. However in December 1947, all controls on foodgrains, imposed in the wake of Bengal Famine and War, were removed all at once. The time for such a dramatic reform was perhaps not opportune and the weather Gods too were not willing to cooperate. There were floods and crop losses. This resulted in steep rise in prices of foodgrains and the controls were immediately reintroduced. Independent India's first experiment with free market economy in foodgrains was, thus, unsuccessful.

Food policy being necessarily a dynamic concept, the 1947 Foodgrains Policy Commission was followed by a number of Commissions which examined the food policy from time-to-time. The Foodgrains Investigation Commission of 1949 again stressed self-sufficiency. Foodgrains Procurement Commission (1950) stressed on maintaining a reasonable level of foodgrains prices to ensure adequate supplies to consumers. To further protect the consumers, it recommended rationing in all the towns with population of more than 50,000, informal rationing in other towns and some regulated supply of grains in rural areas. To carry out this, it recommended monopoly of foodgrains trade in the hands of the Government with procurement at primary markets and levy on the processors. One of the members, R.P. Noronha, gave a dissenting note in which he pleaded for reducing the Government's distribution commitments with sufficient proportion of total effective demand to be met at controlled prices to act as a brake on rise of prices, because according to him, "Democracy is essentially Government by consent and consent to stringent measures ran only be obtained in times of stress and for temporary periods. "He, thus, suggested a policy of via-media, neither total control nor complete free play of market forces. This has been, more or less, the bed-rock of food policy all these years.

A spell of decontrol was again attempted in May 1952, when foodgrain production jumped from 51.99 to 59.20 million tonnes. The rising trend in food production was maintained up to 1956-57 with production reaching a plateau of 66 to 69 million tonnes. However, there was a decline of more than 5.5 million tonnes in 1957-58, forcing the Government to set-up the Foodgrains Enquiry Committee (1957) under the eminent economist Ashok Mehta. The Committee criticised total dismantling of food control mechanism as a hasty step, especially when no buffer stocks were built during the years of good production. It recommended maintenance of a buffer of 1.5 to 3 million tonnes. It also suggested control on foodgrains trading; some regulation of consumption; programmes to increase production but imports pending self-sufficiency; establishment of Price Stabilisation Board; setting up of a Foodgrains Stabilization Board; setting up of a Foodgrains Stabilisation Organisation to undertake purchase and sale operations and constitution of a Central Food Advisory Council at the national level.

The next and a very important landmark was setting up of the Food Corporation of India (FCI) and the Agriculture Prices Commission in 1965. The former was to provide price support to farmers by purchasing quantities that could not fetch minimum support prices in the market, store the grains scientifically, move grains from surplus to deficit areas and make available gains to states to feed the public distribution system. The Agricultural Prices Commission (now known as the Commission for Agricultural Costs and Prices (CACP), a body on which farmers are also represented, was to advise the Government on price policy for agricultural commodities and evolve a balanced and integrated price structure in the perspective of the overall needs of the producers and the consumers. The Commission was, *inter alia,* to keep in view the need to provide incentives to producers for adopting technology for enhanced production; to ensure rational utilisation of land and other productive resources; to take account of the likely effect of the prices on the rest of the economy, broadly on the cost of living, level of wages, industrial cost, etc. and to also keep in view the terms of trade between the agricultural sector and the non-agricultural sector.

These two vital instruments of food policy have come to stay since 1965 and have contributed greatly to the present day situation when India can take pride in having achieved self-sufficiency in foodgrains and banished famines and starvations. To the extent the country acquired self-sufficiency, the food security—at least at the national level, has also gone up dramatically but before we go on to that, it will be better to examine as to how this self-sufficiency was dependent on the fluctuations in the agricultural production, which itself was very much influenced by the behaviour and quantum of the monsoon rains.

FLUCTUATIONS IN FOODGRAINS PRODUCTION AND FOOD POLICY

It is necessary to touch upon the fluctuations in foodgrains production at this juncture itself as these have greatly influenced the food policy. It has already been mentioned as to how a complete decontrol was attempted in 1947 and 1952 when the country had good harvest but how the control were reintroduced when production declined and prices started going up. Stabilization of production along with its increase, therefore, became important goals for Indian agriculture. It must also be appreciated at this juncture that great wisdom was displayed by policy-makers when they kept the agriculture in private sector, although time and again there were occasional pressures for bringing a large part of Indian agriculture under cooperative sector, if not in the public sector. Had the agriculture gone into public or cooperative sector, we could not have reached the comfortable situation as we have done presently.

The First Five Year Plan, launched in 1951, gave highest priority to Agriculture and even though the investment priority shifted to industries in the Second Plan, the foundation laid by the First Plan continued to be the guiding spirit for planning and implementation of agricultural development programmes in India. The first Prime Minister of India, Jawahar Lal Nehru, was convinced that there was no contradiction in pursuing development of both agriculture and industry. "Ever since the demand for the development of modern industry arose in India, we have been told that India is preeminently an agricultural country and it is in her interest to stick to agriculture. Industrial development may upset the balance and prove harmful to her main business—agriculture. The solicitude that British industrialists and economists has shown for the Indian peasant is very gratifying. As if any Indian with an iota of intelligence could forget the peasants. The Indian peasant is our main focus and it is on his progress that India's progress depends. But crisis in agriculture, grave as it is, interlinked with crisis in industry, out of which it arose. The two cannot be disconnected and dealt with separately, and it is essential for the disproportion between the two to be remedied." (Nehru, 1946). The results of such pragmatism are there to be seen today in both agricultural and industrial sectors.

When India embarked on the path of planned economic development in 1951-52, the total foodgrain production was just 51 million tonnes. Within four decades or so, it is estimated to have reached 180 million tonnes in 1993-94. The growth rate of foodgrains production in the long-term period 1949-50 to 1991-92 was 2.7 per cent per annum, which was somewhat higher than the population growth rate of 2.1 per cent per annum during the same period. It may be argued that growth rate of GDP originating in Agriculture could have been even more, especially against the background of many countries in Asia, notably China and Indonesia, having been able to register much higher growth rates. It, therefore, appears that whereas Indian agriculture did make a quantum jump between 1951-52 and 1967-68 with foodgrain production going up from 51 to 95 million tonnes, the growth in the next two decades was not as impressive as made by some other Countries. The production stagnated between 95 and 108 million tones during the next 7 years but recorded another quantum jump in 1975-76, when it went up to 121 million tonnes. For next 12 years, it hovered between 121 and 140 Metric tonnes. Post-1988 period again witnessed a jump from 140 million tonnes in 1988 to almost 170 million tonnes in 1989, a massive increase of 40 million tones or 21 per cent in just one year. The tempo could not again be maintained and while the production hovered around the level of 176 million tonnes achieved in 1988-89 for next two years, it dropped to only 168.4 million tones in 1991-92, a substantial decline of nine million tones as compared to the previous year, forcing the Government to tie up import of three million tones of wheat, the imports being resorted to after a gap of four years. However, this import was just 1.8 per cent of the net production of foodgrains in that year and the country had no difficulty in buying it by making cash down payment in US $. The agricultural production again revived in 1992-93 and reached a healthy 180 million tones. There is a likelihood of a small decline in 1993-94 with expected production likely to be 179.1 million tonnes (*Economic Survey* 1993-94).

As was mentioned earlier, food insecurity is essentially caused either by production or price fluctuations. It is a matter of concern that Indian agriculture is still prone to substantial fluctuations. What is borne out from the above, is that only a small abnormality in the quantum and spread of monsoon rains can still create substantial ups and downs in the agricultural production in India. Such fluctuations can be observed even during the last six year period, starting from 1988-89, when the country is seen to be enjoying average monsoon rains for these six years in a row. The challenge, therefore, is stabilising production and solution lies in expanding irrigation and making optimum use of existing irrigation resources. With the fluctuations in production and buffers being only small fraction of total production, the per capita availability also correspondingly fluctuates as can be seen from the table below:

TABLE I

Productions and Availability of All Foodgrains at All India Level

(In Million Tonnes)

Year	*Net Production*	*Net Imports*	*Change in Govt. Stocks*	*Net availability*	*Per Capita availability per annum (in kg.)*
1951	48.1	4.8	0.6	52.3	144.1
1965	78.2	7.4	1.0	84.6	175.3
1967	65.0	8.7	0.2	73.9	146.5
1971	94.9	2.0	2.6	94.3	171.1
1976	105.9	0.7	10.7	95.8	155.3
1986	131.6	0.6	- 1.6	133.8	163.7
1988	122.8	3.4	- 4.6	130.8	163.7
1989	148.7	1.2	- 2.7	147.2	180.5
1990	149.7	1.3	6.2	144.8	173.9
1991	154.3	- 0.6	- 4.3	158.1	186.5
1992	146.2	0.8	- 3.5	150.5	173.9

Note : Net Production is Gross Production minus 12.5 for seed, food and wastage.

Source : *Economic Survey*, Govt. of India, 1993-94, 1991-92.

It will be seen from the table that it is only during one year i.e. 1991 that the availability of foodgrains crossed the recommended nutritional norm of 182.5 kg. per capita per annum. (cereals plus pulses intake for male sedentary workers). However, the very next year it slipped down to 173.9 kg; a level that was achieved way back in 1965. The population explosion has obviously been the villian. If the estimated foodgrains production of about 180 million tonnes in 1993 is confirmed in final estimates, the availability will again rise to around 180 kg. FAO had estimated (1992) that the Index of food production in India (base 1979-78 = 100) did rise from 123 in 1987 to 147 in 1989 i.e. an increase of 9.7 per cent per year but only by 1.3 per cent per annum in the period of next two years 1989-91. The per capita rise in the index has been an unsatisfactory -0.96 per cent in the entire four year period 1987-91.

BUFFER STOCK POLICY

The availability picture is thus one characterised by sharp fluctuations and becomes an important element to be taken care of in India's food policy. It is, therefore, necessary, to use a part of the bumper production of good years in the subsequent year(s) of lower production by creating buffer stocks during favourable years and using such stocks in the lean years. Buffer stocks also stabilise the intra-year availability, taking care of the lean months. There are some critics of buffer stocking policy of the Government of India, who argue that these involve huge costs, as also some inevitable damage to stored grains and, therefore, suggest imports, as and when required, as an alternative. Practical experience has, however, shown that imports can never provide that sort of the national food security for a big and populous country like India, which buffer stocks can. Most importantly, imports cannot be on the top, as if imports of all the required quantities will materialise as and when one wishes. There is not only a lead time but in the absence of buffer stocks from which quantities can be immediately released in the market, speculative tendencies will not only have a field day in the domestic market but the country's bargaining power in the international market would be seriously eroded with the result that purchases may have to be made at high prices and on the sellers terms. The money required will be in foreign exchange whereas cost of buffer is at least in the domestic currency. Above all, why is it that a natural calamity like drought, flood and cyclone can still impair food security of the affected people very grievously in the developing countries but as observed by Jon Bennett, "No one in USA starves when drought hits the mid-West plains, for the country has mountains of stored grains. And why does

Japan still wants to produce its own rice at great cost when it can buy any amount of rice any time. The moral is try and have your own food buffer. Finally, in the absence of buffer stocks, the nation is prone to be pressured economically as well as politically—the autonomy of the country may itself be in the danger of being impaired. (Jon Bennet, 1987) Buffer stocks provide food security to nation and also give it the required strength and pride at the global level. It has also been experienced that when India enters the international market for imports, which necessarily have to be substantial, the prices tend to harden. Further, the foodgrains, especially rice, in this part of the world also suffers a decline and even the availability goes down. During 1992, when India had to import, Australia, which is the cheapest and ideal source, indicated their inability to spare any quantities out of their 1991 harvest, which had also gone down by 20 to 25 per cent due to poor rains.

THE CHALLENGE FOR THE INDIAN AGRICULTURE

The challenge for the Indian agriculture that lies ahead is to not only increase the agricultural production substantially but also to achieve stability in it. The increase in production has to be achieved by increasing the productivity since the cropped area has remained more or less static at around 120-130 million hectares during the last 25 years. Latest data is available for the year 1990-91, when the cropped area was reported to be 127.52 million hectares with per hectare yield for foodgrains being only 1382 kg. Serious attention will have to be given to rain fed crops especially coarse cereals, where new high yielding varieties will have to be developed. In fact, a second Green Revolution for crops other than rice and wheat and for areas other than Punjab, Haryana and West Uttar Pradesh needs to be ushered in. That the challenge has been accepted in the right spirit is clear from the goals set out both by the Planning Commission and the Ministry of Agriculture for the next fifteen years. Assuming growth rate of population at 2 per cent per annum up to 1997 and 1.8 per cent for the next 10 years, the rate of increase in the demand for foodgrains, after taking into consideration increase in demand on account of rise in incomes, can be assumed to be 2.6 per cent up to 1997 and 2.4 per cent between 1997 and 2007. Based on these assumptions, the Ministry of Agriculture has planned for a total production of 198 million tonnes by 1997 and 251 million tonnes by 2007 AD. This tallies more or less with the foodgrains requirement estimated in the Eighth Five Year Plan document which has stated that "India will have an estimated 941 million people by 1997 AD. This will increase to 1102 million by 2007. With this population and given improvements in consumption levels associated with growth in incomes, the estimated foodgrains requirement for 1997 and 2007 will be around 208 million tonnes and 283 million tonnes respectively". These figures speak for themselves and the big challenge in the attainment of food security is obvious.

CONCLUSION

To sum up, food security seems to have improved in India, both at the national and the household levels. The trends in consumption of energy and protein during the fifteen years covered by surveys conducted by NNMB, FNB and NSSO have been positive but modest. The following suggestions may be proposed:

- Rapid economic growth with steep rise in per capita incomes, backed by effective redistributive policies;
- A second green revolution in crops other than rice and wheat and in areas other than present ones;
- Maintaining and further increasing the tempo in growth of horticulture, animal husbandry and fisheries sectors.
- Special programmes for development of agro and fruit processing industries especially in States/areas with concentration of poverty;
- Technical education and development of human resources, sharply focused and people-led and implemented employment generation and asset building programmes in rural areas;
- Legislation to safeguard interests of agricultural workers who form the hard core of poor in rural areas;

- Targeting of public distribution system to provide an effective safety net, only for identified poor households;
- Integration of nutrition programme with health and education;
- Higher investment on health care, especially maternal and child care as also on elementary education;
- Better utilisation of existing health and educational facilities through awareness development programmes;
- Sanitation and environmental improvement, essentially through people's own efforts;
- Expansion of training and extension in nutrition to achieve optimum use of available and easily producible food stuffs; and
- Finally, and the most important, an effective population control programme.

India appears on the threshold, ready to move on to total food and nutrition security for all. First phase of battle against raw hunger is more or less won. The battle ahead is still more difficult; it must be waged with great resolve on the part of everybody concerned, including of course, the affected people themselves.

References

Acharya, K.C.S. (1983), "Food Security System in India", Concept Publishing Co., New Delhi.

Alderman, Harold (1991), "Food Subsidies and Poor", International Policy Research Institute.

Ahluwalia, D., Public Distribution of Food in India: Coverage, Targeting and Leakages, *Food Policy*, Vol. 1(18), Feb. 1993.

Ahluwalia, Deepak, Public Distribution of Food in India Coverage, *Food Policy*, Vol. 18(1), 1993.

Atkinson, A. (1987), "On the Measurement of Poverty", *Econometric*, 55: 749-64.

Bapna, S.L. (1993), "Options for Ensuring Household Food Security in India", Indian Institute of Management, Ahmedabad.

Bhatia, B.M. (1985), "Food Security in South Asia", Oxford & IBH Publishing Co., New Delhi, 1985.

Bennett, Jon with Susan George (1985), "The Hunger Machine", Polity Press, Cambridge U.K.

Bagchi, Kalyan, "The IDD Problem in India and its Management", Technical Papers, Seminar on IDD.

Chakravarty, Sukhamoy (1988), "Development Planning: The Indian Experience", Oxford University Press, New York.

Chandrashekhar, C.P and A. Sen, Foodgrain Stock: To Feed the Poor Pay for Liberalized Imports? *Business Line*, 30 April, 1996.

Deaton, Augus (1997), "The Analysis of Household Surveys: A Micro-econometric Approach to Development Policy", Washington DC: World Bank.

Dehejia, Rajeev H., and Sadek Wahba (1998), "Propensity Score Matching Methods for Non-Experimental Causal Studies", NBER Working Paper 6929, Cambridge, Mass.

Dev, Mahendra and Suryanarayana, M.H. (1991), "Is PDS Urban-Biased and Pro-Rich?, An Evaluation", *Economic and Political Weekly*, Vol. 26, No. 41.

Geetha, S. and M.H. Suryanarayana (1993), "Revamping PDS: Some Issues and Implications", *Economic and Political Weekly*, Vol. 28, No. 41.

Government of India (2000), "Report of the Expenditure Reforms Commission".

Heckman, J., H. Ichimura, and P. Todd (1997), "Matching as an Econometric Evaluation Estimator I: Evidence from Evaluating a Job Training Program", *Review of Economic Studies*, 64: 605-54.

Sen, A., Poverty and Famine: An Essay on Entitlement and Deprivation, Clarendon Press, Oxford, 1989.

13

Impact of Food Security on Nutritional Health of Rural Women

Arun Kumar Thakur and Umesh Kumar Jha

Food security means physical and economic access to food to all children, women and men at all times. Seen in this light rice occupies a pivotal position in the food security system of India. The future of food security system in this region will depend on over ability to achieve a continuous improvement in the productivity and profitability of nutritional food crop forming system on an ecological and sustainable basis.

The importance of optimal nutrition for health and human development is well recognized. At the time of Independence the country faced two major nutritional problems. One was the threat of famine and the resultant acute starvation due to low agricultural production and the lack of an appropriate food distribution system. The other was chronic energy deficiency due to:

- Low dietary intake because of poverty and low purchasing power;
- High prevalence of infection because of poor access to safe-drinking water, sanitation and health care; and
- Poor utilisation of available facilities due to low literacy and lack of awareness.

The major public health problems were chronic energy deficiency (CED), kwashiorkor, marasmus and micronutrient deficiencies such as goitre, beriberi, blindness due to Vitamin-A deficiency and anaemia.

The country adopted multi-sectoral, multi-pronged strategy to combat these problems and to improve the nutritional status of the population. Article 47 of the Constitution of India states that "the State shall regard raising the level of nutrition and standard of living of its people and improvement in public health among its primary duties". Successive Five-Year Plans laid down the policies and strategies for achieving these goals.

Women are over-represented among the poor. Poverty is associated with higher female employment but lower income, with greater drudgery in domestic work but lower access to support services, and with high fertility. All these contribute to poorer nutrition and health status of families. The persistence of hunger and poverty in India and other parts of the world is due in large measure to the subjugation, marginalization and disempowerment of women. Women suffer from hunger and poverty in greater numbers and to a great degree than men. At the same time, it is women who bear the primary responsibility for actions needed to end hunger, education, nutrition, health.

The major challenge facing rural women of third world today is to overcome the resource constraints that consign them to low levels of productivity and well-being. While women's role in the food chain is essential to produce that all-important resource, food, it paradoxically does not guarantee women even minimum levels of nutrition. This malnutrition adversely affects women's participation in the economic system and their productivity. To break this vicious downward spiral, it is important to focus simultaneously on women's nutrition-related roles and their nutritional status.

Diet and nutrition are important factors in the promotion and maintenance of good health throughout the life cycle. Income, prices, individual preferences and beliefs, cultural traditions, as well as geographical, environmental, social and economic factors all interact in a complex manner to shape dietary consumption patterns and affect the morbidity and clinical status of women. A normal balanced diet must include daily foods from the various food groups in sufficient amounts to meet the needs of an individual and to maintain good heath.

Nutritional stress on women is the outcome of low dietary intake on account of economic and social backwardness, and their high energy output for work and child-bearing. That third-world rural women works more than men when economic and domestic labours are combined seems to be widely accepted. Their reproductive responsibility is inescapable. Among the consequences of this triple burden of market production, home production, and reproduction are the main reasons for high levels of protein-energy malnutrition and anaemia amongst these women. These nutritional problems have received marginal attention in the context of pregnancy and lactation due to focus of WHO programmes. The consequences of inadequate body reserves, deficient dietary intakes, and the resultant low pregnancy weight gains for birth results in the nutritional stress. Maternal depletion on account of high fertility among third-world women has been well recognized, and the consequent high maternal mortality rates of less-developed countries are the subject of great concern. However, less attention has been accorded to these nutritional problems in the context of rural women's general well-being and their participation in economic and social development.

Women are over-represented among the poor. Poverty is associated with higher female employment but lower income, with greater drudgery in domestic work but lower access to support services, and with high fertility. All these contribute to poorer nutrition and health status of families.

However, even among the poor, different groups of women are affected differently by macro-development policies, such as the commercialization of agriculture or family planning. They have different survival/coping mechanisms, including traditional/local resources, and hence require different support strategies. However, to despite their poverty, women have shown exemplary strengths resourcefulness to face these difficulties. Programmes must harness these strengths and build upon them, reaching women through organization, mobilization, and communication.

The conflict between women's (economic) earning role and (biological and social) mothering role results to some degree in a squeeze on child care, with consequences for child health and nutrition. Within the household, women play an important part in health care. They are responsible for water supply, environmental hygiene, food preparation, and preventive health activities.

A central component of effective strategy must be the empowerment of women in ways that enable them to achieve improvements in all key areas that affect their lives and of their families. Women and girls are the most affected by hunger and poverty. Traditionally, women bear the primary responsibilities in the most relevant areas—food production, nutrition, family planning, primary health and education. Ironically, most development inputs continue to go to men. Traditionally, boys are seen as assets to the household while girls are seen as liabilities by the society especially more so in rural background.

The villages face these problems because their women are uneducated, unaware of their capabilities and are denied of their rights. It is so strange that where women bear traditional responsibility for virtually all areas of life-family health, education and nutrition, they are literally denied the information, skills, resources and freedom of action they need to fulfil those responsibilities.

The exceptionally high rates of malnutrition in South Asia are rooted deeply in the soil of inequality between men and women. Malnutrition is far worse in South Asia that is in India, directly due to the fact that women have less voice and freedom of movement. Judgment and self-expression and independence largely denied, millions of women have neither the knowledge nor the means and the freedom to act in their own and their children's best interests.

Gender disparities in nutrition are evident from infancy to adulthood. In fact, gender has been the most statistically significant determinant of malnutrition among young children and malnutrition is a frequent direct or underlying cause of death among girls below age 5. Girls are breast-fed less frequently and for shorter durations in infancy; the diet in childhood and adulthood of males are better than female child. Adult women consume approximately 1,000 calories fewer per day than men according to one estimate from Punjab. Comparison of household dietary intake studies in different parts of the country shows that nutritional equity between males and females is lower in northern than in southern states.

Nutritional deprivation has two major consequences for women: they never reach their full growth potential and are anaemic. Both are risk factors in pregnancy, with anaemia ranging from 40-50 percent in urban areas to 50-70 percent in rural areas. This condition complicates childbearing and result in maternal and infant deaths, and low birth weight infants.

One study found anaemia in over 95 percent of girls ages 6-14 in Calcutta, around 67 percent in the Hyderabad area, 73 percent in the New Delhi area, and about 18 percent in the Madras area. This study states, "The prevalence of anaemia among women ages 15-24 and 25-44 years follows similar patterns and levels. Besides posing risks during pregnancy, anaemia increases women's susceptibility to diseases such as tuberculosis and reduces the energy women have available for daily activities such as household chores, child care, and agricultural labour. Any severely anaemic individual is taxed by most physical activities, including walking at an ordinary pace" (Coonrod, 1998).

Surviving through a normal life cycle is a resource poor woman's greatest challenge. The practice of breast-feeding female children for shorter periods of time reflects the strong desire for sons. If women are particularly anxious to have a male child, they may deliberately try to become pregnant again as soon as possible after a female is born. Conversely, women may consciously seek to avoid another pregnancy after the birth of a male child in order to give maximum attention to the new son.

A primary way that parents discriminate against their girl children is through neglect during illness. When sick, little girls are not taken to the doctor as frequently as are their brothers. A study in Punjab shows that medical expenditures for boys are 2.3 times higher than for girls (Tinker and Anne, 1996).

As adults, women get less health care than men. They tend to be less likely to admit that they are sick and they'll wait until their sickness has progressed before they seek help or help is sought for them. Studies on attendance at rural primary health centers reveal that more males than females are treated in almost all parts of the country, with differences greater in northern hospitals than southern ones, pointing to regional differences in the value placed on women. Women's socialization to tolerate suffering and their reluctance to be examined by male personnel are additional constraints in their getting adequate health care.

A holistic approach to women's health which includes both nutrition and health services should be adopted and special attention should be given to the needs of women and the girl at all stages of the life cycle.

- The reduction of infant mortality and maternal mortality, which are sensitive indicators of human development, should be a priority concern.
- Women's traditional knowledge about health care and nutrition should be recognized through proper documentation and its use should be encouraged.
- The use of Indian and alternative systems of medicine should be enhanced within the framework of overall health infrastructure available for women.
- In view of the high risk of malnutrition and disease that women face at all the three critical stages viz., infancy and childhood, adolescent and reproductive phase, focused attention should be paid to meeting the nutritional needs of women at all stages of the life cycle.

- This is also important in view of the critical link between the health of adolescent girls, pregnant and lactating women with the health of infant and young children.
- Special efforts should be made to tackle the problem of macro and micro-nutrient deficiencies especially amongst pregnant and lactating women as it leads to various diseases and disabilities.
- Intra-household discrimination in nutritional matters girls and women should be sought to be ended through appropriate strategies.
- Widespread use of nutrition education should be made to address the issues of intra-household imbalances in nutrition and the special needs of pregnant and lactating women.
- Women's participation should also be ensured in the planning, superintendence and delivery of the system.
- Steps must be taken to remove drudgery of women both at home and work place.
- Steps should be taken to improve the literacy of rural women.

References

Amrit, Patel (2008), Rural Health in India : Some Issues, p. 77.

B.V. Sandhya Rani (2007), An Integrative Approach for Rural Health Care: NRHM, p. 37.

Rajni Kothari, Rural Health and Nutritional Problem, p. 107.

Shukla (2007), Health Problem of Rural Women, p. 65.

Tenth Five Year Plan (2002-07), p. 315.

14

Issue of Food Security for Poor People and Problem of Public Distribution System in India

SANDHYA RANI AND CHANDRA BHUSHAN KUMAR

INTRODUCTION

In India, the prevalence of poverty remained unchanged from 1950-51 to the mid-seventies. There were year to year fluctuations, but no long-term trend, either downwards or upwards. In the years of good harvests poverty went down; in years of rising foodgrain prices, poverty went up and simultaneously real wages went down. It was established that the level of agricultural output and foodgrains prices were the main determinants of year to year variations in poverty and in real wage rate.

It is a worth-mentioning fact that from the mid-seventies onwards, poverty in India declined continuously up to the end of the eighties, reaching its lowest point ever, at about 34 percent of the population in 1989-90. It again got a slight jump in 1990-91, and recorded a substantial growth in 1992, and subsequently fell down again some what in 1993-94. In absolute terms the reversal of longstanding trends striking. The number of rural poor people declined continuously from 1977-78 to the end of the eighties, reaching an all time low of 2087.863 lakhs in 1989-90. After that the process reversed, and number of rural people began to climb. The absolute number of urban poor had already started to rise during eighties. In the present phase of globalization the people of entire orbit of unorganized sector are victim of poverty.

PROBLEM OF FOOD SECURITY IN INDIA

In India the issue of food security has been a matter of concern for the policy-makers as well as administrator because a large number of people in the country go without food for several days and as a result of that many of them die of hungry. In normal case per capita daily availability of foodgrain has fallen from a high of 503 gms in 1991 to 430 gms in 2003. As lower consumption by the poor can not be a matter of choice, it must be viewed in terms of distress. It is well known that the widespread agricultural growth based on foodgrains and sustainable land and water development and management programmes, has a dual effect—food commodities become available at cheaper prices and employment is generated. Food producers are a large part of the poor and hungry segments of the workforce. This is another reason for precise demarcation of hunger zones—to identify targeted programme. An increase in food prices makes the poor relatively worse-off, as the classic by Radhakrishna and Sharma (1975) has shown. A faster increase in food prices would make the poor justifiably feel relatively more deprived. With high food stocks and large foreign exchange reserves, these trends can be avoided; we must monitor these trends more closely and put into force remedial policies. Our concern is with the identification of the poor in a manner such that in a period of structural reform, targeted groups can be quickly isolated and remedial policy adopted.

The expert group constituted by Planning Commission on Estimation of Proportion and number of poor has missed a good opportunity to provide an analytical framework and database for the next round of food security and employment policies (GOI, 1993). The world over expert groups are identifying the hard core poor and their empirical correlates and developing policies of direct intervention and institutional reform to help them. Recent international conferences show the richness of the material (WFO and FAO, 1993). The Indian report, however, stays as optically away from relevance and has a consequence also created no 'expert' waves.

Beginning with a literature review, the expert group states that the early 1970s generated a rich and extensive literature on poverty, and that the 'Task force on Projections of Minimum Needs and Effective Consumption demand, January 1979, was able to bring together at one place the results of some of these studies and redefine the poverty line.

The Alagh Task Force made four important recommendations, two of which have been accepted by the expert group. *Firstly,* the poverty norm at 2,400 Kcal per person for rural areas and 2,100 Kcal for urban areas, or the poverty line is anchored in a given calorie norm and the corresponding all India consumption basket for 1973-74. *Secondly,* it developed a procedure for updating the poverty norm for years for which house hold consumption surveys were not available. The expert group was in favour of using the same as far as these practices are concerned.

PRODUCTION AND CONSUMPTION TREND OF FOOD

Improving food security is an issue of considerable importance for a developing country like India where millions of people suffer from hunger and malnutrition. It is now widely recognized that food security is not confined only to production, availability and demand for food-ultimately, the key question is that of the ability of the people to access food and utilize it effectively at all times, to lead a healthy life. Nutrition security is an important dimension of food security.

In the post-independence period India has several achievements on the food front. Successive five year plans have laid considerable emphasis on policies and strategies and strategies aimed raising the level of nutritional and standard of living of people. The production of foodgrains has increased more than four-fold since independence—from 50 million tonnes in 1950-51, it has increased to about 210 million tonnes in 1999-2000. As a result, India has moved from a stage of chronic food shortages to self-sufficiency in food production, and has built up substantial buffer stocks. The level of procurement and the reach of PDS has also increased considerably, overtime.

According to a recent report of the FAO over 225 million people of India remain chronically undernourished. Another study conducted by the National Nutrition Monitoring Bureau has estimated that, "in 2000-01 about half of the rural children below five years of age suffered from malnutrition and 40 percent of adults from chronic energy deficiency. This is due to the fact that a substantial proportion of the people are too poor to buy enough food and also exposed to diseases caused by poor sanitation which results in poor conversion of food into energy." The PDS has, therefore, to address the issues of food security in the wider connotations of food as well as nutrition security.

In India for ensuring food management in the country a two-fold strategy becomes necessary. The first is to maintain and steadily increase agricultural production. The second is to procure surpluses and store, transfer and distribute these to those who need food supplies. Procurement of foodgrains in PDS contexts remains an important economic activity of the government and its agencies. The Table 1 indicates the level of procurement of rice and wheat in India from 1995-96 to 2003-04.

Most of wheat procurement in 2003-04 came from the States of Punjab (56.57%), Haryana (32.43%) and U.P. (7.08%). Together these three states contributed 96.67 percent to the wheat procurement of that year. In respect of rice, in 2003-04, only four states, Punjab, Andhra Pradesh, UP and Chhattisgarh contributed nearly 78 percent to the procurement kitty. The position in respect of off-take of rice and wheat from the

Table I
Procurement of Foodgrains in India (Central Pool)

(In million tonnes)

Crop/ Yr.	*1995-96*	*1996-97*	*1997-98*	*1998-99*	*1999-2000*	*2000-01*	*2001-02*	*2002-03*	*2003-04*	*2004-05*
(1)	*(2)*	*(3)*	*(4)*	*(5)*	*(6)*	*(7)*	*(8)*	*(9)*	*(10)*	*(11)*
Wheat (April-March	12.23	8.16	9.3	12.65	14.14	6.35	20.63	19.05	15.8	16.8
Rice (Oct.-Sept.)	10.07	12.97	15.59	12.6	18.23	21.28	22.13	16.42	22.83	NA
Total Wheat + Rice	22.3	21.13	24.89	25.25	32.37	37.63	42.76	35.57	38.63	NA

Source : *Economic Survey*, Government of India, 2004-05.

central pool *vis-a-vis* procurement for the period 1999-2000 to 2003-04 is reflected in Table 2.

TABLE 2
Procurement and Off-take of Wheat and Rice from Central Pool

Year	*1999-2000*	*2000-01*	*2001-02*	*2002-03*	*2003-04*
Procurement	32.37	37.63	42.76	35.57	38.63
Off-take	23.05	18.81	32.93	49.63	49.16

Source : Department of Food and Public Distribution, Government of India.

The Table 2 shows that, while annual procurement of wheat and rice put together rose from 32.37 million tonnes in 1999-2000 to 38.63 m tonnes in 2003-04 (with a midway peak of 47.76 m. tonnes in 2001-02) the off-take was way below it in the first three years of the period in question, i.e., 1999-2000 to 2001-02. The result was that the Centre accumulated huge grain stocks which touched 61 million tonnes in July 2001 and 63 million tonnes in July 2002 against the prescribed buffer stock norm of 24.3 million tonnes at this point of time in a year (i.e., July). The off-loading of such heavy stocks, which meant very heavy locking of funds, very high carrying costs and high storage losses became an urgency a Multiple set of interventions, therefore, became necessary which included the stepping up of exports, larger open market operations and higher foodgrain distribution levels achieved through an expanded Targeted Public Distribution System (TPDS) under BPL, APL, and Antyodaya categories and various other welfare programmes that had food components.

PUBLIC DISTRIBUTION SYSTEM IN INDIA

The genesis of PDS lies in the history of World War II when rationing of food materials was introduced in many parts of the world including India. After Independence, food shortages persisted in the country and, for many years, we had to depend on food imports from abroad. We passed through a critical period during the 50's and 60's of the last century. At one point of time it was said that India was being fed from ship to mouth. Then came a distinct shift in the economic policy with emphasis moving towards the development of agriculture. This shift was immensely facilitated by the advent of what is commonly called the Green Revolution. Both agricultural production as well as productivity steadily increased. From around 50 million tonnes of foodgrains produced at the beginning of the planning era (1951) the production rose to over 200 million tonnes at the start of the present century. For example, in UP, rice productivity shot up from 5.1 qtl/ha in 1950-51 to over 22 qtl/ha in 2000-01. In the case of wheat it increased from 8.21 qtl/ha in 1950-51 to about 25 qtls/ha in 2000-01. but, this is only a part of the story. The demographic rise in the country has been also very sharp. Population grew up from 36.1 crore in 1951 to 102.9 crore in 2001. Poverty persisted continuously. In percentage terms, however, its incidence was coming down. Economists say that over half of India (51.3%) lived below the poverty line in 1977-78. this proportion has now come down to about a fourth of the population (26.1%). In absolute terms the BPL numbers are still enormously high at over 27 crore. In some States the incidence of poverty continues to be very high at between 45 to 50 percent such as Bihar and Orissa.

Poverty means less of income and social security, less of food and nutrition and less of shelter, clothing, education and health cover. It means deprivation, exclusion and un-empowerment for great many people. So, even if the country is more than self-sufficient in food, many cannot buy it. They just do not have the purchasing power to do so. It is their food security and nutrition problems and that of other weaker sections of the society like children, women, the old and the very indigent, that the PDS, TPDS and other poverty alleviation programmes, which include a food component at affordable rates or even free, are designed to address.

PROBLEM OF PUBLIC DISTRIBUTION SYSTEM

The Government of India started PDS with view to tackle the problem of hunger and maintain the food security among rural poor people. But from the day of birth of PDS it has become a shelter of deep corruption. The local officers, leaders, agents and dealers are the components of this corruption and hardly there is a day in a weak when we do not come across reports of malpractice in PD Systems.

There is a long net working of corruption from block level to ministry of food and civil supply in maximum states of country.

The roots of such widespread corruption can be traced to a number of factors. *Firstly*, the very system of procurement and distribution creates distortions that skew normal supply-demand factors that should inform the market. Procurement is a need, as also a compulsion, to ensure, on the one hand, availability of foodgrains for those who cannot afford to pay open market prices and, on the other, to build buffer stocks for meeting emergent food needs at the time of abnormal situations like, for example, crop failures, droughts, floods or any natural calamities. The minimum support price policy is, frankly speaking, both politically and economically driven. Its objectives include protecting the interests of farmers and offering to buy from them grains at prices that are economic to producers. Since procurement is open-ended, heavy accumulation of stocks is one of the consequences that has to be reckoned with. That increases costs sharply and puts severe pressure on the Central Government in financial terms. Grading of procured grains is a stage where malpractices obtain; so are weighing and bagging. In the distribution phase the multiple sets of issue prices, depending upon the target groups to whom foodgrains are to be reached, create opportunities for registering false entitlements and distribution and diverting low priced grains to open market. Distribution takes place through 'quota-holders'. The margins allowed to them to perform this function are reported to be very low. That is said to be yet another reason for the quota-holders resorting to illegal and unhealthy means to make a buck. It is also learnt that the quota-holder system has been politicised in terms of patronage and protection. In this process the collusion of government staff is also enlisted.

The nexus of these corrupt people have led to hunger situation in the society and particularly those states where there are more uneducated people. In this regard states like Bihar. Jharkhand and U.P. are the excellent example where there is loot in public distribution system and people below the poverty live have no reach to the office of action taking officer.

STEPS TO BE TAKEN FOR REVAMPING THE PDS

The public Distribution system of foodgrains in India is a wide national policy which exists in all states. But in some states the PDS works much better than in other states. We would like to place an example of Bihar and Jharkhand states where PDS policy works poorly. It is important to understand why this is the case and a better policy prescription is necessary for those states where P.D.S. is not working as per the norms prescribed by the government. In short, discussion has been made below and what steps should be taken to revamp the PDS are being mentioned here:

1. To protect the interest of dealer by the government. The amount which is given to the dealer by the Government is not sufficient and does not compensate the real wage of dealer in terms of labour/works done by the concerned dealer in functioning of PDS which ultimately compel them to be corrupt or dishonest.
2. The fair price shop dealers pay monthly bribe to the officials of block as well as food and civil supply department which has become a normal tradition that must be stopped by tight checking through any strict agency.
3. Action against Mafias is required on top priority basis. In some of the states mafias are dominating the local offices due to political interference. Under such circumstance the government should recognize the mafia and legal action should be initiated against them so that PDS may come on track and cater the need of poor people.
4. The details of policy and procedural shortcomings and of the economic, social and other factors that

come into play in giving rise to the existing serious distortions and aberrations need to be ascertained through a thorough study so that remedial measures can be identified, and implemented.

5. The PDS system from the stage of procurement to distribution needs to be revamped and remodeled.
6. Government interventions in the foodgrain market should be only strategic and selective rather than of a blanket character like the present procurement system of minimum support prices without any limits on the quantum of purchases.
7. The identification procedures for various categories of the beneficiaries of PDS (e.g., BPL, APL, the old and indigent, the poorest, the unemployed, the special EEP recipients of food, etc.) need to be streamlined, made transparent and be subjected to strict checking, monitoring and periodic corrections.
8. The possibility of introducing an alternative in the form of a food Stamps System needs to be examined with a view to improve the coverage as also the equity focus of PDS and other nutrition supplementing schemes. In his 2004-05 budget speech, the Union Minister of Finance had announced the proposal of introducing a Food Stamp Scheme in certain districts in the country. Under this scheme the plan was that every eligible families could collect their monthly quota of food stamps from a designated distribution centre to exchange these for foodgrains in any shop.
9. Many corrupt practices have entered the vast panoply of food and nutrition-related programmes in the country. There is need to take both preventive as well as curative measures to overcome this menace. This would call for several types of steps like, for example : (i) remodeling procurement policies as well as PDS, (ii) making systems transparent, (iii) intensifying scrutiny, monitoring and supervision over food procurement as well as distribution programmes, (iv) taking speedy and deterrent action against those found to be corrupt

and setting up special fast-track dedicated courts to try and punish them with severity and speed, (v) enhancing public oversight by involving Panchayats, local bodies and civil society formations in the implementation of various types of food and nutrition-related programmes, (vi) providing full right of information to people, and (vii) introducing vigorous audit measures including social audit at village and mohalla (in towns) levels.

CONCLUSION

Though several criticism have been levelled against P.D.S. in India but it is the PDS which has ultimately severed the interest of food security of poor in India. The public Distribution system has proved to be the corner stone of food security in the country and this is evident from several studies conducted on PDS that have high lighted the limitations and role of the PDS in strengthening food security in India. There are two components of PDS—(a) Fair Price Shop (FPS), and (b) Targetted Food Assistance Programmes and both have served the interest of poor. There is defective in operational system and not in public distribution system.

In effectiveness of this government has crippled PDS in many states of India. For example, several scholars have pointed at the governmental ineffectiveness in Bihar (Kohli, 1991) or the withering away of the state (Sharma, 1995, p. 2587). There are at least three inter-related aspects to this governmental ineffectiveness : (a) the deprofessionalisation of the bureaucracy; (b) the criminalisation of politics; and (c) the violence in the state.

Deprofessionalisation is an important feature of Bihar and U.P. states. The more competent civil servants are replaced almost as soon as they do not give into the wishes of their political superiors. What matters to ministers is political loyalty, rather than competence, professionalism is not valid, rather the reverse.

However, several states have not sofar been fully successful in improving the food security through PDS However, in the efforts to achieve this objective it has to face formidable challenge of mafia and rangdar and domination of upper castes. Uncertainties created by the new economic policy, if not handled carefully, can compound the uncertainties created by nature. Hence the need is to correct the operational system of PDS to protect the issue of food security.

References

Alagh, Y.K. (1994), Indian Development Planning and Policy, Second Edition, Vikas Delhi.

Radhakrishna, R. and Sharma, Atul (1975), Price Indices by Income Class in Rural and Urban Areas, Sardar Patel Institute of Economics and Social Research, Ahmedabad.

GoI (1993), Report of the Expert Group on Estimation of Proportion and Number of Poor, Perspective Planning Division, Planning Commission of India, Delhi.

Kanhan, K.P., Food Security in a Regional Perspective: A View from Food Deficit, Kerala, Published in Towards a Food Secure India Issue and Policies, Institute for Human Development. New Delhi.

Radhakrishna, R. (2005), Food and Nutrition Security of the Poor, *E & P Weekly*, 30.4.04.

Saxena, N.C. (2004), Food-based Programmes as Safety nets in India, World Food Forum Workshop, New Delhi, Oct. 2004.

Dhar, T.N., Food Security, Nutrition and Public Distribution (Social Goals And Flawed Delivery Systems). Published in *Indian Journal of Public Administration*, Vol. II, No. 3, July-Sept., 2005.

An Assessment of Targeted Public Distribution System in India and Role of Government in Solving the Problem of Food Security for Poor

Bishwanath Gupta, Bindeshwar Kumar
and As Mahammad

INTRODUCTION

The Government of India launched the Targeted Public Distribution System in 1977 which makes a clear distinction between the people living below poverty line (BPL) and above poverty line (APL) with differential entitlements and prices for the two categories. It was announced that allocations to APL families would be transitory. This kind of targeting was the first step in a process of excluding large number of vulnerable people from the PDS and in changing the character of the PDS was confirmed by the policy announcements in the budget of March 2000.

It may be true to an extent that TPDS has enabled the poor to weather food scarcity shocks caused by droughts, floods, cyclones and other types of disasters and calamities for short durations, but, what is much more true and tragic is that TDPS has not succeeded in achieving its medium and long term objective, namely, economic help and sustained food security for the poor. The farmer complains of MSP being below his production cost. The trade complains of severe restrictions in terms of free market play and unimpeded movement of foodgrains in the country. It also exploits blatantly the opportunities for renteerism that the system provides. The poor complain of getting deprived of the benefits of a policy intended to support and help them on a sustained basis. So, is it a system where the main players seem to be losers all, and the only gainers are those who exploit the system through cross opportunism, corruption, fraud and bribery? It is high time that a fresh look is taken at food management policies and systems. We are told we produce enough food to meet the caloric needs of all. If so why is it said that the food gap for the poor is of the order of ten million tonnes a year?

FOOD AND NUTRITION SECURITY FOR POOR

The government took several steps to ensure food and nutritional security for chronic poor people which costs very high prices. Presently, there are a number of programmes being implemented in the country which directly and indirectly are related to providing various types and degrees of food safety nets and means of poverty alleviation. These programmes target different categories of population. Their means, methods and components vary but their end objectives are addressing poverty problems, enhancing food security and improving nutrition levels of the vulnerable groups of population, e.g. children, pregnant and lactating mothers, the old, the poor, and the very indigent. We would consider here some of the key programmes that are being carried out in these contexts in the country at present, but, before doing so, we may first take a look on the gross off-take of foodgrains from the Central Pool in recent years for different purposes like Targeted Public Distribution System (TPDS), various welfare schemes, open market operations and exports. The position of off-take is reflected in the Table 1.

TABLE 1

Off-take of Foodgrains from Central Pool

Schemes	*Foodgrains (Rice + Wheat)*				
	1999-2000	*2000-01*	*2001-02*	*2002-03*	*2003-04*
(a) TPDS of which	17.07	12.04	13.84	20.13	24.19
(i) BPL	6.99	9.65	10.05	14.51	14.75
(ii) APL	10.08	2.36	2.11	3.08	4.22
(iii) Antyodaya		0.024	1.68	3.54	3.82
(b) Welfare	1.43	3.19	7.18	11.38	13.5
(c) Open Market Sale	4.55	1.49	5.6	5.66	1.33
Export	—	2.08	6.31	12.46	10.14
Total	23.05	18.8	32.93	49.63	49.16

Source : *Economic Survey of India,* GoI (2004-05).

The off-take from the Central Pool has shown a rising trend from 1999-2000 to 2003-04 (in 2004-055 there has been a substantial decline in off-take though final figures are not readily available). The above table shows that TPDS off-take has gone up but the rise has been much sharper through issues covered by various welfare schemes and in the case of allocations for the very indigent, namely, those falling under the Antyodaya category. Exports, too, went up in the period 2001-04 but these have come down very sharply in 2004-05 (less than 1 million tonnes in the period April-November, 2004) due to a deliberate policy change in order to meet the new exigencies of food management in the country.

PROBLEM OF TARGETED PUBLIC DISTRIBUTION SYSTEM (TPDS)

The introduction of TPDS was meant for the chronic poor people but there became many black holes in the system. Though the programme became universal but their quality tend to deteriorate day-by-day and a result of which foodgrains to be distributed among the poor people were too bad to be safe. Since the TPDS was mainly for the chronic poor people so there was no political support to thus programme by the political leaders and ultimately it suffered from different drawbacks such as irregular supply of foodgrains, malpractices on large scale and several other corrupt business started to take place. Though the targeted public Distribution system in the largest food distribution programme in the country that covers about 40-50 percent of the total off-take of foodgrains from the Central Pool. This percentage was much higher (about 65 to 75%) in the earlier years 99-2000 and 2000-01. the TPDS has been defined by some economists as a "producer-price-support-*cum*-consumer-subsidy programme." In its earlier format it was geographically limited to urban areas and those rural areas that were distinctly food deficit ones. It was in the 80's of the last century that food was (through its distribution at subsidized pricing) utilized as a means to providing a safety net to protect the poor "from potential short-run price induced adverse effects." It was made a component of many employment, poverty alleviation and nutrition deficiency-filling programmes. This is when distortions started to surface. The policy of open ended procurement, the rising minimum support prices from year to year, the inexorably high economic costs incurred by FCI on procuring foodgrains that include MSP + procurement charges, warehousing, transport, storage losses, interest charges, etc.), the deliberately fixed lower issue prices for PDS (APL, BPL, etc.) and highly subsidized or even free food supplies for some specified categories of consumers—all these factors put together have created a system that has been, and continues to be conducive to manipulation, fraud, leakages and large scale corruption.

A widespread illegal and criminal diversion of foodgrains meant for the poor in a number of districts in UP and Bihar have come to light in recent time in which scores of people from trade, people's elected institutions, PSUs dealing with foodgrains and government departments are reported to be involved. The widespread scam, covering many districts, in which hundreds of people are involved, is under investigation.

GOVERNMENT STEPS TO PROTECT THE TARGETED POOR PEOPLE

When government came to know the ground reality about the TPDS, the government took alternative steps to ensure food security among the poor people. In other word, the objective of TPDS failed in the eyes of government and it was considered to be the best platform of loot of public property by the dealers, leaders and government officials. So, government constituted many committees to protect the life of poor and on the basis of these reports several programs were launched by the government to solve the problem of food of the poor people which are mentioned below. Now we can say without any hesitation that the programmes mention below came into force as an alternative way of TPDS. Though the TPDS is still in operation and government is trying to bring it back on right path as per its objectives but let us wait for the time when the corruption comes to an end in TPDS so that food for the chronic poor people could be ensured and they may also bring themselves in the mainstream of society. The followings are the alternative programmes for food security for the poor.

(a) Antyodaya Anna Yojana (AAY)

The AAY is mainly for the poorest of the poor, It was launched in December 2000, under it, 25 kg. of foodgrains was to be made available to each eligible family per month at a highly subsidized price of two rupees/kg for wheat and Rs. 3 kg. for rice. This quantitative allocation was raised to 35 kg in April 2002, it was then estimated that one crore families fell in this category. The AAY was later expanded to cover an additional 50 lakh BPL families. In 2004-05 the coverage was yet again increased from 1.5 to two crore families. According to GoI, against the foodgrain allocation of 4.55 million tonnes for AAY in 2003-04, actual lifting was 3.82 million tonnes.

(b) Sampoorna Gramin Rozgar Yojana (SGRY)

SGRY was started by GoI in 2001 after the then Prime Minister, in his Independence Day speech, announced the introduction of a Universal Food for Work Programme to be called SGRY under which five million tonnes of foodgrains valued at Rs. 5000 crore (at economic cost) are provided every year free of cost to States/UTs and another sum of Rs. 5,000 crore is utilized to meet the cash component of wages and material cost. The SGRY is expected to generate 100 crore mandays of employment a year. Under this programme five kg. of foodgrains are provided per man per day and the rest of the wage is paid in cash. The cash component is shared between the Centre and the States in the ratio of 75:25, FCI gets the payment for grains at economic cost. The cost of transportation from the FCI godown to the worksite/PDS location is borne by the concerned State governments. The programme is implemented through PRIs.

(c) Annapurna Scheme (AS)

This scheme covers indigent senior citizens of the age of 65 years and above who are eligible for old age pension but not actually covered by it on account of limited funding available under the National Old Age Pension Scheme (NOAPS). To such indigent old people ten kg. of foodgrains per person per month is supplied free of cost under the Annapurna Scheme, Implementation is again through the States though funding is central. The off-take of foodgrains under this scheme was 1.15 lakh tonnes in 2002-03 (including the backlog of 1-2) and 1.09 lakh tonnes in 2003-04. The allocation for 2004-05 was 1.58 lakh tonnes.

(d) Food-for-Work-Programme (FWP)

The Ministry of Rural Development, GoI, launched the FWI in the rural areas of drought affected States in January 2001, as a part of the employment Assurance Scheme. The Scheme, in its essence, provides for allocation of foodgrains (wheat and rice) free of cost to the affected states/UTs. The scheme was discontinued in March, 2002 but was later allowed to continue as a special Component of Sampoorna Gramin Rozgar Yojana (SGRY). From November 2004, the FWP was merged with the National Rural Employment Guarantee Programme (NREGP) in 150 districts taken up under NREG in the first phase. In the districts not covered by NREGP, SGRY would expectly continue off-take of foodgrains under FWP was 4.5 million tonnes in 2000-03 and 5.44 million tonnes in 2003-04. And several other programmes are inexistence to ensure food for the poor.

CONCLUSION

The present food security system of TPDS needs to be assessed in relation to the broader context of the changing poverty scenario in India and what is urgently required is a thorough going restructuring of the system rather than piece-meal improvement in it. Despite above fact, devoted volunteers should be organized by the government to check the corruption in TPDS so that poor can not be deprived of their right of food.

REFERENCES

Chand, Ramesh (2005), 'Wisher India's Food Policy', *Economic & Political Weekly,* 12.03.05.

Radhakrishna, R. (2005), Food and Nutrition Security of the Poor, *E & P Weekly,* 30.04.04.

Saxena, N.C. (2004), Food-based Programmes as Safety Nets in India. World Food Forum Workshop, New Delhi, Oct. 2004.

World Bank (2003), World Development Indication, 2003, World Bank, Washington, D.C.

SECTION II

Functioning of PDS in Bihar

A Reflection on PDS : Its Operation and Challenges

SUDAMA SINGH

PREFATORY PARAGRAPH

Food security, an unavoidable issue in food management, is based on human consideration. For a man facing insecurity of fooding, clothing and lodging even the cool and calm currents of the Ganges are full of flames:

अषनं वसनं वासः येशां चाविधानतः ।
मगधेन समा काषी गंगा चाप्यंगारवाहिनी ।।

Ashanam Vasanam Vasah Yesham Chhavidhantah,
Magadhen sama Kashi Ganga Chaapyangarvahini.

Hence, state the most powerful institution, is called for managing food supply with a sole objective of facilitating physical and economic access to food grains to those also who remain by-passed in the process of development and are still in the proverty-trap. They can not be left to the market. There emerges an actute need of state-trading in food grains and its supply chain management under a fix-price-model. Public distribution system is an old system of food supply management. The British Government resorted to it in India during the Second World War using quota system for many essential commodities. Greater concern has been shown for food management during the post-Independence period. At the very outset (i.e., during the First Five Year Plan) the Planning Commission laid down,

> ". . . the prices of food grains must be held at the levels within the reach of the poorer sections of the community".

However, an effective step in the direction of state action for implementing its food policy is marked by creation of FCI in 1965 which started operation with its initial buffer stock of 2 million tonnes of foodgrains in 1968-69 for supporting PDS through the country-wide net-work of fair price shops. Surinder Sud (2004) has rightly remarked,

> "India has managed to develop one of the world's most extensive government managed food grains distribution system. Government also claims, "PDS with a network of about 4.74 lakh fair price shops is perhaps the largest distribution net work of its type in the word". For more than six decades, PDS has been a key component of supply management in the nation, but specific concern for the vulnerable section is observable with its revamping by trageted PDS (TPDS) since June 1997, as TPDS contains dual price structure for rice and wheat, keeping lower prices for BPL familes. The state governments were to streamline the PDS by issuing special cards to BPL families and selling essential articles under TPDs to them at specially subsidised prices with better monitoring of the delivery system. Further, taking care of the poorest families, government fixed highly subsidised price for

AAY families i.e. families to be coverd by Antyodaya Annayojana launched in December 2000. Bihar Government has further amplified such categorisation of families, by introducing the category of 'Veshesh AAY' families.

DUAL PRICE SYSTEM UNDER TPDS AND LIFE SUPPORT TO POOR

Dual pricing practices act as helplines for supply management. To quote Prof. B. Ganguly (1974), "whenever there is an imbalance between demand and supply, Government takes recourse to the simple method of dual pricing to ensure minimum supply of essential goods to needy consumers". Dual price system saves the poor ones from the pangs of inflation. Now, since the introduction of TPDS and AAY, administered prices of wheat and rice reflect dual price structure, its system being as follows:

(i) Unsubsidised price for APL families, and
(ii) Subsidised price for BPL and AAY families.

Table 1 shows wheat and rice prices charageable for above types of families.

Before restructuring of PDS, in 1997, PDS issue price was Rs. 402 per quintal for wheat and Rs. 537 per quintal for rice. Now, subsidised price for BPL families and still more concessional one for AAY families are in vogue. The upto-date national norm is 35 kg. food grains to each BPL and AAY families at subsidised rates. Table 1 shows cost-based high price structure for APL families. Undoubtelly considerable expenditure is incurred on food-subsidy. Food-subsidy has shown an annual increase of above 30 per cent during 2000-01, 2001-02 and 2002-03. However, it has become stable since 2003-04. Whatever be the subsidy burden, life support through TPDS and AAY is a commendable step. Dual price system has the merit of providing relief to economically feeble ones.

TABLE I
Issue Price of Wheat and Rice under TPDS

Marketing Season	*Central Issue Price*					
	Wheat			*Rice*		
	APL	*BPL*	*AAY*	*APL*	*BPL*	*AAY*
1997-78	450	250	–	700	350	–
1998-99	650	250	–	905	350	–
1999-2000	682	250	–	905	350	–
2002-03	610	415	200	795	565	300
2003-04	610	415	200	795	565	300
2004-05	610	415	200	795	565	300
2005-06	610	415	200	795	565	300
2006-07	610	415	200	795	565	300
2007-08	610	415	200	795	565	300

Source : Economic Survey, 2003-04, p. 95, and Economic Survey, 2007-08, p. 179.

OPERATION OF PDS/TPDS IN BIHAR

Bihar is one of the states having high incidence of poverty. PDS has much justification for it. Allotment of food grains is made by the Central Government on a previous reporting of 65.23 lakh BPL families in Bihar. But according to Revised Family Survey of Bihar Government, 2007, only in rural areas, number of BPL families stands at, 1,13,40,990. To it may further be added about 8,00,000 urban BPL families. So, actual strength of BPL families stands at 1,21,40,990. The Central Government has not accpted this revised actual number of BPL families. Hence, on the basis of 65.23 lakh BPL families, it allots to Bihar only 2.28 lakh tonnes of wheat and rice per month. Due to such lagged allotment state government is constrained to follow the norm of providing 35 kg food grains to each BPL family which has become national norm from the 1st April 2002. Bihar Government considering much more actual strength of BPL families has reduced this quantum of food supply to 25 kg per family. And such reduced supply too leads to an additional foodgrain requirement of 75209 metric tonnes per month which the state government decided to purchase itself and make available to BPL families.

So far as *modus operandi* of PDS/TPDS in Bihar is concerned, vital points releate to determination of family status, involvement of PRIs and delivery mechanism, etc.

DETERMINATION OF FAMILY STATUS

Beneficiaries of PDS are ascertained on the basis of family status. In Bihar to decide BPL family status, major parameters used are average monthly income of the family, its operational land size and type of that land, average available clothing, drinking water facility, food security, sanitation, labour force, literacy status, livelihood, children status and indebtedness, etc. Families below poverty line are placed into 0-13 grades. At the national level to identify the poorest of the poor families, AAY family category has been introduced. State Government in Bihar has gone one step ahead by introducing the category of 'Vishesh Antyodaya family'. So, Bihar Government has made three categories of BPL families, viz.

(i) Vishesh Antyodaya families,
(ii) AAY families, and
(iii) BPL families.

Families above the poverty line are categorised as APL families. Out of total, 1,21,40,990 BPL families 9,71,437 have been identified as Vishesh Antyodaya families. Vishesh Antyodaya family category has been made with a clear objective that the most deprived families, virtually the destitutes must be the beneficiary of TPDs, and to manage food grain distribution through PDS effectively, the Panchayati Raj Institutions (PRIs) have been involved at the grassroot level.

PARTICIPATION OF PRIS

PRIs as grassroot institutions can play significant role in

administration of such programmes as relating to poverty alleviation, nutrition, disaster and ecological management and public distribution system, etc. As the last panchayat elections have been held with reservation for the weaker section, these institutions are expected to safeguard the interest of vulnerable section with greater concern. Now, the Bihar Government has resolved for creation of 'Panchayat Stariya Nigarani Samiti' in each Panchayat. The Samiti looks after proper distribution of food grains under TPDS and keeps vigil and control over the ultimate points of supply chain.

This samiti is a cent per cent Panchayati Raj Institution, having no berth for official member on it. The Panchayat Stariya Nigarani Samiti is organised as follows:

PANCHAYAT STARIYA NIGARANI SAMITI

1.	Mukhiya of Panchayat	Co-ordinator
2.	Sarpanch of Panchayat	Member
3.	Candidate for Mukhiya defeated by the nearest votes	Member
4.	Candidate for Sarpanch defeated by the nearest votes	Member
5.	Ward Sadasya from coverage area of PDS shops	Member
6.	One representative of each recognised political party, nominated by block/district president/secretary of the party	Member

Thus the panchayat level 'Nigarani Samiti' is formed with all non-official members which may be taken as a step towards facilitating 'power to the people'.

Now following provisions have been made about rights and duties of Nigarani Samiti:

(i) The Samiti will keep supervision over the PDS shops in respect of lifting and distribution of food grains and Kerosene oil among the consumers.

(ii) The Samiti will have to make foodgrains and Kirosene oil available to all consumers as per fixed quota and rate.

(iii) The dealers of PDS shops will have to submit timely the necessary informations related to lifting and distribution to the co-ordinator of Samiti.

(iv) The co-ordinator will have to call at least one meeting of Nigarani Samiti in a month to review allotment, lifting and distribution of foodgrains and Kerosene oil.

(v) The Food and Consumer Protection Department will be responsible to make available any future guideline for supervision work under PDS.

Thus, the Panchayat Stariya Nigarani Samiti has been empowered with sufficient rights to have supervision over the functioning of TPDS. However, overall responsibility of operation of TPDS has been fixed on sub-divisional officer, and as such, he will be personally responsible for its defects and misuse. Under the chairmanship of the sub-divisional officer (SDO), Anusravan Samiti is organised in each sub-division. It has got mixed type, having both official and non-official members and representation of different interests on it. It supervises operation of schemes under TPDS. Further, it reviews lifting of foodgrains by SFC (State Food Corporation) and their distribution by fair price shops among the beneficiaries. It is empowered to look into the operational problems and take decision under the policy formulated by the Government. Anusravan Samiti is linked with PRIs. In the interest of Panchayati Raj all pramukhs of the blocs of concerned sub-division as well as Zila Parishad Sadasya are made its members. Of course this is a very big committee. But it does not miss the grassroot touch. To safeguard the interest of the weaker section, it has been provided that out of 10 State Government nominated members, there must be one member each from minority, SC/ST, backward and woman class. Besides these, other members are Additional District Supply Officer (ADSO), Chairman of Municipal Corporation, or Municipality, representative of all recognised parties, one representative of each local MLA and M.P. and representatives of oil companies. Thus, these two-tier organisations are supervisory which look after food security activities as well as rational distribution of Kerosene oil in the state. Food grain supply is made through coupon system w.e.f. June 2008. For distribution of coupons, the Block Development Officer (BDO) organises camps in the rural areas, wherein the head of the Panchayat (Mukhia) identifies the beneficiaries.

DELIVERY MECHANISM

If one unveils delivery mechanism, a three-tier organisational structure under which PDS operates becomes self-exposed-Food Corporation of India at the apex level, State Food Corporation at the middle level and fair price shops (which, at present, number about 46,000 in Bihar) at the bottom level.

The main agency for supply of foodgrains to PDS in Bihar or in any state is Food Cororation of India. Its primary duty is to undertake the purchase, storage, movement, transport, and distribution and sale of foodgrains and other food stuffs. For similar activities, State Food Corporation in Bihar, stands at the middle level and commission for its services is Rs. 50 per quintal of food supply made to the dealers. At the bottom line are dealers of fair-price shops. Their commission is related to the quantom of actual food delivery to consumers.

Now, the dealer of the PDS shop has to submit the required amount of money as per allotment of quantity through demand draft to the block supply officer by 25th of a month for lifting allotment for the next month. After receipt of amount, the D.M. (District Manager) State Food Corporation is required to give issue order within three days. DM makes store issue order in triplicate, one copy (Yellow) is handed over to the Block Supply officer and two copies to AGM, Godown. The Block Supply Officer makes issue order available to the licencees, and then the AGM godown on production of yellow copy and its comparison with other two copies of the order, issues food grains to the dealers. Then the dealers of PDS shops distribute foodgrains among the consumers at government fixed prices on the basis of coupon system.

THE COUPON SYSTEM

Supply is made under PDS on production of coupon. Coupons are colour–specific as mentioned under Table 2. For food grains, one coupon for wheat and one for rice for each months i.e. 24 coupons in all are supplied to the consumers. Coupon for Kerosene oil is given to APL families also. Validity of coupon for wheat and rice extends upto the last date of the coming month, but in case of Kerosene oil upto the last day of the current month Table 2 shows the types of coupons for different kinds of rural families in Bihar.

On the basis of coupon, as per decision of the Government of Bihar, 25 kg foodgrains (14 kg of wheat and 11 kg of rice) are provided to a BPL beneficiary. Benefit of Annapurna Yojana is made available to severely poor and destitutes on the basis of white coupons. Kerosene oil is supplied under PDS to all types of families on the basis of blue coupon. Undoubtedly PDS operates under well built rule-fabrics, still it can not be claimed that 'zero leakage' operation of the system has been assured. PDS faces many challenges and operational constraints.

CHALLANGES TO PDS/TPDS IN BIHAR

Though both the state administrative wing and PRIs are invovled in operation of the TPDS; still there are many weak spots and challenges. Some of these are focussed below:

1. *Requirement Allotment Gap*: The Central Government makes allotment of subsidised foodgrains at a rate of 2.28 lakh tonnes per month. It is fixed on an old estimate of 65.23 lakh BPL families. But, actual number of BPL families, according to State Government estimates, is about, 1,21,40,990 (including 8,00,000 urban BPL families). Hence, 65.23 lakh BPL families criterion excludes 56,17,990 BPL families from the food-security umbrella. State Government has reduced quantity of food supply to BPL families to 25 kg per month, and to fulfil this norm also the Government of Bihar has to purchase

75,209 tonnes food grains per month. Poor states like Bihar, Orissa and Madhya Pradesh have to face a severe fiscal crunch. In case of Bihar much strain has been created on public exchequer due to 'Kosi-havoc' of recent past. If the Central Government does not accept uptodate number of BPL families in Bihar and fails to revise upward its allotment, in critic's eyes it will be an act of negligence to Bihar and that of failing interest in genuine operation of PDS in this state.

2. *Weak Delivery System*: Ineffective working of PDS/ TPDS owes much to week delivery system. R. Radhakrishna (2002) has observed that even the TPDs has not made a significant impact on the access of food since the delivery systems in the poorer states are weak. Here, one may cite the problem of delay in giving issue order by the DMs of State Food Corporation, which causes non-deposit of DD in time *vis-a-vis* non-release of food grains to the PDS shop keepers. SFC stands as a broker, but dilatory nature of its servcies constrains successful working of the PDS system.
3. *Poor off-take*: One major challenge relates to poor off-take of food grains. APL family food grains are not subsidised, they respond to economic costs and happen to be quite higher than foodgrain prices for BPL and AAY families (*Supra* Table 1). In the past, some times APL prices have exceeded the market prices. In Bihar, complain has been made, from time to time, about substandard grains, such as impurity of grains, insect infected supply and broken grains. PDS shops therefore are not attractive for APL families except Kerosene oil.

Off-takes by BPL, AAY and Vishesh AAY families also happen to be lower from time to time as against allotment for them due to lack of ready cash with them. They are not informed in advance about the actual date of distribution. Jos Mooiji (2001) in her Bihar and Jharkhand-based study has rightly remarked,

"In short, there is a physical access problem in the sense that the commodities may come with irregular intervals or not at all. There is also a problem of economic access in the sense that the poorest people do not have cash ready at the moment stocks arrive".

4. *Problem of leakages*: PDS suffers from the problem of leakages and taking away of benefit by poor-in-disguise. Jos Mooiji in her field work has revealed that many poor families never received BPL ration card. The erstwhile gram panchayats and gram sabhas were highly responsible for such happenings. However, due to formation and working of Gram Stariya Nigarani Samiti and Anusravan Samiti, more transparency in operation of PDS is expected.

Besides, the problem of leakages from PDS arises due to losses in transport and storage and diversion of grains and Kerosene oil to the open markets. Often the dealers resort to such strategy for extra earnings. The issue of bogus sale, e.g. sale to fake consumer as cited by S. Mahendra Dev in case of a village in Dhanu Taluka of Maharashtra is not a state-specific problem, it is much applicable to Bihar also. There is therefore, every need of checking leakages from PDS to safeguard the interest of the vulnerable section of society in this state.

Public Distribution System in Bihar

ANJU JAIN

INTRODUCTION

A well organized and efficient system of Public distribution of essential commodities is a most for Vast developing country like ours, so that the benefits of the new economic programmes filter down to the weaker section of the society. The PDS covers a large area of activity encompassing production, procurement, supply and distribution. The PDS which initially used to be a feature of war economy has gradually become an integral part of our economy. Controlled distribution and price control has been a pre-independence phenomenon. In India both public and private sector of the economy functions in harmony to serve the common people. PDS is an aspect of demand and supply management, its main aim is to meet the basic needs of vulnerable section of the community at reasonable prices who cannot afford to depend on open market as well as to control the prices of those articles of general consumption whose supply is in shortage.

MEANING OF PDS

PDS means distribution of essential commodities to a large number of people through a network of FPS on a recurring basis. The commodities are as follows:

- Wheat
- Rice
- Sugar
- Kerosene

PDS evolved as a major instrument of the Government's economic policy for ensuring availability of foodgrains to the poor at affordable prices and also for enhancing food security for the poorest of the poor.

PDS is operated under the joint responsibility of the Central and the State Governments. The Central Government has taken the responsibility for procurement, storage, transportation and bulk allocation of foodgrains, etc. The responsibility for procurement, storage, transportation and bulk allocation of foodgrains, etc. The responsibility for distributing the same to the consumers through the network of Fair Price Shops (FPSs) rests with the State Governments. The operational responsibilities including allocation within the State, identification of families below poverty line, issue of ration cards, supervision and monitoring the functioning of FPSs rest with the State Government.

Ration Card : A Ration Card is a document issued under an order or authority of the State Government, as per the Public Distribution System, for the purchase of essential commodities from Fair Price Shops. State Governments issue distinctive Ration Cards to Above Poverty Line, Below Poverty Line and Antyodaya families and conduct periodical review and checking of Ration Cards.

THE FRAMEWORK OF PDS

The PDS in India may be looked at from three angles, the Policy Framework, the Legal Framework and the Operational Framework. These three are inter-linked and interdependent with a common objective to ensure the distribution of essential commodities to the common man at reasonable price.

THE POLICY FRAMEWORK

It consists of the broad policy guidelines and direction given by the central and the State governments regarding the PDS. The PDS has been an integrated part of the government's policy ever since the inception of planning in India. It was after the formation of the new Department of Civil Supplies and Corporation in October, 1974 that an integrated policy was adopted covering.

1. Distribution of food and other essential commodities of mass consumption at very reasonable prices to the weaker sections of the community.
2. A system of encouraging and monitoring production of essential consumer goods and their rational distribution with a minimum of formal controls on prices are distribution.
3. Building up of a viable consumer co-operative movement as an indispensable and important element in the consumer-oriented distribution system to provide a regular source of supply at strategic points at reasonable price.

The policy, currently being followed consists of a two-fold approach—"Commodity approach" and "Area Approach". The Commodity approach is based on the economic reality that a demand and supply equilibrium is an essential part to regulate prices. It envisages commodities like foodgrains, pulses, sugar, standard cloth, edible oils and cheap fuel like kerosene and soft coke which are also among the most important essential commodities. A more intensive planning for adequate production supplemented by marginal imports where necessary to match the increasing demand should be attempted to facilities equitable distribution at fair prices. In other words for commodities of basic needs, there should be an annual 'Commodities budget' in the widest sense of terms, including planning of production, availability of inputs to the producing units, as also infrastructural inputs like power, transport and finance. A close watch is kept on production and price trends of certain other items like cement, paper, essential drugs, soap, matches, etc. and these are also made available on a preferential basis to the more vulnerable sections of the society. An effort is also being made to introduce a uniform and country-wide pricing pattern for various consumer products.

The "Area approach" implies that as the streamlining of the PDS for a vast country like ours would require considerable time and effort, a systematic beginning should be made by focusing attention on more vulnerable areas. Areas requiring such attention are metropolitan and large urban areas, labour concentration areas such as industrial and plantation belts, district headquarters, hilly areas and rural areas of districts which are chronically scarcity affected or deficit. In these areas the distribution system should be given constant attention and be strengthened so that more vulnerable and poorer sections of the population are able to receive supplies of essential commodities at a reasonable price.

THE LEGAL FRAMEWORK

The Essential Commodities Act (ECA), 1955 was enacted to provide a legal support in the interest of the general public for the control of the production, supply and distribution of the trade and commerce in certain commodities. The Act is regulatory in its objective. As enunciated under section 3.1, of the ECA, it confers on the Central and State Governments the power to control the production supply and distribution of essential commodities.

The Government has taken various other measures to improve functioning of the TPDS. A Revised Citizens' Charter has been issued and is being implemented since July, 2007. Monthly certification of delivery of allocated foodgrains to FPS and their distribution to ration card holders has been introduced from April, 2008. Training programmes for TPDS functionaries and awareness campaign for TPDS beneficiaries are being taken up. Computerization of TPDS operations has been initiated. Use of new technologies such as Global Positioning System to monitor movement of foodgrains under TPDS has been undertaken on a pilot basis. Policy guidelines have also been issued on distribution of wheat flour under the TPDS, so that the poor families are benefited. For increasing awareness on TPDS, publicity-*cum*-awareness campaign is also being taken up. The Government has given instructions to all State/UT Governments to take action as per law against persons found in possession of bogus or fake ration cards and the Government staff found responsible for issuing ration cards to ineligible persons.

THE OPERATIONAL FRAMEWORK

The organizational involvements in the operational aspects of the PDS presents an ideal instance of management of interlinkage amongst a number of organizations in the private, public and co-operative sectors, under the overall direction and control of the Ministry of Civil supplies at the control and State levels. There-ordination between the Centre and the States is also an added features of this complex mechanism.

Government has been continuously taking steps to strengthen the TPDS by improving its efficiency. Government got evaluated the TPDS by PEO (Planning Commission) and ORG MARG. Certain shortcomings were pointed out in their evaluation reports received in 2005. In view of these reports, to strengthen the TPDS and to curb leakages and diversion of foodgrains meant for TPDS, in consultation with State and UT Governments, the Government evolved a 9-point Action Plan in 2006. This includes measures such as review of BPL and AAY lists for exclusion of ineligible families and inclusion of eligible families, ensuring leakage free distribution by taking penal action against those found indulging in malpractices, involvement of Panchayati Raj Institutions in functioning of FPS, display of BPL and AAY lists at fair price shops, door step delivery of PDS commodities to fair price shops, etc. The Action Plan in under implementation in States and UTs since July 2006 and is being closely monitored by FPS level Vigilance Committees. As a result of this exercise, so far 14 States/UTs have reported deletion of 99.36 lakh bogus/ineligible cards since July, 2006.

PUBLIC DISTRIBUTION SYSTEM IN BIHAR

While Bihar and Jharkhand are among the Poorest and most backward states in India. These states have handily benefited from the PDS system. It is estimated that 5 per cent of Bihar Population lives below the poverty line, while the all India figures in 36 per cent Economic growth rates are much lower than elsewhere in India.

The growth rate in 1990s in undivided Bihar and Jharkhand in November 2000 was 10.12 per cent, as compounded to 6 per cent for the whole of India. The world Food Programme classified the individed state of Bihar as the only State in India suffering from extreme food insecurity.

Currently Bihar distributes 4 types of Ration Cards:

1. Red Card (For Below Poverty Line Family).
2. Yellow Card (For Antyodaya Anna Yojna).
3. White Card (For Annapurna Yojna).
4. Green Card (For Above Poverty Line Family).

The colour coding is because of the introduction of the Targeted Public Distribution System (TPDS) in 1997. The Green cards are meant for families that are above the poverty line, the white ones for those below the poverty line. The red ones for severely impoverished families eligible for the Antyodya Anna Yojna ones for special category families such as families headed by widows or physically disabled. Each card comes with a fixed allow once available for a fixed price. The idea of the TPDS is to direct food subsides to people who really need it, however, its introduction has spelt disaster for villages. This coupon system from January 26 which will provide basic necessities such as foodgrains and Kerosene to all the people.

LEAKAGE IN THE PDS

The most basic problem with the TPDS in that of exclusion. The segregation of the poor into multi-coloured card-holders has put a premium on the yard stick used to measure poverty. Economists believe that the poverty line adopted by the government in an insufficient measure as it represents a bare nutritional minimum divorced from the realities on the ground. Thus, many genuinely poor families in urgent need of ration find themselves categorized as APL.

Another reason for this exclusion is the method of identification with its emphasis on identification of poorest of the poor, the TPDS concentrates all power in the hands of the local Pradhan and Kotwal (ration shop owner) of the area. The Pradhan who is usually a dominant caste member, is charged with identifying the families in the area and categorizing them as eligible for red, yellow, white and green cards. He is also the *de-facto* issuing authority and has complete control over card allotments, given the state government usually issue a fixed number of BPL and Antyodaya Anna Yojana cards for a particular period, most of these cards invariably end up in the hands of the wealthiest and most powerful families in the region, while economically and socially weak sections of society are saddled with APL Cards. This incorrect identification of the desperately poor by APL cardholders, APL families simply can not afford to buy food at APL prices.

While the identification process itself means that many genuinely needy families are unable to afford food, the distribution process ensures that even those who are eligible for ration are unable to buy them.

The full quota of ration costs BPL Cardholders Rs. 205, given that the average family earns between Rs. 300 and Rs. 500 a month, most can not afford to purchase their full quota in a single instalment. They are then forced to buy wheat that cost Rs. 5.65 a kg in the ration shop for Rs. 10 a kg. in the open market and Kerosene that cost Rs. 11 a liter in the ration shop for Rs. 50 a litre in the open market. These restrict restrictions on shop timings and purchase in instalments have meant that families in the region operate on brutally tight budgets. It is not uncommon for families to sleep hungry during the last week of a month, or to ignore an illness until the monthly ration anota have been purchased.

Bihar had recorded a high of around 81.5 per cent in diversions and leakages. Alarmed by the State inability to shore up food security, policy have been contemplating a number of measures.

DUTIES AND RESPONSIBILITIES OF FAIR PRICE SHOP DEALER

The fair price shop owner shall :

1. Sale of essential commodities as per the entitlement of ration card holders at the retail issue price fixed by the food supply and commence department, Bihar, under the PDS.
2. Display of information on a notice at a prominent place in the shop an daily basis.
3. Maintenance of records of ration card holders (APL, BPL, Antyodya and Annapurna) stock register, issue or sale register.
4. Furnishing of copies of specified documents, namely, ration card register, stock register, sale register to the inspecting Authority, Block Supply Officer or as directed by Licensing Authority.
5. Display of samples of foodgrains being supplies through the fair price shop.
6. Production of books and records relating to the allotment and distribution of essential commodities to the inspecting authority and furnishing of such information as may be called by the inspecting of Licensing Authority
7. Accounting the actual distribution of essential commodities and the balance stock at the end of the month.
8. Opening and Closing of the fair price shop as per the prescribed timing display on the notice board.

PUBLIC DISTRIBUTION SYSTEM—A NEW APPROACH IN BIHAR

Bihar will be the first state in the country to modernize its Public Distribution System (PDS) by introducing vouchers to claim benefits. The process of shifting from the existing arrangements of purchasing from ration shops to the voucher system has already began. Under the new voucher system, all targeted households will be supplied with a fixed quota of vouchers which can then be redeemed at any PDS shops of choice. The vouchers collected by these shops can then be encashed by ration shops from the government. This will strengthen the delivery mechanism under PDS.

The number of vouchers collected by a ration shop would act as a performance indicator indicating public preference for "better shops" which would also help accountability. This, in turn would ensure that a large share of civil supplies would then be provided to these outlets. Ration shops have been notoriously famous for malpractices where supplies like wheat, rice, sugar and kerosene oil, meant for the poor is usually diverted to the black market and poor families end up losing substantial part of government subsidies.

CONCLUSION

The solution to leakages in the PDS is a completely new system that gets rid of the old fair price shop, the FCI, the huge infrastructure of transporting and thereby the criminal nexus that has built up around it. Measures to check corruption and malpractices are needed from the government and consumer both. For its success it is necessary that it is implemented in the true spirit of its aims and objectives. Increase in the margin of the profit for the shopkeepers on one hand and control of black marketing, adulteration, under-weighing, quality control of commodities on the other hand can to some extent induce consumer interest in the PDS. Punishing the corrupt officials and consumer awareness will go a long way in making the system successful and popular.

References

Editorial, Bargaining Public Distribution System, *Economic and Political Weekly*, Oct., 1977, p. 1683.

Mishra, For an Effective, Public Distribution System Link, 17 April, 1982, p. 25.

Prasad, J., PDS, A Case Study of Working in Bihar, *Economic Times*, 13 September, 1982, p. 49.

Sundaram, S., The New Public Distribution System, Pedical Humorist, 44 (6), September 29, p. 18.

The Times of India, 22 April, 2003, Probe into Red Card Scam in Selected Districts.

Food and Power in Bihar and Jharkhand PDS and Its Functioning, *Economic and Political Weekly*, 36, No. 34 (Aug. 25-31-2001), pp. 3289 + 3297-99.

18

Significance of Public Distribution System in Context of Food Security in Bihar

RAMANUJ SHARMA

The economy of Bihar is predominantly rural and extremely dependent on agriculture, which generates over 35 per cent of its Gross Domestic Product and engages over 73 per cent of total workers. But in terms of area, production and yield of foodgrains and its major components, Bihar is quite behind in comparison to the agriculturally advanced regions of India. The PDS (Public Distribution System) coverage to people living below poverty line is still inadequate. Hence, it becomes imperative to examine the significance of PDS in context of food security in Bihar.

FOOD SECURITY

Food security involves physical availability of food to the

entire population. Food security and food sovereignty is an essential condition for life with dignity (Ahmad, 2004). World Development Report (1986) defined food security as "access by all people at all times to enough food for an active healthy life". The concept of food security necessities that timely, reliable and nutritionally adequate supply of food should be available on a long-term basis.

Bihar witnessed green revolution and done well. Annual production of foodgrains in the state increased from 53 lakh tonnes in 1962-63 to 119 lakh tonnes in 2000-01. But the overall growth rate of foodgrains production did not keep pace with population growth rate. During 1991-2001, the population growth rate was 2.8 per cent per annum which was very high than production growth rate (1.9 per cent only).

TABLE I

Production of Foodgrains in Bihar

Period	*Production in Lakh Tonnes*	*Production per person in Kg.*
1962-65	53.00	144
1973-76	65.31	142
1988-91	100.21	159
1993-95	109.46	159
1997-99	113.46	150
2000-02	119.55	144

Source : Directorate of statistics, Bihar, Patna (both published and unpublished data of Agricultural statistics at a glance 2003.

The per capita annual requirement of foodgrains based on actual consumption as per 50th round of National Sample Survey in the state comes to 208 kg. But the growth of food production slowed down to 144 kg. per person in 2000-02 from 150 kg per person in 1997-99. This means that the state of Bihar is just in the position to meet hardly 70 per cent of its requirements of its foodgrains from its own production. In other words, there is no food security in Bihar.

RAISON D'ETRE OF FOOD INSECURITY IN BIHAR

Bihar has fertile land, abundant manpower and water resources. But these resources are underutilized and this is the only reason that Bihar has not achieved food security.

Significant correlation has been found between percentage of coverage under irrigation and yield per hectare. The ultimate irrigation potential in Bihar has been assessed at around 127 lakh hectare which far exceeds its total sown area of around 80 lakh hectarcs. The growth of irrigation facilities has been sluggish in the state of Bihar. The created irrigation potential has grown at the rate of only 4.11 per cent per annum (overall) and the state has been able to develop only 51 per cent of its ultimate irrigation potential as compared to 55 per cent for all India. On account of various reasons, the coverage under irrigation in the State does not exceed 43 per cent of the total sown area as compared to 95 per cent in Punjab, 78 per cent in Haryana and 53 per cent in U.P. Due to poor irrigation facility, the cropping intensity comes to 145 per cent in Bihar which is far below the level in Punjab, i.e. 190. Like-wise, in 2001-02, the per hectare productivity of foodgrains in Bihar was only 1679 as compared to 4040 in Punjab. Agriculture production can be increased only through more yield per unit of the cropped area and higher cropping intensity and both are highly dependent on irrigation and as we have seen, Bihar lacs such irrigation facility. The state is favourable endowed with water resources, both surface as well as the ground source. But due to low development and poor management of the water resources about half of agriculture in Bihar is still rainfed which is the main cause of low productivity and food insecurity situation.

PUBLIC DISTRIBUTION SYSTEM AND FOOD SECURITY

In India, food-based safety nets were instated which are :

1. Public Distribution System
2. Antyodaya Anna Yojana
3. Annapurna Scheme

4. Integrated Child Development Scheme
5. Mid-day Meal Scheme
6. Food for Work Programme.

These programmes supply either rice or wheat to alleviate hunger but micro-nutrient problems are not covered by the above schemes.

Public Distribution System (PDS) was introduced to act as a price support programme for the consumer during the periods of food shortage of the 1960s. Later on the coverage of the PDS was extended to rural areas in some states and subsequently it acquired the status of a welfare programme. Food security implies having physical and economic access to food articles that are adequate in terms of quantity, quality and affordability. This raises the question of prices of food articles and the purchasing power in the hands of the population. To help the poor sections, the Government introduced the PDS and adopted dual price mechanism. At the PDS outlet, the issue price of food articles was kept lower than the market price to enable the poor to purchase subsidized food.

The significance of PDS can be reviewed in terms of its efficacy and coverage, PDS supplies and off-take, income transfer to the poor via PDS, impact on poverty and achievement towards food security. The PDS purchases were not able to help the poor. The study of Radhakrishnan *et. al.* (1997) revealed that "Even now the efficacy of PDS in distributing food to the poor seems to be as bad as in 1986-87 and that some of the disquieting features persist the virtual exclusion of backward states such as Bihar and U.P. from the PDS network Obviously there is mistargetting in the distribution of PDS foodgrains. Besides, the coverage was low in Bihar. There is low PDS cereal purchase due to higher poverty levels. In Bihar, 42.6 per cent of total population comes under the category of BPL. In fact, PDS has remained an expensive and largely untargetted programme and has failed to distinguish between the very poor and moderately poor. The very poors suffer not only from chronic food insecurity but are also severely exposed to the risk of uncertainty both in the labour market.

Upward revision of issue price of items under PDS has adversely affected off-take levels since the gap between subsidized issue price and open market price has been narrowed down According to World Bank report, "In poorer states like Bihar and others, the off-take was substantially lower than central allocation partly due to the narrow difference between the central issue price and open market price and partly because of weak fiscal capacity of these states to finance any additional subsidy via lowering the issue price... Ironically the incidence of poverty is high precisely in the states with the lowest off-take of FCI grains."

The basic purpose of the PDS is to transfer income to the poor via ration shops, fair price shops, and control price shops by supplying essential commodities at subsidized prices. But the PDS has failed in serving this very purpose in Bihar. Radhakrishna *et. al.* study supports this fact. The data compiled from this study (Table 2) reveals that income transfer in poor states like Bihar, Orissa, Rajasthan and UP was very small. This is indicative of the regressive nature of the PDS subsidies.

TABLE 2

Income Transfer to Poor, Non-poor and All Classes (1986-87) Due to PDS

States	*Rs. per capita per month*		
	Poor	*Non-Poor*	*All*
All India	3.4	3.8	3.6
Kerala	9.4	8.9	9.1
Bihar	0.7	1.1	0.9
Rajasthan	0.8	0.8	0.8

Source : Compiled from R. Radhakrishna *et. al.*: Public Distribution : A National and International Perspective, p. 42.

In terms of the impact of PDS on poverty, the situation is not encouraging. Bihar does not witness any significant impact as it has still largest percentage of BPL families (42.6 per cent).

Poor impact of the PDS is seen in poor states like Bihar. The Table 3 portrays the real image of Bihar in this perspective with minimum decline in poverty percentages due to PDS. This impact is transient and is not of an enduring nature.

TABLE 3

Decline in Poverty Percentage Due to PDS (1986-87)

States	*Percentage decline in poverty*	
	Rural	*Urban*
All India	1.66	1.71
Kerala	5.49	3.62
Bihar	0.30	0.37
U.P.	0.22	0.88

Source : Radhakrishna, R. *et. al., op. cit,* pp. 44-45.

In nut shell, the PDS has failed in providing food security to the poors in Bihar. The non-poor are taking advantage and benefit from the PDS. The distribution mechanism is entirely faulty. The administrative and management aspects have not clearly been spelt out and formulated in PDS. This is the reality that the FCI buys superior foodgrains and supply them for PDS. But quite a good proportion of these supplies find their way into the open market and PDS outlets supply very inferior grains to ration card holders. The poor consumers have to accept whatever its quality is. The need of the hour is to rectify this mismanagement and corruption so that the intended benefits reach the poor and the PDS can serve the purpose of food security by alleviating poverty.

REFERENCES

Ahmad, S., Yazdani, G. (2004), "Human Rights, Agricultural Deregulation and Food Security", Edited by Bhatt, M.S. in *Poverty and Food Security in India : Problems and Policies,* Aakar Books, Delhi, p. 175.

Directorate of Statistics, Govt. of Bihar, Patna (both published and unpublished), 2003.

Mahendra, Dev S. (1996), "Food Security: PDS *vs.* EGS", *Economic and Political Weekly,* July 6, 1996.

Planning Commission, Ninth Five Year Plan (1997-2002), Vol. II, pp. 529 and 531.

Radhakrishna, R., Subbarao, K., Indrakant, S. and Ravi, K. (1997), "Public Distribution : A National and International Perpective", World Bank Discussion, No. 380, pp. 42-45.

World Bank, World Development Report, 1986.

19

Review of Public Distribution System in India with Special Reference to Bihar

Anjana Kumari and Anju Sinha

Public Distribution System (PDS) mechanism was initiated in India during the period of food shortage of the 1960s. The basic objective of PDS is to maintain a stable price condition of consumer's level, that is to meet at least a part of the consumer's demand at fixed reasonable prices. The seventh plan remarked that "The public distribution is recognised as a permanent feature of the strategy to control prices, reduce fluctuations and achieve equitable distribution of essential goods. Since then the coverage of the PDS was extended to rural areas in some states. It acquired the status of a welfare programme. An effort was made to extend subsidised food grains in 1985 in all the tribal blocks covering about 5.7 crore persons. Ninth Five Year Plan envisaged the strategy to meet the basic food requirements for all. It involved distribution of foodgrains throughout the PDS at subsidised prices to those living below the poverty line. This strategy is continued in Tenth Plan as well as in Eleventh Plan. The PDS in India is perhaps the largest distribution network of its kind in the world covering approximately 17-18 crore families.

The Public distribution is recognised as a permanent feature of the strategy to :

- Control prices
- Reduce fluctuations.

Achieve equitable distribution of essential goods: Under this system, a certain proportion of the output of commodities involved is procured by public agencies or agencies designated by the Government at reasonable prices for distribution through approved channels. This would ensure availability of certain quantities of selected commodities to the consumers, specifically, the vulnerable sections, at reasonable prices and at the same time allow the producers to realise on the whole a fair price for their produce.

SELECTION OF COMMODITIES

In PDS, selective approach for the commodities is adapted. The selective approach is based on the needs of the common man. Applying this criteria, cereals, sugar, edible oil, kerosene, controlled cloth, tea, coffee, soap, etc. is treated as essential items for public distribution. The PDS covers entire country. It is worth mentioning here that the different regions may have different preferences according to their needs. But, having regard to the standard of living of the vast majority of people, it is obvious that the overwhelming majority of commodities needing the care of PDS will be fairly common for the entire country. Besides selective commodities, the Central Government have also been assisting the state government by arrangements with manufacturers of certain commodities of mass consumption at wholesale prices to the state government for distribution through the PDS. The state government can make use of PDS facility fully so that consumers can have access to those commodities at reasonable prices.

INFRASTRUCTURE

At the national as well as state levels, arrangements for procuring essential commodities and supply them through public distribution outlets exists. The necessary operations are undertaken by the Food Corporation of India and/or civil supplies cooperation or cooperatives in most of the states. In states, distribution of essential commodities received from central agencies is being handled by the State Civil Supplies Essential Commodities Corporations, State Level Cooperative federations and other designated agencies.

PROGRESS

In 2003-04, with a network of more than 4.62 lakh Fair Price Shops (FPS) distributing commodities worth Rs. 30,000 crores annually to about 16 crore families, the PDS in India is perhaps the largest distribution network of its kind in the world. It is worth mentioning here that there has been a continuous increase in PDS expenditure due to popular pressure to continue the programme as a welfare measure along with a price stabilisation instrument. As a proportion of Central Government expenditure, it was in the range of 2.9 to 3.1 per cent during 1974-75 to 1985-86. Thereafter, it declined to a low level of 2.22 per cent during the first phase of economic reforms. Since 1997-98 PDS expenditure has increased substantially. As a proportion of total Central Government expenditure, it has increased from 3.23 per cent in 1997-98 to 5.17 per cent in 2002-03. Different items are sold through PDS outlets, but four items—rice, wheat, sugar and kerosene account for 86 per cent of total PDS sales.

It is worth mentioning here that the coverage of PDS in all states is not equally effective. It is mostly effective in southern states of Kerala and Andhra Pradesh whereas in Bihar, Jharkhand and Uttar Pradesh it is not so effective. R. Radhakrishnan in his book 'India's Public Distribution System: A National and International Perspective' has made conclusion on the basis of 42nd NSS round, 1986-87. "The evidence shows that even now, the efficacy of PDS in distributing food to the poor seems to be as bad as in 1986-87 and that some of the disquieting features persist in the virtual exclusion of backward states such as Bihar (including Jharkhand) and Uttar Pradesh from the PDS network." In contrast, to the impressive coverage and high per capita purchase of PDS in the states of Kerala and Andhra Pradesh, the coverage and low per capita purchase is observed in states of Bihar and Jharkhand due to weak fiscal capacity of these states to finance any additional subsidy. The World Bank Report mentions: "In poorer states such as Bihar, Orissa, the off-take was substantially lower than central allocations partly due to the narrow difference between the central issues price and open market price and partly because of weak fiscal capacity of these states to finance subsidy via lowering issue prices. Besides, these states have not yet built up effective institutional mechanism to lift the quotas from FCI depots to fair price shops".

For the success of public distribution system in the state of Bihar depends on the maintenance of supply line of the commodities selected for distribution is of crucial importance. Even a temporary interruption in supply create great hardship to the people particularly disadvantaged sections of society. Hence, adequate arrangements should be made for:

- Procurement of the commodities/items,
- transportation of the commodities/items,
- storage of the commodities/items, and
- distribution of the commodities/items at the central, state and local levels.

CONCLUSION

The PDS in recent years has been characterised by low off-take, increasing economic cost and growing food stocks, the increase in economic cost is due to increase in procurement prices and inefficiency in the functioning of Food Corporation of India in the State.

Recent developments in food subsidy policy seem to indicate that this policy is keeping the surplus farmers more than the poor consumers. Because of the farm lobby, the government has been paying whatever is offered by the farmers instead of buying only the needed commodities. As a result, there has been remarkable accumulation of stocks in recent periods, carrying cost is increasing very fast in the state. Increasing carrying cost is one of the reasons for the higher food subsidy in the state. Another major reason is increase in procurement prices which has raised the economic cost. Persistent in efficiencies in the operation of FCI are another reason for increasing economic cost.

Poor delivery system, inadequate coverage, leakage and poor quality grain plaque PDS in the state.

It is clear from above discussion that the government is following poor strategies for PDS. There is a great need of hours to alter this scenario and take bold initiatives to decentralise and improve the functioning of PDS at central as well as state and local levels.

References

Chand, Ramesh, 'Agricultural Diversifications in India' Mittal Publications, New Delhi.

Datt, Rudar and Sundaram, K.P.M., 'Indian Economy', S. Chand and Co. Ltd., New Delhi.

Jha, Brajesh, 'Indian Agriculture and the Multilateral Trading System', Bookwell, New Delhi.

Kapila, Uma, 'Indian Economy since Independence', Academic Foundation.

Kurukshetra, GoI, New Delhi.

Mishra, S.K. and Puri, V.K., 'Economics of Growth and Development', Himalaya Publication House, Bombay.

Ministry of Agriculture, Annual Report, GoI, New Delhi.

Tyagi, B.P., 'Agricultural Economics and Rural Development', Jai Prakash Narayan and Co., Meerut.

Yojna, GoI, New Delhi.

PDS and its Functioning in Bihar and Jharkhand

LAXMI KUMAR

INTRODUCTION

While Bihar and Jharkhand are among the poorest and most backward states in India, these states have hardly benefited from the public distribution system (PDS). It is estimated that 41.40 per cent of the Bihar population lives below the poverty line, while the all India figure is 27.50.[1] Economic growth rates are much loser than elsewhere in India. The growth rate in the 1990s in undivided Bihar (i.e. before bifurcation into the new states of Bihar and Jharkhand in November 2000) was 1.0-1.2 per cent, as compared to 6 per cent for the whole of India. Education and health facilities are very poor, and malnutrition is endemic. The World Food Programme classified the undivided state of Bihar as the only state in India suffering from extreme food insecurity (Daly and Bhattacharya, 2001).[2] The calorie intake in 1993-94 was just below 2000 kcal per person per day in rural areas which was below the all India rural average and less than it was 20 years earlier.[3] About 31 per cent of the children aged 0-4 years are severely malnourished, and this is more than anywhere else in India (The all-India average is just over 20 per cent). Bihar is not self-sufficient in foodgrains. In the 1990s, the average annual production was 12.2 million tonnes foodgrains (rice and wheat), which is 128 kilos person per year.[4] In this light, one could argue that if there is a need for a properly functioning public distribution system somewhere in India, it would be in the states of Bihar and Jharkhand.

The people in Bihar and Jharkhand have, however, hardly benefited from the food distribution programme. As compared to other states, the undivided Bihar received less foodgrains through the PDS. In 1998, the per capita PDS foodgrains off-take from the central pool was 9.5 kilo, which was about 50 per cent of the all-India average per capita off-take (Swaminathan, 2000). Moreover, a large proportion of what is lifted in Bibar does not reach the cardholders. According to a study conducted to the Tata Economic Consultancy Services (quoted by Ashrana, 2000), the all-India diversion of PDS foodgrains is 31 per cent for rice and 26 per cent for wheat. In Bihar these figures are 64 and 44 respectively. The impact of the PDS on poverty and inequality is small. On the whole, this impact is less than what one would like it to be, but in states like Andhra Pradesh, Gujarat, Karnataka and Kerala, the impact is considerably more than in poor states like Bihar, Orissa, Rajasthan and Uttar Pradesh (Radhakrishna and Subbarao, 1997).

In general, the fact that different states have benefited to different extents from the PDS, and in particular, the fact that Bihar has hardly benefited at all has two main reasons.

1. There are different treatments from the government of India. Some states received much more from the central pool of foodgrains than others. Kerala, for instance, has got a favourable treatment since the mid-1960s onwards. The foodgrain allocation to Bihar on the other hand, has been very low for a long time.

2. There is different political economy within the states. Several factors are important: whether there is surplus foodgrain production or not: the extent to which food distribution is taken up as an issue in populist politics (as in Andhra Pradesh and some other south Indian states); the extent to which there is a powerful, articulated demand from the public for the PDS, etc. In short, the economy, the characteristics of the state and the political processes, as well as the characteristics of the civil society are all likely to be important for understanding the experiences of the PDS in particular states.

The fact that the PDS functions differently in different states calls for a differentiated approach. When there are specific state-wise political economic reasons for good or bad performance in particular states, what is needed are policies which address these issues, i.e. policies adjusted to the local or state-wise constraints and opportunities. This, however, is not happening. The government of India has developed an all-India public distribution system, with all-India guidelines, and it wants these to be implemented in all the states. Individual state governments have made their own adjustments to some extent, and some states have complemented the GOI policies and subsidies with state-wise programmes. Overall, however, policy thinking about the PDS happens in terms of grand schemes and big solutions. The specificities of particular localities are not sufficiently taken into account.

This Article is divided into five sections. Section I deals with "Introduction". Section II describes "About PDS". Section III gives insights on "PDS in Bihar and Jharkhand". Section IV focuses on the "Political Economy of Bihar". The paper ends with "Some general conclusions regarding the processes of policy-making and implementation, as well as some specific conclusions regarding the opportunities for improving the implementation of the PDS in Bihar in Section V".

ABOUT PUBLIC DISTRIBUTION SYSTEM

The main purpose of the Public Distribution System (PDS) was to act as a price support programme for the consumer. It acted as an instrument of price stabilization and became a countervailing force against private traders who were interested to exploit the situation of scarcity to acquire more and more profits. The basic objective of the public distribution system in India is to provide essential consumer goods at cheap and subsidized prices to the consumers so as to insulate them from the impact of rising prices of these commodities and maintain the minimum nutritional status of our population. To run this system, the government resorts to levy purchases of a part of the marketable surplus with traders/millers and producers at procurement prices. The grain (wheat and rice) thus procured, is used for distribution to the consumers through a network of ration/fair price shop and/or for building up buffer stocks. In addition to foodgrains, PDS has also been used in India for the distribution of edible oils, sugar, coal, kerosene and cloth. The most important items covered under PDS in India have been rice, wheat and kerosene. Together these three items covered for 86 per cent of the total PDS sales. The criterion is to issue ration cards to all those households that have proper registered residential addresses. The number of fair price shops (FPS) has increased over the years from 0.47 lakhs at the end of 1960 to 3.12 lakhs in 1984 and is presently 4.74 lakhs. PDS distributes commodities worth more than Rs. 30,000 crore annually to about 160 million families and is perhaps the largest distribution network of its kind in the world.[5]

The Public Distribution System (PDS) evolved as a system of management of scarcity and for distribution of food grains at affordable prices. Over the years, PDS has become an important part of Government's policy for management of food economy in nature and is not intended to make available the entire requirement of any of the commodities distributed under it to a household or a section of the society.

PDS is operated under the joint responsibility of the Central and the State Governments. The Central government, through FCI, has assumed the responsibility for procurement, storage, transportation and bulk allocation of food grains to the State Governments. The operational responsibility including allocation within State, identification of families below the poverty line, issue of Ration Cards and supervision of the functioning of FPS, rest with the State Government. Under the PDS presently the commodities namely wheat, rice sugar, and kerosene, are being allocated to the States/UTs also distribute additional items of mass consumption through the PDS outlets such as cloth, exercise books, pulse, salt and tea, etc.

EVOLUTION OF PDS

Public Distribution System of essential commodities had been in existence in India during the Second World War to address food security concerns in the face of scarcity, with the intention of maintaining price stability and checking dishonest practices in private trade. PDS, with its focus on distribution of food grains in urban scarcity areas, had emanated from the critical food shortages of 1960. PDS had substantially contributed to the containment of rise in food grains prices and ensured access of food to urban consumers. As the national agricultural production has grown in the aftermath of Green Revolution, the out-reach of PDS was extended to tribal blocks and areas of high incidence of poverty in the 1970s and 1980s.

PDS, till 1992, was a general entitlement scheme for all consumers without any specific target. However, despite its expansion, the PDS has been subject to various systemic problems and has faced increasing criticism since 1991:

- Mismanagement has led to a massive increase in operational cost and to market distortion;
- The scheme has an urban bias and has been criticized for neglecting the rural section;
- Below poverty line (BPL) households have not been properly covered owing to leakages through widespread corruption, illegal scales, creation of false cards and the use of facilities by better-off households.

To take these problems, in 1992 the government introduced a Revamped Public Distribution System (RPDS) in 1775 blocks to reach poorer households with more varieties and quantities of foodstuff at cheaper prices.

In June 1997, a Targeted Public Distribution System (TPDS) was introduced. Special cards were issued to BPL families who provided with subsidized foodgrains. Under TPDS, around 60 m 'target' poor families were entitled to 10 kg of foodgrains per month. From 1 April 2000, the allocation to BPL families was increased to 20 kg per month at 50 per cent of cost. However, the off-take of the two major foodgrains, rice and wheat, declined sharply, though it recovered slightly thanks to the *Antyodoya Scheme*.

PDS IN BIHAR AND JHARKHAND

According to the 1997 policy document of the GoI, Bihar would be entitled to 1,031 thousand tones of subsidized foodgrains for the people below the poverty line. There are about 96 million people, of which 55 per cent lives below the poverty line, i.e. 53 million poor people, one can calculate that on average, according to this policy; there would be almost 20 kilo per poor person per year—a substantial increase as compared to the period prior to the introduction of targeting in 1997.

It is, of course, more accurate to look at actual lifting, rather than at allocation. Lifting in Bihar is good, i.e. after 1997. Before the introduction of targeting, lifting was poor. But since Bihar is entitled to a lot of heavily subsidised foodgrains for below poverty line (BPL) families. It lifts almost all wheat (lifting percentage 96 per cent), and 55 per cent of the allocated rice.[6] If one calculates the lifted BPL foodgrains per month, one arrives at an average foodgrain distribution of 1.4 kilo per poor person per month, or about almost 8 kilos per poor family (based on GoI estimate that there are 8.6 million families living below the poverty line). The GoI policy is 10 kilos per poor person per card. So, according to these calculations, distribution in Bihar comes close to the national policy.

In reality, however, only a part of the PDS foodgrains reaches the cardholders in this way. In our study, we found that many poor people have no red card (that is the card meant for below poverty line households), and that the foodgrains are often not reaching the PDS shops in the villages. The network of PDS dealers is quite reasonable, by the way. Altogether there are more than 59,000 PDS dealers, which means that there is one PDS dealer per 1,630.

THE PDS DEALERS

As I mentioned above, there are over 59,000 PDS dealers in Bihar and Jharkhand. Their number has increased considerably in the past decade, partly because licences are given to political followers of the ruling party.

The commission on the sale of the PDS commodities is not large, and the official income to not more than Rs. 400-600 per month. This is comparable to what a landless labourer may earn, and much lower than the salary of the lowest office staff (attendant or sweeper).

Yet, it is obvious that, despite this low income, it is pretty lucrative to be a fair price shop dealer. People are willing to pay large amounts of money to get a licence to become such dealer. One of the ways in which the PDS dealers survive and make money is by having so-called bogus cards—ration cards that do not below to any family but which the dealers themselves keep. The commodities they get for these bogus cards are sold on the open market. Apart from that, they also divert part of the rice, wheat, sugar and kerosene, which is meant for real cardholders.

As long as the fair price shop dealers pay their monthly bribes to the officials of the food and civil supply department these officials usually do not undertake any action to stop the malpractices. On the contrary, they even help the PDS dealers to cover up their activities by informing them when inspection teams come, etc. many dealer are also local level politicians, and several state level politicians started as a PDS dealer- in fact, the food minister in one of the governments in the 1990s also had a PDS shop. In South Bihar we found several examples of block level politicians who had a PDS shop.

Whether the PDS shop is helpful in their political career, is difficult to say. But it is plausible that the political affiliations help to get protection in case of shop suspensions which are done in case of alleged malpractices. Various sub-divisional officials told us that they receive regular telephone calls from local MLAs, with a request to cancel such suspensions.

Interestingly, the PDS dealers are very well organized. There is a PDS dealers association which is very active. Its head quarter is in Patna, where it employs three office workers. In each district and according to some informants even in each block, there are district and block office bearers. For various new policy issues individual PDS dealers wait for instructions from the association, before they decide what to do. A specifically interesting phenomenon is that the leader of this organization—officially he is the secretary—is a very articulate man committed to the PDS. He was a follower of Jayaprakash Narayan, and according to the story he told me, established the PDS dealers organization on the advice of J.P. because at that time the PDS was seen by them as a socialist policy. This leader does not run a PDS shop himself, but has a large charisma, and as far as I can judge, also a considerable command and authority over the PDS dealers. He has initiated many meetings to protest against the harassment of the officials and corruption of the officials, and he has taken up several court cases. For instance, public interest litigation cases to complain about the fact that some rationing inspectors in Patna were posted for 15-20 years in the same posts while they should have been transferred after three years.

But while the association fights corruption and bureaucratic malpractice in Patna, some of the local level office-bearers in the districts pursued mainly their own interests.

THE POLITICAL ECONOMY

The objective of this section is to locate these characteristics of the PDS in Bihar in the wider context of the Bihar political economy. In a sense, there is nothing special about the way the PDS works. Sharma (1995) reviews the implementation of several anti-poverty programmes in Bihar and concludes that: "The measures taken for direct intervention for poverty removal have produced unsatisfactory results, mainly due to deficiencies in the delivery system. The different organs of the delivery system-panchayats, the bureaucracy, cooperatives, etc. have really served the interests of the rich who cornered benefits even from those schemes which were specifically meant for the poor (Sharma 1995: 2601).

Several scholars have pointed at the government infectivity in Bihar (Kohli, 1991). There are at least three inter-related aspects to this governmental infectivity: (a) the deprofessionalisation of the bureaucracy, (b) the criminalization of politics, and (c) the violence in the state.

After having Mr. Nitish Kumar as chief minister, the situation of PDS in Bihar has totally changed. Bihar Chief Minister Nitish Kumar on Friday, 27 January, 2007, launched a coupon system aimed at checking malpractics and encouraging better service at ration shops distributing essentials to below poverty line (BPL) families.

Corruption and malpractice are rampant in the public distribution system (PDS) in Bihar: ration-card holders are often turned away from fair-price shops, they are assigned to and large quantities of grains and kerosene meant for the poor get sold in the open market.

With coupons, beneficiaries can go to another fair-price shop if they turned away at one. Every month each BPL family is entitled for 10 kg wheat, 25 kg rice and five litres of kerosene.

Bihar is the first state to introduce this scheme. Nitish Kumar spoken to the scheme of the shortcomings in the PDS, he said: "for example, kerosene is a necessity for people in our state but most often it gets black-marketed. Now coupons will be issued and people will get kerosene against the coupons."

Launching the scheme at the Jamaluddin Panchayat in Patna district on Republic Day, he said: "It is a simple coupon but a powerful weapon in the hands of the poor. This will empower the poor and stop black-marketing." The coupon scheme has earned laurels from several quarters, and recently Planning Commission member Abhijit Sen praised the effort, saying it must be emulated by other states.

Under the scheme coupons will be distributed every month to BPL families through Elected Panchayat Gram Sabhas. Each BPL family will be given a bunch of coupons for the entire year. The coupons can then be exchanged for kerosene and grain at subsided rates from fair-price shops.

PDS dealers will be given allotments of grain every month only against the coupons they submit. Therefore, they will not be able to corner extra stocks, deny it to the poor, and then sell it in the open market.

The CM said there were more BPL families in Bihar than indicated in the Centre's list. He said the centre should raise the cut-off point for identification of BPL families.

"As per the allotment of food grain and kerosene made by the centre, we can serve only around 65 lakh BPL families in the state. We want that the cut-off point be raised from 13 to 16 points and then we can help around one crore poor families in the state", he said.

CONCLUSION

In this paper I have analysed the way in which the public food distribution is implemented in Bihar (now Bihar and Jharkhand). This analysis showed that there are many problems. There is large scale misappropriation of foodgrains at all levels; the distribution of cards to BPL families is unsatisfactory; the Bihar State Food and Civil Supplies Corporation is financially not able to perform its task. Many people benefit from the way the public distribution system functions at present. Some PDS dealers get a reasonable income, as do many civil servants and others who are involved in monitoring the system. The food minister as well as some other politicians also have vested interests in the way the system works.

The problems with the PDS are not exceptional; in fact, they are part of a larger patterns of governmental in effectivity. The reasons behind this failure on the part of the government are economic stagnation and underdevelopment, and the changing political landscape. Given this political economic context in which the PDS is implemented, the observed problems are not surprising. There is almost no growth, so whatever scarce resources are available, they are appropriated through legal or illegal means. In the case of the PDS, these are public resources. They include foodgrains, post (PDS shop licences, vigilance committee memberships, official postings), and also the discretionary powers to decide about these licences and postings. These are different kind of resources, but they are all scarce and highly valued and people fight for them. These public resources are all misused and the benefits are misappropriated to a large extent. The appropriation happens partly along caste lines, as this is one of the important mechanisms of how access to state resources is organised in Bihar.

So, a firt important point to make is that the form PDS has taken in this state reflects this wider political economy, and cannot be understood without contextualisation within this political economy. A second point is that, when this is the case, proposals for reform and improved performance should take this context into account, and are likely to fail when they do not, i.e. when they assume a political economic vacuum in which policies are implemented.

With the launch of coupon system by Chief Minister Mr. Nitish Kumar, we can expect better services at ration shops and hope this initiative would promote more transparency and beat malpractices and corruption in days to come.

Notes

1. Agri at a Glance 2007, Ministry of agriculture, pp. 12, 13.
2. Daly, Gerald and Deepayan Bhattacharya (2001) 'Food Insecurity and Child Work in Rural India: Space Dimension' Paper presented at the IHD-WFP Consultative Workshop on Food Insecurity and Child Work. 15-17 March 2001.
3. The all-India average in 1993-94 was 2153 kcal. In general, the picture in 1993-94 was worse than twenty years earlier (Swaminathan and Ramachandran, 1999).
4. Data from Department of Agri, Patna, 128 kilos per person per year, means 10.7 kilos per person per month. The per capita cereal consumption in 1993-94 was 14.31 kilos in rural Bihar and 12.82 kilos in urban Bihar (Hanumantha Rao, 2000: Table 1).
5. Government of India, Planning Commission, Tenth Five Year Plan, 2002-07 (Delhi, 2003), Volume II, p. 367.

6. These percentages refer to December 1998. *Source*: Bihar State Food and Civil Supplies Corporation.

REFERENCES

Ashtana, M.D. (2000),: "Rationale for Recent Changes in Foodgrains Distribution under the Targeted Public Distribution System". Paper presented at a seminar "Food Security in India : The Emerging Challenges in the Context of Economic Liberalisation", held at the Centre for Economic and Social Studies. Hyderabad, 25-27 March 2000.

Bhatia, Bela (1997), "Anatomy of a Massacre", Seminar 450, The state of Bihar, *Economic and Political Weekly*. Vol 33, No. 14, pp. 53-59.

Government of India (1997), *Focus on the Poor (Guidelines for the Implementation of the Targeted Public Distribution System)*, Ministry of Civil Supplies, Consumer Affairs and Public Distribution.

Hanumantha Rao, C.H. (2000), "Declining Demand for Foodgrains in Rural India: Causes and Implications". *Economic and Political Weekly*, Vol. 35, No. 4, pp. 201-06.

Jharwal, S.M. (1999), "Public Distribution System in India Reassessed", Manak Publications, New Delhi.

Radhakrishna, R. and *et. al.* (1997), "India's Public Distribution System : A National and International Perspective", World Bank Discussion Paper No 380, *The World Bank*. Washington, DC.

Sharma, Alakh N. (1995), "Political Economy of Poverty in Bihar". *Economic and Political Weekly*. Vol 30, Nos. 41/42, pp. 2587-2602.

Swaminathan, Mabhura (2000), "Weakening Welfare: The Public Distribution of Food in India", *Left Word*, New Delhi.

Public Distribution System in Bihar

An Analysis of Present Scenario

Satyendra Narayan Singh, Rajesh Kumar
and Suresh Kumar

INTRODUCTION

Public distribution of food grains is a very popular measure in India to cater the food need of poor people, which exists in all states. In some states, however, the Public Distribution System. (PDS) works much better than in other states. The state of Bihar is one of the states in which the policy works poorly. It is absolutely necessary to understand why it works as it work, what the main bottlenecks are and where there are possibilities for improvement, if any. The PDS in Bihar not only in terms of how it fails and what it does not accomplish, but also in terms of what it is and what it does.

The PDS experience is put in the context of the wider political economy of Bihar.

Bihar is among the poorest and most backward states in India. This state has hardly benefited from the public distribution system (PDS). It is estimated that 42.6% of the population of Bihar lives below the poverty line, while the all-India figures is 26.1 (Analyzing to data 2000). Economic growth rates are much lower than elsewhere in India. The World Food Programme classified the state of Bihar as the only state in India suffering from extreme food insecurity (Daly and Bhattacharya, 2001). The calorie intake in 1993-94 was just below 2000 kcal per person per day in rural areas, which was below the all-India rural average and less than it was 20 years earlier. About 31 percent of the children aged 0-4 years are severely malnourished, and this is more than anywhere else in India (the all-India average is just over 20 percent). Bihar is not self-sufficient in foodgrains 1990s, the average annual production was 12.2 million tonnes of foodgrains (rice and wheat), which is 128 kg per person per year. In this situation, one could argue that if there is a need for a properly functioning public distribution system somewhere in India, it would be in the state of Bihar.

The people in Bihar has however, hardly benefited from the food distribution programme. As compared to other states, Bihar received less foodgrains through the PDS. In 1998, the per capita PDS foodgrain off-take from the central pool was 9.5 kg, which was about 50 percent of the all-India average per capita off-take (Swaminathan, 2000). Moreover, a large proportion of what is lifted in Bihar does not reach the card-holders. According to a study conducted to the Tata Economic Consultancy Services (quoted by Asthana, 2000), the all-India diversion of PDS foodgrains is 31 percent for rice and 26 percent for wheat. In Bihar these figures are 64 and 44, respectively. The impact of the PDS on poverty and inequality is small. On the whole, this impact is less than what one would like it to be, but in states like Andhra Pradesh, Gujarat, Karnataka and Kerala, the impact is considerably more than in poor states like Bihar.

In general, the fact that different states have benefited to different extents from the PDS, and in particular, the fact that Bihar has hardly benefited at all has two main reasons—

1. *The different treatment from the Government of India*: Some states received much more from the central pool of foodgrains than others. Kerala, for instance, has got a favourable treatment since the mid-1960s onwards. The foodgrain allocation to Bihar, on the other hand, has been very low for a long time.
2. *The different political economy within the states*: Several factors are important—whether there is surplus foodgrain production or not; the extent to which food distribution is taken up as an issue in populist politics (as in Andhra Pradesh and some other south Indian states); the extent to which there is a powerful, articulated demand from the public for the PDS, etc. In short, the economy, the characteristics of the state and the political processes, and of the civil society are all likely to be important for understanding the experiences of the PDS in particular states.

The fact the PDS functions differently in different states calls for a differentiated approach. When there are specific state-wise political and economic reasons for good or bad performance in particular states, what is needed are policies which address these issues, i.e., policies adjusted to the local or state-wise constraints and opportunities. This, however, is not happening. The Government of India has developed an all-India public distribution system, with all-India guidelines, and it wants these to be implemented in all the states. Individual state governments have made their own adjustments to some extent, and some states have complemented the GoI policies and subsidies with state-wise programmes. On the whole, however, policy thinking about the PDS happens in terms of grand schemes and big overall solutions. The specificities of particular localities are not sufficiently taken into account.

PERFORMANCE OF PDS IN BIHAR

The Performance of PDS has never been praise worth which is evident from fact discussed below:

> According to the 1997 policy document of the GoI, Bihar would be entitled to 1,031 thousand tones of subsidized foodgrains for the people below the poverty line. Given the fact that there are about 96 million people, of which 55 percent live below the poverty line, that is, 53 million poor people, one can calculate that on average, according to this policy, there would be almost 20 kg per poor person per year—a substantial increase as compared to the period prior to the introduction of targeting in 1997.

It is, of course, more accurate to look at actual lifting, rather than at allocation. Lifting in Bihar is good, i.e., after 1997, before the introduction of targeting, lifting was poor. But since Bihar is entitled to a lot of heavily subsidized food grains for below poverty line (BPL) families, it lifts almost all wheat (lifting percentage 96 percent), and 55 percent of the allocated rice. If one calculates the lifted BPL food grains per month, one arrives at an average food grain distribution of 1.4 kg per poor person per month, or about almost 8 kg per poor family (based on GoI estimate that there are 8.6 million families living below the poverty line). The GoI policy is 10 kg per poor person per card. So, according to these calculations, distribution in Bihar comes close to the national policy.

In reality, however, only a part of the PDS foodgrains reaches the card-holders in this way. In our field work, we found that many poor people have not red card (that is the card meant for BPL households), and that the foodgrains are often not reaching the PDS shops in the villages (see below). The network of PDS dealers is quite reasonable, by the way. Altogether there are more than 59,000 PDS dealers, which means that there is one PDS dealer per 1630 people.

In this section, the PDS in Bihar will be described in more qualitative terms. The discussion begins with the entry point where various actions are involved.

ROLE OF PDS DEALERS IN BIHAR

There is an organized association of PDS dealers in Bihar and many of them are famous for their criminal history. But the responsibility food for poor rests with them. Recently, there are over 59,000 PDS dealers in Bihar. Their number has increased considerably in the past decade, partly because licences are given to political followers of the ruling party.

Many dealers are local level politicians, and several state level politicians started as a PDS dealer—in fact, the food minister in one of the governments in the 1990s also had a PDS shop. In south Bihar we found several examples of block level politicians who had a PDS shop. Whether the PDS shop is helpful in their political career, is difficult to say. But it is plausible that the political affiliations help to get protection in case of shop suspensions which are done in case of alleged malpractices. Various sub-divisional officials told us that they receive regular telephone calls from local MLAs, with a request to cancel such suspensions.

The commission on the sale of the PDS commodities is not large, and the official income comes to not more than Rs. 400-600 per month. This is comparable to what a landless labourer may earn, and much lower than the salary of the lowest office staff (attendant or sweeper).

As long as the fair-price shop dealers pay their monthly bribes to the officials of the Food and Civil Supply Department these officials usually do not undertake any action to stop the malpractices. On the contrary, they even help the PDS dealers cover up their activities by informing them when inspection teams come, etc.

It is obvious that, despite this low income, it is pretty lucrative to be a fair-price shop dealer. People are willing to pay large amounts of money to get a licence to become such dealer. One of the ways in which the PDS dealers survive and make money is by having so-called bogus cards—ration cards that do not belong to any family but which are kept by the dealers themselves. The commodities they get for these bogus cards are sold in the open market. Apart from that, they also divert part of the rice, wheat, sugar and kerosene which is meant for real card holders.

There is a PDS dealers' association which is very active. Its headquarters is in Patna, where it employs three office workers. In each district, and according to some informants even in each block, there are district and block office bearers. For various new policy issues, individual PDS dealers wait for the instructions from the association before they decide what to do.

MEDIA AND PDS IN BIHAR

There are many other people who take up the cause of the consumers/card-holders, in particular, some reporters of Hindi newspapers. There are regular small reports in these newspapers about the malpractices which are going on. There are also some reporters who have a special interest in the PDS issues and write regularly about them. Doing this is not easy in Bihar. It is a very interesting instance when Bihar was undivided. There was a journalist of the *Ranchi Express*, and he told to an officer that he is regularly threatened when he publishes about the PDS and the mafia involved. He receives anonymous telephone calls, in which he is told that his daughter will be kidnapped or that he will be killed. The following quote is the translation of a newspaper article (September 8, 1999) in the *Prabhat Khabar*, a Hindi newspaper, published from Ranchi":

> "A reporter of a local newspaper, Mr. Rajendra Prasad, was arrested in Khunti for writing against the ration mafia. A first information Report (FIR) was lodged against him by three PDS dealers who had complained to the sub-divisional officer. In the FIR the reporter was alleged to extract money from tribal people and harijans and threaten some PDS dealers to get their licence cancelled if they would not pay him.

It should be mentioned that the reporter Rajendra Prasad has been writing about corruption and black-marketing of the

PDS ration and about smuggling of forest woods of Murhu and Khunti block for the last two years. He has also written several articles about the alleged connection between ration mafia, police and government officials. It is believed that such reports about bungling with the PDS ration in open market have annoyed some PDS dealers who then tried to implicate the reporter in false cases. The reporter has said that police in charge of Murhu and some government officials along with the PDS dealers had already threatened him before for writing such articles. He and his family also used to get threatening telephone calls.

The reporter was arrested at midnight. The police abused him and pulled him forcefully out of the house. They also tried to molest his wife. The three PDS dealers who have lodged the FIR are said to be under the control of a bigger ration mafia operating in the region."

Apart from journalists, there are also a few consumer activists and organizations, mainly active in Patna and other towns. Although food distribution is not their main concern (which is water, electricity supply, etc.), they take some interest in the PDS. Occasionally, they have tried to influence the implementation of the PDS, for instance, by lobbying for the inclusion of a consumer activist in the vigilance committees.

BUREAUCRATIC HURDLE IN PDS

Apart from monitoring the distribution process, card distribution is also a task of the bureaucracy. As per official guidelines from the Government of India, "Gram Panchayats and Gram Sabhas should be involved in the initial identification of the eligible families" (Government of India, 1997, p. 3, What has happened instead is that the red cards have been sent to the district magistrates; they have passed them on to the sub-divisional officers, who have given them to lower ranks officers, and finally, in any places, the cards were given to the PDS dealers themselves to distribute. It is, hence, not surprising that many of them have kept a considerable part of the cards themselves.

Like in all other states, the Department of Food and Civil Supplies has its presence all over the state. The Department is headed by the Commissioner who is also the Secretary. The lowest officials are the supply inspectors. They may have 40-60 PDS dealers to check, and are supposed to visit each of them every month. Above them, in urban areas, there are the marketing inspectors, who are supposed to visit 50 percent of the shops every month. Then there are assistant district supply officers and district supply officers. In four urban zones, there are Special Officers Rationing (SORs). At the block level, there are mainly two people; the block supply officer and the supply inspector.

The department is very corrupt. There are set amounts that the PDS dealers have to pay to the supply inspectors and this money is redistributed with higher-level officers. These higher-level officers themselves may also be involved in money collection and/or black marketeering.

I must say, however, that I can understand the low morale and corruption, especially in the case of the lower level supply officers and inspectors. On one of my trips I visited Karra block in Ranchi. The office of the block supply officer was in a rather dilapidated state. It looked like a shed, with a roof with many holes in it. There was no electricity, also not in construction. In the summer it must be terribly hot; in the rainy season, the rain would come inside through the holes in the roof. The office was hardly furnished. There was one table; and one chair in reasonable condition, and two others on which one could only sit after putting a piece of stone or wood on it. There was one pile of old files somewhere in the corner. Otherwise, there was nothing. The Block Development Officer lived in Ranchi (about three hours by bus), and I would admire him if he would decide to come to this office more than once or twice a week.

But what is also important to mention in a discussion of the bureaucracy is that, although corruption is very widespread and institutionalized, it is not true that each and every officer is involved to the same extent. There are several honest people as well, or people who feel that they are forced to participate in the system of money collection but who do not like it very much.

LACK OF POLITICAL AWARENESS AND WILLINGNESS

There is excessive political interference in PDS. The two politicians who were the subsequent food ministers were both very corrupt, even to the extent that they visited the districts themselves to ask for money from the concerned officials. Most Members of the State Legislative Assembly (MLAs) are not very interested in the PDS. Some have some involvement in the sense that they approach officials to do *pairvi* on behalf of the PDS dealers in case of suspensions, etc., however, there are exceptions: MLAs who take a serious interest in the PDS, who have raised questions in the Assembly, or who have started public interest litigation in relation to wrong and incomplete card issuing and improper distribution.

Yet as compared to south India, there seems to be little interest from the state-level politicians in a properly functioning PDS. In south India, these politicians regard the PDS as something they can give them political mileage, but not so in Bihar. In an earlier paper (Mooij, 1999), I formulated four hypotheses which could explain why politicians in Bihar do not regard the PDS in that way:

1. Politicians in Bihar do not require food to increase their popularity. They pursue other strategies to attract votes.
2. Politicians in Bihar are not capable of making the PDS delivery system function in such a way that they could get political mileage out of it. They do not have sufficient control over the (food) bureaucracy in order to force it to deliver the goods to the people. Or they cannot control the local level vested interests (PDS dealers, local politicians) sufficiently.
3. The present system in which about 85 percent of the commodities are diverted to the black market offers the Bihari politicians more than a system which would benefit the consumers/card-holders.
4. Politicians in Bihar are forced with a different situation than in south India. The poor in Bihar are too poor for the PDS. Households which are

permanently indebted cannot buy the PDS commodities. So, the basic problem is one of demand. This problem cannot be solved by special schemes or proper implementation.

MAFIA RAJ IN PDS

PDS is governed by the mafia in the state. It seems the transporters of the PDS foodgrains—there is no doorstep delivery, and the foodgrains are transported by private contractors from the FCI godowns to the block-level warehouses—are important in this mafia. They divert a part of the PDS foodgrains, possibly assisted by FCI people and/or SFC assistant general managers. For a long time, transportation of the PDS commodities was not a lucrative job. But since the introduction of targeting, the price difference between BPL foodgrains and open market foodgrains is huge. Diversion of the truck (10 tonnes) can give an illegal earning of about Rs. 60,000.

In Bihar there are many petty criminals, the so-called mafia in the form of rangdars who benefit from protection from the local MLAs, and, in turn, these rangdars may play a role at election time in both capturing or threatening people when they cast their votes. Several people told us that rangdars can easily force the PDS dealers to give them some money or food. For instance, when there are political rallies, they harass the PDS dealers and force them to contribute some money. According to a Block Development Officer, some rangdars may also ask for money from local officials.

This description of the main actors in the PDS system in Bihar is rather gloomy. It shows that there are many problems, and also that there are many people who benefit in one way or another from the way the system works at present. But what is also clear is that there is diversity. Not everybody participates to the same extent in all these malpractices. There is an association of the PDS dealers which takes up some important issues; there are committed journalists; there are a few MLAs who have a serious interest in a better PDS; there are some people within the department as well, who would like the system to function differently. Nevertheless, the overall picture is a rather depressing one.

GROWING POPULATION IN BIHAR AND PDS

Bihar is not only a rural but also a very agricultural society. It has the highest proportion of population living in rural areas (87 percent, as compared to the national average of 74.3 percent), next to only Assam (Sharma, 1995, p. 2587), and its population depends to a very large extent on agriculture. There is a retrogression in the employment structure.

One of the main reasons for the slow agricultural growth is the prevailing agrarian structure, which is often characterized as semi-feudal. The abolition of the Zamindari system after Independence mean the transfer of some lands from the upper castes (mainly Yadavs, Koiris and Kurmis). The ceiling legislation was very poorly implemented. It is estimated that about 10 percent of the total cultivated land changed hands from the Zamindars to the intermediate size cultivators. The Green Revolution took place hardly in Bihar, but as far as it took place, it was instrumental in the emergence of a new category of kulak farmers. Many of them belong to the upper backward castes, the Yadavs, the Koiris and the Kurmis (Sharma and Kumar, 1998, p. 404).

The term 'semi-feudal' is used to describe the agrarian structure because 'precapitalist' economic relationships such as sharecropping, usury and bonded labour still perist. Sharecropping is the most common form of tenancy in Bihar, and in some areas share croppers account for about 40 percent of the rural households.

As a result, an increasing number of people depend on agriculture for their livelihood. The agricultural performance is, however, unfortunately, also not very good. During the first decade after Independence, agricultural growth was very poor, and during the Green Revolution period (1964-65 to 1979-80) when cereal production in India as a whole increased at a 1.8 percent compound rate, in Bihar the rate was only 0.1 percent (Blair, 1984, p. 55). Since in mid-1980s the growth rate improved, and became even higher than the national average (Sharma, 1995, p. 2591), but the growth rates decelerated again in the 1990s (Sharma and Kumar, 1998, p. 397). In short, especially in view of the large and increasing population that crucially depends on agriculture for its livelihood, the situation is very problematic.

There were some changes in the 1980s, but according to a more recent study, crop sharing remains the principal form of tenancy.

In this situation of an increasing population depending on a stagnating agriculture, conflicts are bound to arise. The total cake is not growing, but those who dominate the social structure continue to try to increase their share by intensifying surplus appropriation. This is not possible without force, debt bondage, reference to a rigid caste hierarchy and other semi-feudal mechanisms (Kohli, 1991, p. 230; Sharma and Kumar, 1998, p. 399). At the same time, people have become increasingly vocal (see below) and do not accept the extreme exploitation. This has led to very violent rural conflicts.

A study conducted in 1980-81) showed that two-fifths of the rural households leased in land in the plains of Bihar (which the northern part of the State) and about 28 percent of the total cultivated area was being leased in, of which about 70 percent was on crop-sharing basis (Prasad *et. al.,* 1990). Apart from 50 percent share in crop output, even straw was shared and almost the entire cost was borne by the sharecroppers. The survey further revealed that about three-fifths of the rural households were indebted to the traditional sources of loan (money-lenders, employers, etc.), the corresponding percentage for agricultural labourers being more than 80 percent and for poor middle peasants more than 60. Almost one-third of the agricultural labourers were attached to employers and almost invariably they had to work exclusively for them.

CONCLUSION

There is large scale misappropriation of foodgrains at all levels; the distribution of cards to BPL families is unsatisfactory; the Bihar State Food and Civil Supplies Corporation is financially not able to perform its task. Many people benefit from the way the public distribution system functions at present. Some PDS dealers get a reasonable income, as do many civil servants and others who are involved in monitoring the system. Politicians too have vested interests in the way the system works.

The problems with the PDS are not exceptional; in fact, they are part of larger patterns of governmental ineffectiveness. The reasons behind this failure on the part of the government are economic stagnation and underdevelopment, and the changing political landscape. Given this political economic context in which the PDS is implemented, the observed problems are not surprising. There is almost no growth, so whatever scarce resources are available, they are appropriated through legal or illegal means. In the case of the PDS, these are public resources. They include foodgrains. Posts (PDS shop licences, vigilance committee memberships, official posting) and also the discretionary powers to decide about these licences and postings. These are different kind of resources, but they are all scarce and highly valued, and people fight for them. These public resources are all misused and the benefits are appropriated to a large extent. The appropriation happens partly along caste lines, as this is one of the important mechanisms of how access to state resources is organized in Bihar.

So, the first important point to make is that the form the PDS has taken in this state reflects this wider political economy, and cannot be understood without contextualization within this background. A second point is that, when this is the case, proposals for reform and improved performance should take this context into account, and are likely to fail when they do not, i.e. when they assume a political and economic vacuum in which policies are implemented.

Lastly, we can conclude with a very sad remarks that PDS is just like teeth of elephant which is of no use. The government is required to adopt an alternative measure to check the corrupt practice in PDS in Bihar.

References

Bhatia, Bela (1998), "After the Bathe Massacre", *Economic and Political Weekly*, Vol. 33, No. 14, pp. 751-52.

Bose, Pradip K. (1991), "Mobility and Conflict: Social Roots of Caste Violence in Bihar", in Gupta, Dipankar (ed.), Social Stratifica ion, Oxford University Press, Delhi, pp. 369-86.

Das, Arvind N. (1998), "India in the Image of Bihar", *Economic and Political Weekly,* Vol. 33, No. 49, pp. 3103-4.

Government of India (1997), Focus on the Poor (Guidelines for the implementation of the Targeted Public Distribution System, Ministry of Civil Supplies, Consumer Affairs Public Distribution, New Delhi.

Radhakrishna, R. and Subbarao, K., with Indrakant, S. and Ravi, C. (1997), "India's Public Distribution System: A National and International Perspective". World Bank discussion paper No. 380, The World Bank, Washington, D.C.

Sharma, Alakh N. (1995), "Political Economy of Poverty in Bihar", *Economic and Political Weekly,* Vol. 30, Nos. 41/42, pp. 2587-2602.

SECTION III

Various Aspects of PDS

Public Distribution System and Regional Imbalances

ABHISHEK KUMAR AND APRANA BHARDWAJ

INTRODUCTION

The idea of regional development originated with Stalin in Russia and German bombardment on England during Second World War. The backward states can be developed through the development of agriculture, industry, trade or commerce and government policy like PDS. Imbalances in India relate to various aspects like disparity in national resources of the region, development of agriculture and industry, social overheads and government policy of the states. Despite high intended uniform plans and overall growth fruits of development have not been uniform in the states. The basic objective of planning is economic growth, employment and reduction of disparities of income and wealth. In order to achieve balanced development, India has adopted balanced growth (Ragner Nurske) and unbalanced growth (A.O.

Hirshman) as a strategy in the five year plans with the policies of Nehru-Mahalanobis Model, Gandhian Model and Rao-Manmohan model of growth.

Food security depends on the stability in foodgrains production; prices, purchasing power and size of land, unequal distribution of production, irrigated area, etc. There are surplus and deficit foodgrain states. The food security has disturbed due to various factors like food production, per capita availability, unemployment, BPL Population and occupational distribution of population. The implementation of PDS has helped to achieve the balance between surplus and deficit of foodgrain states. Transfer of surplus foodgrains at the deficit area have become financial burden on the federal government. Hence balanced development is important to achieve socio economic equality.

The benefits of growth in India did not trickle down as expected. PCI has increased, but this growth has been unequally distributed among the state and socio-economic groups. Greater equality with development will create sustained growth of the economy. The lowest group of population will spend on necessaries which enhances the production of basic necessitates and on the other hand elite class will spend their income on imported luxurious goods instead of productive investment. Disparity in income can act as psychological disincentive to economic growth. Hence economic policy must focus on trade-off between balanced growth and welfare.

IMBALANCES IN AREA, PRODUCTION AND YIELD OF SURPLUS FOODGRAIN STATES (SFS) AND DEFICIT FOODGRAIN STATES (DFS)

Imbalances of production depends on the land area available for cultivation, cropping pattern, fertilizer consumption and production of food crops. Some states are surplus in foodgrains because of high production and yield.

Table 1 indicates area, production and yield. Average area, foodgrain production in mn hectares and mn tonnes of surplus foodgrain states was 8.08 and 13.75 compared to deficit foodgrain states of 5.08 mn hectare and 6.87 mn tones.

TABLE I

Imbalances in Area, Production, Yield, Per Hectare Consumption of Fertilizer (1996-97)

Surplus foodgrain states	*Area in mn hectare*	*Production in million tonnes*	*Yield in kg./ha.*	*Per hectare Fertilizer Consumption kg.*	*Deficit foodgrain states*	*Area in mn hectare*	*Production in million tonnes*	*Yield in kg./ha.*	*Per hectare Fertilizer Consumption kg.*
(1)	*(2)*	*(3)*	*(4)*	*(5)*	*(6)*	*(7)*	*(8)*	*(9)*	*(10)*
A.P.	7.14	12.68	1776	139.41	Assam	2.73	3.53	1294	14.62
Haryana	4.03	11.45	2843	130.95	Bihar	9.06	14.13	1560	80.61
H.P.	0.82	1.29	1562	35.33	Gujarat	4	5.21	1303	76.23
J & K	0.88	1.32	15.8	40.12	Kerala	0.46	0.86	1863	61.66
Karnataka	7.29	9.27	1272	66.43	Maharashtra	13.79	14.59	1058	62.22
M.P.	17.69	19.56	1106	39.19	Tamilnadu	4.28	7.65	1787	110.5
Orissa	5.54	4.83	873	25.73	Others	1.3	2.12	NA	NA
Punjab	5.69	21.56	3787	158.43	Total	35.62	48.09	8865	405.84

(*Contd.*)

TABLE I (*Contd.*)

(1)	(2)	(3)	(4)	(5)	(6)	(7)	(8)	(9)	(10)
Rajasthan	12.87	12.84	998	36.38	Avg	5.09	6.87	1477.5	67.64
U.P.	20.5	42.69	2083	108.39	Min.	0.46	0.86	1058	14.62
W.B.	6.44	13.74	2133	103.24	Max.	13.79	14.59	1863	110.5
Total	88.89	151.23	18448.8	883.6	Sd.	4.74	5.56	313.47	31.48
Avg.	8.08	13.75	770.21	80.33	Cv	93.1	80.94	21.22	46.54
Min.	0.82	1.29	15.8	25.73	—	—	—	—	—
Max.	20.5	42.69	3787	158.43	—	—	—	—	—
Sd.	6.38	11.61	1027.84	48.89	—	—	—	—	—
CV	78.93	84.48	133.45	60.87	—	—	—	—	—

Source : Rudradutta, Food Security in India, Indian Economy Agenda for 21st Century (2002) (Ed.) Raj Kumar Sen and Biswajit Chatterjee, Deep and Deep Pub., New Delhi.

The per hectare kg of yield and fertilizer consumption of surplus and deficit foodgrain states were 1677.16, 80.33 and 1477.5, 67.64 respectively.

TOTAL POPULATION, BPL POPULATION AND FAIR PRICE SHOPS IN SURPLUS AND DEFICIT FOODGRAIN STATES

Distribution of population, BPL population and fair price shop differ from states to states. Imbalances in the variables are due to imbalances in area under cultivation and irrigation facilities, foodgrain production, cropping pattern and consumption pattern of the population.

Table 2 indicates that total population and BPL population and fair price shops of surplus and deficit foodgrain states. The average population, BPL population and ration cards per fair price shops of foodgrains states were 33.27 mn. 10.55 mn and 418.83 ration cards. Whereas in deficit states it was 28.52 mn, 12.5 mn with 641 ration cards per fair price shop. There is a high rate of variations in surplus foodgrains states compared to deficit food grain states.

DISPARITY IN CENTRAL ISSUE PRICES

It is expected that prices should be uniform throughout the country. Some states have fixed the prices for PDS and RPDS lower than the central issue prices.

Table 3 Transpires the pricing policy of the government. The different states have adopted different prices. The average central prices in surplus foodgrain states of wheat and rice for BPL was Rs. 2.87 and Rs. 5.21, whereas it was marginally low of Rs. 2.15 and 'Rs. 5.16 in deficit foodgrain states. For APL the average price of wheat and rice in surplus foodgrain states was low of Rs. 8.04 and Rs. 8.79. Whereas in deficit area the price was high of Rs. 9.53 and Rs. 11.85.

IMBALANCES IN FOODGRAIN PRODUCTION, TOTAL REQUIREMENT AND PER CAPITA AVAILABILITY

Availability of foodgrains depends on population, food-

TABLE 2

Total Population, BPL Population and Fair Price Shops in Surplus and Deficit Foodgrain States

Surplus foodgrain states	*Total Population (mn)*	*Below poverty line population (mn)*	*Total fair price shops*	*Cards Per fair price shop*	*Deficit foodgrain states*	*Total Population (mn)*	*Below poverty line population (mn)*	*Total fair price shops*	*Cards Per fair price shop*
(1)	*(2)*	*(3)*	*(4)*	*(5)*	*(6)*	*(7)*	*(8)*	*(9)*	*(10)*
A.P.	75.7	11.9	40438	413	Assam	26.6	9.5	32347	131
Arunachal P.	1	NA	945	366	Bihar	82.9	42.6	57535	301
Haryana	21	1.7	7703	545	Goa	1.3	0.1	590	522
H.P.	6	0.5	3895	309	Gujarat	50.6	6.8	14268	741
J & k	10	0.3	2926	461	Kerala	31.8	4.1	14261	434
Karnataka	52.7	10.4	20312	550	Maharashtra	96.8	22.8	45807	424
M.P.	60.4	29.9	24141	737	Meghalaya	2.3	NA	3829	51
Manipur	2.4	0.7	1928	93	T.N.	62.1	13	26514	588
Mizoram	0.9	NA	1003	154	Delhi	13.8	1.1	3167	1128
Nagaland	1.1	0.5	351	573	A & N	0.4	NA	404	213
Orissa	36.7	16.9	24665	329	Chandigarh	0.9	NA	230	922
Punjab	24.3	1.4	13915	388	Daman	0.2	NA	13	2231

Rajasthan	56.5	8.2	18943	541
Sikkim	0.5	0.2	878	75
Tripura	3.2	1.3	1359	505
U.P.	166.1	53	79719	333
W.B.	80.2	21.3	20515	757
D & N	0.2	NA	78	410
Total	598.9	158.2	263714	7539
Avg.	33.27	10.55	14650.78	418.83
Min.	0.2	0.2	78	75
Max.	166.1	53	79719	757
Sd.	43.37	14.88	19992.98	191.36
CV	130.35	141.06	136.46	45.69

Pondicherry	1	NA	396	641
Total	370.7	100	199361	8327
Avg.	28.52	12.5	15335.46	640.54
Min.	0.2	0.1	13	51
Max.	96.8	42.6	57535	2231
Sd.	34.17	14.18	19435.68	567.75
CV	119.81	113.46	126.74	88.64
—	—	—	—	—
—	—	—	—	—
—	—	—	—	—
—	—	—	—	—
—	—	—	—	—

Source : *Statistical Outline of India*, 2002-03 and *Indian Journal of Social Development*, Vol. 1, No. 1, 2001.

TABLE 3

Central Issue Prices in the States (2000) (Rs.)

Surplus foodgrain states	*BPL Wheat*	*BPL Rice*	*APL Wheat*	*APL Rice*	*Rice Grade-A*	*Deficit foodgrain states*	*BPL Wheat*	*BPL Rice*	*APL Wheat*	*APL Rice*	*Rice Grade-A*
(1)	*(2)*	*(3)*	*(4)*	*(5)*	*(6)*	*(7)*	*(8)*	*(9)*	*(10)*	*(11)*	*(12)*
A.P.	—	5.25	9	—	12	Assam	—	6.53	8.74	—	13
Arunachal P.	3	4	5	—	—	Bihar	5.1	6.48	9.84	—	2.89
Haryana	5	—	9.5	—	—	Goa	—	6.3	9.5	—	12.4
H.P.	5	7.2	9.8	—	13	Gujarat	2	3	8	—	10
J & K	5.1	6.5	9.5	12	12.5	Kerala	—	6.4	9.5	—	10.4
Karnataka	5	6.4	9.8	—	12.75	Maharashtra	4	5.4	9.8	—	13.5
M.P.	5	6.4	9.75	—	12.75	Meghalaya	—	6.4	9.6	11.85	12.3
Manipur	—	4	7.6	7.64	9.77	T.N.	2	3.5	9.75	—	—
Mizoram	—	4	7.9	7.5	9.55	Delhi	—	—	9.5	—	12.3
Nagaland	3	4	5.1	6.1	7.6	A & N	5	6.4	10.15	—	12.9
Orissa	—	6.5	—	—	12.9	Chandigarh	4.87	6.28	10.12	—	12.44
Punjab	4.58	5.96	9.06	—	11.86	Daman	5	6.4	9.9	—	12.8
Rajasthan	3	4	7	—	9.7	Pondicherry	—	4	9.5	—	12.3
Sikkim	—	6.4	9.5	—	12.5	Total	27.97	67.09	123.9	11.85	137.23

Tripura	—	6.4	9.75	12.05	12.75	Avg.	2.15	5.16	9.53		10.56
U.P.	3	4	7	7.5	9.55	Min.	2	3	8		2.89
W.B.	5	6.4	9.7	—	12.6	Max.	5.1	6.53	10.15		13.5
D & N	5	6.4	9.7	—	12.4	Sd.	1.41	1.31	0.58		2.88
Total	51.68	93.81	144.66	52.79	184.18	CV	65.58	25.39	6.09		27.27
Avg.	2.87	5.21	8.04	8.79	11.51	—	—	—	—	—	—
Min.	3	4	5	6.1	7.6	—	—	—	—	—	—
Max.	5.1	7.2	9.8	12.05	13	—	—	—	—	—	—
Sd.	0.97	1.21	1.63	2.56	1.68	—	—	—	—	—	—
CV	33.8	23.22	20.27	87.37	16.42	—	—	—	—	—	—

Source : As in Table 2.

TABLE 4

Total Population, Total Foodgrain Production and Per Capita Availability

Sl. No. Surplus foodgrain states	Total Population in Lakh	Total Requirement in (000) mts.	Total Local Production (000) mts.	Diff. (000) mts.	Per Capita Availability kg.	Public Distribution System in kg.	Total in kg.
(1)	(2)	(3)	(4)	(5)	(6)	(7)	(8)
1. A.P.	700.49	10340.5	11176	835.5	159.55	34.21	193.76
2. Arunachal Pradesh	8.9	127.92	200.74	72.82	225.55	96.61	322.16
3. Haryana	182.62	2639.38	10025.67	7386.29	548.99	5.29	554.28
4. H.P.	53.26	787.75	1259.43	471.68	236.47	28.59	265.06
5. J & K	79.51	1164.35	1405.17	240.82	176.73	39.31	216.04
6. Karnataka	476.99	7041.67	7893.63	851.96	165.49	18.87	184.36
7. M.P.	708.19	10269.06	15275.13	5006.07	215.69	12.94	228.63
8. Manipur	18.92	280.66	352.23	71.57	186.17	37.23	223.4
9. Mizoram	7.1	103.22	114.14	10.92	160.76	141.1	301.86
10. Nagaland	12.46	182.64	218.67	36.03	175.5	107.21	282.7
11. Orissa	344.13	5081.83	6645.6	1563.77	193.11	12.29	205.4

12.	Punjab	215.58	3207.79	21052.6	17844.81	976.56	3.39	979.95
13.	Rajasthan	475.79	6812.76	7940.46	1127.7	166.79	13.91	180.8
14.	Sikkim	4.19	60.68	96.63	35.95	230.62	97.73	328.35
15.	Tripura	28.4	413.32	492.57	79.25	173.44	53.7	227.14
16.	U.P.	1452.15	20865.24	35887.83	15022.59	247.14	10.59	257.73
17.	W.B.	709.8	10432.6	13057	2624.4	183.95	20.48	208.43
18.	D & N.	1.43	20.66	27.73	7.07	193.92	31.89	225.8
	Total	5479.91	79832.03	133121.2	53289.2	4616.43	765.34	5385.85
	Avg.	304.44	4435.11	7395.62	2960.51	256.47	42.52	299.21
	Sd.	391.0203	5656.247	9546.877	5304.264	200.1003	40.58779	190.4502
	Cv	128.44	127.53	129.09	179.17	78.02	95.46	63.65

(*Contd.*)

TABLE 4 (Contd.)

Sl. No.	Deficit foodgrain states	Total Population in lakh	Total Requirement in (000) mts.	Total Local Production (000) mts.	Diff. (000) mts.	Per Capita Availability kg.	Public Distribution System in kg.	Total in kg.
	(1)	(9)	(10)	(11)	(12)	(13)	(14)	(15)
1.	Assam	270.49	3889.92	3470.63	419.29	128.31	24.53	152.84
2.	Bihar	963.08	13797.27	12193.1	1604.17	126.21	13.17	139.77
3.	Goa	12.05	185.98	137.97	48.01	114.5	56.19	170.69
4.	Gujarat	452.85	6702.84	3871.63	2831.21	85.49	17.69	103.19
5.	Kerala	317.91	4874.27	272.87	4601.4	30.6	55.88	86.48
6.	Maharashtra	841.67	12448.85	10404.17	2044.68	123.61	17.69	141.31
7.	Meghalaya	18.28	259.48	147.67	111.81	80.78	78.48	159.27
8.	T.N.	579.84	8828.28	6843.85	1984.43	149.06	17.43	166.5
9.	Delhi	97.03	1442.77	128.8	1313.97	13.27	65.9	79.18
10.	A & N	2.89	42.63	32.4	10.23	112.11	96.71	208.82
11.	Chandigarh	6.61	100.18	0	100.18	0	23.92	23.92

12.	D & N	1.05	15.51	1.8	13.71	17.14	20.57	37.71
13.	Lakshadweep	0.53	7.77	0	7.77	0	90.38	90.38
14.	Pondicherry	8.32	126.43	62.36	64.07	74.95	13.81	88.76
	Total	3572.6	52722.18	37567.25	15154.93	1056.03	592.35	1648.82
	Avg.	255.19	3765.87	2683.38	1082.495	75.43	42.31	114.77
	Sd	333.9497	4889.249	4207.332	1397.997	53.18344	30.54792	53.31011
	Cv	130.86	129.83	156.79	129.15	70.51	72.2	46.45

Source : Annual Reports, Ministry of Food Supplies, GoI, 1997-98.

grain production and the PDS of the states. Considering the criteria of nutritional norm of 440 gm per capita per day (160 kg per year), it is observed that average Indians will get as per this norm. The problem of foodgrain availability relates to inequality in income, population and foodgrain production of the states. Some states like A.P., Haryana, Karnataka, Punjab, Orissa, U.P. and West Bengal the annual production of the food grain as well as per capita availability was higher as compared to the rest of the states.

Table 4 indicates imbalances in the foodgrain production, total requirement and per capita availability in the states. The average foodgrain production and its availability of surplus states was 299.21 kg (per capita availability of local production 256.47 + PDS 42.54). Whereas it was 144.77 (Per capita availability of local production 75.43 kg + PDS 42.34 kg) in deficit foodgrain states as against all India availability of foodgrains 210.58 kg. Low per capita availability in the states created heavy burden on PDS.

CONCLUSION

Imbalances in India relates to natural resources of the region, development of agriculture, industry and social overheads. Despite intended plans and overall balanced growth strategy, the fruit of development has not been uniform in the states, i.e. planning has failed to achieve the balanced development in the country. Benefits of growth also did not trickle down as expected. The high growth of national income and per capita income unequally distributed among the states and socio-economic groups. Disparity in development can act as psychological disincentives to economic progress. The idea of regional development originated with Stalin in Russia and German bombardment on England. Backward states can be developed through the development of various sectors of the economy and government policies like PDS and also other developmental programmers. There are imbalances in socio-economic development of the economy like population growth, sectorial imbalances in production of foodgrains, prices, BPL population, and infrastructural rural facilities results into distortions in food security of the states. The per capita availability of the foodgrains depends on the total population, area under cultivation, foodgrain production and distribution of the states. So far as total requirement is concerned out of 32, 18 states are surplus in foodgrains. The average area and production of surplus foodgrains states was quite higher as compared to deficit foodgrain states. Simultaneously the average population in surplus foodgrain states is higher and BPL population is lower as compared to deficit foodgrain states. In order to achieve the balance between surplus and deficit foodgrain states, the government started effective implementation of PDS under uniform pricing policy. The surplus foodgrain production was transferred to deficit area. Hence the per capita availability of the deficit foodgrain states was 144.77 kg per year as against the requirement of 160 kg. The imbalances in the states have created heavy burden on PDS. The problem of imbalances should not be discarded in the globalized era.

References

GoI Report (1997-98), Ministry of Food Supply, New Delhi.

Statistical Outline of India, 2002-03.

Indian Economy Agenda for 21st Century (2002) (Ed.) Raj Kumar Sen and Biswajit Chatterjee, Deep and Deep Publications (P) Ltd., New Delhi.

Global Food Crisis and its Impact on India

D.K. Bhattacharya and Niyati Chakraborty

Food security refers to the availability of sufficient foodgrains at a reasonable price so that each and every individual in a country can access foodgrains as per his/her requirements. Even when the pace of economic development has been accelerating, the problem of food insecurity is still persisting in most underdeveloped countries of the world. Most of the African and South Asian countries still are not able to provide sufficient foodgrains to their people at an affordable price. The situation in India in this regards is not much better. Still a sizeable section of the Indian society is deprived of adequate quantity of foodgrains at a reasonable price. Nearly 20 per cent of the total population are living below poverty line and realing under absolute poverty. This figure itself explains the grim situation of food insecurity in India.

INTERNATIONAL SCENE

Global food prices witnessed a very sharp increase in 2007 and they are continuing to rise. Initially it was thought that the increase in food prices was a part of their cyclical nature, aggravated by the adverse impact of weather on production in some parts of the world. However, the continuous surge and the high level of global food prices seen so far in 2008 make it abundantly clear that the recent trend cannot be attributed to any volatility of international prices and there are fears that food prices may stay at these levels or may rise even more. This is causing worldwide concern. The severity of the problem can seen from the fact that food price based on IMF food price index increased by 95 per cent between April 2006 and April 2007 and by 45.6 per cent over the next 12 months. Food price inflation stared building up around August 2005, it reached the double digit level in mid-2006, crossed 20 per cent in September 2007 and accelerated to 43 per cent in March 2008. The rise in prices has been much higher for staple foods. Wheat, rice and maize prices in international markets in the first quarter of year 2008 were 107 per cent, 71 per cent and 29 per cent higher, respectively, as compared to the previous year and this came on top of substantial jump in 2007.

It seems that both the market fundamentals caused by shifts in demand and supply as well as speculative trade are jacking up food prices. The major factor on the supply side is the increase in the price of crude oil and other forms of energy that have an impact on the cost of agricultural production. Most of the farm operations are now mechanized and the increase in the price of oil naturally enhanced total cost. Energy prices are also a significant factor in the price of fertilizers. Urea prices in the international market were around 50 per cent higher in 2007. While these two factors and the rise in transportation charges have raised the cost of farm production, other events have directly led to food shortage. The diversion of maize and vegetable oils for ethanol and biodiesel production, severe drought in Australia in 2006 and 2007 and adverse weather in East Europe led to a significant reduction in grain production. The amount of corn used for ethanol in just the United States is around 5 per cent of global production and is equivalent to 40 per cent of global trade cereals. The use of one food crop as feedstock for biofuel has a spillover effect on others.

Some long term factors have also contributed to build up of food shortage. The terms of trade for food in most countries deteriorated between 1998 and 2003, discouraging private investments in farming. Due to low food prices and an increase in the export surplus in many developing countries in the post-WTO period, the priority to food self sufficiency and higher food production was considerably reduced by many countries and international development agencies. So far no concrete action is being contemplated at the international level to mitigate the severity of the food scarcity and rising prices.

Although this scarcity offering a good opportunity for speculative trade and global agri-business companies are making huge profits from the sale food to the poor and hungry in the third world. High prices are also very beneficial for food surplus countries like U.S.A., Canada and the European Union as they will then not have to dole out large subsidies to protect the income of their farmers. In contrast, according to the Food and Agricultural Organisation, as many as 37 developing countries are in food crisis and require external assistance. These include China and all countries of South Asia, except India.

Although grain production reached a new peak in 2007-08 and was more than 4 per cent higher than in 2006-07. But the medium-term trend by and large looks worrisome. Energy prices are continuing to rise, the natural resource base for food production is shrinking and climate is exacerbating production uncertainties. Developing countries need to understand the gravity of the crisis before it becomes too late.

IMPACT ON INDIA

Food inflation in India is below 10 per cent and much lower than what is being experienced globally. An important reason for this is that India has not passed on the increase in energy prices to the cost of agricultural production. The price of urea has not been raised for a couple of years and diesel prices have gone up by far less than in global markets. The minimum support prices of wheat and paddy were raised by around 20 per cent in 2007 and that for wheat by 18 per cent in 2008, increases which have to be reflected in wholesale and retail prices. What is causing worry in India is that despite strong measures taken to insulate the domestic market from global effects may witness high inflation in the future.

Although India's population is growing by 1.44 per cent per year and per capita food demand is also increasing. But the growth in cereal and pulse production is not keeping pace with the rise in population. The soaring global food prices will adversely impact government finances in India and Pakistan and may result in bloating of their deficits by over 5 per cent of the G.D.P. India with revenue at less than 20 per cent of their G.D.P. have put these economies in a precarious position of large deficits and narrow underlying revenue bases as reported by Standard and Poors report. The other main pressure points would be on fiscal balances, which would likely be from both the expenditure and revenue side.

The situation in India regarding food security is not much better. Still a sizeable section of the Indian society is deprived of adequate quantity of foodgrains at a reasonable price. Nearly 20 per cent of total population (more than 20 crores of the total population) are living below poverty line and this figure itself explains the grim situation of food insecurity in India.

Now question arises here that what should India do? Does farm loan waiving policy of the government mean an end to food insecurity problem? Is there need to adopt 2nd green revolution to increase food production? Or it is technological fatigue or policy failure? Thus we have to analyse all these aspects in detail.

(A) Government Policy of Waiving Farm Loans

During the recent past, suicides by the farmers owing to their debt burden (specially in Vidharva regions of Maharashtra and some backward regions in Andhra Pradesh) has aroused hot debate and discussions in the Parliament and among informed academicians. Taking into account UPA Government initiated a policy measures to waive the farm loans to end the debt-trap of the farmers and ensuring them food security. In 2008-09 budget speech, Indian Finance Minister P. Chidambram announced the farm loan waiver scheme for small and marginal farmers who were in acute economic distress due to heavy pressure of debt burden. This policy decision of the government was supposed to give relief to nearly four crore farmers at an estimated government outlay of Rs. 60,000 crores.

However, this farm loan waiver scheme has been criticized by politicians and academicians. Specially the people with leftist and rightist blend of mind have criticized on its different points. According to them, firstly, this policy may not end the debt-trap to the farmers because the loans taken from non-institutional sources are not included into the waiver scheme, as money owned to private lenders accounts for around 70 per cent of the total debts of the farmers. Thus, substantial position of the debt amount will not be waived off, as this policy is only focusing on the institutional sources of loans. Secondly, the definition of small and marginal farmers has to be different for the irrigated and non-irrigated (dry farming) areas because farmer's income who owns 4 to 5 hectares of land in the dry farming areas is often less than of those owing even less than a hectare of land in irrigated (double crop) areas. Thirdly, there is no relief for the farmers who are working in the informal sector. This policy did not indicate any provision in the budgetary allocation, nor was there any explanation on resource mobilization for the one time waiver. So this policy thus ignored about 42.3 per cent farmers in the informal sectors who pay high rate of interest to money lenders as debtors to them. Fourthly, farm loan waiver scheme would not end farmers indebtness, because farmers would fall back into debt-trap again as it is a one time waiver, what happens tomorrow? They will be thrown from one round of indebtness to another.

Now question arises here that whether this scheme would end the problem of the food crisis. As we know, nearly 20 per cent of the total population is living below poverty line and it is deprived of even two square meals a day. Although government expects that this waiving policy of farm loans would certainly help these sections in ensuring minimum quantity of foods for consumption. However, merely by offering a one-time loan waiver, we cannot expect the small and marginal holders to achieve riddance of their problems of poverty and food scarcity emanating from low productivity and low level of income. They need to be constantly and consistently helped by the way of infrastructural facilities besides an affordable farming technology. Farmers should get remunerative price from their produce. This can be possible if agricultural marketing system is strengthened. Another step is to consider a change in the definition of small and marginal farmers with regard to irrigated and non-irrigated areas. Also assistance should be given to the farmers who have taken loans from non-institutional sources. Thus even though the loan waiving policy of the government is an important step, it is certainly not sufficient to end the problem of food scarcity in India.

(B) Need of 2nd Green Revolution

The adoption of Green Revolution Policy succeeded in a record grain output of 131 million tons in 1978-79. Yield per unit of farm land improved by more than 30 per cent between 1947 and 1979. The crop area under HYV varieties grew from 7 per cent to 22 per cent of the total cultivated area during the 10 years of the Ist Green Revolution. More than 70 per cent of the wheat crop area, 35 per cent of the rice crop area and 20 per cent of the millet and corn crop area used the HYV seeds. Due to these achievements of Green Revolution, India became world's biggest agricultural producers. No other country in the world which attempted the Green Revolution recorded such level of success. India also became an exporter of foodgrains. India became most successful rice producers and is now a major rice exporter, shipping nearly 4.5 million tonnes in 2006. India saw annual wheat production rise from 10 million tonnes in 1960s to 73 million tonnes in 2006.

The impact of 1st Green Revolution can be seen to limited areas. Only rich states like Punjab, Haryana, Gujarat, Maharashtra and other few states have been benefited, but its impact on other states, like Orissa, Assam, Bihar, Madhya Pradesh and other poor States cannot be seen. These States are still found to be backward in agriculture production. These

States could not gain the benefit of this policy, may be due to political discrimination done by central government. The transition from traditional agricultural in which inputs were generated on-farm to Green Revolution agriculture which required the purchase of inputs, lead to the widespread establishment of rural credit institutions. Smaller farmers often went into debt, which in many cases result in a loss of their farmland. Because wealthier farmers had better access to credit and land, the Green Revolution increased class disparities. Because some regions were able to adopt Green Revolution agriculture more readily than others, inter-regional economic disparities increased as well. Many small farmers are hurt by the dropping prices resulting from increased production overall.

New economic difficulties of small holder farmers and landless farm workers led to increased rural urban migration. The increase in food production led to a cheaper food for urban dwellers, and the increase in urban population increased the potential for industrialization. India paid back all loans it had taken from the World Bank and its affiliates for the purpose of Green Revolution. This improved creditworthiness in the eyes of the lending agencies. Some developed countries, specially Canada, which were facing a shortage in agricultural labour, were so impressed by the India's Green Revolution that they asked the Indian government to supply them with farmers experienced in the methods of Green Revolution. Green Revolution created plenty of jobs not only for agricultural workers but also industrial workers by the creation of lateral facilities such as factories and hydroelectric power stations in different places. Green Revolution was a product of globalization as evidenced in the creation of international agricultural research centres, that shared information with foreign institutions. The inputs required in Green Revolution agriculture created new markets for seed and chemical corporations.

In fact, these are different practico-theoretical implications of Green Revolution in India but the major theme of the revolution is that it has not been considered at the macro level and hence has many limitations. Even then Green Revolution has shown many good results to improve the productivity in rice and wheat in India and this country became self-sufficient in food production. Seeing its results some of the prominent economists suggested that country needs 2nd Green Revolution specially keeping in mind to those backward States which needs strong support of the central government for the success of 2nd Green Revolution It may definitely benefit to these States to increase their productivity in agriculture sector. Let the 2nd Green Revolution start from Eastern sectors of the country so that they can get more benefits, which they could not get in previous Green Revolution due to many political reasons.

(C) Technology Fatigue or Policy Fatigue?

It comes into view from the deliberations at the 53rd meeting of the National Development Council and other documents prepared for the 11th Plan focusing on agriculture, that there is a technology fatigue, which needs to be addressed in order to increase the production of foodgrains and overall growth of agriculture. Though the situation assessment survey (SAS) carried out on various aspects of farming by the ministry of agriculture clearly showed that over 40 per cent of farmers are willing to get out of farming because it had become non-viable, no-body seems to have highlighted the cost and price related issues in the meeting. Is it correct to say that technology fatigue is the reason for poor performance of agriculture? Can we achieve a 4 per cent growth rate in agriculture during the 11th Plan period by addressing the technology issue?

Even if one accepts the view of technology fatigue, it is not a new phenomenon, not common to all crops and all regions. Technology fatigue has existed in certain crops in India for many years now and it was never an issue earlier. We have been importing large quantities of pulses from various countries over many years because there is an absolute "technology failure" (not fatigue) in pulse crops. Despite the fact that we know that there is an increasing demand for pulses, we have not tackled this issue so far. Is it not policy fatigue? Stagnation in productivity crops, the ratio became less than one in crops like cotton, paddy, sugarcane and groundnut. This is the result of policy fatigue because prices for different crops were not announced in consonance with the cost of cultivation.

Besides price policy fatigue the sector has been encountering quite a few policy-related problems that have hampered its growth over the last 10 years. Despite knowing that there is a close complementarity between public and private investment in agriculture policy-makers somehow did not make concerted efforts to step up public investment in agriculture. This reduction in public investment in agriculture is also considered to be one of the reasons for poor performance of agriculture in recent years. Another example of policy fatigue is related to institutional credit which is very essential for agricultureal development. In spite of realising its importance, there has been a significant reduction in the growth of institutional credit to agriculture during the post reform period. Non-availability of institutional, credit in time has forced farmers to rely on non-institutional sources to meet their credit requirements for crop cultivation in most places in India. Since the rate of interest charged by the money lenders is exorbitant and the returns from crop cultivation are also very low, farmers were unable to repay loans in time and find themselves into debt-trap. In spite of knowing these current weaknesses in agriculture, our planning commission has fixed target of 4 per cent growth rate for the 11th plan period. This is going to be a herculian task for policy-makers in Planning Commission and ministry of agriculture.

CONCLUSION

In this paper, the various factors that have been tried to identify as responsible for the current global crisis in the availability of food and for the rise in prices of cereals. It has been argued that the crisis is different from the one in 1960s and 1970s in that there is now likely to be a permanent upward shift in real prices. It is important that developing countries place renewed emphasis on self-sufficiency to ensure food security, since they are unlikely to be able to afford expensive food imports.

The soaring global food prices will adversely impact government finances in countries like India and Pakistan and may result in bloating of their deficits by over 5 per cent of the GDP, according to an S & P report. India, Pakistan and Egypt would be hardest hit by the rise in food costs, with a general government deficits 5.9 per cent, 6.5 per cent and 6.9 per cent of GDP respectively, projected for 2008-09. Even developed countries are vulnerable to food price inflation and political instability if there is a mismatch between higher revenues from food exports or domestic supply. The other main pressure points would be on fiscal balances, which would likely be from both the expenditure and the revenue side.

Governments around the world will need to bring about significant investment in agriculture and infrastructure to address the problem long-term, which, for the low-income savings, could mean more resource to borrowing or increase in aid. Russian President has blamed the 'egoistic' policies of the U.S. for dragging the global economy into crisis and alleged that due to American greed 'most people on the planet have become poorer'. He slammed Washington for pursuing a version of global free trade, tailored to the interests of U.S. alone, which has resulted in a spreading financial meltdown and food shortages in many parts of the world. It is the gap between the U.S. formal role in the world economy and its actual capabilities that was a key reason for the current crisis.

References

A. Narayan Moorthy, Deceletation in Agricultural Growth—Technology Fatigue or Policy Fatigue? *Economic and Political Weekly*, June 23, 2007, pp. 2375-77.

Bala Sahib Vikhe Patil, 'Agricultural Indebtness: Crisis and Revival', *Economic and Political Weekly*, February 2, 2008, pp. 47-52.

Bidyadhar Majhi, 'Food Security in India *vis-a-vis* the policy of waving Farm Loans', *Southern Economists*, 15 January 2009, pp. 42-44.

BrownLester, R., 'The Next Crisis Food', *Foreign Policy*, No. 13 (Winter) 1975.

GoI (1991), "Cost of Cultivation of Principal Crops in India", Ministry of Agriculture, Govt. of India, New Delhi.

Johnson, D. Gale, "Food Security and World Trade Prospects", *American Journal of Agricultural Economics*, 80(5), 1998 November, pp. 941-47.

M. Raghavan, 'Changing Pattern of Input use and Cost of Cultivation', *Economic and Political Weekly*, 28 July, 2008, pp. 123-29.

Planning Commission (May 2007), Agricultural Strategy for Eleventh Plan: Some Critical Issues: Planning Commission, Govt. of India, New Delhi.

Sujit Kumar Chaudhary, 'Second Green Revolution'—Need to Implement at Macro Level, *Civil Services Chronical*, June 2008, pp. 28-30.

Swaminathan, M.S., "Community led Approaches to Ending Food Insecurity and Poverty", M/s Swaminathan Research Foundation (2000).

Report, CACP (various issues), Report of the Commission for Agricultural Costs and Prices, Ministry of Agriculture, Govt. of India, New Delhi.

News Reports, News Reports from Different News Papers Published during 2007 and 2008.

24

Who Does the Public Distribution System Target?

KAMINI JHA

INTRODUCTION

The second world war had compelled the then British Government to introduce the first structured Public Distribution System of cereals in India through the rationing system, with the sale of a fixed quantity of ration to card holders in certain selected cities. Firstly, it was started in Bombay in 1939 and by 1946, 771 cities were covered. With the end of the Second World War India like other countries decided to close the programme. But on attaining independence India reintroduced the rationing system in 1950. The food policy committee under the chairmanship of Sir Purushottam Das Thakur in 1947 recommended the continuance of the old system. Food Corporation of India and Agriculture Price Commission was set-up to provide price support to cultivators by purchasing foodgrains from them on fixed price and to move the grains from surplus area to deficit area. By the end of First Five Year Plan PDS had changed from the typical retaining system to a social safety system. In short, it can be said that the PDS as an instrument of government to moderate market price and to ensure food security at the household level, involved management and maintenance of supply and distribution of essential commodities such as wheat, rice, sugar, edible oil, kerosene oil, etc. at affordable price to the public even in the interior areas through various fair price shops. However, the TDPS as it now stands has been widely criticized for its failure to reserve the population below poverty line, its urban and rural bias both as well as lack of transparency therein realizing this, the central government proposed to streamline by issuing special ration card to families BPL and selling essential commodities to them, at specially subsidized prices with monitoring the delivery system. Besides providing foodgrains to target families the government also proposed to extend this facility to the beneficiaries under the various employment schemes.

PUBLIC DISTRIBUTION SYSTEM

Public Distribution System has immense importance in providing food security to the weaker section of society. But it was also realized that if PDS is not targeted it will fail in its purpose. Hence the United Front Government adopted a new scheme The Targeted Distribution Scheme in February 1997, this scheme became operational on June 1, 1997 and mainly aimed at overcoming the deficiencies of the PDS which had failed in its goal to make food available to the poor at affordable rates. The Targeted Public Distribution System has been designed to provide food security especially to those below the poverty line on the basis of subsidized foodgrain prices. In India it operates through a network of ration shops and fair price shops. The Targeted Public Distribution system is a poverty eradication programme and in a poverty stricken country like India it has immense potential and possibility. The aim of the Targeted Public Distribution System (TPDS) is to raise the quality of the people below the poverty line by upgrading their nutritional status through the supply of essential consumer goods at cheap and subsidized prices. Essential commodities such as wheat, rice, etc. are distributed through a network of ration and fair price shops the principal agency providing foodgrains to these fair price shops is the Food Corporation of India which undertakes purchase of surplus foodgrains from the farmers and distributes these foodgrains to consumers through different fair price shops across the country at a uniform price level fixed by the Government of India.

The allocation is made to various states on the basis of the population below the poverty line, the national co-operative consumers federation Ltd. is the central agency nominated for the distribution of all commodities.

The beneficiaries of the Targeted Public Distribution System would be the poor and vulnerable section of the society living below the poverty line. It will largely include landless agricultural labourers, marginal farmers, rural artisans, craftsmen, etc. would also encompass slum dwellers and persons earning their livelihood on a daily basis like rickshaw puller, fruit and flower seller on the pavement in the urban areas. It does not discriminate among the poor when providing help, on the basis of their caste class or religion, its only aim is to help the poorest of the poor.

FOOD SECURITY AND TARGETED PUBLIC DISTRIBUTION SYSTEM

Food is a basic necessity without which survival is not possible. India suffers from inequality of income the 'haves', the rich class enjoys all kind of luxuries whereas the 'have nots' the poor find it difficult to have two square meals. In India the food problem has been viewed primarily as that of ensuring a certain minimum supply of foodgrains at reasonable prices particularly to the poor. Failure to ensure this minimum supply has serious consequences on the health and efficiency of the general mass. The government thus started the Public Distribution System to restrict urban bias to food distribution, it later started the TPDS which not only provided food security to the poor but at the same time reduced food subsidy and hence the budgetary deficit of the government. It issues special ration cards to families below poverty line and provides essential commodities to them at subsidized rates with better monitoring of the delivery system. Even without leakages and even when the poor only get subsidies it will require 45 thousand crores of rupees per year if all the poor are to be lifted above the poverty line. As the subsidy burden falls on the government and as it has increased considerably over the years it has led to the argument for 'targeting' subsidies only to the vulnerable and poor sections of the population. The issue of targeting has to be decided on two fronts—

1. Persons needing food subsidy and therefore to be targeted have to be identified.
2. Persons not belonging to the above group have to be eliminated from the system.

Since the inception of planning considerable progress has been made establishing a National food Security System. Through a lot more needs to be done to develop it into an adequate system.

The TPDS as practiced in India involves a sub-division of the whole population in two sections:

Below Poverty Line (BPL) and Above Poverty Line (APL), the policy is that BPL families receives 10 kilos of foodgrains per month at subsidized price while APL families receives a variable quantity for a higher price. Its other essential features were as follows:

1. States were to identify families BPL. The maximum income level for the population to be covered under PL was kept at 15,000 per annum.
2. As against the ruling issue price of Rs 4.02 per kg for wheat in 1997, BPL consumer were to be provided wheat at subsidized price of Rs 2.50 per kg.

In the early 1999 a further price rise of APL foodgrains was introduced in order to reduce the subsidy for APL families. This policy implies not only a reallocation of foodgrains between BPL and APL families but also a reallocation of foodgrains between the various states within India. The new allotment of foodgrains to the states is based on the number of households below the poverty line. According to the initial plan the allotment of foodgrains to all states was reduced. However in some cases the actual supply increased which was intended. Bihar for instance lifted less than a quarter of the allotted quantity in 1995-96.

Under the new scheme it lifts much more since foodgrains have become cheaper. Some states with high levels of poverty but relatively little food distribution prior to the TDPS, benefits from the new policy. While other states with lower levels of poverty and higher levels of PDS in the past are bound to receive less foodgrains. It has been acknowledged that a substantial percentage of over 80 lakh Red cards distributed in Bihar was cornered by those who did not qualify in the BPL category while a matching number of deserving household found themselves denied. Officially it has been recognized that 37,741 such cards were issued to such persons other than the surveyed BPL households. However, the actual number of such cards is stated to be much higher.

Difficulty

Targeting the poor under TDPS is a difficult task. As correctly pointed out by Tamarajakshi it is one thing to estimate the number of poor on an ex-post basis from the surveys of consumers expenditure and an assured poverty household but it is an entirely different things to identify the poor on the basis of poverty line like APL and BPL. Moreover, the chances of corruption and leakages in the new TDS are many. The temptation for many people falling under the category of non-poor to get themselves classified as APL and BPL consumers. To achieve this purpose they will not hesitate to grease the various palms at regional card offices. Many shopkeepers may also succeed in diverting supplies meant for BPL consumers to the open market and sell grains at such higher prices prevailing there pocketing the differences.

The delivery system in Bihar is very corrupt, dealership of PDS commodities as well as membership of vigilance committees are seen as positions in which it is easy to earn an illegal income. The procedure to appoint people to appoint people to these posts is fully politicized members of the legislative assembly or other politicians are appointed ex-officio or make recommendations. As a result, it is mainly local level politicians or clients of MLA who are appointed. Secondly, the Bihar state food and civil supplies corporation which is the only PDS wholesale agent does not have the infrastructure to distribute the foodgrains properly. For example in the whole district of Gumla there are only 8 godowns for 18 blocks and the nearest gowdown is at padra was 12 kms away from the depot at Ranchi.

Apart from lack of warehouse the corporation is in an extremely poor financial shape. There is no working capital to purchase the PDS commodities from FCI, it is the PDS dealers who have to advance money every month the mobile van meant to bring the foodgrains from the godowns to the shops are all in need of repairs or there is no driver and money for fuel, there are districts in which the depot manager and other corporation staff members have not received salaries for 12 to 18 months or longer, malpractice such as illegal sales of the commodities and misappropriation of money occur regularly.

Though the major inconveniences and difficulties for the beneficiaries do not arise at the shop level, yet in his own way the dealer can act to lessen the inconvenience to the beneficiaries. He should not keep back information from the customers there should be transparency in his dealings with the people and he should not adopt unfair means to earn profits. He should understand that it is the poor who are really in need of subsidized food items for their existence and should prefer them in his dealings some other necessary items like edible oils should be made available to the consumers. He should also be able to store the goods properly.

It is an irony that in a country like India where majority of the people are poor poverty alleviation measures lack the drive, the administrative dedication that is called for. This was evident by the casual approach adopted in the manner of supply of goods for the fair price shops. India cannot hope to stand up to face the world's competition if majority of its people go without basic nutritional requirements with the achievements of self-sufficiency in food production, the TPDS can act as an effective agent of food security for the poor masses, but only if it is efficiently administered. In the 1990's the public distribution system has come under increasing critique. The system is deemed to be costly as well as insufficiently capable to address the issue of food security. There are considerable leakages in Public Distribution System. Most of the time it fails to reach the real beneficiaries, the cardholders because it gets lost, stolen or sold illegally to others. Another point of critique is related to the persistence of malnutrition. Despite the huge subsidy and the large scale of this intervention the food security of many vulnerable household is still marginal or insufficient, distribution to the states has not been proportionate to the number of poor people in each state and within states the available supplies have not gravitated in favour of the poor. As the number of households below poverty line grew from 1.40 crores in 1991 to 1.56 crore in 1995 the actual quantum of subsidized foodgrains reaching them is estimated to have declined owing to the many ills plaguing the PDS. All this only added to the feeling that drastic measures were needed.

In general Targeted Public Distribution System has been widely criticized for its failure the problems of TPDS are as follows :

1. to find the population BPL it was proposed to adopt the methodology of expert group headed by late professor Lakrawala which is controversial. According to this committee 35.97 per cent of the country is BPL, whereas according to planning committee it is only 18.17 per cent,
2. under TPDS only wheat and rice is distributed whereas maize and millet is not which is low price and affordable for them,
3. under TPDS only 10 kg of cereals is distributed among the needy and the rest they have to buy from the open market at high prices,
4. lack of fund and purchasing power leads to the BPL family not able to purchase the amount of 10 kg together,
5. under TPDS, fine rice is not distributed from fair price shops,

6. according to late professor Lakrawala Committee of 1993-94 about 75 per cent of the poor section reside in villages whereas fair price shops are often seen in urbanized areas, and
7. people face difficulties from administration in receiving red cards.

Government is very keen that the foodgrains supplied at subsidized rates reach the real beneficiaries and not diverted to the open market for which, a proper monitoring of the targeted public distribution should be maintained in this sphere, a checklist pertaining to inspection should be drawn up, right from the district magistrate to supply inspector, remedial action should be provided when shortcoming emerge or noticed at the time of inspection card holders should be invited at the shop during inspection to ascertain their views about functioning of TPDS at the district level too, weekly review meetings on TPDS should be held by the district magistrate and shortcomings should be brought to notice of higher authorities. If steps are taken timely and remedial measures implemented the TPDS can be a beneficial scheme which would be a great asset for the socio-economic development of Bihar.

Strengthening Public Distribution System

SHAILESH KUMAR

The Role of the Public Distribution System (PDS) has undergone change during the last four decades. Earlier, the PDS was viewed as a mechanism to mitigate misery caused by shortages. At present, it is considered to be a conduit to achieve national objectives like growth with stability, social justice and improvement in the consumption standards of the vulnerable sections of society. The PDS has emerged as an anti-inflationary measure in a climate of uncertainty of foodgrain output.

While the Central Government has taken up the responsibility of procuring, storing, allocating and transporting foodgrains to godowns for the PDS, the state governments and the Union Territory administrations have to ensure uninterrupted supply of essential items to consumers through a network of fair price shops.

It is the responsibility of the Government to ensure reasonable price stability in the interest of the nation, particularly for the benefit of the weaker sections. The Government has been trying to achieve this objective through the instruments of direct subsidies or price controls. These measures are generally resented to by businessmen as they fear that they would deprive them of a fair return on investment. How to help the weaker sections without harming the producers and traders is the dilemma facing the Government.

It is in this context that the Programme Evaluation Organisation (PEO) of the Planning Commission had suggested, in its Study made in 1985, a dual pricing policy in respect of all commodities made available through fair price shops. Most prestigious companies of the day do not utilise their technologies and managerial skills towards provision of low cost product or service to the society. It should therefore be made obligatory on the part of a company to produce at least one low cost brand.

The total foodgrain output may be of the order of 173 million tonnes during the current year, 1989-90, as against 170 million tonnes in 1988-89. Yet, the level of stock of foodgrain has been coming down in recent years. In March 1984, the Government expressed its desire to maintain a buffer stock of 10 million tonnes. This buffer stock would be over and above the operational stocks which may range between 11.4 million tonnes on July 1 to 6.5 million tonnes on April 1. Of course, the averse situation in respect of food stocks is mainly due to reduced procurement (13.42 million tonnes) and foodgrain output (138.41 million tonnes) in 1987-88.

PRESENT POSITION

A disturbing development in recent years has been the dwindling buffer stock which stood at 23.6 million tonnes at the end of 1986. This declined to 21 million tonnes by July 1987 and further to 14.14 million tonnes by December-end 1987. By mid-March 1988, it further declined to 9.18 million tonnes. Under the present circumstances, buffer stock falling below 10 million tonnes should be viewed with alarm.

The declining trend in buffer stock is not only due to higher off-take of foodgrains from the PDS, but equally due to fall in procurement of foodgrains by the public sector agencies. The drought conditions in 1987 too contributed to this worsening situation. It may however be noted that the country is able to withstand a drought without depending upon food imports only because of buffer stock which provides a cushion between good and bad years.

The country is now having an enlarged PDS which caters to the needs of the population, especially those living in rural, backward, tribal and remote areas. The number of fair price shops in the country steadily increased from 2.39 lakhs in 1979 to 3.40 lakhs at present. About 80 per cent of these are in rural areas.

Transporting foodgrain to hilly, tribal and inaccessible areas is a difficult task. The PDS has to depend on mobile fair price shops to serve these areas. The Central Government has been providing financial assistance to states to purchase vans for the PDS. To ensure fair quality of items supplied through PDS, a joint inspection system for wheat, rice and sugar at the time of lifting from Food Corporation of India has been evolved.

In areas having humid climate, the Central Government, by entirely subsidising packaging, has ensured supply of iodised salt and levy sugar in small packs. In recent years, the PDS has been viewed as an instrument of poverty alleviation. Thus, to those living in integrated tribal development project areas, wheat and rice are supplied at a specially subsidised rate. Also, the Government has been organising training programmes for the personnel associated with PDS with a view to upgrading their managerial skills and reorienting their attitudes.

The performance of PDS has not been uniform throughout the country. In some states, the administration has been weak, corrupt and unresponsive to public needs. In these states, the deficiencies noticed include huge shortages in stocks particularly in respect of palmolein, rice, sugar and kerosene and also fake supply entries in family cards with a view to diverting commodities for sale to the open market.

SUGGESTIONS

In a study (sponsored by the Ministry of Food and Civil Supplies) conducted by the Indian Institute of Public Administration, New Delhi in 1987, it has been pointed out that the PDS becomes less effective because of seasonal pattern of off-take in some of the states. There are month to month fluctuations in PDS off-take. According to the study, the number of fair price shops, their location, periodicity of permitted purchases, behaviour of the dealer, long queues, unsatisfactory quality and fear of incorrect weighing erode the credibility of the PDS. To make PDS popular, the study suggested that it should cover coarse grains and supply them with a price advantage when compared to the market.

The PEO study in 1985 relating to 11 commodities pointed out that the PDS suffers from irregular supply and poor quality of commodities made available through fair price shops. In case almost all the commodities the incidence of not lifting of sanctioned quotas by fair price shopkeepers was observed to be higher in rural as compared to urban areas. As a result of poor quality especially in respect of rice and wheat, there has been low off-take of these cereals from fair price shops by beneficiary households.

The study also revealed that easy availability in the market of some commodities like rapeseed oil, wheat flour, palm oil, rice and wheat is another reason for not lifting these commodities especially in rural areas.

The study further revealed considerable delay in supplying commodities to shopkeepers. It observed that 49 per cent of the total selected shopkeepers has to make more than one visit per month for lifting the monthly quota of different commodities. Most of them felt that running of fair price shops was not profitable. The reasons given for this include low rate of commission, high cost of overheads, underweighing at the warehouse supply points and poor quality of commodities supplied leading to unsold stocks.

The study however pointed out that the weakness and deficiencies of the PDS do not consist in either the lack of sufficient coverage or want of necessary administrative machinery but in certain inadequacies in its operational aspects and the degree of coordination required.

RURAL COOPERATIVES

It is true that 80 per cent of fair price shops are in rural areas. However, the working of PDS in these areas is far from satisfactory, particularly in remote and inaccessible areas. As a result of the mischief played by middlemen, there has been diversion of good quality items to open market, while fair price shops keep poor quality foodgrains and other items.

We have to assign an enlarged role to the rural consumer cooperatives. Consumer goods routed through cooperatives are at present valued at Rs. 3,000 crores a year, sales being accounted for equally by the rural and urban cooperatives. Consumer cooperatives cover about 40 per cent of the fair price shops. Consumer cooperatives handle a number of items like foodgrains, groceries, oil, textiles, cosmetics, toiletories, household/electrical/electronic travel goods, vegetables, medicines, cooking gas, petrol/diesel, novelties, footwear and stationery. However, the consumer cooperative movement is weak in the North Eastern States, Rajasthan and Jammu & Kashmir.

The primary agricultural service cooperative face a number of problems: the range of articles being offered for sale is minimum the supply line is often irregular and counter service remains poor. They do not get proper support from higher tier organizations in respect of bulk procurement, packaging and transportation, easy credit and convenient deliveries. There is therefore need for strengthening the village level cooperative shops by increasing the range of articles for sale in order to meet most of the needs of an average rural household, ensuring timely, uninterrupted and cost effective supplies and by integrating the consumer business of the primary agricultural service cooperatives with the other agriculture-related operations of credit, farm input supplies, extension, storage and marketing of agricultural produce.

It is also necessary to do away with multiplicity of organizations in the wholesale business, and multiplicity has often resulted in overlapping of functions, failure to derive the economies of scale and higher administrative and related operating costs. A few measures may be taken to improve the motivation of the personnel manning village level cooperatives.

STRENGTHENING PDS

The PDS is a consumer-oriented system and as such it cannot be run successfully unless the public is involved in vigilance work at the grassroots. Some states have not shown positive interest in the constitution of watchdog panels at the shop level.

The PDS is also greatly handicapped by the presence of bogus ration cards. In some states, the menace of bogus cards has been eliminated to a large extent, by insisting on two attested photographs—one for pasting on the ration card and other for keeping in government records.

The PEO study made certain suggestions for improving the efficiency and performance of the PDS. These include:

1. The food and civil supplies departments in the states should not take staff on deputation from other departments. The association of revenue officials with the implementation of the programme should be eschewed;
2. Computerization of the distribution mechanism at the all-India and state levels could be resorted to minimise delay and to make essential commodities available to fair price shops in time and at prescribed frequencies;
3. Steps should be taken to ensure that the commodities made available through fair price shops are of clean and of good quality; and
4. All village panchayats should have powers and authority to check and supervise the working of air price shops in the respective jurisdiction.

The PDS should be strengthened not only to ensure price stability in respect of essential commodities, but to mitigate the misery of the vast masses below the poverty line. The PDS should form an integral part of the anti-poverty drive.

Public Distribution System and Panchayati Raj Institutions

SAROJ KUMAR

THE INDIAN PUBLIC DISTRIBUTION SYSTEM

The rural Indian spend 64 per cent of its budget on food. Food share is an inverse indicator of welfare (e.g. Deaton, 1997): it follows that food security should be a major focus of policies concerned with well-being in this society. In terms of both coverage and public expenditure, the most important food safety net is the Public Distribution System. Of the 200 million tonnes of food grains produced in 1999-2000, about 29 million were produced by the government under PDS, which now support the largest network of "fair price shops" in the world. (4,58,499 shops in 1999). These provides rice, wheat, sugar, edible oil, soft cake and kerosene oil at subsidized prices. The PDS is managed by state governments. The central government based on the population state and its share of below poverty line households and above poverty line.

The institutional structure of the Panchayati Raj, the local self-government system in India, and the implementation of rural development programmes in the context of a participatory approach have been examined in this paper. Although the Panchayati Raj institutions have existed for many years, owing to inherent weaknesses in the systems they were not very effective in the implementation of rural development programmes. Through constitutional amendments a third tier of local self-government has been set-up and steps have been taken to remove the inherent shortcomings of the system. It is expected that the new Panchayati system should now provide the much needed non-bureaucratic institutional support to rural development programmes. With a more aware rural population, the prospects for success are perhaps brighter. The functioning of the new decentralized system has been examined with three case studies concerning rural roads planning and their implementation. Policy conclusions are drawn based on a general analysis of the new set-up, past experience and the findings from the three case studies.

INTRODUCTION

This paper examines the institutional structure and the implementation of rural development programmes in the context of participatory approaches in a decentralized framework. The description of the structure is accompanied by detailed case studies of rural roads planning. The paper is divided into three sections. The first sets out a brief background of decentralized development efforts in India and the considerable attempts at reorganizing the system in the late 1980s and early 1990s. It then sets out the institutional framework of implementation, particularly around and after the Seventy-second and Seventy-third Amendment of the Constitution of India on Panchayati Raj (setting up a "third" tier of local self-government). The second section gives three case studies of rural roads planning and development. The first is a study of a successful project in Ahmedabad district of Gujarat.

The second relates to a plan for the development of a road network in a watershed development project in India's first major cooperative sugar factory area in western India. The third is the Marathwada study of local planning in Aurangabad district, which has as yet not taken off. The third section draws policy conclusions for institutional development to enhance the effectiveness of participatory approaches to rural development in India. The research is largely based on secondary data. The three case studies were developed by field visits followed by data collection by the author and selected field collaborators. Data and reports from the Rural Development Division of the Planning Commission gave an up-to-date assessment of the countrywide situation. The concluding section is based on these sources and the author's own experience.

SOURCES OF DATA AND METHODOLOGY

Historical Background

Recognizing the importance of democratic institutions at the grass-roots level, the Indian Constitution laid down in Article 40 of Part IV of the Directive Principles of State Policy that the state would take steps to organize village panchayats and endow them with such powers and authority as might be necessary to enable them to function as units of self-government. The Panchayati Raj institutions became a state subject under the Constitution. The Balwant Rai Mehta Committee was appointed in 1957 to study the Community Development and National Extension Service programmes, especially from the point of view of assessing the extent of popular participation, and to recommend the creation of institutions through which such participation could be achieved. The Committee recommended the constitution of statutory elected local bodies with the necessary resources, power and authority devolved to them and a decentralized administrative system working under their control. It also recommended that the basic unit of democratic decentralization should be located at the block/samiti level. The Committee envisaged directly elected panchayats for a village or group of villages, an executive body called Panchayat Samiti for a block with directly elected and co-opted members, and an advisory body called Zila Parishad at the district level constituted mainly through ex-officio members from the lower tier and others with the district chief as Chairman. The National Development Council affirmed the objective of democratic decentralization. This was the genesis of the Panchayati Raj system and when ushering it in, Nehru described it as "the most revolutionary and historical step in the context of New India". In 1972, the Planning Commission advised the state governments to set-up state planning boards as apex planning bodies with the Chief Minister as the Chairman and the Finance Minister, Planning Minister, and technical experts representing various departments and disciplines as members. The plans envisaged the decentralization of the planning process to districts and ultimately to the block level. District planning bodies were constituted in all the states except Tripura and Arunachal Pradesh. However, the district planning machinery has not really started functioning in some states. The current status is as follows:

The Committee envisaged directly elected panchayats for a village or group of villages, an executive body called Panchayat Samiti for a block with directly elected and co-opted members, and an advisory body called Zila Parishad at the district level constituted mainly through ex-officio members from the lower tier and others with the district chief as Chairman. The National Development Council affirmed the objective of democratic decentralization. This was the genesis of the Panchayati Raj system and when ushering it in, Nehru described it as "the most revolutionary and historical step in the context of New India". In 1972, the Planning Commission advised the state governments to set up state planning boards as apex planning bodies with the Chief Minister as the Chairman and the Finance Minister, Planning Minister, and technical experts representing various departments and disciplines as members. The plans envisaged the decentralization of the planning process to districts and ultimately to the block level. District planning bodies were constituted in all the states except Tripura and Arunachal Pradesh.

Ferment in the 1980s

A number of committees and study groups reviewed the situation and made recommendations to strengthen the systems of integrated decentralized planning. The Ashok Mehta Committee reviewed the situation in 1978, recommending an institutional design for the Panchayati Raj in the light of the developmental thrust and technical expertise required for the planning and implementation of rural development programmes. Working groups were appointed by the Planning Commission. The Working Group on Block Level Planning headed by Professor M.L. Dantwala in November 1977, and the Working Group on District Planning headed by Dr. C.H. Hanumantha Rao, Member of the Planning Commission in September 1982, studied various aspects of decentralized planning at the district and block levels. Both Working Groups recommended that the basic decentralized planning function had to be at the district level. The Working Group on District Planning recommended that:

For decentralized planning to make headway, institutional mechanisms had to be more broad-based with the active involvement of local representatives and endowed with a greater degree of autonomy in local decision-making.

Panchayati Raj institutions and other local government institutions should play a crucial role in the district planning process. The Committee to Review the Existing Administrative Arrangements for Rural Development and Poverty Alleviation headed by Dr. G.V.K. Rao, Member of the Planning Commission (March 1985), also went into the question of decentralized planning and recommended that:

(a) Rural development should be the major component of district planning, though the District Plan should encompass the total activity of the district;
(b) The district should be the basic unit for policy planning and programme implementation. The Zila Parishad should, therefore, become the principal body for the management of all development programmes that could be handled at that level;
(c) Panchayati Raj institutions at the district level and below should be assigned an important role in

respect of planning, implementation and monitoring of rural development programmes;

(d) Some of the planning functions at the state level might have to be transferred to the district level for effective decentralized district planning; and

(e) In order to give some leeway and maneuverability in planning and decision-making, it was necessary to make some funds available to the District Planning Body, funds which were not tied to any departmental schemes and which might be used towards small schemes meant for the local priorities, needs and aspirations of the local community.

The mid-1980s saw the emergence of an influential movement to revitalize local self-government structures in India and link them with the agricultural and rural development process. There were two basic reasons for this. The first was the belief with the then Prime Minister Rajiv Gandhi that India was too 'large' a country to be ruled from a central place. The responsibility of the centre for many functions had to be at the local level.

This would lead to accountability in the long-run, although in the short-run resources would have to be allocated at the local level and these resources could be misused. Rajiv Gandhi, however, believed that in the long-run democratic policies would take care of such abuse and so insisted on the political and economic enfranchisement of poorer groups (Scheduled Castes, Scheduled Tribes and women). The second reason was the fact that India's initial agricultural planning systems were somewhat linear in nature, emphasizing, for example, canal and tube-well irrigation and high-yielding varieties and led to the favoured region, favoured crop strategy. The mid-1980s saw this strategy being questioned and the whole issue of widespread agricultural growth raised in terms of an agro-climatic plan. This in turn raised the question of local participation and voluntary organizations and the associated question of resource allocation and functioning of decentralized markets. The question raised was the manner in which special programmes for employment and rural development could be integrated with the agricultural development. The mid-term appraisal of the Seventh Five-year Plan had anticipated these problems, as the following abstract shows: "However, it is noticed that wherever the Panchayati Raj institutions have been actively involved, the implementation of rural development programmes has been better and the selection of beneficiaries and designing of schemes have been more satisfactory. The Planning Commission has been impressing upon the states that various rural development programmes will be realistic and meaningful only if people's representatives are actively involved and associated in local level planning, design formulation and implementation of those programmes and the selection of beneficiaries in the anti-poverty and employment programmes such as IRDP, NREP, RLEGP, etc. and that there is no better instrument to meet this need other than the Panchayati Raj institutions' (Government of India, 1987:16). The original Panchayati Raj Bill (1989) was an initiative not only to decentralize power, but to politically enfranchise the poorer sections of society, such as Scheduled Castes, Scheduled Tribes and women, who form a large part of the landless labourer and artisan populations. The Jawahar Rozgar Yojana (JRY), a nationwide employment scheme, attempted to put economic power behind this change.

CONCLUSION

The basic local institutions for participatory planning in India have been set-up. However, these institutions ought to have adequate autonomy as units of self-government so as to decide on the local needs and priorities and design and implement the necessary action. The challenge of making this new phase of democratic decentralization successfully depends on the commitment of the political leadership, bureaucracy and the people themselves. The state governments have the responsibility of transferring schemes as provided in the 11th Schedule of the Constitution and also of transferring corresponding funds to the Panchayats. Similarly, the staff available for the implementation of schemes related to these subjects should also be placed under the control of the Panchayats. Sufficiently clear and workable regulations have to be framed to streamline the inter-tier relationships and functions of each tier. The change which has been initiated by the Seventy-third Constitution Amendment needs to be managed and sustained effectively through innovative strategies. Panchayats have been empowered by this Amendment. Access to and effective control over resources is a critical component of this empowerment. The real issues of such access are knowledge and awareness of the needs of the people, legal rights, and availability and accessibility of social and economic resources. These changes in procedures and organizations have as yet not fully taken place as envisaged in the legislation. It also requires restructuring relationships, including looking at gender issues at both the micro and macro-level. A culture of equality has to be evolved not only between men and women representatives but also between officials and non-officials manning the decentralized development structure. The district has been recognized as the basic unit for decentralized planning functions. Operationalizing the concept of district planning requires functional local institutions. The District Planning Committee is the statutory authority for preparing plans for local development area planning. The involvement of the people in the planning process is necessary to take into account their felt needs, to Mobilize local resources, to increase the speed of implementation by securing the people's cooperation, to increase the acceptance of the planned projects and also to bring about a change in the power structure in people's institutions in favour of the poor. Strong leadership and political will are the necessary conditions for facing the challenge of enabling the local self-government institutions to become effective instruments of social and economic development of rural areas.

References

Alagh, Y.K. (1990), Agro-Climatic Planning and Regional Development, *Indian Journal of Agricultural Economics*.

Alagh, Y.K. (1993), Institutional Framework for Implementation of Anti-poverty Programmes, ILO-ARTEP, New Delhi.

Business Standard.

Economics Times.

Economic Survey of India (2007-08)

Government of India (1987), Mid-term Appraisal of the Seventh Five-year Plan, Planning Commission, Delhi.

Government of India (1993), Agro-Climatic Planning, District Level, Planning Commission, New Delhi.

Government of India (1997), Approach to the Ninth Five-year Plan, Planning Commission, Delhi.

International Labour Organization (ILO) (1997), Employment Poverty and Economic Policies, New York.

Swami Ramanand Teerath Research Institute, undated, Marathwada Study, Aurangabad, India.

(2005), "Globalization and Inequality", *Indian Economic Journal*, Vol. 53, No. 2, pp. 71-86.

(1997), "Regional Variation in the Growth of Crop Output in West Bengal—An Inter-district Analysis", *Artha Beekshan*, Vol. 6, No. 2, pp. 57-65.

(2005), "State and Transformation of Rural Workforce Structure in West Bengal 1961 to 2001", *The Indian Journal of Labour Economics*, Vol. 48, No. 4, Oct.-Dec., pp. 959-80.

Modern Economic Growth: Rate, Structure and Spread.

Sagar, Vidya (1980), "Decomposition of Growth Trends and Certain Related Issues", *Indian Journal of Agricultural Economics*, Vol. 35, No. 2, pp. 42-59.

PDS and Panchayati Raj Institutions (PRIs)

SANJAY KUMAR

In this titles, we briefly review the current situation of local institutions for participatory planning in India. The basic constructs of the system have been set-up. Effectiveness depends on three factors. The first is a genuine attempt at giving flexibility to local institutions in implementing major developmental initiatives such as the Basic Minimum Services Programme and the Special Employment Programme (JRY). The second is the need to involve local institutions in the country's economic liberalization and restructuring programmes. The Ahmedabad Municipal Board issue focuses on this issue, which is basic to the success of participatory planning for infrastructure development in India. Without restructuring, local bodies will not be able to mobilize resources for such development. This restructuring has to be done at three levels—local, state and central. Finally, when the three-tier system has been set-up, its development will need continued emphasis on transparency, genuine transfer of power and administrative coordination and reform, particularly in planning and implementation.

The first aspect to underline is that while local government, as a part of the process of democratic decentralization, is over four decades old in India, it was the Seventy-third Amendment to the Constitution which was indeed a far-reaching, if not a revolutionary step. It gave constitutional validation and empowerment to the third tier of government. Elected leadership at the local level became mandatory.

The provision of positive affirmation mandated through the constitutional 21 law that one-third of the elected leadership at the local level had to consist of scheduled castes, scheduled tribes and women, was indeed a major breakthrough. The process of transfer of power has begun and in the long-run there will be no going back. The discussion in this paper underlines the fact that there is a need for greater focus on the central resources made available to the Panchayats through JRY. The system of responsibility and resource-raising at the state level has as yet not been set-up in an organized way and the question of restructuring and reform needs urgent attention. As regards roads, the problem of rural connectivity is still to be solved in some regions, but in others, the quality of the road link is becoming the issue. Resources for the purpose will involve a restructured system of local finance.

The basic minimum need for roads is an accepted norm in India. The situation at present is that in some large states substantial progress lies ahead. In Arunachal Pradesh, Bihar, Madhya Pradesh, Orissa, Punjab and Rajasthan, less than 40 per cent of villages are connected. The Annual Plan for 1996/97 contained a long-term policy on the provision of seven basic common services throughout the country in a time-bound manner, including rural roads. An allocation of 24.6 billion rupees for basic common services was made under the heading 'Central Assistance to State Plans'.

For this, a group of Chief Ministers working with the author evolved a strategic approach to the State Plan. This indicated development options by the Planning Commission, leaving details to the state authorities, and the stipulation of much stronger evaluation procedures. The Planning Commission indicated the overall ceilings of additional resources to the state and they, in turn, decided on the phasing of priorities in areas such as drinking water, rural literacy, health programmes and rural roads. The state governments were requested to take similar initiatives towards decentralization at the local level (for details, see Government of India, 1997).

This approach, which is included in the approach paper to the Ninth Plan, was described by the present author as follows: "Economic growth and employment opportunities in themselves may not be sufficient to improve the living conditions of the poor. They need to be accompanied by measures which enhance the quality of life. For concretising this approach, a number of steps have already been taken which provide the initial outlines of the larger initiatives that will be contained in the Ninth Five-year Plan. At a conference of Chief Ministers held in July 1996, it was decided to implement a programme for the achievement of total coverage of seven basic minimum services in a time bound manner. It was agreed to raise the outlays of these programmes by 15 per cent in spite of the stringent fiscal situation. The Ninth Five-year Plan will continue this commitment in real terms through each of the five years. While the objectives of this programme have been decided through the process of mutual consultation, the states have been given full opportunity to decide on the phasing of the target for each specific sector. The achievement of these targets will be jointly monitored by the state and the central governments. This approach is an ideal blend of national commitments with local initiatives.

The method of planning for agriculture-related infrastructure, irrigation and water planning, and other infrastructure such as power, railways, communications and information technology and science and technology will be a variant of the methods developed for the basic minimum services programme. Plans will be set-up with well defined targets set at the national level in detailed consultation with the states. Policies will be explored in each sector to provide for more investment from the private sector, from cooperatives and voluntary organizations and international private investment. However, the slack in these selected sectors will be taken by public investment. The objectives will be defined nationally but the states and local governments will be given much larger freedom for choice of programmes, phasing of schemes and choice of appropriate instruments of finance.

The system of greater involvement of Panchayats in rural development was institutionalized in 1989/90 with the launching of JRY where there was a substantial flow of funds to the village level, every village having access to JRY funds, though the amount varies. In addition, the village Panchayats prepare an inventory of assets and give details of the projects taken up by them under JRY. This acts as a social audit. The works to be taken up are decided in the meeting of the Gram Sabha and these are prioritized according to the felt needs of the local people. It is thus possible to take a holistic view of the development needs of the area. This enables the village Panchayat to meet the critical gaps in rural infrastructure and also to generate income via supplementary wage employment to those willing and able to do manual.

References

Alagh, Y.K. (1990), Agro-Climatic Planning and Regional Development, *Indian Journal of Agricultural Economics*.

Alagh, Y.K. (1993), Institutional Framework for Implementation of Anti-poverty Programmes, ILO-ARTEP, New Delhi.

—— (2005), "Globalization and Inequality", *Indian Economic Journal*, Vol. 53, No. 2, pp. 71-86.

—— (1997), "Regional Variation in the Growth of Crop Output in West Bengal—An Inter-district Analysis", *Artha Beekshan*, Vol. 6, No. 2, pp. 57-65.

—— (2005), "State and Transformation of Rural Workforce Structure in West Bengal 1961 to 2001", *The Indian Journal of Labour Economics*, Vol. 48, No. 4, Oct.-Dec., pp. 959-80.

Business Standard.

Economic Survey of India, (2007-08).

Economics Times.

Sagar, Vidya (1980), "Decomposition of Growth Trends and Certain Related Issues", *Indian Journal of Agricultural Economics*, Vol. 35, No. 2, pp. 42-59.

Modern Economic Growth: Rate, Structure and Spread.

Public Distribution System and Panchayati Raj Institutions in Bihar and Jharkhand

BINOD PRASAD AND PANKAJ KUMAR

The Public Distribution System initially visualised in terms of checking inflation and protecting vulnerable sections from the vagaries of the market mechanism, is an organisational asset of considerable significance for achieving wider socio-economic objectives.

While looking at the management aspect and overall operationalised network of the Public Distribution System it shows good results in Andhra Pradesh for the government machinery and organisational set-up devised for handling the mechanism of all the aspects of the PDS have suitably fitted into the Central-policy which aims at strengthening and revamping the entire scheme creating viable economic growth for poor masses of the community in the country. Also, based on the delivery system evolved. It could be conceptualised that the people in Andhra Pradesh are making use of the PDS and deriving economic profits.

In this empirical study, findings and contacts with officials, non-officials and other beneficiaries have created the impression that Andhra Pradesh is one of the successful States in handling the scheme of Public Distribution System and this success. Of course is due to the introduction of Mandal System initially and the associated changes in administrative mechanism right from the level of state to grassroots.

It has also been observed that PRIs have as such, no role to play except the Sarpanch being the Chairman of Village Food Advisory Committee. His role on 'participation' in the process of implementation of PDS is very less and confined limitedly. Hence PRI's involvement in the extension of PDS is very poor and thereby image prevails at the lowest degree. However, the unique and more attractive feature is that ill Andhra Pradesh die mould of changes brought into the system of Panchayati Raj consequent upon the 73rd and 74th Constitutional Amendments which has thereby bestowed upon the people 'empowerment', has undeniably forced 'decentralisation and democratic footing of administration' which in turn, would effect the Public Distribution System for further improvement and thus the common man can enjoy the fruits of the scheme.

PANCHAYATI RAJ IN BIHAR

There are several deficiencies in the Bihar state conformity act. These deficiencies exist both at the gram sabha and the panchayat levels.

The gram sabha has not been given enough power, making it an ineffective body. The act has no guidelines on convening gram sabha and gram panchayat meetings and does not impose penalties for failing to conduct them. No quorum is specified for adjourning a panchayat meeting.

The functions of panchayats are not clearly spelt out. Overlapping functions at different levels cause considerable confusion and conflict.

Gram panchayats do not have the power to borrow from banks and financial institutions.

The state government has the power to post and transfer officials in panchayats. It can also remove elected functionaries and dissolve elected bodies. These powers erode the autonomy of the panchayats.

Panchayat elections were held in Bihar after a gap of over 20 years in 2001.

PANCHAYATI RAJ IN JHARKHAND

Jharkhand is yet to hold its first panchayat elections. The state government exercises complete control over the functioning and powers of the gram sabha and can even withdraw its powers.

MLAs and MPs can become members of the panchayat samiti and zilla parishad and even nominate persons to attend meetings on their behalf. The state government can nominate 'distinguished' persons to panchayats.

Key positions in a panchayat are held by government employees. The government can also depute any government servant to a panchayat.

The government can amend any function or responsibility entrusted to a panchayat. It can even dissolve the panchayat on grounds of illegalities and irregularities, without inquiry. During the period of dissolution, the affairs of the panchayat are managed by a committee appointed by the state government, giving it further control over the functioning of the panchayat.

Panchayats have no financial freedom. Grants-in-aid given to them are conditional. On the other hand, panchayats do not have the power to raise revenue independently.

There is no provision for consulting with gram sabhas and panchayats :

- before making land acquisitions for development purposes,
- before granting prospecting licences or mining leases,
- on enforcing prohibition,
- on regulating the sale of intoxicants,
- on preventing land alienation, and
- on exercising control over money-lending, etc.

INVOLVEMENT OF PANCHAYATI RAJ INSTITUTIONS

The Government feels that the Targeted Public Distribution System (TPDS) should be strengthened to ensure its proper coverage and make it more efficient. It is also felt that the system should be transparent and accountable with built-in provisions for social audit. The Government of India feels that there is a complete lack of information to the citizens with regard to functioning of the Fair Price Shops (FPSs) leading to a large number of malpractices. Another area needing improvement seems to be in the issue of the ration cards to the targeted group. Yet another problem seems to be that the wrong set of people maybe drawing rations and other commodities at BPL rates, which are highly subsidised. It is felt that a more transparent and accountable system with provision of social audit can eliminate most of the ills of the system. It is felt that a set of simple administrative measures would go a long way in reforming the system. They are enumerated in the following paragraphs:

RIGHT OF INFORMATION REGARDING THE FAIR PRICE SHOPS (FPSs)

The villagers and interested persons should have the right to know the address of the FPSs along with the number of cards attached to each of them. Each FPS should also maintain the basic information with regard to each of the cards like the name of the card holder, the number of units of each card and the identity of the residence of the card holder. The details of BPL cards should be marked distinctly.

BPL BENEFICIARIES

The list of BPL beneficiaries should also be displayed on the fair price shop and the office of the Gram Panchayat for public scrutiny. This will help in elimination of undeserving families which may be drawing BPL supplies at highly subsidised rates.

RIGHT OF CONSUMERS WITH REGARD TO CERTAIN INFORMATION

The consumers have also the right to know the per capita entitlement of each of the commodities being distributed under the TPDS. They also need to be informed about the price of the commodities. This information is liable to change from time to time. For example, the entitlement of sugar may increase during festival seasons or there may be supply of additional items which are not usually supplied in the area. Entitlements may also be affected on account of natural calamities. Arrangements need to be made for this information to be passed on to the consumer. The possible modes could be the publicity through the local newspapers, a notice to be pasted in the office of the Gram Panchayats, Blocks, Tehsils, etc. The official audio visual media may also be utilised to achieve this objective.

DISPLAY OF STOCK POSITION

The date of arrival of the commodities, as also the stock position on each of the days is an important information which should be displayed prominently on the FPS. It should also display the price of each of the commodities. Non-fulfilment of this provision should be a serious matter.

FURNISHING THE COPIES OF CERTAIN DOCUMENTS CONCERNING PDS TO INTEREST GROUPS

Each FPS maintains ration card register, stock register and sale register. Each page of the register should have a tear-off page, so that at the time the entries are being made, a copy is easily and automatically made on the tear-off by inserting carbon. This can easily be detached from the register and the copy sent to the Gram Panchayats. The tear-off should be available for inspection by any interest group in the premises of the Panchayats. If anybody wishes to take its copies for the purposes of cross-checking, it should be made available by charging nominal fees. The fee should be no more than the cost of making the copies. The State Governments should evolve guidelines for manner in which the copies of the FPS documents which may be indented by any interested person from the Gram Panchayats should be made (manually, photocopying, etc.) and by whom. The time period should be fixed in which such documents will be delivered to the indentor.

SOCIAL AUDIT-FORMATION OF AN FPS COMMITTEE BY EACH GRAM PANCHAYAT

The Gram Panchayats should be encouraged to form a FPS Committee which should include the Members of the existing Vigilance Committees for the Fair Price Shops of the area under its jurisdiction as also the representatives of the TPDS groups, women and SC/ST/OBC panchayat members to keep a watch on the functioning of the FPS. They should be given the right to inspect the records of the FPSs, the periodicity of which should be prescribed by the State Governments. The Committee should be required to report their findings to the Gram Sabha. They should also endorse a copy of the report to the prescribed civil supplies authority for action wherever required.

Those states where properly constituted Gram Panchayats are not in position for some reason, the State Governments should evolve an alternative mechanism to discharge the aforesaid responsibilities of Gram Panchayats. The existing Vigilance Committees could be one such machinery.

INVOLVEMENT OF THE GRAM SABHA IN THE RUNNING OF THE FPS

The Government of India has already written to the States that Gram Sabhas should be convened four times in a year on January 26th (Republic Day), May 1st (Labour Day), August 15th (Independence Day) and October 2nd (Gandhi Jayanti). It is expected that the State Governments would have also prescribed the venue and time (publicized in advance) for these meetings because lack of information or insufficient information on these vital items is often made use of by the unscrupulous Gram Panchayat functionaries in preventing the larger body of Gram Sabha from attending its meetings. The extraneous considerations may be the motive in changing of the venue and time at the last moment thereby defeating the very purpose of transparency with regard to the Gram Sabha meetings. The report of the Gram Panchayat Committee on the functioning of the FPS of the area should be compulsory item on the agenda of the Gram Sabha to which the FPS owners should also be invited. Their presence in fact should be insisted upon. If the Gram Sabha does not find the functioning of the FPS satisfactory, a report to that effect shall be made to Government functionary prescribed by the State Government. This shall be done within one week of the Gram Sabha meeting.

DUTY OF THE PRESCRIBED AUTHORITY ON RECEIPT OF THE REPORT OF GRAM SABHA ABOUT THE FPS FUNCTIONING

The prescribed authority on receiving a report from the Gram Sabha about the unsatisfactory functioning of the FPS and the details thereof shall conduct and complete the enquiry in a time bound manner as prescribed by the State Government. If the charges preferred by the Gram Sabha are found to contain substance, the licence of the FPS shall be suspended forthwith and he will be dealt with in accordance with the provisions of the law, again within a stipulated time frame to be prescribed by the State Government. Alternative arrangements regarding running of the suspended/cancelled FPS shall be made by the prescribed authority in accordance with the prescribed procedure for the purpose.

MAKING OF NEW RATION CARDS

The present procedure of issue of ration cards needs to be simplified so that within a stipulated number of days (30-45 days), the applicant's claim for a ration card is verified and his claim either accepted or rejected, under intimation to the applicant. It should be possible for the applicants to file their application with the Gram Panchayat who should forward it to the competent prescribed authority, responsible for issue of ration cards.

CHECKING OF RATION CARDS

The Gram Panchayats/Gram Sabhas should also be responsible for checking of the ration cards occasionally to find out whether the card is genuine and the number of units contained on it are correct. The FPS Committee of the Gram Panchayat will report to the Gram Sabha the results of its occasional checking. It would contain details like the number of checks carried out and the outcome of its efforts to eliminate bogus ration cards and the number of units contained on the ration cards checked.

Public Distribution System in India

SYED ALAY MUJTABA, PANKAJ PURUSHOTAM AND KAMLESH KUMAR

A well targeted and properly functioning Public Distribution System (PDS) is an important constituent of the strategy for poverty alleviation. Public Distribution system under the Government Control System i.e. (PDS) evolved as a system of management of scarcity and for distribution of foodgrains at affordable prices. Over the years, PDS has become an important part of Government's policy for management of food economy in the country. PDS is supplemental in nature and is not intended to make available the entire requirement of any of commodities distributed under it to a household or a section of the society. PDS is operated under the joint responsibility of the Central and the State Governments. The Central Government through FCI, has assumed the responsibility for procurement, storage, transportation and bulk allocation of foodgrains to State Governments. The operational responsibility including allocation within State, identification of families below the poverty line, issue of Ration Cards and supervision of the functioning of FPS, rest with the State Governments. Under the PDS presently the commodities namely wheat, rice, sugar and kerosene, are being allocated to the States/UTs for distribution. So States/UTs also distribute additional items of mass consumption through the PDS outlets such as cloth, exercise books, pulse, salt and tea. The Revamped Public Distribution System (RPDS) was launched in June, 1992 with a view to strengthen and streamline the PDS as well as to improve its reach in the far-flung, hilly, remote and inaccessible areas where a substantial section of poor live. It covered 1775 blocks wherein area specific programmes such as the Drought Prone Area Programme (DPAP), Integrated Tribal Development Projects (ITDP), Desert Development Programme (DDP) and certain Designated Hill Area (DHA) identified in consultation with State Governments for special focus, with respect to improvement of the PDS infrastructure. Foodgrains for distribution in RPDS areas were issued to the States at 50 paise below the Central issue Price. The scale issue was up to 20 kg per card. The RPDS included area approach for ensuring effective reach of the PDS commodities, their delivery by Governments at the doorstep of FPSs in the identified areas, additional ration common requirements like additional Fair Price Shops, storage capacity, etc. and additional common requirements, etc. for distribution through PDS outlets. Procurement higher than the off-take had in a build-up of excessive stocks of tins during the two successive years, 2001-02 and 2002-03. Subsequently, however due to increased offtake under TPDS other welfare schemes, stocks of tins stood at 18.8 million tonnes on January 1, 2006, lower than not only of 21.7 million tonnes on January 1, 2005 but also the buffer stock norm of 20 million tonnes. The main reason for the decline was the lower stock of wheat. Coarse grain procurement was higher at 1.14 million tonnes in 2005-06 as against 0.8 million tonnes in 2004-05. Wheat stocks depleted down to 2 million tonnes in April 2006 against a buffer stock norm of 4 million tonnes. Poor procurement of wheat further reduced the actual stocks relative to buffer norms. To make up for the shortfall of wheat procurement in the rabi marketing season (RMS) 2006-07, Government decided to import 5.5 million tonnes of wheat through the State Trading Corporation (STC) for an average weighted price of tonne, of which 4.5 million tonnes arrived by end of January 2007, addition, one million tonnes of wheat import on account of private traders was also contracted. On the sugar front, adequate domestic availability is ensured with a supply of 22.7 million tonnes as against estimated consumption of 19.0 million tonnes. In so far as rice and wheat are concerned, accelerated procurement of rice together the augmentation of stocks through import of wheat has ensured adequate consumption stocks in foodgrains. Government timely decision of importing wheat checked the deficit and augmented the domestic availability of foodgrains, pre-empting major negative impact on food security for the nation.

The year 2005-06 was a normal agricultural year with adequate procurement of foodgrains. Rice procurement dam kharif marketing season (KMS) 2005-06 at 27.7 million tonnes was higher by around 3 million tonnes compared to 2004-05. Wheat procurement during RMS 2006-07 (as on November 30, 2006) stood at 9.2 million tonnes was, however, substantially lower by 5.6 million tonnes than that during RMS 2005-06 in KMS 2006-07, which started from Oct., 2006, procurement of rice upto Jan. 2006 was satisfactory at 11.1 million tonnes compared to 11.5 million procured corresponding period of 2005-06. The data from 1951 to 2005 of net availability, procurement and public distribution of foodgrains is presented underneath.

Recently, it was a common grievance of many States that their farmers have not benefited much from the price support operations, since the procurement of foodgrains by the Food Corporation of India (FCI) has been largely concentrated States such as Punjab, Haryana, Uttar Pradesh and Andhra Pradesh. These four states for nearly 74 per cent of rice procured for the central pool in KMS 2003-04 while only two states, Punjab and Haryana accounted for more than 91 per cent of wheat procurement in RMS 2005-06. The procurement of rice in traditional states, which have adopted the decentralized procurement scheme, like Chhattisgarh, Orissa, Tamil Nadu and West Bengal, has gone up substantially from 7.8 million tonnes in KMS 2003-04 to 10.9 million tonnes in 2005-06. The decentralized procurement scheme of the Government of India that is in operation since 1997 has evoked good response from the State Governments. Under this scheme, the designated States procure, store and also issue foodgrains under TPDS. The difference between the economic cost of the State Governments and the central issue price (CIP) is passed on to the State Governments as subsidy. The decentralized system of procurement, helps to cover more farmers under the MSP operations, improves efficiency of the PDS provides varieties of foodgrains more suited to local taste, and reduces transportation costs of the FCI. 11 States/UTs (West Bengal, Uttar Pradesh, Madhya Pradesh, Chhattisgarh, Uttarakhand, Gujarat, Orissa, Tamil Nadu, Union Territories Andaman & Nicobar islands, Karnataka and Kerala) are undertaking decentralised procurement. There was record procurement of 10.9 million tonnes under this scheme by these States in 2005-06. Wheat and rice are issued by the Central Government at uniform CIP to states and Union Territories for distribution under TPDS. There has been no revision of CIPs for BPL since July 2000, and for APL since July 2001 (except for a reduction in APL, prices for 3 months in 2002-03).

The main purpose of the Public Distribution System (PDS) in India was to act as a price support programme for the consumer during the periods of food shortage of the 1960s. Thus, it acted as an instrument of price stabilisation and became a countervailing force against private traders who were interested to exploit the situation of scarcity to acquire more and more profits. The basic aim was to provide essential commodities such as rice, wheat, sugar, edible oil, soft coke and kerosene at subsidised prices. Since the mid-1980s, the coverage of the PDS was extended to rural areas in some states. Thus, it acquired the status of a welfare programme. An effort was made to extend subsidised foodgrains in 1985 in all the tribal blocks covering about 51 million persons. With a network of more than 4.62 lakh fair price shops (FPS) distributing commodities worth Rs. 30,000 crores annually to about 160 million families, the PDS in India was the largest distribution network of its kind in the world. In several employment generation programmes, subsidised foodgrains were distributed as apart of wages. The food subsidy component of the Central Government is given in table. It may be noted that there has been a continuous increase in PDS expenditure, which rose from Rs. 650 crores in 1980-81 (at current prices) to Rs. 2,450 crores in 1990-91. There was a big jump in expenditure during. As a proportion of Central Government expenditure, it was in the range of 2.9 to 3.2 per cent during 1980s and 1990s. Since 1997-98 PDS expenditure has been shooting up from Rs. 7,500 crores to Rs. 12,120 crores in 2000-01 and further to a record level of Rs. 25,800 crores in 2003-04. But responding to popular pressure to continue the scheme as a welfare measure along with a price stabilisation instrument, food subsidies went up sharply to 3.6 per cent in 2000-01 and 5.2 per cent in 2003-04.

Rice, wheat, sugar, edible oil, soft coke and kerosene are sold through PDS outlets. Of these 4 items, viz., rice, wheat, sugar and kerosene account for 86 per cent of total PDS sales. Sugar alone accounts for 35 per cent, followed by rice (27 per cent), wheat (10 per cent) and kerosene (15 per cent). Coarse cereals (bajra, jawar and other coarse grains), which are largely, consumed by the poor account for less than one per cent of total PDS sales. The share of pulses, the main source of protein for the poor, is less than 0.2 per cent. Dr. M.H. Suryanarayana concludes: "A up for rural and urban sector separately shows sugar, rice, and kerosene are relatively more important items sold through the PDS in the rural sector, while sugar, kerosene, wheat and edible oils in the urban sector. Thus, there is some basis for the general impression that the PDS commodity composition is weigh favour of items supposed to be consumed largely relatively richer sections of the society.

Data about commodity-wise composition of market dependent population reveal that the bulk of the PDS purchases of these commodities go to benefit the non-poor in urban and rural areas. On the basis of the poverty line as used by the Planning Commission, a major factor is the calorie norm and on an average, cereals account for 85 per cent for the poorer households, particularly in the rural sector. Hence cereals consumption is an important indicator of food security.

For the poorest decile, consumption of cereals was in the range of 8 to 11 kg in the rural sector during 1989-90. Similarly, in the urban sector, for the poorest decile consumption of cereals is around 10.0 kgs during 1989-90. This is below the subsistence level norm of the Indian Council of Medical Research (ICMR) for minimum cereal consumption of 11.6 kg. per month. Thus, from the point of view of food security, it is necessary bring the cereal consumption to the minimum consumption norm of 11.6 kg fixed for subsistence level by ICMR. Food security is intended in the first stage to achieve the minimum level of 11.6 kg per month. The lowest 30 per cent are not able to reach the minimum level of cereal consumption prescribed by ICMR by the year 1990. This is a sad commentary on our achievement towards food security. The basic question, is whether PDS purchases are effectively help the poor. Radhakrishna *et. al.* studied this problem on the basis of 42nd NSS Round 1986-87. Their study brought out many disquieting points.

(i) The virtual exclusion of backward states such as Bihar and Uttar Pradesh from the PDS network.

(ii) In states, like Kerala and Andhra Pradesh, PDS purchases were relatively high in all expenditure groups but generally the poor purchased less while the non-poor purchased more. In this sense, the PDS scheme was regressive.

(iii) In contrast to the impressive coverage of PDS in the states of Kerala and Andhra Pradesh, the coverage was low in all-India; the monthly per capita purchase was 0.9 kg in rural areas and 1.3 kg in urban areas.

The low PDS cereal purchases in all-India can be attributed to the extremely low cereal purchases from the PDS in the prosperous states such as Punjab and Haryana, as well as in the states with high poverty levels such as Bihar, Orissa, Madhya Pradesh and Uttar Pradesh.

(iv) The monthly purchase from PDS was lowest for the very poor uniformly across all the states, both in rural and urban areas. In other words, impressive

> coverage of PDS and/or additional state-level spending on the subsidy is no guarantee that the very poor are better served. They further states:
> PDS has thus remained an expensive and largely untargeted Programme. The basic question is : how to improve the efficacy of PDS in transferring food to the poor cost-effectively. The government should distinguish between the very poor and moderately poor, and attempt at improving the efficiency of PDS in transferring food to the former (that is very poor) since the ultra poor suffer not only chronic food insecurity but are also severely exposed to the risk of uncertainty both in the food and labour markets.

Upward revision of issue price of cereals by PDS adversely affected off-take levels since and the gap between subsidised issue price, open market price was narrowed down. As a result, in all states, off-take was lower than the Central allocation.

But persistence by certain State Governments to implement subsidised PDS was responsible for higher off-take in certain States, such as Kerala and Andhra Pradesh. The rigid adherence to Rs. 2 per kg. rice scheme in Andhra Pradesh by late Mr. N.T. Rama Rao is a case in point. Similarly, Kerala has been pushing the implementation of subsidised foodgrains very enthusiastically.

In poorer states such as Bihar, Orissa and Madhya Pradesh, the off-take was substantially lower than Central allocations partly due to the narrow difference between the Central issue price and open market price and partly because of weak fiscal capacity of these states to finance any additional subsidy *via* lowering of issue prices. Besides these states had not built up effective institutional mechanisms to lift the quotas from FCI depots to fair price shops. Ironically, the incidence of poverty was high precisely in the states with the lowest off-take of FCI grains. The per capita off-take was low in food surplus states with low incidence of poverty such as Punjab, Haryana, as well as in poorer states (with low fiscal capacity) such as Bihar, Orissa, Madhya Pradesh and Uttar Pradesh. From the point of view of food security, states with higher poverty ratio should have higher per capita off-take of PDS foodgrains. But this hypothesis is not confirmed by statistical analysis. It is only the social commitment of the state that is responsible for higher per capita off-take of foodgrains. This is true in case of Kerala and Andhra Pradesh. Besides, Jammu & Kashmir and Assam are two other states with higher off-take. Weak commitment to the programme is observed in Orissa, Bihar, Uttar Pradesh, and Madhya Pradesh—the very poor states of India. Economically better-off states such as Punjab and Haryana have also a very low commitment to PDS. Radhakrishna Report has also studied the decline in poverty as a result of PDS subsidies. Taking India as a whole, the impact of all consumer subsidies on poverty was moderate; subsidies were estimated to have reduced poverty by 1.6 percentage points in rural areas and 1.7 percentage points in urban areas. About 12 million persons (9 million in rural and 3 million in urban areas) may have moved out of poverty in 1986-87 due to income transfers from PDS. As the absolute number of poor in India was 274 million in 1986-87, these numbers are small. To bring about 5.4 per cent decline in rural poverty in Kerala, 4.6 per cent in Andhra Pradesh, 4.3 per cent in Karnataka and 3.8 per cent in Gujarat indicates a significant contribution by these states in poverty reduction in 1986-87. Had the scheme been not universal, but properly targeted, this impact would have been much greater.

Moreover, the poor impact of the scheme in poor states also underlines the need for strengthening PDS in these states. To underestimate the over-all impact of the scheme in reducing poverty by 1.6 per cent in rural and 1.7 per cent in urban areas is to do injustice to the impact of the scheme. Besides, as long as the development process is not able to reduce poverty effectively in Bihar, Uttar Pradesh, Madhya Pradesh, Orissa and Rajasthan, the continuance of the PDS in poor states stands justified. Rather, the need of the hour is to encourage proper targeting to achieve better results and to build commitment on the part of the poorer states to pursue PDS.

CONCLUSION

In last 58 years India's food problem has changed.

Fundamentally in the beginning, India's Food problem was one of scarcity, shortage of Rice after the separation of Myanmar and shortage of wheat also after partition of the country in 1947. Initially, the major concern of the government was to increase the domestic supplies either through increased production or through imports or through both. Recently (2005-06) PDS has shortage control the food problem. The severe feminine conditions of 1964-65, the huge imports of foodgrains from America under the P.L. 480 Agreement and the American threat to stop supplying P.L. 480 food support during Indo-Pak war compelled the Indian Government to formulate a new food policy-push through the green revolution, create a surplus and became self-sufficient in foodgrains. Over a period, this policy was successful and govt. accumulated huge stocks of major foodgrains—rice and wheat through the FCI. PDS has three purposes :

1. Stabilise prices of major foodgrains,
2. Supply foodgrains at subsidized prices to lower income groups later called below poverty line families (BPL), and
3. During the First year of the 11th Plan (2007-08) the Government of India is importing over 5 million tonnes of wheat. A big country like India cannot depend on imports of essential goods, India's imports alone can push international prices of essential goods.

New Yojana is created by government to benefit the people of India. It is known as Antyodaya Anna Yojana (AAY). AAY is a step in the direction of making TPDS aim at reducing hunger among the poorest segments of the BPL population. A National Sample Survey Exercise points towards the fact that about 5 per cent of the total population in the country sleeps without two square meals a day. This section of the population can be called as "hungry". In order to make TPDS focused and targeted towards this category of population, the "Antyodaya Anna Yojana" (AAY) was launched in December, 2000 for one crore poorest of the poor families. AAY contemplates identification of one crore poorest of the poor families from amongst the number of BPL under TPDS within the States and providing them foodgrains at a highly subsidised rate of Rs. 2/per kg for wheat and Rs. 3/per kg for rice. The States/ UTs are required to bear the distribution cost, including margin to dealers and the transportation cost. Thus the entire food subsidy is being passed on to the consumers under the scheme. The scale of issue that was initially 25 kg per family per month has been increased to 35 kg per family per month with effect from 1st April 2002. The government is also implementing a scheme especially in the tribal areas at a price well below the already subsidized price in the PDS. An important aspect of the Government's policy in the strengthening of the PDS even covering rural areas. The government has set-up a network of fair price shops numbering nearly 4,00,000 which cover a population of over 500 million and which distribute wheat, rice, sugar, imported edible oils, kerosene, etc. The public distribution system serves two purposes. Firstly, it helps to hold down prices. It provides essential commodities to low income groups. Now commonly called Below Poverty Line (BPL) families at relatively low price but whenever the PDS is hard pressed due to inadequate supply, Price of essential goods tended to rise.

References

Chaudhri, D.P., New Technology and Income Distribution in Agriculture in Agrarian Reforms and Agrarian Reformism, Edited by Davin Lehman.

C.H. Hanumantha Rao, Technological Change and Distribution of Grains in Indian Agriculture (1975).

Department of Food and Public Distribution (www.indiabudget.nic.in).

Etiennie, G. (1988), Food and Poverty: India's Half Won Battle.

Economic Survey, 2005-06.

Hanumantha Rao, C.H. and Radhakrishna, R., National Food Security: A Policy Perspective for India (Mimeo).

Ruddar Datt and K.P.M. Sundaram, Radhakrishna, R, Subbarao, K., Indrakant, S., and Ravi, K. (1997), Public Distribution: A National and International Perspective, World Bank Discussion, p. 380.

Planning Commission, Ninth Five Year Plan (1997-2002), Vol. II.

Report of Foodgrains Strategy—Lesson of First Three Years, *Economic and Political Weekly*.

Single, D.P., The Impact of the Green Revolution on the Poor, Agricultural Situation in India, August 1980.

Tenth Five Year Plan (2002-07), Vol. II.

V.K.R.V. Rao, New Challenges before Indian Agriculture, Pause Memorial Lecture, 25-28 April, 1974 (Mimeographed).

Developmentalism through PDS Mechanism

Towards a New Regime—Paradoxical Situation

Nisha Kumari and Swarnim Ghosh

"A hunger-free Bihar is not only a state's pride but can make a huge contribution to national food security through PDS effective delivering mechanism."

Paradoxically; Bihar attained State food self-sufficiency 35 years ago, yet about only 35 per cent of its population remains food insecure; how incomes and high food prices prevent individual food security. Another aspect of Bihar's food security situation is that after over three decades of operation, PDS meets less than 10 per cent of consumption of PDS grains—rice and wheat—by the poor. Attaining long-term food security requires the raising of incomes and making food affordable. To ensure food security for the vulnerable section of the society; a multi-pronged strategy is to be evolved. To begin with; all the existing social safety not programmes and amalgamation and should fours on vulnerable and under privileged regions and groups. Simultaneously PDS needs to be reformed by improving incentives, increasing investments, etc.; so that PDS will be work effectively.

Designing a policy options for Reform of PDS

↓

The supreme intension of helping the poor

↓

Identifying the poor (basic problem)

↓

Development of strategies

↓

Ability to minimize the

↓

Accrual of benefits of PDS

↓

To the non-poor

Designing the consideration should be taken into account while identifying the poor by delivery mechanism

FOR THE RURAL AREAS

- All households participating in employment programmes may be included.
- Single mothers with children or widows without support should be included.
- All non-income tax paying household (less than 5 acres of irrigated land/10 acres of unirrigated land should be included.
- All landless agricultural laboures, Petty artisans should be included.

FOR URBAN AREAS

- Careful selection of areas; slums, areas occupied by traditionally poor communities such as potters, cobblers, construction workers, poor home-based workers, etc.
- All non-income tax paying households should be included.
- Households, which do not possess expensive consumer durable and services (cooking gas, Refrigerators, washing machines, telephones, etc.)

In this paper, I am trying to my best to prompt or pathway to achieving sustainable food and nutrition security through PDS effective delivery mechanism framework interns of operational efficiency and quality aspects. But Bihar has today certainly a good chance to do that if only it tries/with eanestness and determination.

Over 35 per cent BPL cards issued to bogus families; the fresh evidence has once again undersigned the serious problems that be devil the PDS. But while there are mounds of evidence of PDS grain being diverted to private players and increasingly even living exported; the political class scoffs at suggestions for reforms. They have brushed aside those who have advocated alternations life food-vouchers. Further as in the case of other programmes; the implementation of this scheme lacks information, education and communication (IEC) activities which resulted in such riots in many places or food revolution as claimed by many; thus is not much correlation between starvation and per capita grains availability. Hence, the problem is not of production but of distribution. Moreover owing to irregular delivery schedule of FPS quota and several other reasons like irregular income wage payments in food grains and low market price in harvest season, etc., many BPL families donot left their ration quota regularly fully in Bihar, the obstensible propose of the TPDS was to take food to the poor; in practices. It has resulted in the large-scale exclusion of the poor and food secure from the public food system.

In Bihar; 82 per cent of households held on APL card or no card; the NSS Data shows that 70 per cent or more of SC

In Some Areas, PDS Diversion is 100% Grain Drain

	BPL	*AAY*
Wheat		
Arunachal Pradesh	100	0
Bihar	47	39
West Benngal	83	77
Haryana	80	38
Delhi	53	38
Rice		
Arunachal Pradesh	78	100
West Bengal	30	67
Madhya Pradesh	40	67
Manipal	98	97
Goa	61	39

households had no card or an APC card in the rural areas of Bihar turning to households belonging to the STs; again, large number of households do not have access to the PDS. Again the conclusion is that a very high proportion of landless and near landless households did not posse BPL or any cards and were effectively excluded from the PDS. I defined inclusions as obtaining on BPL or Antyodaya card. Our results show that a significant proportion of households falling below the official poverty line did posses on BPL or Antyodaya card. The proportion of such households was to illustrate; 77.5 per cent in Bihar and 67 per cent in Jharkhand. In striving for or efficiency by means of narrow targeting households that should be entitled to basic food security through the PDS have been leftout.

The only immediate remedy to the problem is to make the PDS universal against, and to ensure that a monthly ration of basic food commodities including grain, pulses and oil is available at affordable prices to all households.

A state programme of coordinated action with specific goals and dead lines are needed. However, PDS to be tried out to bridge the gap between demand and supply. The question is; what is most challenging is to find effective policies related to PDS mechanism to deal with the consequences of extremely asymmetric expansion of the Bihar economy. The success of TPDS depended largely on the state Government of Bihar identifying the genuinely poor families and issuing the BPL ration cards to them so that they are able to buy more quantity at a higher subsidized price.

The denial of the right to food for a large sections of the Bihar's population reflected in increased malnourishment, stunted growth, ill-health and loss of energy and therefore productively is an issue that desires more state attention with co-ordination of national attention. An associated problem with targeting is that of identification of the poor. If only those who are officially identified as 'Poor' can have access to food, then clearly the method has to be one that ensures accuracy. The prevailing method of identification is entirely unsatisfactory, what needs to be done is to improve the system? whether of the procurement agencies, the fair price shops (FPSs) or the methods of distribution—but not to destroy them. But that is, what the food and PDS department secures to be proposing people centered reform requires a return to the PDS; target-oriented *v.* Universalisation. The basic questions which needs to the probed; is whether PDS purchases are able to effectively help the poor. The evidence shows that even how the efficiency of PDS in distributing food to the poor seems to be as had as in 2008 and that same of the disguisting features perist—the virtual exclusion of backward states such as Bihar from the PDS network and the universal character of PDS in various states including Bihar in which PDS off-takes were significant. None of the four villages surveyed in Bihar received any PDS supplies, nor did there out to four villages surveyed in other BIMARU states. Obviously, there is mistargetting in the distribution of PDS food grains. In that way of state with higher poverty levels such as Bihar, it may be observed that monthly purchases from PDS was lowest for the very poor uniformly across all the villages in Bihar both in small and urban areas.

To verify the relationship between off-take of rice and wheat from FCI and its correlates number of factors, i.e.

- per cent of population under BPL,
- Per capital state domestic product, and
- State Government's per capita expenditure.

The evidence shows, work commitment to the programme is observed in BIMARU states like Bihar—the very poor state of India. Its needs to be understood that the impact is transient and is not of an enduring nature. But so long as the development process is not able to reduce poverty effectively in Bihar. Rather the need of the hour is to encourage proper targeting to achieve letter results and to build commitment on the part of the poorer states to pursuer PDS mechanism effectively. The cost-effectiveness of a program depends very much on the choice of a particular targeting method and the design and delivery of the program; which, in turn, depend on the needs of beneficiaries and on state-specific-constraints.

References

Alagh, Y.K.; Towards a Policy System for Food Security.

Economic Survey, 2006-07.

Radhakrishna, R., Subbarao, K. Indrakant, S.; and Ravi Kr.; (1997), Public Distribution : A National and International Prospective; World Bank Discussion Paper No. 380.

Tenth Five Year Plan (2002-07).

Yojana, July, 2008.

31

The Efficiency of Public Distribution System as a Poverty Eradication in India

CHANDRIKA PRASAD

The Public Distribution System has been playing a vital role as a poverty alleviation measure and eradication of hunger. Supporters of PDS, who see it as a major instrument for ensuring food security for the poor, strongly appose this prescription even as they recognize the need for restructuring the programme. The PDS is one of the instruments for improving food security at the household level in India. The PDS ensure availability of essential commodities like rice, wheat, edible oils and kerosene to the consumers through a network of outlets or fair price shops. These are supplied at below market price to consumers. PDS is run through food procurement in the domestic market at a pre-announced procurement price, although imports have been resorted to in some countries. A major objection raised against this method of ensuring food security is that it becomes difficult to target supplies to the poorer households, and arrangement becomes, in effect, universal. The poor get only marginal assistance. Even countries where PDS in its original form continues, the difference between the market price and the issue price is reduced to curtail subsidies on food save budgetary resources. Such a more takes away the benefits of PDS as far as the poor are concerned. PDS also acts as market outlet in areas where private trade is reluctant to operate. It can discipline the market by providing effective competition to private trade.

HISTORICAL DEVELOPMENT

In India, the PDS has involved through various stages since the colonial times. It started as war-time rotating in 1939 in Bombay and was extended eventually to several other cities. It was also taken to rural areas to meet situation of food shortage. In 1947 it was terminated, and in 1950 it was reintroduced as part of the planning process. As the country was facing serve shortage of crop production, the system had to rely on imports. Through the 1970s and 1980s, the PDS in India became increasingly robust with the accumulation of buffer stock following rapid growth for some crops in some areas. In 1997 the government introduced Targeted Public Distribution System (TPDS).

PRESENT STATUS

National Sample Survey Organisation (NSSO) in its 55th Round in 1999-2000 collected information on purchase of rice, wheat, sugar and kerosene made in fair price shops. According to 1999-2000 data, the PDS is accussible to about 30 per cent of Indian rural households for rice and only 17 per cent for wheat. The corresponding figures for states show large variations from 75 per cent for Tamil Nadu to 17 per cent in West Bengal in case of rice and 34 per cent in Gujarat to 0.21 per cent in Punjab in case of wheat. Access to PDS in poorer states like Bihar, Madhya Pradesh, and Uttar Pradesh is low. At the all-India level, the share of rice construction due to PDS in rural areas was 9 per cent in 1993-4. The corresponding numbers for rural wheat, urban rice, and urban wheat 5.6 per cent, 14.2 per cent, and 9.2 per cent, respectively. There shares were higher for Kerala, Gujarat, A.P., and Tamil Nadu. The share of PDS for rice in rural areas increased from 9.4 per cent in 1993-4 to 12.1 per cent in 1999-2000. The shares increase significantly for Orissa, Tamil Nadu, and J&K. In the case of rural wheat, rice and wheat in urban areas, the shares have not increased at all India level. Various micro studies have documented about the prevalence of hunger and starvation deaths in many parts of the country. A public hearing on hunger and the right to food held in Manatu Block of Palamu district of Jharkahnd following starvation death rivals gross irregularities in food-related programs and a disastrous level of public services.

India is perhaps the largest distribution network of its kind in the world. Access to the PDS until 1997 was universal. The targeted PDS (TPDS) was introduced in 1997 and under this scheme special cards were issued to families below poverty line (BPL) and foodgrains were distributed at a lower price for these families compared to those above the poverty line, known as APL families.

There were some disturbing trends in food policy in the first few years of this decade. Procurement of food grains increased significantly in the late 1990s from about 20 MT in 1996-7 to 42.8 in 2001-2 almost 20 per cent of food grains production. Buffer stock increase from 16 MT to 51 MT during the same period. As a result of accumulation of food grains the food subsidy increased significantly in the late 1990s. The food subsidy at current prices increased from Rs. 24.1 billion in 1990-1 to Rs. 262 billion in 2005-6. As per cent of GDP, the food subsidy increased from 0.43 in 1990-1 to 0.98 per cent in 2002-3. Similarly, food subsidy as per cent of total public expenditure also increased significantly from 2.3 per cent in 1990-1 to 5.7 per cent in 2003-4. The related issue under food subsidy is that the producer subsidy has increased while the consumer subsidy has declined. In spite of high food subsidy, the impact of TDPS on food security of poorer has been marginal. The main problems of present TDPS are: (a) large exclusion and inclusion errors; (b) the impact on the poor is marginal particularly in poorer states; (c) large leakage and diversion of food grains to open market.

PDS TO TPDS

As the TDPS was designed to use food-subsidies more specifically for the poor, the state governments were expected to identify the population "below the poverty line" (BPL) so that every BPL family could be offered certain quantity of food grain at specially subsidized rates. In fact, the price for the BPL was set at half the economic cost which the APL population was expected to pay. Besides, while food grain available for the BPL families was fixed, initially 10 kilograms, revised to 20 kilograms from April 2000, no such quality was assigned for the APL population. So, the declared goal of the TPDS was to insure food-subsidy for the poor, guarantee regular supply, cut down on wastage and leakage, and exclude the under-serving section of the population from the government's largesse.

SHORTCOMINGS

Although the public distribution system has been giving assistance to very good, the poor PDS is meant to provide nutritional security to the poorest in the country but that is exactly where it fares the worst. In some states highly failure of the system are identification of BPL families and flows in the delivery mechanism like in Bihar. There is collusion between the various agencies to divert a large part of the subsidized grain from supply chain of PDS. The characteristics of the delivery system of those states that have shown relatively low leakages.

A combination of factors have been responsible for the incidents in late 2007 involving the public distribution system in West Bengal. While the central policy of Targeted Public Distribution System and decreased allocations to the state have been primary contribute factor, local level dynamics that have affected the panchayati raj system are also of significance. A recent study has put the number of ghost public distribution system cards at a staggering 2.3 crore and, what is even more damning revealed that as many as 1.21 crore "deserving" poor have been left out of the food security umbrella. The food grain is being diverted to the black market. The quality of grain is not so good. The purpose of PDS to provide nutritional security to the poor is defeated. The study found Bihar to be worst off. Almost 90 per cent households in case of rice and 70 per cent in case of wheat complained of impurity, insect-infested supply and broken grain.

There are three principal reasons put forth regarding why the PDS does not deliver food subsidies efficiently. There are: (a) targeting errors, i.e., income transfers to non-target groups; (b) excessive cost of procurement, strong, and distribution, relative to the private sector; and (c) leakage or fraud, i.e. illegal diversions of subsidized grain to the open market.

To minimize leakages and distributions of subsidized grains there is need of bringing down the economic cost of grains through rationalization of cost of grains through rationalization of cost structure of handling food grains, procurement, storage, transport, etc. through public agencies. Doorstep delivery to retail outlets authenticated by the pros, releasė of ration quota to the beneficiaries in weekly instalment and efficient monitoring system will also improve the delivery system. Basically people in many places do not know their rights and entitlements regarding PDS. Dalit and tribal women are not aware of their entitlements. Right in terms of legal action helps in better implementation.

Apart from corruption, negligence on the part of the government to establish a viable distribution channel for the scheme in several states has resulted in this situation.

CONCLUSION

There are many reasons, of diversion of resources at such a massive scale and ineffective working of PDS suggests serious failure on the part of government to discharge its obligation to provide. Right policies and implementation are needed regarding the PDS problems. Rights approach in terms of legal measures, democratic participation and demand from public due to increase in awareness and transparency can improve the effectiveness of the programmes.

References

Dev, S. Mahendra, Inclusive Growth in India, Oxford University Press, New Delhi, 2008, pp. 114-21.

Economic and Political Weekly, Feb. 2-8, 2008, p. 63.

Vyas, V.S., India's Agrarian Structure, Economic Policies and Sustainable Development, A.F., New Delhi, 2003, pp. 182-83.

Yojana, July 2008, p. 44.

Public Distribution System

Issues and Challenges

Ashok Kumar Jha, Mirza Ehshan Haidar "Sham" and Gori Shankar

The Public Distribution System (PDS) in India, which was initiated as an *ad-hoc* war time measure to mobilize food supplies to prevent undue rise in prices, is now one of the largest such systems in the world. Over the years, the system has been developed as a stable and permanent feature of the strategy to contain rise in prices and to achieve equitable distribution of essential commodities. Through its supplemental role, the system strives to insure food security for millions of consumers across the country by making available some important and essential food items viz. wheat, rice, sugar, and edible oils at cheaper rates. As part of its two pronged strategy, the PDS also intends to play a crucial role in ensuring remunerative prices to the producers of these food items by the system of procurement during the post-harvest season when the prices normally tend to decline. Its efficacy in stabilizing food prices could be gauged from the fact that nearly one-third of the marketed surplus in respect of wheat and about one-fourth in respect of rice is being purchased and distributed by the public agencies every year. In the case of sugar about 40 per cent of the total sales in the country is being made available through the PDS network. With regard to edible oils, the system has tried to bridge the gap between the demand and supply by providing additional quantities of edible oils through imports.

In the recent years, PDS has occupied a prominent place in the public policy debate in this research work while tracing the origin, course and progress of PDS, an attempt has been made to provide a quantitative assessment of the benefits from PDS to the people in rural areas poor in particular, both in terms of quantity and income and its impact on the market prices.

The public distribution system (PDS) has received considerable attention in recent years in analyses and evaluations. PDS has been criticised for neglecting rural areas and for not doing enough for the poor. The consequences of these weaknesses it is being argued by some, are likely to be particularly adverse when the policy regime is strongly influenced by the philosophy of liberalisation and globalisation, it is believed that the promotion of agro-exports which is priority objective of the new policy regime would cause domestic foodgrain prices to rise affecting their economic move away from food crops to other more profitable crops. Above all, the newspaper reports were made even a layman aware of the puzzling paradox that while hunger persists in our land, unsold stocks of foodgrains remain locked in godowns and market price remain high.

Over the years the concept of PDS has evolved as a major policy instrument to : (i) reach essential commodities to the people particularly the weaker sections of the society, on an assured and regular basis at reasonable prices, (ii) work as an effective anti-inflationary measures, and (iii) make significant contribution in raising the nutritional standard of the poor. The system has acquired a vital position in our country. In the present context, it was extremely relevant to know the extent to which the avowed objectives of the PDS have been achieved.

The concern for ensuring food security to the teeming millions in the developing countries has been at the top of their agenda as these countries are invariably plagued by a high degree of inequality in income distribution widespread poverty and concomitant problem of malnutrition on under nutrition. Enhancement and maintenance of per capita entitlements deserves greater attention in view of the low per capita income and lack of social security cover of any meaningful magnitude in such countries. In India, the focus of attention during the sixties and seventies was mainly on increasing the food production and productivity coupled with the notion that the distributional aspects could be tackled subsequently. Although during the early eighties, foodgrain production reached a record level of 151 million tonnes, the estimate of 271 million persons below the poverty line aptly explained the proverbial "poverty amidst plenty" situation, fortunately, the segregated analysis and debate pleading for growth only and neglecting the distributional aspects user relegated to the background both in practical and conceptual terms during the eighties and it come to be realized that the gains of growth must be equitably distributed.

In India, about 30 per cent of the people belong to the poorer sections of the society. Food constitutes about 71 and 67 per cent of total expenditure of a poor household in rural and urban areas respectively. A large segment of the population, covering both the producers and the consumers, is vulnerable to the fluctuations in the prices of essential items. Even a marginal fall in consumption either due to an increase in price on due to a fall in income can bring the poor closer to starvation levels. In this context, in a free market situation, given the wide differences in production levels in various states with imperfections in the market, it is also essential to recognise that even if supply exceeds the demand at the country level, it does not necessarily mean adequate supplies in every region and in every market.

It is observed that the per capita availability of cereals fluctuated widely while recording only a marginal improvement over the years. During the sixties, the per capita availability fluctuated between 360 and 419 grams per day. It ranged between 366 and 442 grams during the seventies and between 398 and 453 grams per day during the eighties. Due to such variations, in shortage situations the free operation of the market forces tend to carry the supplies to those markets which buyers with incomes high enough to pay the market prices. In the process, some states get more than the other cities and towns than the rural areas while the groups with lower income find the supplies beyond their means. The far flung and hilly areas may not get enough supplies because of high handling and transport costs. Even if they do, lack of purchasing power at that price may not sustain such supplies for long. Thus, given this scenario, inequality in consumption may increase in a free market situation. The problem gets aggravated farther market situation. The problem gets aggravated further when these are inter-year fluctuations and wide inter state variation in production.

Further, the low income rural households mostly depend for their food purchases on the small traditional markets and for them the time is a crucial variable as for as demand is concerned. During, and a few months following harvest, rural households are by and large self-sufficient in food. However, small and marginal farmers sell a part of their output of grain to meet cash obligations; even though they subsequently buy back. Later in year, pressure in the market increases as most households exhaust their own stocks and begin to depend increasingly on the market. It has been the Indian experience that wide fluctuations in prices take place owing to the fluctuations in production aggravated by speculative behaviour of the traders. More importantly, the dependence on the market for foodgrains by the poorer section during the lean season of the year has been observed to lead to a high dependence on consumption loans taken from the traditional sources viz. local money lenders, petty shop keepers, etc. It is the setup that the availability is needed to be improved through the Public Distribution System (PDS) network so that in a situation of high prices, its presence and effectiveness could be felt.

In the Indian agriculture scene, a major share of the surplus foodgrain production comes from a small number of states. Only three states namely, Punjab, Haryana and Uttar Pradesh offer about 90 per cent of the total quantity of foodgrains purchased by the public agencies at support/ procurement prices. While in the case of rice, these states contribute about 83 per cent of total procurement, in the case of wheat, almost the entire lot comes from them. As the procured foodgrains are transported to the deficit states, the average lead of haul by rail from the surplus producing states to the consuming states is more than 1400 kilometers, these long leads involve enormous transport costs and thus result in higher market prices, if no subsidy is provided, which may not be affordable for the consumers in the far flung areas. Therefore, supplies in such areas through PDS at reasonable prices after incurring a subsidy assumes special significance.

The relational of such a policy is also derived from the observed fact that price elasticity in respect of essential commodities, such as cereals, pulses edible oils and sugar is relatively high for those below the poverty line *vis-à-vis* for those in the higher income classes both in urban and rural areas and, therefore burden of any decline in the availability and consequent increase in price hurts disproportionately the poor particularly during the years of high prices. This necessitates that in such years, a larger proportion of the quantities procured by the public agencies be made available quantities procured by the public agencies be made available to the vulnerable sections of the society. In the years of abundant production of foodgrains, a policy of procurement is also to help the producers secure remunerative price for their output. In view of this, the PDS is favoured on a continuous bases irrespective of the level of production. It is also expected to render better support to the vulnerable sections, if activated on a much larger scale in drought and scarcity situations. Given the size of the country, degree of instability in agricultural production wide inter-state variations in production of food items, nature of price elasticity of demand for these products and low per capita incomes and its skewed distribution it appears necessary to protect the vulnerable sections of the society through distribution of food items at reasonable prices.

The Public Distribution System (PDS) in India which started as an *ad hoc* war time measure to mobilize food supplies to support undue rise in price, is now one of the largest such system in the world over the years, the system has been developed as a stable and continuous feature of the strategy to contain rise in prices and to achieve equitable distribution of essential commodities. Through its supplemental role the system strives to ensure food security for millions of consumers across the country by making available the essential food items viz. wheat, rice, sugar, and edible oils at cheaper rates. As part of its two pronged strategy, the PDS also intends to play a crucial role in ensuring remunerative prices to the producers of these food items by the system of procurement during the peak marketing period when the price normally tend to decline. Its efficacy in stabilizing food price could be gauged from one-fourth in respect of rice is being purchased and distributed by the public agencies every year in the case of sugar, about 40 per cent of the total sales in the country is being made available through the PDS network with regard to edible oils the system is expected to bridge the gap between the demand and supply by providing adequate quantities through imports.

However, despite the elaborate network involving handling of PDS has been free from criticism. The universal coverages has massive quantities of food items, the performance drawn adverse comments because of the large subsidy burden on the state exchequer. The system has also been blamed for its reported bias towards urban, middle and rich classes of the population ignoring the need for targetting towards the vulnerable section of the society and thus diluting the principal objective of achieving equitable distribution and providing food security to the needy. However, such notions were not derived on the basis of any systematic study but often on the basis of general perceptions based on partial observations. Further, these perceptions gained currency due to a visibly higher density of PDS network in relatively small geographical urban areas as compared to the rural areas. It was only after the 42nd round of National Sample Survey Organization's (NSSO) country-wide survey of 1986-87 on utilization of PDS, which reported certain facts contrary to the general observation, that the misconception were partially removed.

Over the years, the concept of public distribution system has evolved as a major policy instrument to : (i) Such essential commodities to the people, particularly the weaker sections of the society on an assured and regular basis at reasonable prices, (ii) work as an effective anti-inflationary means use, and (iii) make significant contribution in raising the nutritional standard of the poor. The system has acquired a vital position in our country. In this context, it would be very relevant to know the extent of which the avowed objectives of PDS has been achieved. Some of the earlier studies found that PDS remained mainly urban-oriented and biased towards middle and rich classes. Gupta (1977) found that even during the abundant supplies through PDS, the economically vulnerable section could not be protected from erosion of foodgrain consumption. Subbarao (1988) supported this view and observed that the poor in rural areas did not benefit much but the urban population undoubtedly benefited from PDS. Joh (1989) also viewed that the food subsidies went overwhelmingly to urban areas in preference to the rural area. However, some recent studies viz. by Dev and Suryanarayana (1991) and Auluwalia (1993) have found that the PDS is not pro-urban and the rural areas were nearly as well served by it as the urban areas. These studies also concluded that PDS is not biased towards any particular group. Most of the other micro and macro-level studies concentrated on the day-to-day operational problems faced in the implementation of PDS and did not assess, in a systematic manner the extent to which the system had helped the poor and rural population. A particular mention needs to be made of the serious limitation of the studies as they concentrated more on process evaluation and did not ply adequate attention to the impact evaluation with particular reference to the rural and poor people. The aspect of income transfer and redistribution through PDS remained almost unattended. The Price advantage over a period of time has also not been analyzed, in detects, and of the studies. The analysis given in the book is intended to fill up this research gap.

References

Although no precises estimates of the exact size of the marketed surplus are available based on the available micro-studies. S.S. Acharya came to conclusion that the marketed supplies out put ratio is around 0.15 for paddy and wheat, see S.S. Acharya *et. al.* "Agricultural Marketing in India", Oxford & IBH Publishing Co. Pvt. Ltd., 1992.

Department of Civil Supplies, Annual Report, 1988-89. Also, see, *Economic Survey,* 1987-88, Ministry of Finance.

Economic Survey 1992-97, Ministry of Finance, p. 24.

In 1980, The Government decided to make the PDS a Permanent Feature of the Economy and an Integral part of the price stabilization policy. This is also evident from the objectives tested in the Seventh Five Year Plan (1985-90), Planning Commission and the focus on PDS was sharpened in the revised Twenty-point programme, 1986, and by including it as one of the important components in the minimum needs programme in 1987-88.

Planning Commission, Eighth Five Year Plan (1992-97), Government of India, p. 27, also see *Economic Survey,* 1991-92, Ministry of Finance, p. 126.

Sen, Amartya, "Poverty and Famines", Published on behalf of the ICO by Clarenton Press, Oxford (UK) 1982. Also see, Sen "Poverty and Entitlements" in "Food Policy Integrating Supply, Distribution and Consumption", World Bank (1987).

Planning Commission, Draft Sixth Five Year Plan (Revised) 1978-83, p. 129.

World Bank, The World Development Report, 1986, New Yark, Oxford University Press.

Working of PDS/TPS and Food Management

MUKUL KUMAR SINGH

INTRODUCTION

State trading in foodgrains through public distribution system is a good device for food management. PDS structure as prevalent in India is most extensive. Economic Survey, 2002-03 lays down, "PDS with a network of about 4.74 lakh fair price shops is perhaps largest distribution network of its type in the world. It operates as a joint venture between the centre and the states with the FCI as an apex body for procurement and distribution. Arora (1997) rightly observes: "The public Distribution System (PDS) is a key component of supply management in the nation". Its revamping by TPDS is pro-poor as TPDS contains subsidised price system for the BPL families. Under it, AAY families are supplied most subsidised foodgrains. Central Government makes an allotment of 2.28 lakh tonnes of wheat and rice per month to Bihar. This allotment lags behind the actual requirement for subsidised food in the state. In this respect inter-state disparity is marketable. The poor states despite high incidence of poverty and population pressure are subject to some sort of negligence. The poorest states of Uttar Pradesh, Bihar, Madhya Pradesh, Rajasthan and Orissa account for as much as 52 per cent of population and even a larger proportion of the country's poor. But these states receive only 20 per cent of Central allocation of foodgrains. Bihar is the worst sufferer in this respect.

PDS ALLOCATION AND OFF-TAKE VIS-A-VIS THE CASE OF BIHAR

On allocation off-take front, a gap is noticeable. According to Prof. R. Datt, "Sharp fluctuation in PDS off-take is either due to narrow margin between open market and issue price or low releases of PDS supplies by Government to dealers or lack of commitment to PDS programme. Table 1 presents allocation and off-take of foodgrains (wheat and rice) in different years.

TABLE I

Foodgrains Allocation and Off-take under Public Distribution System

(Million tonnes)

Year	*Wheat Allocation*	*Rice*	*Allocation Offtake*	*Offtake*
1992-93	9.25	7.47	11.48	9.55
1993-94	9.56	5.91	12.41	8.87
1994-95	10.80	4.83	13.32	8.03
1995-96	11.31	5.81	14.62	9.75
1996-97	10.71	8.52	15.10	11.14
1997-98	10.11	7.08	12.83	9.90
1998-99	10.11	7.95	12.93	10.74
1999-2000	10.37	5.76	13.89	11.31
2000-01	11.57a	4.07	16.26	7.97
2001-02	13.4a	5.68	17.23	8.16
2002-03	13.4a	9.78	36.02	10.35
2003-04	37.11a	10.71	34.46	12.08

Note : a—Including Antyodaya.
Source : *Economic Survey*, 2003-04, p. 94.

From the table, it is clear that off-take of wheat and rice under PDS has been always less than allocation. Allotment off-take gap is more marketable in 2002-03, and 2003-04. Off take of foodgrains has lagged behind in recent years also. Total procurement of rice and wheat was 37.2 million tonnes in 2003-04, 41.6 million tonnes in 2004-05, 42.4 million tonnes in 2006-07 whereas off-take of wheat and rice for TPDS was 24.2 million tonnes in 2003-04, 2.97 million tonnes in 2004-05, 31.4 million tonnes in 2005-06 and 31.6 million tonnes in 2006-07. In 2003-04, to sale out the surplus, Government took help of open sales and exports to the extent of 11.6 million tonnes. But it is surprising that in spite of excess stock available with F.C.I., why does the central government not raise the allotment to Bihar on the basis of its actual BPL families as per revised survey made by Ministry of Rural Development of the Government of Bihar. Agrawal has rightly remarked,

> ". . . the PDS has evolved in a way that the regional variations in it have nothing to do with foodgrains deficits of the states or with the requirements of States.

The case of Bihar: In Bihar there are 46,000 fair price shops through which public distribution system operates. Each fair price shop is envisaged to serve a population of 2000. The FPS dealers get commission for foodgrains distribution or sale which is released to the quantum of food supply to consumers. In this respect State Food Corporation too has a broker status, it receives foodgrains from the FCI and releases it from its godowns with the help of district manager and AGM of Godown. It charges Rs. 50 per Quintal of foodgrain supply to dealers for its services.

In operation of PDS, PRIs are deeply involved. BPL AAY and Vishesh AAY families are identified by the Mukhiya of Gram Panchayat in the camp organised by the BDO. It is on the basis of such identification that BPL families receive red coupons, AAY families yellow and vishesh AAY families orange colour coupons. To keep vigile over operation of PDS in foodgrains, Bihar Government resolved for creation of 'Panchayat Stariya Nigarani Samiti'. This is totally a

Panchayati Raj institution having no berth in it for any official member. Likewise there is due representation of Panchyati Raj on Anusravan Samiti that operates at the sub-division level. However, sub-divisional officer is responsible for its overall operation and commission.

Now the subsidised foodgrain price is Rs. 4.15 per kg. of wheat for BPL families and Rs. 2 per kg for AAY families. In case of rice, it is Rs. 5.65 per kg for BPL families and Rs. 3 per kg for AAY families.

But one shortcoming is worth mention. The Central Government has accepted the number of 6523 lakh BPL families but according to the revised survey of BPL families, total number of rural and urban families has been reported to 1.2 crores. Hence, the State Government has to fix subsidised food supply to BPL and AAY families at 25 kg i.e. 14 kg wheat +11 kg rice. On the other hand, Central Government has decided to supply 35 kg subsidised food-grains to poor families. As a matter of fact this would be possible in Bihar only when its allotment is raised. APL families can also purchase from fair price shops but at higher prices which respond to the economic costs. Now, PDS in Bihar has got many contradictions and constraints as detailed under following sub-section.

PROBLEMS AND WEAK-SPOTS OF PDS

There has been various weaknesses in the working of the public distribution system such as failure to serve effectively even the BPL families, bias in favour of urban areas, lack of due care *vis-a-vis* inappropriate coverage in Poor states with large population of the rural poor and wide leakages of PDS foodgrains procured from the Food Corporation of India to open market and supply of inferior grains in the ration shops. Arora has remarked :

In states like U.P. and Bihar the performance of PDS particularly in rural areas, is found very dismal. A concerted and sincere effort is needed to bring the performance of the PDS to a satisfactory level. Dagli Committee also questioned the operational efficiency of PDS and its role in securing social justice. R. Radhakrishna (2002) has pinpointed weakness of delivery system in poor states. In Bihar much complexities are caused due to low performance at the level of District managers of State Food Corporation. Practically due to poor staffing one D.M. of FCI has to look after grains supply to many blocks. Issue order is consequently delayed. So the fair price shop dealers often fail to make foodgrains supply to consumers on particular date. Such uncertainty goes against the interest of the poorest of poor families. Due to irregularity, in supply and communication of right time for distribution of foodgrains the poorest people have the problem of economic access. And as such they do not have cash ready at the moment when stock arrives at the shops.

In Bihar one most needed item, i.e. Kerosene oil is also supplied through the PDS. Kerosene oil is sold to APL families also. For all types of families blue coupon is provided. Here leakages to open market the price being higher are more rampant. The problem of leakages of foodgrains to open market is also a common matter. The fair price shop dealers manage such leakages to have earnings from the market. Of course, the great problem with the poor ones, in Bihar or in such other states, is that they are not awakened.

No doubt progressive parties, specially the revolutionary leftists are awakening them, as it is evident from challenges to BPL lists. Yet any scheme meant for the poor can be successful if the poor ones themselves are fully awakened and capable to avail the benefit. Without co-operation of the beneficiaries, leakage managements of PDS in Bihar in the interest of the dealers will continue. The problem of leakages of foodgrains to open market has been rather intensified under TDPS (Targeted Public Distribution) which is in operation since June 1997. It happens, so because, to provide food security to vulnerable section some sort of poverty-based price discrimination has been effected by the government. Prices of foodgrains for BPL and AAY families have been kept very low (the difference between cost and price being subsidised); so it is more paying to divert such highly subsidised foodgrains to the open market. Hence, the poor families which face the problem of economic access and remain uninformed of due arrivals, remain deprived and through leakage channels the PDS shop licences maximise their earnings. Such stigma on TPDS must be removed.

A RESUME

Public distribution system in India specially the revamped one as TPDS is not only a device for food management but also a consignment of the stages for poverty alleviation. It has been claimed by the Government.

"A well targeted and properly functioning public distribution system (PDS) is an important constituent of the strategy for poverty alleviation. But unfortunately in case of this device too, in stead of trickle down there is the problem of 'trickle across' or 'trickle up'. Poor and defective delivery system has facilitated leakage of foodgrains from fair price shops to open market kerosene oil is also black marketed. On the one hand there has been enormous burden of subsidy on the government that it accepts to safeguard the interest of the poor families. But subsidisation has led to black marketing through leakages to open market. PRIs no doubt have been involved but what ever be the reasons, zero leakage is still a dream unless the poor ones are awakened and invited, capable to raise their voice and fight irregularities and leakages of PDS, improvement will be rather a shifting horizon in Bihar. Equally important is the role of state which through its administrative personnel involved in implementation of PDS, can facilitate physical access to food, besides economic access through subsidised price system. In respect of food management, determination of state machinery can be a very much effective in controlling leakages of public distribution system.

REFERENCES

Govt. of India, *Economic Survey*, 2002-03, p. 94.

Arora, V.P.S. (1997), 'Agricultural Marketing Senario in India', *The Bihar Journal of Agricultural Marketing*, Vol. 3, p. 284.

Agrawal, A.N. (2008 ed.), Indian Economy, New Age International Publishers, New Delhi, p. 358.

Datt, R. (2006 ed), Indian Economy, S. Chand and Co., New Delhi, p. 503.

Govt. of India, *Economic Survey*, 2007-08, p. 175, Table 723.

Ibid.

Op. cit., p. 359.

Government of Bihar, Resolution No. 4124/Khadya, Patna dt. 26.09.2001.

Op. cit.

Radhakrishna, R. (2002), Food and Nutrition Security in Kirit S. Parikh and R. Radhakrishna, India Development Report, 2002, New Delhi, p. 55.

Govt. of India, *Economic Survey*, 1997-98, p. 72.

Social Aspects of Public Distribution System
Some Issues

Jagdish Prasad and Arun Kumar

During periods of high inflation in food prices, governments must provide a basic minimum quantity of foodgrain and other food items at low prices through public distribution systems to low-income, food-insecure, and vulnerable populations. In India, the ostensible purpose of the Targeted Public Distribution System (TPDS) was to take food to the poor; in practice, it has resulted in the large-scale exclusion of the poor and food-insecure from the public food system.

The 61st Round of the National Sample Survey (NSS), establishes that targeting has led to high rates of exclusion of needy households from the Public Distribution System (PDS) and a clear deterioration of coverage in States like Kerala where the universal PDS was most effective.

The Targeted PDS was begun in 1996. In March 2000, the prices of grain for above poverty line (APL) cardholders were hiked and the gap between prices for below poverty line (BPL) and APL households widened. In many States, APL prices of grain were close to market prices and, as a result, households with APL cards stopped buying grain from the PDS. The Antyodaya programme introduced a new category, the "poorest of the poor", for whom rice and wheat are available at even lower prices than for BPL households. In the present situation, a person who belongs to a household that has neither a BPL nor an Antyodaya card is effectively excluded from the PDS.

The government has acknowledged in the Lok Sabha that 3.7 crore below poverty line (BPL) card-holders or a staggering 35 per cent of the total number of beneficiaries did not exist, solidifying the already strong evidence of rampant misuse of the food subsidy for purposes other than the well-being of the intended beneficiaries.

Food and agriculture minister Sharad Pawar confirmed that 10.28 crore BPL cards were issued which was way above Planning Commission's estimate of there being only 6.52 crore BPL families.

The disclosure naturally had members expressing their apprehension that benefits of other central schemes might not be reaching the intended beneficiaries.

Various central schemes, such as for self-employment, housing and health insurance among others, are made available to the poor across the country based on the BPL card. Pawar said several state governments had initiated action to cancel bogus cards. As many as 13 states, including Andhra Pradesh, Assam, Gujarat, Madhya Pradesh, Delhi and Orissa had cancelled more than 67.45 lakh bogus ration cards since July 2006.

"Instructions have been issued to all state and UT governments to take action as per law against persons found in possession of bogus of fake ration cards and against government staff found responsible for issuing ration cards to ineligible families," the minister said. The fresh evidence has once again underscored the serious problems that be-devil the PDS. But while there are mounds of evidence of PDS grain being diverted to private players and, increasingly, even being exported, the political class scoffs at suggestions for reforms. They have brushed aside those who have advocated alternatives like food vouchers.

The recent report of the National Sample Survey gives us an insight into the magnitude and nature of this exclusion from the PDS. At the all-India level, 70.5 per cent of rural households either possessed no card or held an APL card. Since households with APL cards are effectively excluded from the PDS, the majority of rural households in India are excluded from the PDS.

To take some State-level examples, in Bihar, 82 per cent of households held an APL card or no card; the corresponding proportion was 87.7 per cent in Assam, 83.5 per cent in Uttar Pradesh, 83.2 per cent in Himachal Pradesh, 81.5 per cent in Rajasthan and 74.3 per cent in Uttaranchal. In Kerala, the State where the universal PDS was most effective 70 per cent of households now have been excluded from the PDS. The magnitude of exclusion was also high in the State of the North East (for example, in Nagaland, 90 per cent of households are reported to have no ration cards) but this may reflect poor quality data. The only two States where a simple majority of households were not excluded and did possess a BPL or Antyodaya card were Andhra Pradesh (56.5 per cent), and Karnataka (51.7 per cent). Tamil Nadu is an honourable exception. Although 68.9 per cent of households have APL cards (and 11 per cent have no ration cards), there is a uniform price and allocation for APL and BPL cardholders. In practice, there is a system of universal PDS in Tamil Nadu.

The NSS Report also allows us to classify—by caste, occupation, land ownership and consumer expenditure category—the households that are excluded from the PDS.

EXCLUSION BY OCCUPATION

The NSS defines five types of rural households, based on information 011 sources of income: self-employed (agriculture), self-employed (non-agriculture), agricultural labour, other labour and other households. We focus on agricultural labour, since manual agricultural labour households are undoubtedly among those most in need of access to the PDS. The all India average indicates that 52 per cent of agricultural labour households either had no card or an APL card. The corresponding proportion was 96 per cent in Manipur, 68 per cent in Rajasthan and Assam, 71 per cent in Bihar and 73 per cent in Uttar Pradesh. Can 70 per cent of agricultural labour households be considered as ineligible for the PDS? There were only four States in which two-thirds or more of agricultural labour households were not excluded from the PDS (that is, held a BPL or Antyodaya ration card). These States were Andhra Pradesh, Karnataka, Jammu and Kashmir and Tripura.

SOCIAL BACKGROUND

The social background of households, focusing on Scheduled Caste and Scheduled Tribe households. We have selected only those States where the rural Scheduled Caste population is more than 10 per cent of the total population. In rural areas, there is known to be substantial degree of overlap between the Scheduled Caste status, landlessness and poverty. The NSS data shows that 70 per cent or more of Scheduled Caste households had no card or an APL card in the rural areas of Assam, Bihar, Himachal Pradesh, Jammu and Kashmir, Punjab, Rajasthan and Uttar Pradesh. Among these States, only Punjab is a cereal-surplus State. At the all-India level, 60 per cent of the Scheduled Caste households in rural areas were effectively excluded from the PDS. States with a lower degree of exclusion of Scheduled Caste households were Karnataka (27 per cent excluded), Andhra Pradesh (31 per cent), and Kerala (38 per cent).

Turning to households belonging to the Scheduled Tribes, again, large number of households do not have access to the PDS : to illustrate, 90 per cent of rural Scheduled Tribe households in Assam, 79 per cent in Arunachal Pradesh and 68 per cent in Chhattisgarh were excluded from the PDS. Surprisingly, the North Eastern States did not perform too well on this count (though again there may be a problem of data quality). There were only four States—Andhra Pradesh, Orissa, Gujarat and Maharashtra—where more than 50 per cent of rural Scheduled Tribe households had received a BPL or Antyodaya card.

The NSS Report has classified households by the extent of land they possessed. It is to be noted that land possessed refers to all types of land and includes agricultural land, homestead land and non-agricultural land. It is not surprising, then, that a very small proportion of households is reported as landless. I have therefore grouped together the two categories of landless and near-landless households, and only considered those States in which this category comprised 20 per cent or more of the total population. Again, the conclusion is that a very high proportion of landless and near landless households did not possess BPL or Antyodaya cards (86 per cent in Sikkim, 80 per cent in Goa, 79 per cent in Uttar Pradesh, 76 per cent in Haryana, 75 per cent in Jharkhand, and 74 per cent in Uttaranchal, for example) and were thus effectively excluded from the PDS.

A classification of households on the basis of per capita household expenditure class: Using the official poverty line (an all-India level of Rs. 360 per capita per month), we classified all households with a monthly per capita expenditure (MPCE) less than Rs. 365 as "poor" households. It needs to be noted that the official Indian poverty line reflects absolute deprivation. Again, it may be defined inclusion as obtaining a BPL or Antyodaya card. Our results show that a significant proportion of households falling below the official poverty line did not possess a BPL. or Antyodaya card. The proportion of such households was, to illustrate, 77.5 per cent in Bihar, 74 per cent in Uttar Pradesh, 67 per cent in Jharkhand and 54 per cent in Madhya Pradesh and Chhattisgarh. In all these States, even the majority of those below the official poverty line were excluded from the PDS.

In starving for "efficiency" by means of narrow targeting households that should be entitled to basic food security through the PDS have been left out. The data from the 61st round of the NSS make it quite clear that a high proportion of agricultural labour and other labour households, of households belonging to the Scheduled Castes and the Scheduled Tribes, of households with little or no land and households in the lowest expenditure classes, are effectively excluded from the PDS today. The exception is Tamil Nadu, which is the only State to have introduced a universal system of PDS, with rice available at Rs. 2 a kilogram to all households irrespective of the type of ration card. The only immediate remedy to the problem is to make the PDS universal again, and to ensure that a monthly ration of basic food commodities including grain, pulses and oil is available at affordable prices to all households.

References

Report of the Public Distribution and Other Sources of Household Consumption, 2004-05, Govt. of India, 2007.

Report of National Sample Survey, 2005.

Report of the Ministry of Agriculture, 2008.

Economic Survey, 2008-09.

Approach paper of 11th Year Plan, 2007-12.

Administrative Aspects in Delivery Mechanism of Public Distribution System

R. Rahman and Md. Ayub Rayeen

The Public Distribution System (PDS) evolved as a system of management of scarcity and for distribution of foodgrains at affordable prices. Over the years, PDS has become an important part of Government's policy for management of food economy in the country. PDS is supplemental in nature and is not intended to make available the entire requirement of any of the commodities distributed under it to a household or a section of the society.

PDS is operated under the joint responsibility of the Central and the State Governments. The Central government, through FCI, has assumed the responsibility for procurement, storage, transportation and bulk allocation of foodgrains to the State Governments. The operational responsibility including allocation within State, Identification of families below the poverty line, issue of Ration Cards and supervision of the functioning of FPS, rest with the State Governments. Under the PDS presently the commodities namely wheat, rice, sugar and kerosene, are being allocated to the States/UTs for distribution. Some States/UTs also distribute additional items of mass consumption through the PDS outlets such as cloth, exercise books, pulses, salt and tea etc.

EVOLUTION OF PUBLIC DISTRIBUTION SYSTEM

Public Distribution of essential commodities had been in existence in India during the inter-war period. PDS, with its focus on distribution of foodgrains in urban scarcity areas, had emanated from the critical food shortages of 1960. PDS had substantially contributed to the containment of rise in foodgrains prices and ensured access of food to urban consumers. As the national agricultural production had grown in the aftermath of Green Revolution, the outreach of PDS was extended to tribal blocks and areas of high incidence of poverty in the 1970s and 1980s.

PDS, till 1992, was a general entitlement scheme for all consumers without any specific target. Revamped Public Distribution System (RPDS) was launched in June 1992 in 1775 blocks throughout the country.

The Targeted Public Distribution System (TPDS) was introduced with effect from June 1997.

REVAMPED PUBLIC DISTRIBUTION SYSTEM (RPDS)

The Revamped Public Distribution System (RPDS) was launched in June 1992 with a view to strengthen and streamline the PDS as well as to improve its reach in the far-flung, hilly, remote and inaccessible areas where a substantial section of the poor live. It covered 1775 blocks wherein area specific programmes such as the Drought Prone Area Programme (DPAP), Integrated Tribal Development Projects (ITDP), Desert Development Programme (DDP) and certain Designated Hill Areas (DHA) identified in consultation with State Governments for special focus, with respect to improvement of the PDS infrastructure. Foodgrains for distribution in RPDS areas were issued to the States at 50 paise below the Central Issue Price. The scale of issue was up to 20 kg per card.

The RPDS included area approach for ensuring effective reach of the PDS commodities, their delivery by State Governments at the doorstep of FPSs in the identified areas, additional ration cards to the left out families, infrastructure requirements like additional Fair Price Shops, storage capacity, etc. and additional commodities such as tea, salt, pulses, soap, etc. for distribution through PDS outlets.

TARGETED PUBLIC DISTRIBUTION SYSTEM (TPDS)

The PDS, till 1992 was a general entitlement scheme for all consumers without special targets. The RPDS was launched in 1992 in 1775 blocks in tribal, hill and drought prone areas. PDS as it stood earlier, had been widely criticized for its failure to serve the population Below the Poverty Line (BPL), its urban bias, limited coverage in the States with high concentration of the rural poor and lack of transparent and accountable arrangements for delivery.

In June 1997, the Government of India launched the Targeted Public Distribution System (TPDS) with focus on the poor. Under the TPDS, States are required to formulate and implement foolproof arrangements for identification of the poor for delivery of foodgrains and for its distribution in a transparent and accountable manner at the FPS level.

The scheme, when introduced, was intended to benefit about 6 crore poor families for whom a quantity of about 72 lakh tonnes of foodgrains was earmarked annually. The identification of the poor under the scheme is done by the States as per State-wise poverty estimates of the Planning Commission for 1993-94 based on the methodology of the "Expert Group on estimation of proportion and number of poor" chaired by Late Prof. Lakdawala. The allocation of foodgrains to the States/UTs was made on the basis of average consumption in the past, i.e. average annual off-take of foodgrains under the PDS during the past ten years at the time of introduction of TPDS.

The quantum of foodgrains in excess of the requirement of BPL families was provided to the State as 'transitory allocation' for which a quantum of 103 lakh tonnes of foodgrains was earmarked annually. Over and above the TPDS allocation, additional allocation to States was also given. The transitory allocation was intended for continuation of benefit of subsidized foodgrains to the population Above the Poverty Line (APL) as any sudden withdrawal of benefits existing under PDS from them was not considered desirable. The transitory allocation was issued at prices, which were subsidized but were higher than the prices for the BPL quota of foodgrains.

Keeping in view the consensus on increasing the allocation of foodgrains to BPL families, and to better target the food subsidy, Government of India increased the allocation to BPL families from 10 kg. to 20 kg. of foodgrains per family per month at 50 per cent of the economic cost and allocation to APL families at economic cost w.e.f. 1.4.2000. The allocation of APL families was retained at the same level as at the time of introduction of TPDS but the Central Issue Prices (CIP) for APL were fixed at 100 per cent of economic cost from that date so that the entire consumer subsidy could be directed to the benefit of the BPL population.

The number of BPL families has been increased w.e.f. 1/12/2000 by shifting the base to the population projections of the Registrar General as on 1.3.2000 instead of the earlier population projections of 1995. With this increase the total number of BPL families is 652.03 lakh as against 596.23 lakh families originally estimated when TPDS was introduced in June 1997.

The end retail price is fixed by the States/UTs after taking into account margins for wholesalers/retailers, transportations charges, levies, local taxes, etc. Under the TPDS the States were requested to issue foodgrains at a difference of not more than 50 paise per kg over and above the CIP for BPL families. Flexibility to States/UTs, has been given in the matter of fixing the retail issue prices by removing the restriction of 50 paise per kg over and above the CIP for distribution of foodgrains under TPDS except with respect to Antyodaya Anna Yojana where the end retail price is to be retained at Rs. 2 a kg. for wheat and Rs. 3 a kg. for rice.

IDENTIFICATION OF BPL FAMILIES UNDER TPDS

To work out the population below the poverty line under the TPDS, there was a general consensus at the Food Minister's conference held in August 1996, for adopting the methodology used by the expert groups set-up by the Planning Commission under the Chairmanship of Late Prof. Lakdawala. The BPL households were determined on the basis of population projections of the Registrar General of India for 1995 and the State-wise poverty estimates of the Planning Commission for 1993-94. The total number of BPL households so determined was 596.23 lakh. Guidelines for implementing the TPDS were issued in which the State Governments had been advised to identify the BPL families by involving the Gram Panchayats and Nagarpalikas. While doing so the thrust should be to include the really poor and vulnerable sections of the society such as landless agricultural labourers, marginal farmers, rural artisans/craftsmen such as potters, tappers, weavers, black-smith, carpenters, etc. in the rural areas and slum-dwellers and persons earning their livelihood on daily basis in the informal sector like potters, rickshaw-pullers, cart-pullers, fruit and flower sellers on the pavement etc. in urban areas. The Gram Panchayats and Gram Sabhas should also be involved in the identification of eligible families.

The number of BPL families has been increased w.e.f. 1.12.2000 by shifting the base to the population projections of the Registrar General as on 1.3.2000 instead of the earlier population projections of 1995. With this increase the total number of BPL families is 652.03 lakh as against 596.23 lakh families originally estimated when TPDS was introduced in June 1997.

ANTYODAYA ANNA YOJANA (AAY)

AAY is a step in the direction of making TPDS aim at reducing hunger among the poorest segments of the BPL population. A National Sample Survey Exercise points towards the fact that about 5 per cent of the total population in the country sleeps without two square meals a day. This section of the population can be called as "hungry". In order to make TPDS more focused and targeted towards this category of population, the "Antyodaya Anna Yojana" (AAY) was launched in December, 2000 for one crore poorest of the poor families.

AAY contemplates identification of one crore poorest of the poor families from amongst the number of BPL families covered under TPDS within the States and providing them foodgrains at a highly subsidized rate of Rs. 2 per kg. for wheat and Rs. 3 per kg. for rice. The States/UTs are required to bear the distribution cost, including margin to dealers and retailers as well as the transportation cost. Thus the entire food subsidy is being passed on to the consumers under the scheme.

The scale of issue that was initially 25 kg. per family per month has been increased to 35 kg. per family per month with effect from 1st April 2002.

The AAY Scheme has been expanded in 2003-04 by adding another 50 lakh BPL households headed by widows or terminally ill persons or disabled persons or persons aged 60 years or more with no assured means of subsistence or societal support. With this increase, 1.5 crore (i.e. 23% of BPL) families have been covered under the AAY.

As announced in the Union Budget 2004-05, the AAY has been further expanded by another 50 lakh BPL families by including, *inter alia*, all households at the risk of hunger. Orders to this effect have been issued on 3rd August 2004. In order to identify these households, the guidelines stipulate the following criteria:

- Landless agriculture labourers, marginal farmers, rural artisans/craftsmen, such as potters, tanners, weavers, blacksmiths, carpenters, slum-dwellers, and persons earning their livelihood, on daily basis in the informal sector like porters, coolies, rickshaw pullers, hand cart pullers, fruit and flower sellers, snake charmers, rag pickers, cobblers, destitutes and other similar categories irrespective of rural or urban areas.

- Households headed by widows or terminally ill persons or disabled persons or persons aged 60 years or more with no assured means of subsistence or societal support.
- Widows or terminally ill persons or disabled persons or persons aged 60 years or more or single woman or single man with no family or societal support or assured means of subsistence.
- All primitive tribal households.

With this increase, the number of AAY families has been increased to 2 crore (i.e. 30.66% of BPL) families.

As announced in the Union Budget 2005-06, the AAY has further been expanded to cover another 50 lakh BPL households thus increasing its overage to 2.5 crore households. (i.e. 38% of BPL)

The status of identification of households under AAY (Normal, 1st expansion, 2nd expansion and 3rd expansion) is given in Annexure. The defaulting States/UTs are reminded regularly as a part of monitoring.

IDENTIFICATION OF ANTYODAYA FAMILIES AND ALLOCATION OF FOODGRAINS

The identification of the Antyodaya families and issuing of distinctive Ration Cards to these families is the responsibility of the concerned State Governments. Detailed guidelines were issued to the States/UTs for identification of the Antyodaya families under the AAY and additional Antyodaya families under the expanded AAY. Allocation of foodgrains under the scheme is being released to the States/UTs on the basis of issue of distinctive AAY Ration Cards to the identified Antyodaya families. The present monthly allocation of foodgrains under AAY is around 7.27 lakh tonnes per month.

Since 1997, the Scale of issue of the BPL families has been gradually increased from 10 kg. to 35 kg. per family per month. The scale of issue was increased from 10 kg. to 20 kg.

per family per month with effect from 1.4.2000. The allocation for APL families has been retained at the same level as at the time of introduction of TPDS (i.e. 10 kg. per family per month). The allocation of foodgrains for the BPL families has been further increased from 20 kg. to 25 kg. per family per month with effect from July, 2001. Initially, the Antyodaya families were provided 25 kg. of foodgrains per family per month at the time of launching of the scheme. The scale of issue under APL, BPL and AAY has been revised to 35 kg. per family per month with effect from 1.4.2002 with a view to enhancing the food security at the household level.

MEASURES TAKEN TO STRENGTHEN TPDS

The Central Issue Price for wheat and rice for BPL families is Rs. 4.15 per kg. and Rs. 5.65 per kg. This has remained constant since 25.7.2000 and has not been increased since last two and half years taking into account their low purchasing power. This is approximately 48 per cent of the economic cost of FCL. The CIP for MY families has also remained unchanged.

As per the latest Poverty Estimates of the Planning Commission (1999-2000), the poverty ratio at national level has come down from 36.15 per cent in 1993-94 to 26.10 per cent during 1999-2000 (with State-wise variations). The allocation of foodgrains under the TPDS however, continues to be made on the basis of estimates of poverty of 1993-94, which are higher. This allocation based on 1993-94 poverty estimates, have been further revised upwards, and based on the population projection, as on 1st April 2000 thereby increasing the monthly allocation to the State Governments.

The Citizens' Charter (issued in November 1997), for adoption by the State Governments, is to provide services in a transparent and accountable manner under PDS.

The Order, *inter alia,* covers a range of areas relating to correct identification of BPL families, issue of Ration Cards, proper distribution, and monitoring of PDS-related operations. Contraventions of the provisions of the Order are punishable under the Essential Commodities Act, 1955.

From February 2000 the Ministry has appointed Area Officers for different States/UTs to coordinate with the State Governments/UTs for regular and effective monitoring of PDS.

This Department organized five Regional Conferences for strengthening the Targeted Public Distribution System during 2005-06. A Conference of State Food Ministers/Food Secretaries was organized on 29.3.2006 at New Delhi for the purpose of strengthening of TPDS. The minutes of the meeting have been sent to all the concerned for taking necessary action thereon.

References

Economic Survey, 2005-06.

Planning Commission, 1992.

Report of the Expert Group on Estimation of Proportion and Number of Poor, 1993-93.

Report of the Income Estimation Committee, 1967.

Report of the Poverty Estimation Commission, Planning Commission, 2000.

Tenth Five Year Plan, 2002-07.

Panchayati Raj and Public Distribution System in India

BIPIN PD. SINGH AND MD. AIYUB RAYEEN

After Independence of India a number of states have statutory set-up village Panchayat. Panchayati Raj are of three-tire system of local self-Government consisting Panchayat at village level, Panchayat Samiti at Block level and Zila Parishad at District level was first set-up in 1959. However in several states the two-tire or even a one-tire system exist. The States design the structure of these institutions in the light of the local conditions. Special representation is given to interests like backward classes, women and corporative society elected directly from and by the village. The Panchayats are responsible for promotion of agriculture, rural industries provisions of medical relief, maternity and child distributions. They also provide primary education in all the rural areas and collect land revenue.

The Main Objectives of Panchayati Raj are:

1. To secure the maximum participation of people in the socio-economic development of the country.
2. To decentralize the administrative apparatus down to the village level and to enable the rural population to participate in the decision-making processes.
3. To carry the democratic processes and local self-government institutions to rural areas.

The panchayat, the co-operative and the school are the basic institutions at the village level for carrying out programme of rural development. The elected Panchayat is responsible for many development programmes within its territorial jurisdiction. The village school, is also a community centre, looks after the Educational recreational and cultural needs of the people. Associate bodies such as organizations for women and the youth, farmers and artisans, Associations, work in co-ordination with the Panchayat in order to perform various developmental activities. At present Government is introducing *'Nyaya Panchayat' or 'Village Court'* which provides a speedy and inexpensive system of justice to the villagers which are functioning in some of the states in India.

In India, system of public distribution has aims at supplying foodgrains and other essential commodities through a wide network of fair price shops to the consumers particularly to the weaker sections of the society at reasonable prices. It also includes mobile shops to meet the needs of industrial workers and people living in isolated pockets and remote areas. The number of fair price shops under Panchayati Raj System has been increased from year to year and at present nearly seventy-eight (78 per cent) per cent shops are located in rural areas. The food items made available at controlled prices include wheat, rice, levy sugar and imported edible oils.

Eleventh Plan continues to lay emphasis on to maintain the food security. India is self-sufficient in producing foodgrain throughout the plan period. This plan has given greater stress on vegetable oils, pulses, horticulture vegetables, hand forestry, decide improve dry land farming to increase productivity. There are a number of programs which would convert these objectives of foodgrains security through Panchayati Raj System.

Factious and frictions among the villagers, lack of proper leadership, too much political interference, overpowering influence of the big landlords or money lenders or some other vested interests, major financial resources are some of the reasons which have weakened this institution of democratic decentralization and decentralize planning. It is true that sometimes Panchayati Raj has acted as a hand maiden of vested interests. But there is no evidence that the plutocracy is any better.

In this way we can say the dynamics of development required that a high level of technical expertise be made available at the district level where planning of a more comprehensive and sophisticated kind can be undertaken, and concomitant administrative functions can be discharged more fruitfully.

References

Alok Ghosh, Indian Economy, World Press, Kolkata.

Govt. of India, Various Issues of Five Year Plans, New Delhi.

Govt. of India, Economic Survey, Various Issues, New Delhi.

Rudra Datt and K.P.M. Sundharam, Indian Economy, 2008, S. Chand and Co., New Delhi.

Shridhar Pandey, '*Bharat Ka Aarthik Vikas*', Motilal Banarasi Das, Patna.

Public Distribution System, Panchayati Raj and Women's Empowerment

Key Steps for Accelerating Gender Justice

Vandana Kumari

Actress Manisha Koirala, Goodwill Ambassador of UNFPA (United Nation's Population Fund) and whose grandfather Girija Prasad Koirala was the Prime Minister of Nepal shared her personal experience of attitudes towards girl children in Nepal even in the well-known families where it is difficult to imagine that expression of such attitude could be there. Apparently, attitudes for girl children do not change if they are viewed from a perspectives of honor, burden and some certain religious perspectives where son is privileged and desired for performing the last rites. The statement of Manisha Koirala in this regard is an example: "I feel angry about the domination of men in family and society. In Nepal, my great grandmother could not even breast-feed her daughter. Even today widow remarriage is unheard there. My mother once told me that my grandfather made faces when he learnt that the first child (Manisha) was a girl. She did not speak to him for a month after that. My mother then resolved to make me a strong, independent and successful woman". Such expressions are not very uncommon and it can be found in the narration of thousands of women in South Asia. On the one hand, father did not welcome the girl child, on the other the mother showed the resolve but this resolve in many cases remain absent and the girl child remains discriminated.

Ecologically hostile and Gender unjust socio-economic policies had an adverse affect on lives of women in India especially in rural areas. The sexual division of labour though relevant in low technology phase of Indian history in India is both a cause and the effect of monopoly of man of key position in social, economic and political hierarchy and control of societal institutions and this coupled with low education levels of women especially in the rural areas are one of the major reason of poor implementation of government schemes and governance of public services. There are several examples that show how women's empowerment makes economic and ecological sense. In Uttar Pradesh only 5 per cent of population avails of subsidized food through public distribution system while in Kerala 95 per cent of the population take benefit of it. The forces that have helped Kerala achieve such a success rate in obtaining subsidized food are universal primary education, emphasis on girl child, economic equality and better health care. Educated and empowered women doing justice to the duties are also conscious of the rights and entitlements that are due to them. Example of Kerala demonstrates the importance of education though it is a universal fact that education plays a critical role in the development of critical thinking. Key argument of this article is to seek equal participation of women in the distribution network especially in the public distribution system with representative justice to social groups while sharing key concerns, key challenges and suggestion for policy advocacy. At this stage, it would be important to recall the six basic principles of the Beijing Conference formally known as the 4th World Conference on Women convened in Beijing in 1995, where following six basic principles were emphasized:

1. Violence against women must be dropped.
2. Girls must be valued against the boys in their families and within society.
3. Women must have access to high quality education and health care and to economic resources and political power.
4. Family responsibility must be shared.
5. Women must have right to control their own fertility and equality in sexual relations.
6. Human rights and women's rights are intertwined and based on freedom of expression.

In order to translate the commitment made by our country during the world conference, a national policy on empowerment of women was finalized in 2001. The primary objective of the 9th Five Year Plan was empowerment of women. It was committed to creation of enabling environment where women can freely exercise their rights both within and outside home as equal partners along with men. Experiences in China indicated that women's control over land rights during 1940s gave women a stronger sense of self and the means to leave unhappy marriages. Lack of property rights is an obstacle to women's empowerment in India. Land also provides social status and political power as well as economic security. Women's landlessness reduces women's power in the household even for wealthy women. This demonstrates the need to ensure education for women so that they are enabled with the entitlements, participation in governance, business and they are equal partners in ownership of land as a means of ecologically sustainable livelihoods.

In the National Population Policy 2000, emphasis is laid on convergence service delivery at village level by involving the Para-professionals including anganwadi workers and mention is made about the establishment of maternity huts in each village to be used as village delivery room with storage space for supplies and medicines. It is also emphasized that meaningful decentralization will result only if convergence of National Family Welfare Policy with ICDS programme is strengthened. Experience over the years has shown that Universal Immunization Programme became successful when it was converged with ICDS. Convergence is in itself a way for empowerment of women through improved health and nutritional status. However, monitoring and surveillance system needs to be strengthened for ensuring that anganwadi services are accessed in totality with better remuneration for the anganwadi workers.

The Government of India had ushered in the new millennium by declaring the year 2001 as 'Women's Empowerment Year' to focus on a vision 'where women are equal partners like men'. The most common explanation of 'women's empowerment' is the ability to exercise full control over one's actions. The last decades have witnessed some basic changes in the status and role of women in our society. There has been shift in policy approaches from the concept of 'welfare' in the seventies to 'development' in the eighties and now to 'empowerment' in the nineties. This process has been further accelerated with some sections of women becoming increasingly self-conscious of their discrimination in several areas of family and public life. They are also in a position to mobilize themselves on issues that can affect their overall position. These mobilization to a great extent has paid-off though there is much that is needed across the social groups for acceptance the new found assertion of right in a social milieu where women have been assigned some roles to which they are supposed to attend first before getting in the non-conventional domains of social, political, cultural and economic life.

The latest news items regarding violence committed against women reveal that women's position has worsened. Tulsidas' verse from Ramayana 'Dhol, janwar, shudra, pashu, nari ye sub nindan ke adhikari' highlights the discrimination and deep-rooted gender bias which still exists in all sectors on the basis of caste, community, religious affiliation and class. The Constitution of India grants equality to women in various fields of life. Yet a large number of women are either ill-equipped or not in a position to propel themselves out of their traditionally unsatisfactory socio-economic conditions. They are poor, uneducated and insufficiently trained. They are often absorbed in the struggle to sustain the family physically and emotionally and as a rule are discouraged from taking interest in affairs outside home. Oppression and atrocities on women are still rampant. Female infanticide continues to be common. Statistics show that there is still a very high preference for a male child in states like UP, MP, Punjab, etc. The male to female ratio is very high in these states. Domestic violence is also widespread and is also associated with dowry. Leaving a meager number of urban and sub-urban women, Indian women are still crying for social justice.

A review of government's various programmes for women empowerment such as Swashakti, Swayamsidha, Streeshakti, Balika Samrudhi Yojana and another two thousand projects reveal that little has been done or achieved through these programmes. The national programmes such as National Programme for Education of Girl Children, Kasturba Gandhi Bal Vidyalaya for educational backward blocks are significant milestones under Sarva Shiksha Abhiyan (SSA) and these programmes are likely to generate large number of educated girls in the rural areas. The discrepancy in the ideology and practice of the empowerment policy of women in India constitutes its continued social, economic and social backwardness. Women make up 52 per cent of our country's population. Hence there can be no progress unless their needs and interests are fully met. Empowerment would not hold any meaning unless they are made strong, alert and aware of their equal status in the society. Policies need to be framed to bring them into the mainstream of society. It is important to educate the women. The need of the hour is to improve female literacy as education holds the key to development.

Empowerment would become more relevant if women are educated, better informed and can take rational decisions. It is also necessary to sensitize the other sex towards women. It is important to usher in changes in societal attitudes and perceptions with regard to the role of women in different spheres of life. Adjustments have to be made in traditional gender specific performance of tasks without losing the specific knowledge of women in certain domains. A woman needs to be physically healthy so that she is able to take challenges of equality. But it is sadly lacking in a majority of women especially in the rural areas. They have unequal access to basic health resources and lack adequate counseling. The result is an increasing risk of unwanted and early pregnancies, HIV infection and other sexually transmitted diseases. The greatest challenge is to recognize the obstacles that stand in the way of their right to good health. To be useful to the family, community and the society, women must be provided with best health care facilities. Access to quality public health care for all should be a cross-cutting policy imperative without leaving health care to the issues of affordability and private sector. There are several examples where health care costs have been an important factor for the indebtedness of poor.[1]

Most of the women work in agricultural sector either as workers, in household farms or as wage workers. Yet it is precisely livelihood in agriculture that has tended to become more volatile and insecure in recent years and women cultivators have therefore been negatively affected. The government's policies for alleviating poverty have failed to produce any desirable results, as women do not receive appropriate wages for their labour. There is also significant amount of unpaid or non-marketed labour within the household. The increase in gender disparity in wages in the urban areas is also quite marked as it results from the employment of women in different and lower paying activities. They are exploited at various levels. They should be provided with proper wages and work at par with men so that their status can be elevated in society. Also, there is a need to ensure monetization of unpaid labour of women. Sustainability Project in Canada as part of 7th Generation Initiative calls for development of alternative measurement of GDP where women's unpaid labour and the ecological costs of development are accounted for getting an ecologically safe and gender just model of development operation across the nations.[2]

Empowerment needs to be viewed as a process in which all voices are encouraged to be heard for ultimate goal of securing mutually beneficial solutions. Spouses, partners and mother-in-laws often make decisions for women on contraceptive choice and use. Women are also financially weak to pay for the health services. This needs to be addressed through ensuring access to quality health care. Access to interest free loans,[3] affordable public health care through strengthening of primary health centre is an important step that needs to be taken. UPA government's initiative to universalize access to secondary education following the success of SSA goals in the rural areas, bridging of social groups disparity in access to education is laudable and it must be followed up by government as large number of girl children can not get education beyond the upper primary level without access to secondary education at manageable distances.

Another hope lies in Panchayati Raj System. In India, there are a million elected women representative at the village council level. This number is higher than the total number of women leaders in the rest of the world. If we can train these one million women, then they will carry forward the message of women's empowerment. Formation of self-help groups (SHG's) has contributed in further empowerment of women in the rural areas. In spite of the positive stories, there are still many areas that are extremely backward, says Hemlatha Patil. In Marathwada, many of the women sarpanches have no role in decision making. "They attend the meetings but do not even sit. When we went to those areas, we realised how poor, illiterate and unaware they were. Furthermore, caste continues to play an ugly role in politics." Vibhuti Patel, an economist at the Centre for Women's Studies, University of Mumbai, was part of a gender audit of the budget. She says, "We have repeatedly seen that elected women leaders look into issues such as construction of schools, area development, immunisation, garbage collection, marriages—anything that affects the family and daily life. In most cases, there was no corruption, and funds were used wisely and not diverted to irrelevant activities." Even before reservation for women was enforced in 1993, Maharashtra had initiated a 30 per cent quota for women in municipal councils. It was among the first few States to have an all-women panchayat body. There are 13 such inexistence today. There is need to multiply success stories for women participation in the local governance institutions. Allotment of public distribution system to educated married women in the rural areas would be another critical step for enhancing the role of women in ensuring access to food.

The major areas of challenges before the Government and policy-makers are:

- Access to interest free loans for setting up small enterprises in rural and urban areas made possible through public creation of interest-free money.
- Access to ecologically sustainable livelihoods and employment.
- Right to ownership of land, property and assets especially for the women belonging to the landless and marginalized on a priority basis.
- Elimination of social evils such as trafficking in women and girls through strict enforcement of laws and protection of girl child.
- Access to ICT enabled services, information technology and participation in food processing industries.
- Support services like child care facilities, crèches at work places.
- Continued increase in the number of Kasturba Gandhi Balika Vidhyalayas upto secondary level both in the urban and rural areas.
- Care of women in difficult circumstances like extreme poverty, destitute women, conflict situations, natural calamities, etc.
- Development of surveillance system for maternal health.
- Establishment of maternity huts in close proximity of anganwadi centres.
- Effective coordination between para-professionals at village level.
- Supportive supervision.
- Involvement of panches and sarpanchs at the village and sub-centre level in the planning and review the programmes.

- Emphasis on literacy to girl-child through community-based enrolment drive.
- Skill development of para-professionals for interacting and educating women.
- Involving adolescents as a link between an anganwadi centre and the village household.
- Involvement of women in social, economic and political hierarchy.

Notes

1. http://muhammad_mukhtar_alam.tigblog.org
2. www.sustainwellbeing.net
3. Advocacy if interest-free loan is part of national and international movements. Global Justice Movement www.globaljusticement.net has been calling for public creation and control of interest-free money for generation of productive capacities.

References

http://www.solutionexchange-un.net.in/decn/cr/res21070804.doc

Reservation for Women in Panchayati Raj Institutions has yielded Excellent Results, *Frontline*, Volume 25, Issue 11, May. 24-June 6, 2008 http://www.hinduonnet.com/fline/fl2511/stories/20080606251101200.htm

Public Distribution System in Backward Region of Jharkhand

A Need for Efficient Governance

Ram Kumar Prasad and B.K. Pandey

INTRODUCTION

In recent time the Public Distribution System is being hotly debated. Even in the oath Session of 15th Lok Sabha the issue of poor and process of PDS got a very hot debate. According to views of some of the renowned social scientist the PDS is functioning in a ailment condition since its birth. Though the birth of PDS in new form has come from the garb of world war II but practically and legally it was adopted in India after independence which was extended into a universal welfare measure in the sixties designed to ensure that food rations are accessible to all households in both rural and urban areas of the country. Presently, the PDS is a rationing mechanism that entitles households to specified quantities of selected commodities at subsidized prices. Deserving households have been issued ration cards that gives an entitlement to purchase fixed ratio of commodities. Though the system was initiated by central government at its own cost but the responsibility of its distribution rests with the states.

In this paper we have to study this article mainly in two parts : (a) Role of efficient Governance, and (b) Position of PDS. In second part we have to study the PDS in context of backward areas of Jharkhand. Again we have to examine whether PDS is feasible in present time and why the Public distribution system is being criticized by the social scientists.

In view of the growing poverty as well as higher incidence of hunger as perceived by the households in the region, ensuring food security becomes a challenging task. There are two aspects of achieving this objective—first is to ensure adequate supply of food and second is to help households to have enough income to purchase food.

In the absence of a developed knit market mechanism in the region, adequate supply of food is to be ensured through the PDS.

Though the PDS is being criticized through many agencies at several fronts but despite the failure of mechanism of PDS it has ensured food to a larger portion of poor people in Jharkhand State. In true sense the people of Jharkhand are victims of several natural calamities. That is why after a long gap of 62 years of independence a major portion of people particular STs are compelled to lead a wild life in forest or nearby the forest areas.

Under such circumstance the distribution of food for poor through PDS requires an efficient governance of state machinery.

Need for Governance—Improving the quality of governance requires a system of checks and balances in society that restrains arbitrary action and harassment by politicians and bureaucrats, promotes voices and participation by the population, reduces incentives for the corporate elite to engage in state capture, and fosters the rule of law. A metritocratic and service-oriented public administration is a salient feature of such a strategy. However, synthesizing the strategy of key reforms for improving governance and combating corruption is particularly a daunting challenge, as is the task of detailing and adapting a strategy to each country-specific reality. Governance is more than fighting corruption. Improving governance should be seen as a process integrating three vital components: (a) knowledge, with rigorous data and empirical analysis, including in-country diagnostics and dissemination, utilizing the latest information technology tools, (b) leadership in the political, civil society and international arena; and (c) collective action via systematic participatory and consensus-building approaches with key stakeholders in society for which technology revolution is also assisting.

The threshold of the new millennium has furnished us with a good occasion to reflect upon and evaluate India's experiences in administrative development towards its pursuit of good governance and ponder over the likely emerging trends and the lessons learnt for the future. Reflecting upon the realities of public administration system in India over the last half a century is not a simple exercise, for India is a complex society composed of diversity of languages, social systems, ethnic, tribal and caste groups, various religions, regional disparities, different cultural patterns, and unlimited environmental factors that shape the behavioural pattern of masses and public functionaries at all levels, which affect the idea of rationalism in administrative behaviour. It is indeed very difficult to objectively evaluate the impact of all these factors on governance. The Government of India has since Independence in 1947 taken a number of steps to revamp the system of administration at different stages of its evolution with a view to secure objectivity, transparency, efficiency and responsiveness in the administrative process—the basic ingredients of good governance in a democratic system based on the concepts of rule of law and public welfare.

As it appears, the search for the elusive goal of good governance in India has been simultaneous with the evolution of a constitutional democratic government—a government which is limited, stable and truly representative of the majority of the people, maintains its territorial integrity and national sovereignty, accelerates economic growth and development, upholds the rule of law and renders justice without fear or favour and without delay, and ensures welfare of all sections of the people. These objectives were sought to be achieved through the adoption of the Republican Constitution in 1950. However, despite the lofty ideals and the values of good governance enshrined in the Constitution, we find ourselves today in a state where the system has not been able to provide either a stable government or stable policies. What has gone wrong in our constitutional and administrative system during the last fifty years has been a subject of endless debate and discussions, and a number of prognosis have been made by constitutional and administrative experts, political leaders and policy-makers, and various commissions and committees to reform and restructure the system to be able to achieve the objectives of good governance. "Has the system of government failed in India or we have failed the system" is an oft repeated question being raised again and again without any satisfactory answer.

In India poor are still poor and have even increased in absolute numbers. Economic gains have been wiped out by population growth. Though India has an economically powerful middle class, a vibrant software industry, and nuclear capability, but a huge number of India's population continue to eke out a living under conditions of extreme poverty and deprivation. The government's capacity to perform is still weak; resources available for public investment and development are still scarce, local jurisdictions are particularly starved. The critical basic needs in education, health, welfare, infrastructure and the very basic need of clean drinking water for the masses still go unmet. Many of the poor are in fact worse-off now than they were a decade or so ago. No wonder that India ranks very low in the Human development Report prepared each year by the UNDP. Human development is the strand which holds together concerns on political institutions and governance, social institutions and culture, and science and technology.

Pointing out a number of deficiencies in the system of governance in India, the Approach paper to the Tenth Five Year Plan has noted its views in the following way:

"While the functions of the state in India have steadily

increased, capacity to deliver has declined over the years due to administrative cynicism, rising indiscipline, and a growing belief widely shared among the political and bureaucratic elite that the state is an arena where public office is to be used for private ends. In almost all states" people perceive bureaucracy as wooden, disinterested in public welfare and corrupt. The issue of reform in governance has acquired critical dimensions in poorer states in the light of low economic growth and fiscal crisis. Weak governance, manifesting itself in poor service delivery, excessive regulation, and uncoordinated and wasteful public expenditure, is seen as one of the key factor impinging on growth and development. The paper emphasizes that the agenda of reform in governance should include not only a reshaping the bureaucracy by adopting a comprehensive reform of civil services, and a multi-faceted strategy based on ensuring security of tenure, increasing accountability, civil service renewal, open and responsive government, tackling corruption and strengthening the rule of law, and e-governance.

FOOD PROBLEM

The task of providing food security poses many obstacles in backward areas where we find chronic poverty. Given the fragile base of agriculture, growth processes remain sluggish. Shifting to commercial crops, and more recently, I-tech agriculture, are promising sources of growth but their impact on food security could be far from favourable. Commercial crops raise the incomes of farmers but also make them more vulnerable to vagaries of the market and fluctuations in production. More importantly, commercial crops divert land from coarse cereals which are the local staple foodgrains in backward areas. As regards hi-tech agriculture, it usually remains confined to small enclaves; while it would contribute handsomely to the value of agricultural output, it is far from certain that it would have a beneficial impact on the income and employment of the vast majority of the poor.

FEATURES AND FEASIBILITY OF PDS IN BACKWARD REGION

It is necessary to note the features of PDS and also estimate the feasibility of the same in current scenario of reform period which are being discussed below separately.

Features of PDS and PRIs

1. The coming into being of the third tier of government at the district and lower levels (Panchayati Raj Institutions, i.e., PRIs) would build up an institutional structure which has a constitutional status and the powers and resources associated with that status. It would be the responsibility of the PRIs to formulate and implement development programmes in their areas including those meant for the poor. The PRIs would have to organize the tasks associated with the food security system, viz., identification of the poor, location of households eligible for receiving subsidized food assistance and provision of food assistance to such households. Thus, irrespective of the food security system, its decentralization now appears to be certain.
2. The present system is likely to move towards a breakdown in the not-too-distant future. Removal of food subsidy and linking of issue prices to economic cost of grains procured and distributed by FCI would lead to reduction in off-take. As the prices charged to the poor for the PDS grains are a fixed proportion of the issue price (currently 50 percent), the poor also would have to pay a higher price for the PDS grains and the off-take by them may also decrease. On the other hand, given the political clout of the farmers in green revolution areas, the support prices paid to them would continue to rise in future along with the quantities of grains they offer to the government. It is necessary to remember that FCI has to purchase whatever the farmers offer, which in

years of bumper production could be enormous even for the government to handle. It should be fairly obvious that the growing economic and physical burden caused by the system must eventually exceed its capacity to bear the same.

3. The years since the early eighties have witnessed the spread of agricultural growth to areas and crops far beyond the limited pockets where the green revolution took place in the seventies. The yields of most crops improved during the later phase. Two recent studies of agricultural growth since the early eighties visualize a continuation of the trend towards broad-base (area-wise and crop-wise) growth (Sawant and Achuthan, 1995; Ray, 1998). The prospective situation would then be favourable for the emergence of local surpluses in a wide range of foodgrains, provided the policy regime remains conducive to broad-based agricultural growth.

Feasibility of PDS

1. Identification of the poor, selection of those eligible to receive food security assistance and delivery of assistance to them should be organized by local representative bodies in which representatives of the poor participate. There should be provision for a watchdog body to ensure that the system covers all the eligible households. Beneficiary groups, local organizations of people and NGOs may be associated with the operation and monitoring of the system.
2. The system should be based on the local staples consumed by the poor. This would make it possible to decentralize the food security system and economise on the logistic arrangements need to operate the system. A further advantage of a local staple would be that it would ordinarily figure low in preference ranking by the non-poor and, hence, would be less prone to leakages. The policy support given to the local staples as a constituent of the food

security system would benefit the poor as producers and also stimulate growth in the areas of local staples which are usually backward and receive little policy attention.

3. When disaster strikes, all the tiers of the government-from the central government downwards—would get together to handle the crisis. In normal times, the role of the higher tiers would be minimal, confined to laying down norms for assistance, devolution of funds and overall supervision of the working of the system and its results.
4. Physical handling of foodgrains involving purchase, storage, distribution by the local body organizing the food security system, may be minimize. For example, in an employment programme linked system, the beneficiary may receive part of wages in the form of food coupons which could be exchange for foodgrains in a designated local shop. Similarly, the mid-day meal programme for school children could be operated by the organization running the school.

PUBLIC DISTRIBUTION SYSTEM IN JHARKHAND

It is important to place the fact on forefront that a field work was carried out in the area of Palamu and Ranchi by Dr. Alok Deo Singh in 1999 who finds the worst system of PDS in this region and Dr. Singh has narrated in his field work that poor are being thrown out from the PDS net. Hence, name of a few villages is quoted here to know the reality of PDS and Card holders by Dr. Singh.

Card distribution is poor in Jharkhand, so there are many poor people who should have a card, but who have never received one. We found many people complain about the fact that they have never received a card, or that the foodgrains never arrived, or that the dealer made false entries in their cards. On the other hand, he also found villages in which many people were satisfied.

The main problem (Table 1) is that PDS commodities arrive late and irregular, if at all. The villagers are poorly

TABLE 1
Position of PDS in Jharkhand

Palamu District		
Chandwa Block	Village 1	Almost everybody satisfied. The PDS shop run by a cooperative.
	Village 2	Reasonable supply, but rice not available for last few months. Sometimes people have no money when shop is open.
	Village 3	Many poor households without red cards. Erratic supply and false entries in the cards.
	Village 4	Many poor households without red cards. Erratic supply and false entries in the cards; Foodgrains finished within 1-2 days.
	Village 5	Erratic supply, except to local Vigilance Committee members; villagers not informed about stock arrival.
Ranchi District		
Silli Block	Village 1	Poor distribution of red cards; those with red cards purchase the commodities, but often do not have money when foodgrains have arrived; influential people close to the PDS dealer have no problem in lifting.
	Village 2	Random distribution of red cards. Those with cards were satisfied, although supply was irregular.
	Village 3	Reasonable distribution; some complaints about late arrival of stocks, and stocks finished within three days.
	Village 4	No major complaints. Many people do not take sugar.
	Village 5	Many people without red cards. Some people with red cards had problems to arrange the money when stock had arrived.
Ranchi District		
Kanke Block	Village 1	Village with two shops; one doing well, the other much less: irregular supply of foodgrains, late arrival and foodgrains finished within a day.
	Village 2	Many deserving people without cards, false entries in the cards; Irregular supply of

	foodgrains; sugar and kerosene somewhat better.
Village 3	Preferential treatment to people close to the PDS dealer, rice and wheat often not available.
Village 4	Many people without red cards. Small quantities of rice and wheat in the shop, and poor people sometimes not able to purchase on the day the stocks are available.
Village 5	Irregular supplies. False entries in the cards. If the foodgrains arrive at all, they are sold out within no time.

Source : Fieldwork done by Alok Deo Singh, 1999 the chart summaries the main findings in 15 villages on the basis of 10 interviews in each village with randomly selected villagers and occasional group interviews. The villages are spread over the blocks. Some close to the block capital, others more remote.

informed, and certainly not in advance. This means that the poorest among them may not have sufficient cash readily available when the foodgrains arrive in the shop. The PDS dealer will only transport so much as he expects to sell within one or two days. In short, there is a physical access problem, in the sense that the commodities may come at irregular intervals or not at all. There is also a problem of economic access, in the sense that the poorest people do not have cash ready at the moment the stocks arrive. Yet, on the positive side, all villagers we interviewed knew about the PDS and knew what a 'red card' (a card meant for the BPL population) was. This, he has been told, was very different 15-20 years ago.

Since 1997, as per Government of India guidelines, vigilance committees have been introduced at various levels: district, sub-divisional, panchayat or ward, and shop level. Membership of the first three types of vigilance committees is almost completely politicized, and it is mainly local level politicians who are appointed. At the shop level, the members are usually selected by the PDS dealers themselves and are often not aware of the tasks they have to do.

During the fieldwork, he tried to find out whether there are examples of positive experiences, for instance, villagers who organized themselves to fight for a better PDS system. In short, we can say that the position of PDS is still worst in this region. Because neither the governance is prevailing nor PDS in the state and particularly after the decline of the government of Babu Lal Marandi the position is very worst.

GROUND FOR CRITICISM OF PDS

There are several grounds which form the basis for criticism of P.D. system. A few famous researchers have outlined their views which are being discussed below:

The present Public Distribution System (PDS) has been criticized by researchers and policy analysts for the following reasons. (See Radhakrishna and Dinns Tsp. 1997; Jharwal, 1998; Mahendra Dev, 1996; Mahendra Dev and Suryanarayana, 1993; Swaminathan, 1998).

1. The system is inherently costly as it is based on surpluses of two superior cereals—rice and wheat—generated in a few green revolution pockets; Punjab, Haryana and western Uttar Pradesh. These surpluses have to be procured, stored and distributed all over the country.
2. The system is too far centralized, hierarchical and bureaucratic to achieve cost-effectiveness, respond quickly to distress in localized areas and distinguish those in real need for assistance from those who do not need it.
3. Judged by the yardsticks of (a) coverage of vulnerable groups, (b) quality of food security provided, and (c) the impact on the conditions of beneficiaries, the performance of the system is rated as poor. The system is practically absent in some of the hard-core poverty areas as well as backward areas. When we observe the cases of Jharkhand region, we find that the area is dominated by STs and Backwards where people are exploited by the dealers, local leaders and also by the junior officers.

To an observer from outside India, the present food security system must indeed seem paradoxical. Out of a wide range of cereals grown in India, the PDS has chosen rice and wheat—two superior cereals preferred by the well-to-do consumers rather than the numerous local staples consumed by the poor for generations. While the system is ostensibly for the benefit of the poor, it is not targeted on the poor and has shown little concern to extend its reach to areas where food distress is widespread among the poor. Ideally, a food security system should have a dependable provision to ensure that the poor have the capacity to pay for the foodgrains made available to them. This is not the case in India. Employment programmes and the PDS operate as separate activities. A link between them could have improved the access of the poor to foodgrains. While good subsidy is growing, one can not be sure that it is really going to the poor.

The observer during the seventies, on the other hand, would have been full of admiration for the food security system which helped India overcome one of the worst crises it faced since independence. However, it originated as an appendage of the green revolution, the chief concern of which was with a quick breakthrough in foodgrain production—which necessitated concentrating on rice and wheat—and not with food security for the poor or to increasing the production of staples consumed by them. The centerpiece of the green revolution was the farmer in the green revolution areas. Subsidies inputs and credit, research and extension, price support through procurement by the government agencies, were all focused on the green revolution farmer to help him raise yields and production. With the increase in production, the dependence on imports and food aid was eliminated. As the upsurge continued, the surpluses became an embarrassment. Simultaneously, the number of the poor and the deprivation suffered by them—particularly their foodgrain needs—assumed a prominent role in Indian policies and in policy research and analysis. The outcome was the coming into being of a countrywide network of the Public Distribution System. Over the decades which have followed, the network has expanded considerably, spatially as well as in terms of quantities of foodgrains handled. However, price support to green revolution farmers continues to be the major objective of food policy with the poor providing only an excuse for the huge subsidies and physical losses in foodgrains involved in the operations of Food Corporation of India. The limited purpose here is only to suggest that the present food security system, viewed as a safety-net for the poor needs to be streamlined.

CONCLUSION

It is clear from the above discussed facts that in backward region of Jharkhand even today poor people do not know what is the "red card". Hence, at the initial stage a better governance be set-up in this area which could make a better interaction with the poor people with honest effort. Secondly, the operational system of PDS may be corrected by involving the grass-root level governance as well as imposing a regular check by vigilance department or any antonomous checking agency.

The present food security system in Jharkhand reflects two basic flaws in our policy-making for promoting agricultural and rural development. First, the problem of the relatively better-off sections of farmers receive far more attention in policy-making than the deprivations suffered by the poor. Second, while the areas lagging in development like backward areas urgently need investment and an infrastructure to support and sustain the development process, the emphasis in policies remains on temporary and *ad-hoc* relief measures. In fact, the PRIs as visualized in the recent constitutional amendments, would need a long time to become operational even in the few states like Jharkhand regarded as being backward in promoting the PRIs.

Thus, the present system is likely to drift towards the system approximating that described in this paper. Discussion on the present food security system often revolves around how it can be improved by : (a) focusing the PDS on the poor; (b) excluding the better-off; and (c) reducing leakages and corruption. While improvements in the system are welcome, our plea is that the present food security system needs to be assessed in relation to the broader context of the changing agricultural and poverty scenario in India and the officers should change their mindset and should adopt a welfare measure so that food supply may be ensured to the poor people.

References

Approach Paper to the Tenth Five Year Plan (2002-07), Planning Commission, New Delhi.

Daniel Kaufman, New Empirical Frontiers in Fighting Corruption and Improving Governance—Selected Issues", a paper presented at the OSCE Economic Forum 2001, Brussels, 30-31 January 2001, pp. 1-3.

Mahendra Dev, S. (1996), "Food Security: PDS *vs*. EGs: A Tale of Two States", *Economic and Political Weekly*, Vol. 31, No. 27.

Radhakrishna, R. and Subba Rao (1997), "India's Public Distribution: A National and International Perspective", World Bank Discussion Paper, No. 380, Poverty and Social Development Department, World Bank, Washington, D.C.

Swaminathan, Madhura (1998), "Understanding the Costs of the Food Corporation of India", *Economic and Political Weekly*, Vol. 34, No. 52, December 25.

Public Distribution System in India
An Introspective View

Asim K. Karmakar and Sangeeta Kundu

INTRODUCTION

Public Distribution System (PDS) is a rationing mechanism that entitles households to specified quantities like wheat, rice, sugar, edible oils, kerosene (only for below poverty line) and coals, whereas additional commodities like pulses, salt, tea are supplied selectively made available through a network of fair-price shops. In many of the most parts of India, PDS has been universal and all households, rural and urban, with a registered residential address that are entitled to rations. Eligible households are given a ration card that entitles them to buy fixed rations though varying with households size and age composition of the above mentioned commodities. The exact entitlement varies across Indian states. There is at present a network of about 4.61 lakh PDS retail outlets in the country, raising from 4.5 lakh PDS retail outlets in 1998.

PDS is operated under the joint responsibility of the Central and State Governments. The Central Government bears the responsibility of procurement, storage, transportation and bulk allocation of foodgrains, rice and wheat at subsidized prices, while the responsibility of distribution to consumers rests with the State Governments. The PDS also helps to modulate open-market prices for commodities that are distributed through the system. The Department of Food and Civil Supplies, Government of Delhi, manage the PDS in Delhi for regulating supply and distribution of, and trade and commerce in, essential commodities with a view to maintain or increase supplies thereof and secure their equitable distribution and availability at fair prices by enforcing the Essential Commodities Act, 1955, and various Control Orders made thereunder.

The objectives of PDS in India are the following:

- rationing during situations of scarcity,
- maintaining price stability,
- keeping a check on private trade, and
- raising the welfare of the poor by providing basic foods to the vulnerable population at reasonable prices.

In the above backdrop the present paper focuses the operation, problems and reform aspects of PDS in Section II. Section III is the concluding observations.

PDS : OPERATION, PROBLEMS, REFORMS

India's Public Distribution System is built around a network of roughly 462,000 'Fair Price Shops'. They are often referred to as 'ration shops', making it one of the biggest such systems in the world. India's Planning Commission estimates that 160 million families purchase commodities at ration shops every year. This includes mainly foodgrains, but also such items as sugar and kerosene (used as cooking fuel). The 'food subsidy', as calculated in the Government of India's budget estimates for fiscal year 2007-08, accounts for more than six percent of total central government expenditure—up from roughly 2.5 percent before India embarked on its programme of market-oriented economic reforms in the early 1990s. This does not include the amounts added by state governments, which often 'top up' central subsidies.

The PDS is not only enormous in terms of its expenditure and its reach, but also in terms of the range of agencies involved in its operation. These include agencies of both the central and state governments, as well as private-sector traders and even representatives of civil society, who can be appointed—along with elected officials—to the official 'vigilance committees' constituted under PDS regulations.

At the central level of India's federal system, the Commission on Agricultural Costs and Prices recommends minimum support prices (or 'procurement prices') of key commodities. These are then subject to adoption or modification by a cabinet sub-committee and the full cabinet. Commodities are procured primarily through the Food Corporation of India, which operates not only a vast network of warehouses and distribution centers, but also operates through private agents. The central government allocates state governments procurement and distribution quotas.

State-level ministries of food and civil supplies regulate networks of ration shops within their jurisdictions, and are thus responsible for allocating licenses to the private traders who operate the shops. State governments also issue 'ration cards' to their residents (at one time on a nominally universal basis, but more recently on a 'targeted' basis), and determine the quantities to which consumers are entitled. These vary from one commodity to the next. The prices are also partly determined by state governments, but as with questions relating to shop-licensing and regulation, commodity entitlements, oversight and vigilance arrangements, and other matters pertaining to the operation of the system, state governments are bound (or on some issues merely informally constrained) by guidelines issued by central government agencies.

The PDS, despite its many successes, has over the years manifested a broad array of problems. The PDS suffers from chronic management shortcomings concerning: the extent and timing of procurement, poor forecasting capacity, antiquated logistical systems to support storage and delivery functions, inappropriate product mix, cost inefficiencies, poor quality foodgrain. Moreover, unsatisfactory quality of commodities, the rude behaviour of the shopkeepers and malpractices in weights and measures have eroded the credibility of PDS.

Many of these problems stem from systemic corruption, which infects virtually every component of the bureaucratic machinery responsible for operating the PDS. India's Central Vigilance Commissioner supports his assertion that in India 'corruption is anti-poor' by stating that '31% of the foodgrains and 36% of the sugar meant for the [PDS], which is designed to provide food security to the people below the poverty line, gets diverted to the black market'.

That a dual-price system should produce leakages is axiomatic to economists. And, indeed, the illegal diversion of PDS commodities to the open market, through a highly institutionalized network of agents and other middlemen, is a routine practice, and severely undermines the capacity of the system to serve the needs of the poor. Widespread theft of supplies by the workers and managers who operate the vast network of PDS warehouses and fair-price shops means that consumers who rely on subsidized rations are faced with chronic shortages. Those products that are available are often adulterated to mask leakages from stocks. In many areas, to obtain five kilograms of grain, consumers must sign a shop register recording that they had received ten kilograms. This is another means of fixing the otherwise out-of-balance books produced by the shop-keepers' continued creaming. A huge range of actors receive a share in the institutionalized looting of the PDS: from warehouse night watchmen to drivers, to politicians, to audit officials and so forth.

Corruption also plagues the process of issuing 'ration cards', which households require in order to purchase stipulated quantities of various commodities at government-determined prices. The level of bribe payable in order to obtain a ration card should, in theory, be moderated by the very leakiness of the system. Poor people, in other words, will refuse to pay large sums of cash for a card that buys them very few *de facto* benefits. But there is more to it than this.

People are willing to pay the going rate of $100 for a ration card because it can purchase, in addition to diluted kerosene and grains that in some instances have been declared unfit for human consumption, basic citizenship rights. Possession of a ration card is widely required as a precondition for verifying identity and domicile, without which access to many public and private services would be impossible. It is a *de facto* identity card, and obtaining one is a major preoccupation of many poor families.

Local—mainly political—factors can sometimes exacerbate this situation for certain groups. During the late 1990s, for instance, the preoccupation with obtaining a ration card increased dramatically for Muslim slum-dwellers in Mumbai, and so did the price they were willing to pay for one, even as the level of benefits provided was being (officially) curtailed. This which included the rabidly Hindu chauvinist Shiv Sena party—had begun a drive to rid Mumbai of what it considered 'illegal' migrants from Bangladesh. Muslim residents were required to prove their nationality (not just their municipal residency), and the ration card was the standard means for doing so, though even this was often considered insufficient evidence. The ration card became, for Muslims, a means for not just food security, but for physical security as well. The resulting increase in demand for ration cards meant that the 'commission' payable to obtain one went up—for Hindus as well as Muslims.

One additional problem in making the PDS responsive to the needs and concerns of poor people is that state-level ruling parties differ significantly in their political perceptions of food security. Some state-level parties see the efficient distribution of food as critical to their main objective: maintaining political support and gaining (or retaining) state power. Mooij has examined the discrepancy between, on the one hand, the willingness of state governments in Karnataka to use the PDS as a political tool, and on the other, the aversion shown to such a strategy by their counterparts in Bihar. As Mooij puts it, 'the PDS in Karnataka works reasonably well. Most poor people receive some subsidized foodgrains every month. Karnataka politicians see the scheme as important and use it to enhance their popularity and attract votes.' Politicians in Bihar behave differently: they 'take an interest in the PDS, but because of the different features of the overall political processes in these two States, this leads to a different type of influence as well as outcomes for the beneficiaries'.

Systemic problems in the operation of the PDS have worsened significantly in the last few years (or at the very least are widely perceived to have worsened). The image of government warehouses overflowing with grain, while people in some parts of India suffer from malnutrition and starvation deaths, has become part of the political landscape. This has led to the continued politicization of food security—manifested most visibly, perhaps, by the public interest litigation filed in the Supreme Court by the People's Union for Civil Liberties, supported by a large range of non-party political formations.

The PDS's increasing failure in recent years has much to do with the political constraints facing the ruling coalition government in New Delhi. Because the government relies for its parliamentary majority on the support of regional parties from key grain producing states—in particular, Haryana, Punjab, Andhra Pradesh and Tamil Nadu—the government has increased the price paid to farmers by the Food Corporation of India. When these 'procurement prices', or Minimum Support Prices (MSPs), go up, the government is faced with a choice. One option is to absorb the extra cost as a subsidy burden on the government. The government has sometimes done this, though fiscal constraints—and competing claims on resources—have limited its appeal. The second option, to which the government has increasingly resorted, is to pass on the cost increases generated by higher procurement prices to the people who buy government procured grain through the PDS outlets—that is, to shift the fiscal burden onto the poor. As the government-determined prices at which commodities are sold in the ration shops has increased, the level of purchases (or 'off-take') has gone down—hence the overflowing warehouses.

REFORMING THE PDS

The PDS's many shortcomings like that : (a) it imposes an unsustainable fiscal strains, (b) it is not progressive scheme like food-for-work programmes, (c) in many states it has failed to provide nutritional support to the poor, have been acknowledged by representatives of governmental, non-governmental, and international agencies, though the emphasis has varied considerably, as have the recommendations for reform. Efforts to improve the system—on both a general basis and through piecemeal experimentation—have been undertaken almost since the system came into being. The reform agenda has broadened and become more intense during the last ten years. Reform efforts fall into three main categories: (1) restructuring of oversight mechanisms, (2) targeting of benefits, and (3) experimentation with voucher systems.

From time to time, officials in the central governments will issue new guidelines to encourage improvements in the way in which the PDS is overseen. During the 1970s and 1980s, these centered mainly on the creation of new oversight bodies, and a restructuring of reporting relationships among officials. On the whole, they achieved very little, except in some cases to widen the range of officials able to gain a share in the illicit spoils. By the late 1990s, however, an increasingly high profile was given to various efforts at increasing public oversight of key actors in the system. One initiative launched by the Food Ministry in New Delhi, for instance, sought to make the PDS more accountable to local representative institutions. There is little evidence that it produced tangible results. Another similarly ineffective edict from Delhi came in late 2001. The central government forced state governments to finalise lists of BPL families, issue ration cards, and 'monitor the Public Distribution System effectively'. The directive, issued under the Essential Commodities Act, called for 'fixing responsibility' and 'invoking punitive measures against shirkers', instructions that were greeted with some amusement by lower-level officials. The central government has also made several attempts to tighten the rules governing the official vigilance committees that are supposed to exercise oversight over the functioning of the PDS at the local level. Comprising civil society representatives and local elected officials, these committees exist mainly on paper, or when in operation contribute further to corruption. What one planning commission study concluded about their operation in Bihar is equally true for Maharashtra: 'membership of vigilance committees is seen as positions where money can be made' and the procedure to appoint them is highly politicized, and mostly clients of MLAs.

During the 1990s, Indian policy circles began seriously to discuss the idea of targeting—that is, making subsidies go further by ensuring that they reached only poorer citizens. The idea of targeting was pushed particularly by the World Bank and other international donor agencies, but had many supporters within India's policy establishment as well. The process of moving from a universal system to one targeted at specific groups unfolded in a phased manner. In the early 1990s, the Congress government announced the 'Revamped PDS', or RPDS, which was to be rolled out in certain districts. This was ultimately replaced, under the centre-Left United Front government by the Targeted PDS, or TPDS, which introduced the idea of differential entitlements for different categories of citizens—based on formulae that identified Below Poverty Line (BPL) households.

As with any targeted system, the BPL basis for PDS eligibility has been plagued by errors of both exclusion and inclusion—that is, the exclusion of certain families that should have qualified, and the inclusion of families that should not have been. The extent of these errors is a subject of much debate. In Mumbai there have been controversies surrounding the definition of the poverty line, the procedures used to screen families to determine whether they conform to the stipulated criteria, the creation of a multiple-tier system with differing benefit levels, and the suitability of the benefit levels themselves.

The idea of using food vouchers or food stamps is nothing new, either in India or internationally. A recent paper argued that food vouchers (perhaps combined with cash transfers) could provide a 'more effective basis for social protection' than the current system. Food stamp systems are usually designed to allow their targeted beneficiaries to select which private-sector outlets to purchase from. This does away with the hugely inefficient government procurement, storage and distribution operations. Moreover, the resulting competition among shops to attract these stamp bearing consumers would eliminate irregularities: customers with food stamps would frequent shops that did not impose illicit fees or shortchange customers on either quantity or quality.

Because politicians are fearful of the political backlash that might ensue were they to propose the wholesale abolition of the current PDS—even if replaced with a voucher system—there has been increasing discussion of the potential of hybrid systems. These sometimes envisage retention of the existing infrastructure of ration shops for far-flung rural areas, where private-sector competition might be inadequate and monitoring a voucher system would be difficult. Another hybrid is found in the food-stamp system being pilot-tested by the Government of Andhra Pradesh. This provides eligible families with serial-numbered food stamps, which also indicate the number of the shop where they are to be tendered. These can be exchanged only in existing ration shops. While providing less client choice than would be the case under a classic voucher system that used non-PDS shops, the system allegedly makes cheating on the part of shop owners more difficult, though there are questions as to whether this is indeed the case.

CONCLUSION

Regardless of its problems, the Public Distribution System (PDS) is widely considered an essential element of a multi-pronged strategy to both alleviate and reduce poverty. In recent days in April, 2009 following the General Elections, many existing Ministers of the Centre and the States in their Election Campaign have vociferously articulated that a genuine PDS system will solve the problem of acute poverty in the country because it is the only safety net for the poor, especially useful in the context of deregulation and inflation. Indeed, the PDS is a critical resource for the food security of the poor and particularly women, who manage household food supplies. The continued value of such a mechanism has long been questioned by those who consider market reforms better able to increase food availability to poor people. The political reality, however, is that while neglect of the PDS may well continue, it is very unlikely to be disbanded entirely. The question thus becomes how to make it serve its objective—of increasing food availability to the poor with an effective delivery system and without uneven distribution system—better than it has. Greater involvement by civil society organizations, different NGOs in monitoring the PDS's activities is a potential solution that has received increasing attention in recent years.

References

Arvind Vermani and P.V. Rajeev, 'Excess Food Stocks, PDS and Procurement Policy', Working Paper No. 5/2002-PC, Planning Commission, New Delhi, May 2002.

Bapna, S.L. (1990), "Food Security through the PDS: The Indian Experience" in D.S. Tyagi and V.S. Vyas (eds.), Increasing Access to Food: The Asian Experience, New Delhi: Sage

Dasgupta, P. (1993), An Inquiry into Well-being and Destitution, Oxford: Clarendon Press.

http://planningcommission.nic.in/wrkpaper/wp_pds.pdf.

Problem of Food and Hunger

A Need for Introducing Targeted Public Distribution System for the Poorest in India

Dhananjay Kumar, Arun Kumar
and Iswari Prasad

INTRODUCTION

The PDS in India works alongside a free market. It makes available quotas of foodgrains through ration shops at subsidized 'ration' or 'issue' prices. The role and working of the PDS has undergone several changes since its inception. Initially, its objective was to stablise prices and consumption in the light of fluctuations in foodgrain output. Later, it also assumed importance as one of the government's most significant anti-poverty programs. The changes witnessed in the last decade were a result of the liberalization process underway and the structural adjustment programmes undertaken by the government since 1991, the year of economic crisis. The reforms in the system focused on removing existing inefficiencies, particularly in costs. The costs of operating the PDS consist of two major components: subsidy costs and administration costs. The subsidy costs occur mainly because the cost at which foodgrains are procured is higher than the price at which they are sold in the PDS. In addition there are procurement incidentals, storage, transport and other administrative costs involved in the procurement and distribution of grain. Theft, damages and other kinds of losses in storage and transit add to these costs. In spite of incurring these costs the effectiveness with which the PDS provides food security to the poor has been low. This is mainly due to two reasons. Since the provision of food subsidy through the PDS has until recently been universal and not specifically targeted at the poor a large proportion of the subsidy has gone to the non-poor. There is also the phenomenon of corruption leading to leakage of a large amount of subsidized grain into the open market. In her study on Bihar, Mooij (1999) found that it was difficult for the PDS dealers to make profits without being corrupt. The administrative efficiency and the level of corruption vary with the state. For the nation as a whole, the estimates of diversion of grain from the PDS to the open market is close to one-third (Ahluwalia, 1993; Howes and Jha, 1992 and GOI, 2000).

PROBLEM OF HUNGER

Since a large proportion of the population continues to be poor, food security concerns have assumed great importance in India. Widespread poverty and lack of purchasing power implies limited market demand for foodgrains. Increases in food supply without adequate increase in demand means lower prices for farmers, which in turn necessitates price support for farmers from the government. At the same time price support operations can result in excessive stocks with the government in the absence of a food distribution program. Food subsidy to consumers and price support to farmers, are, therefore, complementary to each other. But the current food scenario is marked by a high level of foodgrains output coupled with a large grain reserve in public storage. This is largely due to the efforts of the government to protect farmers through regular increases in the procurement price of grains. These two factors together impose a heavy drain on the exchequer, which responds by increasing the issue price of subsidized grain. The ultimate effect of these policies is to reduce the per unit subsidy to consumers leading to a shortfall in the off-take.

Thus, despite the achievement of self-sufficiency in foodgrains and the prevalence of subsidized distribution of grains since World War II, per capita consumption of the poorest sections of the population continues to be lower than the recommended nutritional levels and as a result a large percentage of children remain underweight. At historical growth rates, Bhalla *et. al.* (1999) estimate a gap between the demand for and supply of cereal to be 25 million tonnes by 2020 even though consumption preferences are shifting towards non-cereal foods, the food gap may, still be substantial. In this paper, we, therefore, examine the costs and benefits associated with the operation of the PDS and discuss the ways of both cutting costs to improve efficiency and better targeting methods to improve the food security of the poor.

PROVISION OF FOOD FOR TARGETED PEOPLE

The recent changes in the food distribution system have been motivated mainly by the need to reduce the food subsidy bill. The infrastructure for integrated bul handling, storage and transportation of foodgrains.

SUPPLY OF FOOD THROUGH FCI

The FCI plays an important role in the distribution of foodgrains in India. The FCI and other public procurement agencies purchase their supplies from producers at pre-announced 'procurement prices' fixed by the central government and sell it to the state civil supplies or food corporations at an issue price, which is also fixed by the government. The state agencies in turn distribute the grain to the public through their network of fair price shops. In the case of wheat the procurement price has mostly acted as a support price, whereas for rice it is a levy on the millers. Of late, however, there has been a situation of surplus, even of rice and pressures are building up for its procurement by the FCI at support rather than levy price. Even in the case of wheat, at times the farmers used to be compelled to sell to the FCI at the procurement price when it fell below the market price. This happened in several ways such as traders not being allowed to bid in the procurement season until the FCI achieved its procurement target. Currently, however, the MSP has become a misnomer. It is fixed at such a high level that the FCI is forced to purchase almost the entire market arrival and there is no element of compulsion or coercion to sell to FCI.

On behalf of the central government, the FCI carries out operations and takes care of all aspects of the system including procurement, renting of warehouses and storage and allocations to the states. The net costs that it incurs in this operation over and above sales realization through the PDS is reimbursed to it by the central government and is referred to as food subsidy. The FCI maintains a buffer stock in order to stabilize grain prices and to provide minimum support prices to protect the farmers. These prices have been rising significantly, partly due to pressure from various interest lobbies. The economic cost consists of the purchase or procurement price, procurement incidentals, storage or carrying cost and the distribution cost. In the last five years of the nineties each cost component for each grain has grown at a slower rate compared to the growth in the previous five years. The growth rate of total cost has declined by 5 percentage points for rice and 4 percentage points for wheat between these periods. This may be due to better management practices and more efficient use of resources in recent years. For example, storage capacity utilization has increased from 53 percent in the early 1990s to 85 percent in 1999-2000 (Gulati *et. al.*, 1996, and GoI, 2001). However, due to various erroneous policies that are being followed including that of steadily raising issue prices and exclusion of a large deserving population by the TPDS, the off-take has declined resulting in falling average sales realization. The net effect of the rising costs and falling revenue has been that growth rate in unit subsidy, which was lower in the early 1990s (17.7 percent and 9.8 percent per annum, respectively for rice and wheat), has risen to 23.8 percent per annum for rice and 19.7 percent for wheat in the late 1990s.

ADVENT OF TARGETED PUBLIC DISTRIBUTION SYSTEM

In order to increase the share of the poor in the benefits from the PDS, the government has in recent years introduced new schemes such as the Revamped PDS (RPDS) and the TPDS. The performance of the TPDS so far does not seem to be satisfactory. Although the ration quota for the poor (the BPL population), has been increased, they are unable to make full use of this quota due to their limited purchasing power. For example a study by Srivastava (GoI, 2000), shows that the performance of the TPDS in Uttar Pradesh has been highly unsatisfactory. Food subsidy to the poorest groups increased by a meager amount (1.1 percent to 1.3 percent) due to the introduction of the TPDS. The large difference between open market and TPDS prices provided a great incentive for the diversion of grain to the black market with the estimated leakage being 41 percent. The selection of beneficiaries was not transparent and the basis for selection was "too complicated for the local officials to administer". In the case of Bihar too, the corruption levels are found to be high (Mooij, 1999). The delivery system was weak even before the introduction of the TPDS and not much could be expected in terms of increasing the benefits to the poor.

Replacing a system of universal provision of subsidies with a finely targeted one can lead to serious problems if no provision is made for a safety net to cover those excluded through poor targeting. In particular, such targeting, by leaving out large sections of the so-called APL families, given the controversies surrounding the poverty lines that are being used, is likely to lead to a rising exclusion error. Studies have also shown that since a substantial part of poverty is transient in nature, targeting based on current consumption status is likely to have a lesser impact on chronic poverty as compared to the case of uniform distribution of subsidies to the poor and the non-poor (Jalan and Ravallion, 1998). In short, the whole objective of protecting the poor consumer could get vitiated.

At present, the APL prices are higher than the ruling market prices, which in effect has driven the APL families out of the system. While the central issue price (CIP) was frozen for the BPL families until it was revised upwards last year, there has been a substantial increase in the price for APL families (Table 1). This has led to a lower off-take in the APL category. The net effect seems to be increasing food stocks with the FCI adding further to its storage costs. Due to the poor off-take in the APL category there is not much scope for growth in FCI's average sales realization. The introduction of the TPDS has also led to the perverse outcome whereby allotment of foodgrains was increased to states with a weak delivery system and reduced to those with greater administrative efficiency since the allotment was based on the prevailing poverty levels in these states (Mooij, 1999).

Several studies have highlighted the different problems associated with the TPDS. One of the major problems with targeting the scheme specifically to the poor is the high cost involved in the correct identification of the target group. Narrow targeting at the level of individual households, for example, requires very detailed data for all households and a complex and expensive process of testing in order to identify the eligible households. The effectiveness of such mechanisms depends on the magnitude of the two possible errors—the errors of exclusion and inclusion. The exclusion error indicates the extent to which the poor are excluded from the list of beneficiaries and the inclusion error, the extent to which the non-poor are included in the list. Direct targeting of the poor through means testing, entails high administrative costs due to the need for repeated periodic identification. The cost of identification of the poor, which is of a recurring nature, can be very high and implementation of such schemes could become cumbersome going by the experiences of other countries.

The costs are further augmented due to widespread leakage to non-poor households by misrepresentation of information. The incentive for leakage has increased due to the larger difference between the open market and ration market prices for BPL families. Thus, although the off-takes are higher for BPL than for APL foodgrains it is not clear how much actually reaches the poor. With persisting distributional problems, it is also not clear as to whether and how the entire allocation would be lifted by the states and then by the consumers. In addition, it was originally envisaged that the APL families will be slowly phased out of the system.

CONCLUSION

The introduction of the TPDS has only magnified the problem. The off-take of foodgrains for distribution to APL families has fallen since the ration prices have risen close to (and at times are even higher than) the open market price. The off-take from the BPL, allocation has been impressive, but a large part of the grains is diverted to the black market. The TPDS thus appears to have failed in serving both its objectives. It has succeeded neither in reducing the food subsidy bill nor in providing food subsidies to a greater proportion of the poor. The government should, now concentrate on tackling the real issues, namely reducing the cost inefficiencies in the procurement and distribution system and controlling the diversion of grain from the PDS to the open market. In the effort towards realizing these objectives, while some functions of the FCI can be left to the market, there is a large scope for improving the efficiency of the remaining operations of the FCI. For example, while the FCI's role can be limited to price stabilization and maintenance of buffer stocks, the central government could provide food subsidy to the states in the form of specific grants linked to their requirements so that the state agencies, private or public, can find the best possible way to procure grains to serve their PDS. This would also lead to decentralization of storage activities thereby avoiding cross hauling of grain that takes place in a centralized system. The restrictions raced by the private traders under the essential commodities Act need to be removed to facilitate this process. Further, liberalizing external trade in foodgrains and the use of other instruments of price stabilization like variable levies would also reduce the high costs of buffer stocking.

Our analysis in the context of rural India shows that there are positive benefits from choosing smaller geographic units for targeting, although at the level of the district the gains are modest. The exercise also clearly suggests that the universal provision of subsidies is desirable for poorer states such as Bihar, Orissa, Rajasthan and Madhya Pradesh since most of the districts in these states belong to the 'poor' or 'very poor' category. In the other states, on the other hand, universal subsidies could be provided only to the poorer districts. In respect of other districts, self-targeting mechanisms or other direct targeting criteria based on characteristics such as landlessness, old age, widowhood, etc., could be used.

References

Balakrishnan, P. and Ramaswami, B. (1995), Public Intervention and Private Speculation: The Case of Wheat Procurement in India,". *Journal of Quantitative Economics*, Vol. 11, No. 2, pp. 59-83.

Bhalla, G.S., Hazell, P. and Kere, J. (1999), "Prospects for India's Cereal Supply and Demand to 2020," Food, Agricultural and the Environment Discussion Paper 29, International Food Policy Research Institute (IFPRI), Washington, D.C.

GoI (2001), Background Note on Public Distribution and Food Security, Government of India, Development Policy Division, Planning Commission, New Delhi.

Jha, Shikha, and Srivassan, P.V. (1999), "Grain Price Stabilisation in India: Evaluation of Policy Alternatives," *Agricultural Economics*, Vol. 21, pp. 93-108.

An Analysis of Targeted Public Distribution System in Backward Areas of India

PRITA YADAV AND RAM DULAR SINGH

INTRODUCTION

The Government of India launched many programmers for poverty eradication in tribals areas backward as well as social groups and Targeted Public Distribution system has been given top priority to fulfil the need of food security of poor people. Food security issue is an alarming issue in tribal areas as well as backward region where large number of tribals people have died of hungry and in some areas their population have declined due to lack of food security and proper health care. Under such circumstance, the study of an analysis of problem of Targeted Public Distribution System in underdeveloped areas of country is necessary to know that what steps have been taken to strengthen the TPDS in the said area so that one can say that the TPDS is ensuring food for the poor people of country and TPDS has been a successful programme for poor people.

Though it is being stated that it involves high cost. Infact the TPDS Programme was launched in 1997 by the government of India by making a distinction between people falling below the poverty line (BPL) and above poverty line (APL) with differential entitlements and prices for the two categories. The government of India made a very important announcement in Budget 2000 stating that targeting was the first step in a process of excluding large number of vulnerable people like ST, SC and OBC from the PDS. The new policy aimed at targeting households on the basis of income criterion which implied using the income poverty line to demarcate poor and non-poor households. The Targeted Public Distribution System differs form earlier variants of PDS in certain key aspects. In other words, the people falling under APL category will have to pay more for the goods purchased form PDS shops.

However, some of the problems of targeting, in principle and in practice, are quite visible. The new policy of targeted food distribution has impacted on entitlements, the quantity of foodgrains distributed, prices and, finally, on coverage. There are some features of Targeted Public Distribution System which are being discussed below:

1. The scheme provides for a dual price policy: while prices of foodgrain for allocation to families identified as BPL are lower than was the case earlier (that is under the universal PDS scheme), central issue prices of grains for allocation to families in the APL category have been raised substantially. As a consequence, in most states, the prices of wheat and rice for APL allocations have risen steeply after the introduction of the Targeted PDS. The Budget of March 2000 increased prices further, and brought them on par with market prices for APL consumers (see below).
2. The entitlement of a household have been reduced sharply so that each poor household is entitled to

> only 10 kg of grain each month. As against the entitlement the annual level of cereal intake recommended by the Indian Council of Medical Research (ICMR) is 135 kg per person (or 11.25 kg per month). Thus, for a five-member family, the new ration scale of about 2 kg per person per month provides less than 18 percent the recommended intake.

The principle of entitle has been altered from a per capita norm to a family nom. As per the earlier policy, ration scales were typically defined in terms of fixed quantities per person or per unit (with an adult equivalent to two units, and a child equivalent to one unit). Under the Targeted PDS, however, each poor family, irrespective of size and need, is entitled to a uniform quantity of foodgrain.

The pattern of allocation as between poor and non-poor categories of households differs significantly across states. This can be illustrated with the help of data on purchases for the period, January to December 1998. In Bihar, a states where the functioning of the PDS is known to be weak, purchases form the PDS have risen sharply consequent to the introduction of the Targeted PDS: purchases of rice and wheat under the BPL category were about five times higher than those under the APL category. Given a weak distribution system and relatively low level of distribution in the past, the state now appears to be only purchasing the cheaper grain allocated for distribution to BPL households. It is difficult to say whether this grain actually reached BPL households or whether it was siphoned off to other consumers at a profit. In Kerala by contrast, purchases for the APL families were 16 times greater than BPL purchase in the state. This shows that the state was allocated higher quantities of APL grains on the basis of past allocation, and was committed to supplying a certain quantity of foodgrains to the entire population served by the PDS. The state government offered a higher quantity of foodgrains for BPL households than the allocation form the center besides providing for the APL population. As there is a price different between BPL and APL allocations, (additional allocations being even more expensive), it is clear that state governments that are committed to provide a certain minimum quantity of foodgrains to their population have to now bear the burden of higher costs.

Foodgrains were now allocated on the basis of to a new set of principle, according to which 10 kg of foodgrains were to be reserved for allocation to the officially recognised poor population and restrictions were placed on the quantity supplied to the 'non-poor'. States that were providing more than 10 kg of foodgrain per family now have to buy the additional quantity at higher prices even for distribution to the BPL population. As a result, the share of different states in the distribution of foodgrains has altered with the introduction of the TPDS- the states that were earlier ranked at the top in terms of share of all-India distribution lost their position after 1997. The new policy thus constitutes an "attack on the PDS in those states where it has been functioning well" (Chandrasekhar and Ghosh, 1977).

The method of targeting-based on the income poverty line-has already led to the exclusion of million of under-nourished people who face the risk of undernourishment from the BPL category. Identification of beneficiaries in the basis of a narrow income poverty line is, as I have argued elsewhere, faculty conceptually and difficult to implement, resulting in large errors of exclusion (Swaminathan, 2000). The entire process of selection of households has been slipshod and arbitrary and has led to the exclusion of many of them. Even the Comptroller and Auditor General of India has been critical of the method of targeting and pointed out that 18 out of 31 states and union territories had not conduction any survey for the identification of BPL families (*Business Line*, February 6, 2001).

Beside deviating from the official guidelines of the Government of India on the subject, the authors argue that each of the three criteria was arbitrary and provided and unjust basis for the exclusion of a family from the system of subsidised food-provision. Take the criterion of employment in a 'service' job. A service job, as understood by local officials, referred to any non-agriculture employment. It included regular salaried workers such as teachers and government employees as well as persons employed as watchmen or office attendants in private organizations. This argued that in the absence of any information on the actual earning, size and composition of each household covered, it cannot be known if the salary of one member was adequate to ensure food security to the entire family. The authors then examined household information from their survey of 2000 on household that had been classified as BPL and APL for the purposes of availing the benefits of the PDS and found major mismatches between the Government of India's official criteria for the exclusion of household from the BPL list and the actual procedures adopted at the ground level.

There were three main criteria on the basis of which government differentiated the BPL and APL households. Though in the tribal areas poor people fall under BPL category but government fixed certain criteria to make distinction between BPL and APL people.

IMPACT OF BUDGET PROVISION (2000-01) ON TARGETED PEOPLE

The provision made regarding Targeted Public Distribution System in budget 2000-01 has great impact on the price of rice and wheat. It was experienced that there was a steep price increases for rice and wheat supplied through fair price shops and a clear change in policy.

Henceforth, central issue prices, that is prices at which the Food Corporation of India (FCI) sells foodgrains for the PDS to state governments were to be set at half the 'economic cost' incurred by the FCI for BPL households and at the full 'economic cost' for APL households. In effect, wheat would now be available at Rs. 8.40 (against Rs. 6.82) per kg and rice at Rs. 11.70 (against Rs. 9.05) per kg for APL families. BPL families would thus be charged Rs. 4.20 (against Rs. 2.50) per kg of wheat and Rs. 5.85 (against Rs. 3.50) per kg of rice. These prices were revised downloads slightly after a few months when the estimates of economic costs were lowered. The new prices were Rs. 8.30 and 11.30 for wheat and rice for APL families and Rs. 4.15 and Rs. 5.65 for wheat and rice respectively for BPL families. These policy changes have had a marked and immediate impact on consumers. This is set out below:

> In the first place, the increase in prices of basic foodgrain issued through the PDS have been substantial and will have an adverse impact on the real incomes of millions of consumers. For impact BPL families, the price of rice was hiked by 61 percent and that of wheat by as much as 65 percent (after the download revision). For APL families, the price of wheat has increased by 22 per cent and that of rice, by 25 percent. Taking a long-term perspective, in real terms, although BPL prices were lower than prices in the universal PDS in 1996, the rise in prices for BPL families is higher than the rise in 1991 and that of wheat is approximately the same. In other word, the introduction of the TDPS has not resulted in lower prices for the BPL population relative to changes in wholesale prices.

The new policy has introduced as in-built mechanism for raising prices, so that every rise in procurement prices results in a rise in the issue prices of foodgrains for the poor. It bears an emphasis that procurement prices have raised regularly each year and in recent years (including the most recent announcement) the increased have actually been above those recommended by the Commission on Agricultural Costs and Prices. The inflationary effects of the new policy can hardly be overstated.

The hike in procurement prices, in effect, excludes APL families from the PDS. A comparison of the economic costs of the FCI with wholesales prices and retail in different states shows a steady decline in the price advantage enjoyed by the FCI in the 1990s compared to that the 1980s. In situation where the economics cost is higher than the market price, APL consumers will have to pay more for grain in the ration shop than in the open market as is the case in several north Indian states. The exclusion of APL households from the PDS has implication for (a) the consumption and nutrition of a large part of the population, (b) the quality of the programme,

(c) the effectiveness of the delivery system, (d) stocks of foodgrains, and, ironically, (e) the central government's food subsidy bill.

For BPL families, allocations have been doubled (from 10 to 20 kg per family per month) for BPL households. However, despite this increase, which was long overdue, due to the steep rise in the prices, genuinely poor families will have to spend more now on acquiring the same quantity of foodgrains. This will compound the existing hardship for BPL families, who, under the PDS system as it works in many parts of the country are required to buy the total monthly allocation in one or at best two instalments.

Millions of undernourished persons and the persons vulnerable to under nutrition have already been exclusion from the BPL category by means of income targeting. Under the proposed dispensation, the excluded population can no longer have even the limited benefits available to it as a possible part of the APL category.

Finally, the central government is abdicating its responsibility with respect to the provision of a minimum quantity of cheap food to consumers in all parts of the country. It has decided to transfer the cost of the food subsidy to state governments. Of course, the current policy affects different states differentially, but it targets and penalizes states that performed well—state government that have shown some commitment to the PDS in the past and wish to continue to provide a sufficient quantity of foodgrains to vulnerable section of the population at low prices will have now to pay the bill themselves. On the other hand, in states such as Bihar, where the delivery network and administration are already weak and fail notoriously to reach the poor, the new scheme is likely to increase the incentive and scope for diverting foodgrains meant for BPL households to the open market.

POSITION OF FOODGRAINS AVAILABILITY AND DISTRIBUTION

Now we observe the effect of change in the Budget on availability, distribution and allocation of foodgrains. We find a poor performance of supply of foodgrains. It is also important to note that the off-take by BPL households in relation to allocation has fallen.

The impact of the new changes in policy is visible clearly from the available data on quantities distributed under the PDS. First, let us look at the board pattern of change during the last 15 years of rice and wheat distributed through the PDS network fell from 20.8 million in 1991 to 14 million tonnes in 1994. The quantity of foodgrains supplied through the PDS rose again thereafter but the introduction of targeting has clearly led to a sharp reduction of intake. The provisional estimate for off-taken in 2000 was 12 million tonnes.

More detailed data on quantities allocated and purchased by commodity after the introduction of the targeted PDS demonstrate that the main factor behind the decline is the total collapse in demand for grain from APL consumers. In the case of wheat, for example, 76.7 percent of allocations to APL households in 1998-99 were 'lifted' (or distributed); the ratio fell to 38 percent in 1999-2000 and to a mere 3.8 percent in 2000-01. A similar pattern can be observed in the case of APL purchase of rice: the ratio off-take to allocation fell from 82.8 percent in 1998-99 to 73.2 percent in 1999-2000 and further to 21.6 percent in 2000-01 (The off-take of rice by APL consumers has not fallen to the same extent as wheat because of the higher demand from the southern states, which have maintained their own subsidy to the PDS). The policy announcement equating issue prices with economic cost thus had the desired affect of excluding APL consumers from the PDS.

It is noteworthy that the off-take by BPL households in relation to allocation has also fallen, particularly in the case of wheat. This could be due to several reasons including, among others, the lack of access of BPL card-holders to ration shops and foodgrains therein. With the exclusion of the APL from the PDS, it is likely that many fair-price shops became unviable and ceased to operate regularly for a small number of BPL households. Further, even BPL households may not make the effort to buy foodgrains from the ration shops on the few days when it is usually available given the small quantities involved.

PROBLEMS OF TPDS

The system of TPDS had been surrounded from problems since the day of its birth. There are several problems which proved to be abstracts in the smooth functioning of TPDS and are provided a large platform for the criticism. The problems are being discussed in brief:

Decline in Quality of Food Materials

When programmes that are universal become targeted, their quality tends to deteriorate as the oft-heard phrase 'programmes for the poor are poor programmes suggests van de Walle *et. al.* (1995). For example, the quality of food targeted to the poor tends to deteriorate. Targeted programmes therefore, often end up being inferior to universal programmes. And worsening quality can undermine the objective of the original programmes, as for example, if the quality of food distributed is too bad to be unsafe. To take another example, delivery may become irregular when only the poor are to be provided the benefits.

Selection of Non-eligible Person

In any targeted welfare programme there are two types of errors that occur due to imperfect measurement. Errors of wrong exclusion refer to the exclusion of genuinely poor of deserving households from a programme, while those wrong inclusion of non-eligible persons or households in a programme.

Loss of Social Cohesion among People

Targeting can be invasive and intrusive and result in greater social divisions. Segregating households on the basis of incomes in a country where the poverty line reflects a very low absolute level of income, and where there is a fluidity of households around the poverty line, can lead to social tensions and polarization. To put it more explicitly very narrow targeting is like to lead to the exclusion of some genuinely poor households from the programme, and create divisions among the poor. Such division can exacerbate existing forms of caste and gender oppression.

The Administrative Cost

A second major cost in developing countries is that of the administrative of targeted programmes. The costs of administration of a welfare programme depend on the nature of instruction and delivery mechanism in an economy, and on the extent of information available. Targeting raises the costs of delivery and administration, as the target group has to be identified on the basis of specified criteria, say incomes. Given the structure of our economy (which has a large agriculture and self-employed sector) and the ability of administrative organizations to collect accurate information, the costs of administering a targeted programme are likely to be high. This cost, however, vary with the type of targeting on the basis a criterion such as geographical residence may be easier to implement and is less costly than on that of income or nutritional status.

LOSS OF SUPPORT OF POLITICAL PARTIES AND LONG RUN COSTS

Lastly, any programme which targets the poor is likely to get less political support than a universal programme resulting in lower allocations for a targeted programme. In other words, the budgetary allocation for the welfare programme depends on the type of the programme, i.e., whether it is a targeted or a universal programme—and typically, allocations fall when a programme becomes targeted. If the budget support for a programme is made endogenous, then targeting may be worse for the poor than a system of universal transfer. There is a good body of evidence from developed and less developed countries to show that political support differs as between universal and targeted transfers. The differences in political support get reflected not only in the size of transfers, both in per capita terms and in terms of total transfers, but also in the very continuation or dismantling of a programme. So the inclusion of the middle classes in a welfare programme may be done on 'purely pragmatic' grounds for they 'play a crucial role in creating, expanding, sustaining, reforming and dismantling the welfare state' (Goodin and Le Grand, 1987).

Targeting is far from costless, and when all the costs are accounted for the benefits of targeting may vanish. We thus need to openly recognise and assess the relative costs and benefits of factor, perhaps, is the cost of exclusion. If the errors of exclusion are large, and costs attached to these errors are high, then universal programmes are preferable.

SUGGESTION FOR IMPROVEMENT IN TPDS

On the basis of above discussion, it is the need of the time as well as social scientists to chalkout a way for better functioning of TPDS so that fruits of this programme may reach to the entire chronic poor in general and tribal people in particular. Hence, in view of the above fact, there are certain suggestions which deserve to be taken into consideration.

Firstly, targeting is very costly in a country with a large population that is undernourished and venerable to undernourishment. At the very least, we need to include around 70 to 80 percent of the population (and a much higher proportion of the rural population) in a scheme of providing minimum nutritional and income support such as the PDS. So, the first step of the reform process must be to redefine the population that is to be included in the PDS. Once the size of the population whose nutrition needs are to be covered by the public distribution system, which includes all vulnerable sections of the population, is determine then administrative, fiscal and welfare concerns all indicate that—universal coverage is a better way to reach the target group than a complicated process which involves the exclusion of those in the highest consumption quintile. A belated recognition of this problem has led to be announced (in July 2001) that price for APL consumers in the PDS will be lowered to 70 percent of the economic cost of grain. This announcement, it is hoped, will bring the consumers back to the fair-price shops resulting in a higher off-take from the PDS.

Secondly, ration quantities should be fixed on a per person norm and the entitlement of each person should be raised so as to provide a measure of minimum nutritional support. Consumption requirement are age and sex-specific and it makes little sense to allocate the same quantity to a one person adult family as to a ten person family. It needs to be added here that prior to the introduction of the TPDS, state government had set such norms. In Kerala, for example, the norm was 1302 kg per adult per month—an entitlement that went some way in meeting the cereal requirement of a person.

Thirdly, beside being expanded to cover a wider section of the population the PDS must be geared to provide for higher entitlements per person, thus ensuing that all vulnerable groups are able to meet their nutrition requirements. For instance, the provision of about 60 kg per annum per adult (the average off-take in Kerala) to 80 percent of the population (say 520 million adults and 280 million children) requires that the PDS supplies about 40 million tonnes of foodgrains. At current production level, this amounts to one-fifth of production. Distribution of foodgrains on this scale is feasible and sustainable if appropriate production and procurement policies are pursued.

Fourthly, there must be greater accountability and transparence in the administration of the PDS at all levels of the delivery network (that is from the FCI to the fair-price shop owner). The government, academics, and mass organisations in India have recommended of ensuring such transparency.

CONCLUSION

1. The targeted PDS is an ill-conceived measure and the introduction of targeting was, as the changes in the Budget for 2000-2001 confirm, the first step in the dismantling of the PDS in India. As expected, the increase in grain prices and restrictions in coverage in the wake of the introduction of the scheme have led to a spiral of lower off-take, higher stocks and higher prices. Further, there is little doubt that the frequent changes in policy in the last few years combined with the exclusion of a large majority of the population from the PDS have undermined the exiting delivery network.
2. The provision for ensuring effective food security at reasonable costs to the government requires

> integration of production of production, procurement and distribution policies. Unless all parts of the food system are strengthened, any talk of isolated issue such as the high costs of the FCI is meaningless. Taking a ling-run perspective, if it is only with an expansion of foodgrain production and acceleration in the growth of yields of major foodgrains in relatively backward areas that a system such as the PDS can be sustained. Greater localised procurement and storage as a consequence of higher production in hitherto less developed areas in one way of keeping a check on the costs of distribution. Another suggestion is to set the final procurement price inclusive of taxes (CACP, 1998). These issues deserve to be studies separately. The main point to be noted here is that the costs of the PDS are closely linked to changes in production and production-related policies.

So far the problem of food security of tribals of India in concerned, it is an alarming problem in the state According the census of 2001, the total population if ST constitutes 26.30% in the state out of this population the larger number of ST are Santhal (20,60,730) the required in Santhal Pargana while Qrann has got the second position in the matter of population of tribals in Jharkhand thoughout of total districts of state there is a heavy concentration of tribals in 13 districts.

The food security problem is alarming in the state became there is a pancity of agriculture land in the state. The poor people particularly the STs have to remain dependent on agriculture products on small land as well as forest eating materials which does not meet the food requirement of STs. As revealed in several reports of NGOs and other agencies a large number of tribals are dying hungry. The Targeted Public Distribution System launched for these people dose not cover the food needs of these people. Moreover, the foodgrains supplied for these people are being sold in the market by the dealer. Since the tribals are not well education and people living in rural areas are quite illiterate. Hence, the foodgrains of their share is sold in the market and they are forced to put their thumb impression in grains distribution register and for that thumb impression they receive a small quantity of country made liquire. This is the real picture of tribal area. So, there is an urgent need to educate the tribal people and distribution of foodgrains among them should be made before an authorized office and videography be made. So that the actual needy tribe may be benefited from TPDS scheme. Otherwise the entire money spent on this programme will be Siphoned of till a strict system is adopted.

References

Chandrasekhar, C.P. and Ghosh, I. (1997), "Targeted Public Distribution System: Is It Getting Some Food to the Poor', *Business Line*, July 22.

CACP (1998), Reports of the Commission for Agricultural Costs and Prices for the Crops Sown during 1998-99, Commission for Agricultural Costs and Prices, Government of India, Ministry of Agriculture, New Delhi.

Dutta, B. and Ramaswami, B. (2001), 'Targeting and Efficiency in the Public Distribution System: Case of Andhra Pradesh and Maharashtra," *Economic and Political Weekly*, Vol. 36, No. 18, May 5, pp. 1524-32.

GoI (2001), Economic Survey, Government of India, Ministry of Finance, New Delhi

———, (2001), Foodgrains Monthly Bulletin, Ministry of Food and Consumer Affairs, Department of Food and Civil Supplies, March 2001, New Delhi.

———, (1997), Focus on the Poor, Ministry of Civil Supplies, Consumer Affairs and Public Distribution, New Delhi.

Gupta, S.P. (1999), "Globalisation, Economic Reforms and the Role of Labour", Society for Economic and Social Transition, New Delhi (mimeo).

Indrakant, S. (1995), "Food Security and Public Distribution System in Andhra Pradesh", Workshop on Food Security and Public Distribution System in India, Planning Commission, New Delhi, April.

Index